# THE NURSE PSYCHOTHERAPIST
# IN PRIVATE PRACTICE

**Jerry D. Durham** is Associate Professor and Director, School of Nursing at Illinois Wesleyan University, Bloomington, Illinois, and a nurse psychotherapist in private practice in Fairbury, Illinois. Dr. Durham earned a B.S. Ed. from Southeast Missouri State University; an M.A. in English from Bradley University; a B.S.N., M.S.N. (medical-surgical nursing), and Doctor of Philosophy (Education) degree from Saint Louis University. He also received an M.S. in psychiatric community mental health nursing from the University of Illinois, Chicago. He holds membership in the American Nurses' Association, Council on Psychiatric and Mental Health Nursing, American Assembly for Men in Nursing, Sigma Theta Tau, and the Midwest Nursing Research Society. Dr. Durham's research interests lie in the areas of private practice in nursing, men in nursing, and writing for publication. In addition to his present roles, he has worked as a staff nurse, nursing supervisor, and consultant.

**Sally Brosz Hardin** received her B.S.N. and M.S.N. (psychiatric nursing) degrees from the University of Illinois College of Nursing, Chicago. She earned the degree of Doctor of Philosophy in Communication Science at the University of Illinois, Urbana. She is currently Associate Professor of Psychiatric Nursing at the University of South Carolina, Columbia, where she teaches in the graduate program. Dr. Hardin has also practiced as a psychiatric nurse clinical specialist, psychiatric nursing coordinator, and nurse psychotherapist. She is affiliated with the American Nurses' Association, Sigma Theta Tau, the Council of Nurse Researchers, the Midwest Nursing Research Society, and Sigma Xi Research Society. Her research interests include nurse psychotherapy, nurse-patient communication, and maternal-child mental health. After receiving a research grant from Alpha Lambda Chapter of Sigma Theta Tau, Dr. Hardin was the principal investigator of a three-year research project on the structure, process, and effectiveness of nurse psychotherapy.

# The Nurse Psychotherapist in Private Practice

Jerry D. Durham, R.N., Ph.D.
Sally Brosz Hardin, R.N., Ph.D.
*Editors*

SPRINGER PUBLISHING COMPANY
New York

Springer Publishing Company, Inc.
536 Broadway
New York, NY 10012

86 87 88 89 90 / 5 4 3 2 1

**Library of Congress Cataloging-in-Publication Data**

The Nurse psychotherapist in private practice.

  Includes bibliographies and index.
  1. Psychiatric nursing—Practice.   2. Psychotherapy.
I. Durham, Jerry D.   II. Hardin, Sally Brosz.
[DNLM: 1. Private Practice.   2. Psychiatric Nursing.
3. Psychotherapy—methods—nurses' instruction.
WY 160 N9733]
RC440.N85   1986          610.73'68          86-14266
ISBN 0-8261-5000-4

Printed in the United States of America

*To my parents, Irene Trawinski Broszniowski
and Nick Broszniowski*
—Sally Brosz Hardin

*To Kathleen, for her patience and love*
—Jerry Durham

# Contents

## Part II: Patients of Unique Concern to the Nurse Psychotherapist

# Contributors

**Olga Maranjian Church, R.N., Ph.D., F.A.A.N.**, Associate Professor of Psychiatric Nursing at the University of Illinois College of Nursing, Chicago, IL

**Alice J. Dan, Ph.D.**, Associate Professor of Medical-Surgical Nursing, University of Illinois College of Nursing, Chicago, IL

**Marguerite A. Dixon, R.N., Ph.D.**, Assistant Professor of Psychiatric Nursing, University of Illinois College of Nursing, Chicago, IL

**Laina M. Gerace, R.N., M.S.**, Acting Clinical Chief, Psychiatric Nursing, University of Illinois College of Nursing, Chicago, IL; and Lecturer, Graduate Program in Psychiatric Nursing, St. Xavier University College of Nursing, Chicago, IL

**Mary R. Haack, R.N., Ph.D., C.A.C.**, Research Associate, University of Illinois College of Nursing, Chicago, IL; Nurse Consultant, Chem-Stress, Rush-Presbyterian-St. Luke's Medical Center, Chicago; and nurse psychotherapist in private practice

**Sally A. Hutchinson, R.N., Ph.D.**, Associate Professor, University of Florida College of Nursing, JHEP, Jacksonville, FL

**Donna K. Ipema, R.N., Ph.D., C.S.**, Professor and Director of Nursing, Trinity Christian College, Palos Heights, IL

**Sherry Johnson, R.N., Ph.D., C.S.**, Nurse Psychotherapist at the South Shore Pastoral Counseling Center, Hingham, MA

**Joan M. King, R.N., D.N. Sc.**, Professor of Psychiatric Nursing, University of Illinois College of Nursing, Chicago, IL

**Diane Kjervik, R.N., M.S., J.D.**, Director of Governmental Relations, American Association of Colleges of Nursing, Washington, DC

**Ruth Dailey Knowles, Ph.D., A.R.N.P., C.S.,** Educational Director of PEERS, Inc., and nurse psychotherapist in private practice in Miami, FL

**Janet Konat, R.N., M.A.,** doctoral candidate in psychology at DePaul University, Chicago, IL

**Suzanne Lego, R.N., Ph.D.,** nurse psychotherapist in private practice in New York City and in Demarest, NJ

**Linda L. Lewis, R.N., M.S.,** doctoral candidate in nursing sciences at the University of Illinois College of Nursing, Chicago, IL

**Maxine Loomis, R.N., Ph.D., C.S., F.A.A.N.,** Professor and Director of Doctoral Studies, University of South Carolina College of Nursing, Columbia, SC

**Rose Odum, R.N., D.N.Sc., A.A.M.F.T.,** Assistant Professor of Psychiatric Nursing, University of California School of Nursing, Los Angeles, Los Angeles, CA

**Anita O'Toole, R.N., Ph.D., C.S.,** Professor and Director, Graduate Psychiatric Nursing Program, Kent State University School of Nursing, Kent, Ohio

**Lynne Parsons, R.N., M.S.,** nurse psychotherapist in private practice in Oak Park, IL; and doctoral candidate at the Chicago School of Professional Psychology, Chicago, IL

**Kathryn R. Puskar, R.N., Dr.P.H., C.S.,** Assistant Professor of Psychiatric Nursing, University of Pittsburgh School of Nursing, Pittsburgh, PA

**Karen Skerrett, R.N., M.S., M.A.,** nurse psychotherapist in private practice in LaGrange, IL

**Shirley Smoyak, R.N., Ph.D., F.A.A.N.,** Professor of Psychiatric Nursing, College of Nursing, Rutgers, The State University, New Brunswick, NJ

**Jan Pleak Spunt, R.N., M.S.,** Psychiatric Clinical Nurse Specialist, University of Illinois Hospital, Chicago, IL

**Lois Sullivan-Taylor, R.N., M.S.N.,** Assistant Professor of Nursing, Illinois Wesleyan University School of Nursing, Bloomington, IL; and nurse psychotherapist in private practice

**Joyce Torpey, R.N., M.S.,** nurse psychotherapist at the Institute for Motivational Development, Lombard, IL

**Denise Webster, R.N., Ph.D., C.S.,** Assistant Professor of Psychiatric Nursing, University of Illinois College of Nursing, Chicago, IL; and nurse psychotherapist in private practice

**Ruth Weinstein, R.N., Ph.D.,** nurse psychotherapist (and psychologist) in private practice in Silver Spring, MD

**Anne Wells, R.N., Ph.D.,** Assistant Professor of Psychiatric Nursing, University of Illinois College of Nursing, Chicago, IL

**Jane Howarth White, R.N., D.N.Sc., C.S.,** Assistant Professor and Chairperson, Graduate Program in Psychiatric-Mental Health Nursing, Catholic University of America School of Nursing, Washington, DC; a nurse psychotherapist in private practice

**D. Jean Wood, R.N., Ph.D.,** Professor and Director, Department of Psychiatric Nursing, University of South Carolina College of Nursing, Columbia, SC

# Foreword

When I began my private practice of psychotherapy in 1965 there were few psychiatric nurse therapists in private practice around. Most of us were students of Hildegard Peplau at Rutgers or June Mellow in Boston. We opened our practices nervously and tentatively.

My first two private patients were people I had treated in the county hospital when I was a graduate student at Rutgers. Their discharge coincided with my graduation. They each paid $2.00 per visit, and when I took an apartment in New York they had the additional cost of bus fare from New Jersey to my apartment.

I continued to see patients in my home until 1974 when I rented a suite of offices because my patient load was large enough to support the rent. The next year I stopped teaching because I was seeing enough patients to justify it as a full time job. Now, ten years later, I have an office in New York City, and one in my home in New Jersey, a full practice.

My progress as a private practitioner is a reflection of the progress of the psychiatric nursing profession over the past two decades. This began with the establishment of graduate programs in psychiatric nursing in 1947, the coining of the term "clinical specialist" in 1956, and the certification of clinical specialists in psychiatric nursing, first by the New Jersey State Nurses' Association in 1972 and then by the American Nurses' Association (ANA) in 1980. In the past few years psychiatric nursing leaders have worked successfully to have state laws passed mandating that nurse psychotherapists be reimbursed by insurance companies. Through the work of the Council of Psychiatric and Mental Health Nurses of the ANA, we are now represented on the mental health advisory panel of CHAMPUS, the largest third party payer of mental health benefits in the world; and certified psychiatric nurse specialists are providers and peer reviewers for CHAMPUS.

So, we've come a long way, and this volume provides yet another milestone. To my knowledge it is the first book by psychiatric nurses describing the private practice of psychiatric nurses. It covers both core issues and patients believed to be of unique concern to nurse psychotherapists. It provides the reader with a very broad and rich view of the myriad of practices by psychiatric nurse psychotherapists. I commend the editors and contributors for a fascinating and far-reaching book that should help establish us once and for all as valuable providers of psychiatric and mental health care.

SUZANNE LEGO, R.N., Ph.D., C.S.
Private Practice
New York City and Demarest, New Jersey

# Preface

Practitioners of psychiatric-mental health (PMH) nursing have worked diligently over the past few years to identify their unique knowledge base and practice niche, both within nursing and within the mental health services arena. This has been no mere intellectual exercise. At a time when PMH nursing content has been integrated into many undergraduate curricula, those arguing for its primacy in nursing have met with resistance. PMH nurses have seen their roles diluted by the employment of less experienced (and, not coincidentally, often less costly) "mental health technicians" in a number of their traditional practice settings. Other non-nurse specialists have proclaimed that only they are qualified to provide a broad range of primary mental health services to patients, including those which PMH nurses of an earlier time provided when no one else would. These changes have culminated in something of an identity crisis for psychiatric nurses and psychiatric nursing.

In the 1950s, a movement developed whereby nurses began studying and practicing psychotherapy, although they used other labels to describe their efforts and achievements. As greater numbers of nurses completed graduate degrees and as the collective self-esteem of women and nurses grew, PMH nurses began to envision ways to use their knowledge and skills. Initially many became head nurses, supervisors, and teachers; eventually, however, more became skilled nurse clinicians, using their expertise to foster change in individuals, families, groups, and communities. These change agents frequently met resistance to the implementation of their roles since their colleagues from other disciplines were unaccustomed to seeing nurses work so autonomously; however, issues of professional territoriality and turf-sharing were more frequently the real, if not always expressed, concern of these colleagues.

Well-prepared and highly-skilled PMH nurses have demonstrated that their services can meet the mental health needs of a large portion of our population. Several studies suggest that this practitioner is capable of initiating and sustaining a therapeutic relationship that results in improved health for patients. Moreover, the nurse psychotherapist (NPT) can provide this therapy in a cost-effective manner. Recognizing this ability, increasing numbers of PMH nurses are entering private practice as NPTs. Working for the most part on a fee-for-service basis, many are solo practitioners, while others practice in partnerships or corporations with nurses and other health professionals. Unfettered by institutional gatekeepers, NPTs have direct access to patients to whom they are accountable.

Little has been written about the nurse psychotherapist; thus, this book provides NPTs an opportunity to share their insight and expertise with others. We have a clear understanding of what this book is not. It does not attempt to catalog all therapeutic interventions employed by NPTs; it does not discuss all issues relevant to initiating and maintaining a private practice in nurse psychotherapy; it does not identify all patients who might benefit from NPTs' efforts; and, finally, it is not meant as a primer for inexperienced students or nurses who hope they can become expert NPTs merely by reading its pages. Rather, it explores selected issues and therapy with patients of unique concern to NPTs. We hope that the book will prove beneficial, perhaps even inspiring, to those nurses who have considered adopting the role of NPT or who are already working in this role. We believe the contributing authors have demonstrated how PMH nurses with advanced education, rich experiences, and ongoing supervision can play a vital role in the health of Americans.

# Acknowledgments

The authors would like to acknowledge the support and assistance of several individuals who have made this book a reality. Janice Wagoner provided intelligent and tireless proofreading and word processing for several months as contributing authors submitted manuscripts. Alma Woolley arranged for secretarial services and offered her critical reading skills and encouragement. A number of our colleagues at Illinois Wesleyan University School of Nursing and the University of Illinois College of Nursing offered suggestions and support throughout this project. We would like especially to acknowledge the nurse psychotherapists and nurse scholars whose contributions to this volume have enriched psychiatric mental health nursing. Finally, our families provided considerable understanding, love, and patience.

# Part I
## Core Issues for the Nurse Psychotherapist

# Chapter 1

# Introduction and Historical Perspective: The Nurse Psychotherapist as Private Practitioner

*Olga M. Church, Sally B. Hardin, Jerry D. Durham*

Multiple forces have shaped psychiatric nursing practice as it is interpreted today by its myriad practitioners who work in a wide variety of roles and settings. One such force was an Act of Congress, which influenced a shift in the role of the psychiatric nurse from custodial caretaker to increasingly autonomous practitioner. The Mental Health Act of 1946 marked the beginning of significant federal support that improved opportunities for graduate psychiatric nursing education. Four years later, nursing education leaders convened to define psychiatric nursing formally and elucidate the characteristics of its practitioners. At this Conference on Advanced Psychiatric Nursing and Mental Hygiene Programs, jointly sponsored by the National League of Nursing Education and the University of Minnesota, the nurse leaders concurred that psychiatric nursing was that branch of nursing concerned with the total nursing care of the psychiatric patient through development of the interpersonal relationship, creation of therapeutic situations, and application of nursing skills (Peplau, 1956). They further emphasized education and credentialling as key elements basic to psychiatric nursing practice.

Following these major events, the powerful influence of the curative/ medical model on the development of the psychiatric nurse's role began to erode. The influence of the curative/medical model on psychiatric nursing can be traced to Dr. Edward Cowles, Superintendent of the McLean Asylum in Waverly, Massachusetts. Dr. Cowles established the first training program for psychiatric nurses at McLean where his goal was to "medicalize" the asylum. Twenty years later, Euphemia Jane Taylor established the first nurse-organized psychiatric training program at Johns Hopkins Hospital School of Nursing. The differences in the orientation and scope of practice expected by graduates of these two programs provide early examples of the differences in the prevailing treatment-oriented medical ideology and health promotion and disease prevention nursing ideology (Church, 1985). The history of psychiatric nursing is riddled with this persistent conflict between medical and nursing orientations.

That a causal relationship exists between this conflict and the roles women and nurses have played in our society is supported by Ashley's assertion that ". . . the role of nursing in the health field is the epitome of woman's role in American society" (1975, p. 125). The commonly held observation during the first half of this century with regard to the American woman's aspirations for work was that she had two choices: (1) "Either she proclaimed herself a woman and therefore less an achieving individual or an individual and therefore less of a woman" (Church, 1982, p. 23); or (2) by staying within the confines of the male-dominated system of health care and extending her "natural" maternal role, the woman as nurse was successful in establishing an acceptable niche in the world outside home and hearth. The historical fact that psychiatric nursing emerged in isolation and separate from the development of general nursing gave rise to even greater inter- and intraprofessional problems. These relate to the traditional concerns of the workplace, such as professional boundaries, economics, and education, which in turn relate to and reflect the subordinate position of women working in a man's world.

In 1967, the American Nurses' Association took a critical step in extending the role of the psychiatric nurse with its *Statement on Psychiatric Nursing Practice*, which identified individual, group, and family psychotherapy as direct patient care functions of psychiatric nurses (Church, 1982). This pivotal document reinforced the definition of the nurse leaders of a quarter-of-a-century earlier. Such expansion in the nurse's role had been articulated by the pioneers in nursing education for ". . . the rhetoric from the turn of the century implied direct involvement in patient care and management of the therapeutic environment"

(Church, 1985, p. 45). In this emergent role, the psychiatric nurse did not merely administer somatic treatments and medications, restrain or seclude patients, or respond to physicians' orders (Huey, 1975). The modern psychiatric nurse now maintained a therapeutic environment and developed a therapeutic relationship with the patient, the latter being enhanced by psychotherapy knowledge and skills.

Over the next two decades, psychiatric nurses expanded their knowledge base, conducted nursing research, became certified, and obtained advanced degrees. Exposure to active, multidisciplinary approaches provided a broader foundation for psychiatric nursing. The addition of sociocultural concepts required for this growth facilitated the expansion of the nurse's role in the community. Psychiatric nurses began to enjoy not only expanded roles, but even more importantly, autonomous ones. Psychiatric nursing care by these specialists became increasingly characterized by the use of theory, independent nursing judgment, and decision-making. By 1976 psychiatric nursing was defined to encompass

> theories of human behavior as its science and purposeful use of self as its art. It is directed toward both preventive and corrective impact upon mental disorders and their sequelae and is concerned with the promotion of optimal mental health for society, the community, and those individuals who live in it. [Church, 1982]

As an accommodation to changing community-wide concerns in psychiatric-mental health care, the role of the psychiatric nurse expanded to include a challenging variety of opportunities and responsibilities, including the provision of psychotherapy services in increasingly independent roles.

As recently as the 1960s, however, nurse leaders still argued about whether nurses should function as psychotherapists (Huey, 1975). Debate about the appropriate use of psychiatric nurse specialists continues today. Controversy also surrounds the issue of whether psychiatric nursing specialists are qualified to treat all patients, regardless of their psychiatric problems. For example, British clinicians who devised a two-year program to prepare nurses as psychotherapists cautioned that only neurotics and patients with personality disorders should be seen by nurse psychotherapists (Bird, Marks, & Linley, 1979). Carter (1971) believed that female therapists (and at this time most psychiatric nurses are women) should treat only women, children, and psychotic patients.

In spite of these controversies, psychiatric nurse specialists are practicing in ever-increasing numbers as primary psychotherapists with individuals, couples, families, and groups (Calnen, 1972; Ledney, 1971; Lego,

1973; Sills, 1983). Several factors support this development. Lego (1973) argues that the nurse psychotherapist (NPT) perceives patients in a holistic way, is not restricted by traditional psychiatric models, and is comfortable in dealing with patients in crisis situations. Patients themselves report that nurses are very important to their recovery (Zaslove, Ungerledier, & Fuller, 1968). Furthermore, the use of NPTs by mental health service consumers makes economic sense; nurses can deliver psychotherapy services to consumers both effectively and economically (Carter, 1971; Fagin, 1983; Ginsberg & Marks, 1977; and Marks, 1977). Moreover, the current preoccupation with cost control in health care places the NPT in an excellent market position if one accepts the finding of Pardes and Pincus (1983) that only 25% of those needing mental health services require a psychiatrist's attention; they concluded the remainder can be effectively treated by non-physician mental health practitioners, including nurses.

While a few nurses opened private practices in the early 1970s, this movement didn't gain momentum until 1975 when thirty-four private practitioners from throughout the United States, including a significant number of psychiatric nurses, convened at the University of Iowa to share their experiences (Jacox & Norris, 1977). Since that time, increasing numbers of anecdotal reports by psychiatric nurses in private practice have appeared in the literature. It is impossible, however, to estimate the number of these nurses who treat patients. This problem stems from the paucity of research relative to this role and from a lack of sources to identify and locate these practitioners. However, one can conclude, on the basis of reports in the literature, conference papers, networking and lobbying activities, and the increased enrollment of nurses in graduate psychiatric nursing programs, that the number of these practitioners continues to grow.

In 1982, during an individual psychotherapy seminar for psychiatric nursing graduate students, several participants remarked that although they knew of nurses who had nursing psychotherapy practices, they had very little information about them. The students were curious about how the nurses structured their practices, whom they treated and what they actually did with patients. Our extensive literature search uncovered little systematic research in this area. Interest in these nurses and their work led to our completing several exploratory and descriptive studies (Durham & Hardin, 1985a & b; Durham & Hardin, 1983; Hardin & Durham, 1985; and Spunt, Hardin, & Durham, 1984).

While conducting our research, many psychiatric nurse leaders and NPTs discussed their work and shared their ideas with us. Often there was confusion, if not outright disagreement, about the appropriate label for this unique practitioner. One difficulty was the use of the term "independent" to describe this role. Sills (1983), for example, pointed out that to some extent all nurses practice independently; and, conversely, no nurse, not even the nurse psychotherapist, is totally independent of other practitioners.

A second disagreement occurred over our use of the term "psychotherapist." Several research subjects argued that they are "not psychotherapists," but rather "counselors," or, as one nurse stated, she is, "simply a nurse who performs nursing care." Still an additional concern centered around our using the label "nurse" psychotherapist. Several psychiatric nurse educators said the term was redundant; others believed that the label combined opposing concepts. We concluded that not only was nursing somewhat unclear about this role that we had begun to study, but also that these entrepreneurial practitioners were in disagreement over whether their identities as nurses and as psychotherapists were discernable, or, in fact, even should be.

Through our research, we also discovered that many patients who were treated by nurses did not identify their therapists as such, especially if their NPTs held advanced degrees in other disciplines (many held doctorates in areas other than nursing). We also wondered whether some nurses might consider it more prestigious to identify themselves as simply "counselors" or "therapists" since several shared the view of one subject who informed us that "My patients do NOT identify me as a NURSE!" Parsons (1984) alluded to this identity conflict when she wrote about her self-perception as both a psychotherapist and a nurse.

> I have never felt it necessary to call myself a "Nurse Psychotherapist." To do so would be to divide my sense of self. I don't feel it is necessary to carry my awareness of my being a nurse in the foreground. The term "nurse psychotherapist" may be a small example of a large problem within nursing— blurred professional identity. Is using the word "nurse" before anything else we do a natural reaction to the very complexity and ambiguity that encompasses what nurses do? To me it is this very breadth of scope and lack of closure that does us credit as a profession. Too easily are we captured in nursing by the ubiquitous human tendency to seek boundaries and tight definitions to aid our tenuous sense of control. Hypersensitivity about our professional identity demeans us. Dignity is a quiet virtue that nursing richly deserves.

One cannot help but wonder about the impact of the professional origins of non-nurse psychotherapists as they practice and identify themselves to their world of patients and colleagues. For us, the issue is not resolved. However, in the interest of clarity, and acknowledging that we may sound defensive or overly sensitive concerning this practice role, we use the label *"nurse* psychotherapist" (or NPT) throughout the book. We emphasize the term "nurse" because we believe this functional role is still a relatively new one for our profession. We shall also refer to the NPT in this book as "she" because about 97% of all nurses are women. In light of this fact, our choice of pronouns seems warranted. Finally, we use the term "patient" in preference to "client" in the sense that Pellegrino (1980) described: "patient" (from the Latin) means "to suffer, to bear something," while "client" implies "a vassal or dependent." We do not mean to imply that "patients" are those who are treated on an inpatient basis while "clients" are those who are seen in outpatient clinics, offices, or other similar settings.

What is it that NPTs do? How does what they do differ from the work of other psychotherapists? In this book we offer the contributions of nurse psychotherapists in private practice to provide initial answers to these questions. However, conclusive answers may elude us since experts do not agree upon what constitutes psychotherapy. Victor Raimy, for example, has wryly defined psychotherapy as an "undefined technique applied to unspecified cases with unpredictable results. For this technique, rigorous training is required" (London, 1964). In a less humorous vein, Churchill (1967) described psychotherapy as a process in which persons are helped to become aware of attitudes and feelings in a specialized relationship that involves the deliberate application of theory and concomitant techniques to treat particular disturbances.

Beuker (1966), Biddle (1966), and Strupp (1978) have described the "art of psychotherapy" in which skills of a personal nature, compassion, and empathy play a critical role. Most evaluation research on psychotherapy (including that with patients who are themselves therapists) indicates that effective therapists are those who demonstrate empathy and warmth as primary characteristics (Grunebaum, 1983). We maintain that nurse psychotherapy is an art, as well as a science.

London and Klerman (1982) catalogued psychotherapeutic approaches into four broad categories as having: (1) verbal dialogues (e.g., psychoanalysis, group psychotherapy, client-centered, or nondirective therapy); (2) dramatic verbal interactions with behavioral rehearsal or altered states of consciousness (e.g., psychodrama, hypnosis, sex therapy); (3) chemical or physical manipulation of the body (e.g., aversion therapy, biofeedback, and rolfing); and (4) biological interventions in the brain (e.g., the use of psychotropic drugs). Although debate continues on how to classify and label the various psychotherapies, Lazarus found that most therapies had more commonalities than differences across styles (1978). In their work as nurse psychotherapists, practitioners can use one or a combination of these four major approaches.

We see psychotherapy as consisting of several major elements: verbal and nonverbal interactions that occur between two or more people over a prolonged period of time; mutually established goals determined both by the patient's needs and therapist's orientation; a mutual commitment to the therapeutic relationship; and knowledgeable use of theory and techniques. We conclude that the NPT is a registered nurse whose minimal academic qualifications include the master's degree in psychiatric-mental health nursing and whose practice is guided by the American Nurses' Association's *Standards of Psychiatric and Mental Health Nursing Practice* (1982) and "Guidelines for Private Practice of Psychiatric and Mental Health Nursing" (1985).

We believe that the nurse is a unique psychotherapist in certain respects. Although these unique aspects will be discussed and amplified in Chapter 2, here we can interject that we agree with Sedgwick's (1974) view that nursing as a discipline has a unique form of problem conceptualization. The nurse psychotherapist selects, modifies, and applies theory and interventions in a manner discernable from other disciplines in her work with individuals, families, and/or groups. In addition to these professional dimensions of her role, the NPT's work also involves entrepreneurship: creativity, risk-taking, business acumen, energy, self-direction, autonomy, and interdependence. A central purpose of this book, therefore, is to illustrate how psychiatric nurses synthesize their unique knowledge and skills to effect change in patients through the interpretation of an entrepreneurial nursing role, that of nurse psychotherapist.

## SELECTED RESEARCH FINDINGS ABOUT THE ROLE OF THE NPT

While most NPTs currently work as solo practitioners, others provide their services within a partnership, corporate, or noncorporate group arrangement. The NPT has direct access to patients to whom she is accountable and from whom she collects fees-for-service. Patients who have been treated by NPTs have a very positive attitude toward the concept of nurse psychotherapy and toward their individual nurse therapists (Hardin & Durham, 1985). Our research suggests that the typical patient tends to be a young, unmarried, well-educated professional woman whose reasons for seeking treatment include depression, low self-esteem, insecurity regarding control over their own lives, and difficulties with interpersonal relationships. (Many NPTs do, of course, treat men, children, families, and groups.) NPTs generally help patients to increase their independence, self-esteem, and insight, and to decrease anxiety and guilt. Patients describe therapy as a satisfying, successful experience with a therapist who is empathic, warm, and competent, and who is a good listener.

The typical NPT is a highly experienced and educated female who works independently in a private office, treating patients on a weekly basis for approximately fourteen months. In 1983, she charged about $40 per fifty minute session (about half of most psychiatrists' fees) in a practice that is usually not her primary source of income. Many structural aspects of the NPT's practice mimic the medical model (i.e., NPTs maintain office practices, use verbal therapies, and rely on medical supervisors and medical continuing education), even though the NPT functions in a unique manner on a process level (Hardin & Durham, 1985).

Nurse psychotherapists typically use multiple theories to guide their work, although these are seldom nursing theories (Spunt, Durham, & Hardin, 1984). This finding supports Peplau's (1982) contention that psychiatric nursing is in a stage of transition from medically-oriented to nursing-oriented models of practice. The tasks of this transition are the reformulation of old theories within the nursing perspective, as well as the articulation of nursing theories (Fitzpatrick, Whall, Johnston, & Floyd, 1982). The first of these functions seems to characterize the practice of nursing psychotherapy at the present time. The bridge connecting theoretical models and concomitant interventions is not particularly obvious, possibly reflecting psychiatric nursing's historical tendency to be practical, as well as action and goal-oriented, and to divorce theory from practice (Hoeffer & Murphy, 1981; O'Toole, 1981; Spunt, Durham, & Hardin, 1984). Or perhaps it is too early in the era of the NPT to clearly articulate theoretical and interventionist linkages. A more thorough description and discussion of the theoretical models underpinning nursing psychotherapy is found in Chapter 3.

The authors were concerned that the ideas and skills of educated and experienced nurse psychotherapists (who might potentially generate or reformulate psychiatric nursing theory) were being lost. We speculated that the NPT might be less encumbered by institutional restrictions and freer to conceive and enact her role in a creative and highly autonomous way. We also observed there were few published reports to guide nurse psychotherapists wishing to establish a private practice. Neither was there a readily available forum in which nurse psychotherapists could share their theoretical perspectives, clinical approaches, and practice experiences.

Therefore, this book focuses upon issues, concerns, and considerations in beginning and maintaining a private practice in nurse psychotherapy and upon the NPT's interpretation of her clinical role. We are unable here to debate the ethical aspects of private practice as a phenomenon within nursing today. However, others have offered somewhat opposite views of the ethics of the private practice movement within nursing. Hoeffer (1983), for example, expressed concern that private nursing practices do not provide for distributive justice, just as medical treatment is often not available to those who cannot pay for it. Fagin (1983) noted, however, that NPTs can provide excellent psychotherapy services inexpensively and should, therefore, continue to develop this role. These, as well as other ethical concerns related to the role and work of the NPT, merit further discussion.

We maintain that the role of the NPT is a viable option and legitimate role for psychiatric nurse specialists. We are fully aware that some skilled and well-educated psychiatric nurses may not wish to deal with the machinations of this entrepreneurial role. Most nurses who do become private practitioners are motivated, according to Jacox and Norris (1977), by the desire to achieve greater patient contact, power, renumeration, independence, and prestige; to fill unmet community needs; and to educate the public about what nursing has to offer. Regardless of the NPT's reasons for entering private practice, those who are experienced in this role should have a forum in which to share their knowledge and experience with other nurse psychotherapists or those who are contemplating this role. We hope this book generates both interest and debate among its readers.

# REFERENCES

American Nurses' Association Council on Psychiatric and Mental Health Nursing. (1985). Guidelines for private practice of psychiatric and mental health nursing. *Pacesetter, 12*(1), p. 3.

American Nurses' Association. (1982). *Standards of psychiatric and mental health nursing.* Kansas City: American Nurses' Association.

Ashley, J. A. (1975). Nursing and early feminism. *American Journal of Nursing, 75,* 1465–1467.

Beuker, K. (1966). The treatment role of the psychiatric nurse—one point of view. *Perspectives in Psychiatric Care, 4,* 15–19.

Biddle, B. J., & Thomas, E. J. (1966). *Role theory: Concepts and research.* New York: Wiley.

Bird, J., Marks, I. M., & Lindley, P. (1979). Nurse therapists in psychiatry: Developments, controversies, and implications. *British Journal of Psychiatry, 135,* 321–329.

Calnen, T. (1973). Whose agent? A re-evaluation of the role of the psychiatric nurse in the therapeutic community. *Perspectives in Psychiatric Care, 10,* 210–214.

Carter, C. A. (1971). Advantages of being a woman therapist. *Psychotherapy: Theory, Research and Practice, 8,* 297–300.

Church, O. M. (1982). That noble reform: Emergence of psychiatric nursing in the United States, 1880–1963. Unpublished doctoral dissertation, University of Illinois Health Sciences Center, Chicago.

Church, O. M. (1985). Emergence of training programs of asylum nursing at the turn of the century. *Advances in Nursing Science, 7*(1), 35–46.

Churchill, J. (1967). An issue: Nurses and psychotherapy. *Perspectives in Psychiatric Care, 5,* 160–162.

Durham, J., & Hardin, S. (1985-a). Nurse psychotherapists' experiences in obtaining individual practice privileges. *The Nurse Practitioner, 10*(11), 62–67.

Durham, J., & Hardin, S. (1985-b). Promoting advanced nursing practice. *The Nurse Practitioner, 10*(2), 59–62.

Durham, J., & Hardin, S. (1983). Promoting independent practice in a competitive marketplace. *Nursing Economics, 1*(1), 24–28.

Fagin, C. M. (1983). Concepts for the future: Competition and substitution. *Journal of Psychosocial Nursing and Mental Health Services, 21*(3), 36–40.

Fitzpatrick, J., Whall, A., Johnston, R., & Floyd, J. (1982). *Nursing models and their psychiatric-mental health applications.* Bowie, MD: Brady.

Ginsberg, F., & Marks, I. (1977). Costs of benefits of behavioral psychotherapy: A pilot study of neurotics treated by nurse therapists. *Psychological Medicine, 17*(3), 685–700.

Grunebaum, H. (1983). A study of therapists' choice of a therapist. *American Journal of Psychiatry, 140,* 1336–1339.

Hardin, S., & Durham J. (1985). First rate: Structure, process, and effectiveness of nurse psychotherapy. *Journal of Psychosocial Nursing and Mental Health Services, 23*(5), 8–15.

Hoeffer, B. (1983). The private practice model: An ethical perspective. *Journal of Psychosocial Nursing and Mental Health Services, 21*(7), 31–37.

Hoeffer, B., & Murphy, S. (1982). The unfinished task: Development of nursing theory for psychiatric and mental health nursing practice. *Journal of Psychosocial Nursing and Mental Health Services, 20*(12), 8–14.

Huey, F. L. (1975). *Psychiatric nursing, 1946–1974: A report on the state of the art.* New York: American Journal of Nursing.

Jacox, A., & Norris, C. (1977). *Organizing for independent practice.* New York: Appleton-Century-Crofts.

Lazarus, A. (1978). Styles not systems. *Psychotherapy: Theory, Research, and Practice, 15,* 359–362.

Ledney, D. M. (1971). Psychiatric nursing: Breakthrough to independence? *RN, 34*(8), 29–35.

Lego, S. (1973). Nurse psychotherapists: How are we different? *Perspectives in Psychiatric Care, 11,* 144–147.

London, P. (1964). *The modes and morals of psychotherapy.* New York: Holt, Rinehart, and Winston.

London, P., & Klerman, G. (1982). Evaluating psychotherapy. *American Journal of Psychiatry, 139*(6), 709–717.

Marks, I. (1977). Recent results of behavioral therapy of phobias and obsessions. *Journal of International Medical Research, 5*(5), 16–21.

O'Toole, A. (1981). When the practical becomes theoretical. *Journal of Psychosocial Nursing and Mental Health Services, 19*(12), 11–19.

Pardes, H., & Pinkus, H. A. (1983). Report of the Graduate Medical Education National Advisory Committee and Health Manpower Development: Implications for psychiatry. *Archives of General Psychiatry, 40*, 97–102.

Parsons, L. (1984). Beginning a nurse psychotherapy practice. Chicago School of Professional Psychology, Chicago.

Peplau, H. (1956, November). *Historical development of psychiatric nursing: A preliminary statement of some facts and trends.* Paper presented at the Working Conference on Graduate Education in Psychiatric Nursing, Williamsburg, VA.

Peplau, H. (1982). In J. Fitzpatrick, A. Whall, R. Johnston, & J. Floyd (Eds.), *Nursing models and their psychiatric-mental health nursing applications* (p. vii). Bowie, MD: Brady.

Sedgwick, R. (1974, September). Nursing's contribution to social psychiatry: A holistic approach to personhood. Paper presented at the Fifth International Congress of Social Psychiatry, Athens.

Sills, G. (1983). The uncertain future. In I. L. Abraham, B. K. Hagerty, K. P. Krone, & G. D. Reed (Eds.), *Psychiatric nursing under conditions of economic uncertainty* (pp. 1–12). Ann Arbor, MI: University of Michigan.

Spunt, J., Durham, J., & Hardin, S. B. (1984). Theoretical models and interventions used by nurse psychotherapists. *Issues in Mental Health Nursing, 6*, 35–51.

Stevens, B. (1979). *Nursing theory.* Boston: Little, Brown.

Strupp, H. (1978). The therapist's theoretical orientation: An overrated variable. *Psychotherapy: Theory, Research and Practice, 15*, 314–316.

Zaslove, M. O., Ungerleider, J. T., & Fuller, M. (1968). The importance of the psychiatric nurse: Views of physicians, patients, and nurses. *American Journal of Psychiatry, 125*, 74–78.

# Chapter 2
# The Nurse Psychotherapist as Unique Practitioner

*Shirley A. Smoyak*

Psychiatric nurses in the United States celebrated their 100th birthday in 1982 at the Century Celebration held in Washington, D.C. For years, the title, "psychiatric nurse," was applied to any nurse who had trained in a psychiatric hospital or who was currently working in one. Occasionally, psychiatric aides or attendants were also addressed as "nurse." It was not until the American Nurses' Association first published *Standards for the Practice of Psychiatric Nursing* (1965) that this title was reserved for nurses holding the master's degree in psychiatric nursing.

In 1950, Arnhoff, Rubinstein, and Shriver (1969) observed that there were 7,100 psychiatrists and child psychiatrists, 7,300 psychologists (belonging to the American Psychological Association, but few of them practicing as clinicians), and virtually no psychiatric nurses. While in 1950 nurses worked in psychiatric settings, they were not identified by these authors since they did not hold advanced degrees. In a sense, psychiatric nurses were invisible practitioners.

In 1980, there were an estimated 1.1 million registered nurses in the United States (U.S. Department of Health and Human Services, 1981). About 5% of these reported psychiatric-mental health as their area of clinical practice. To identify the body of psychiatric nurses who are at least master's-prepared and who are in private practice as nurse psychotherapists in the United States today is an impossible task. No national organization represents this group of practitioners, nor is there any specific, country-wide licensing mechanism to allow their being systematically counted. In a 1977–78 Inventory (ANA, 1981), of the 51,564 nurses who said psychiatric-mental health was their clinical area, most (approximately two-thirds) had earned less than the baccalaureate degree and a mere 13% (6,579) had at least a master's degree. (Some of these advanced degrees, however, were in areas other than psychiatric nursing.) Today, approximately 70% of all mental health nurses (including all levels of preparation) work in hospitals, and an additional 10.6% in community health, including mental health. From these statistics, one might approximate the current number of master's-prepared, private-practicing, nurse psychotherapists as 1,000–2,000; however, projections are for this number to increase dramatically over the next decade.

Psychiatric nursing has the highest proportion of nurses educated at the graduate level of any field of nursing (NLN, 1977; Taube & Barrett, 1983). From 1965 through 1975, about 25% of all master's degrees in nursing were earned by psychiatric nurses. Since then, this percentage has dropped, but the absolute number of degrees awarded in the field has continued to rise. The integrated curriculum in nursing education is often cited as the reason for the decline in the selection of psychiatric nursing as a career by recent graduates. The effect of the loss of federal funds for graduate study may also partially account for the decrease in psychiatric nurse careers.

## THE FOUR CORE MENTAL HEALTH PROFESSIONS

Psychiatric nursing is one of the four core mental health professions, the other three being psychiatry, psychology, and social work. Psychiatrists and nurses are most often on the staff of inpatient facilities, especially state and county mental hospitals and the psychiatric units of non-Federal general hospitals. Psychiatrists, unlike nurses, are usually not employees of the institutions, and social workers and psychologists are most heavily concentrated in free-standing, outpatient clinics and community mental health centers. The educational preparation of the core professions differs also, with psychiatrists accounting for the most years (usually four years of medical school followed by a four-year residency in psychiatry), followed by psychologists (a doctorate and some type of clinical internship), and then social workers (the majority of whom hold master's degrees).

Even though the preparation, work settings, and gender (more men in psychology and psychiatry and more women in social work and nursing) of the four core mental health professions vary considerably, all four practice psychotherapy and its variants—group therapy, family therapy, behavioral therapy—very similarly. Moreover, ten or fifteen years ago, a popular topic at conventions and conferences was, "Should there be a generic psychotherapist?" The four core professions soundly rejected the idea of a "fifth profession" and the debate seems to have ended.

When the core mental health professions work together or convene at conferences and workshops to discuss their perspectives and jurisdictions of practice, each is concerned with delineating and promulgating the unique aspects of its group. In partial recognition of this interest, The Joint Commission on Interprofessional Affairs (JCIA) was founded in 1975, with members representing the American Nurses' Association, the American Psychiatric Association, the American Psychological Association, and the National Association of Social Workers. The Commission was convened after one organization critically commented on another organization in testimony before the United States Congress. Following this commentary, the organizational leaders realized the destructiveness of the professions' divisive stance and created the JCIA. The American Orthopsychiatric Association also takes into account the perspectives of all of these groups and frequently organizes panels and workshops to consider issues pertinent to all the mental health professions. At the Century Celebration (1982), each of the four groups was represented in a panel presentation on the state of the art.

The Committee on Governmental Agencies (1983) of the Group for the Advancement of Psychiatry has prepared a manuscript entitled, "Changing Roles of Mental Health Professionals." They invited a psychologist, a social worker, and a psychiatric nurse (this author) to meet with them over several years to discuss the issues of what the similarities and differences in the four professions were; how practice jurisdictions were handled in various settings; how authority and responsibility for patient care were defined and implemented; and how colleagueship was managed. Each nonpsychiatrist prepared a chapter on the unique dimensions of her/his profession, which was discussed and debated by the others. The psychiatrists prepared their chapter and also subjected it to dialogue. These manuscripts are currently being reviewed by the parent body, the Group for the Advancement of Psychiatry, before publication.

## What Is Unique About Nurse Psychotherapists?

In attempting to define for the Committee on Governmental Agencies the "unique characteristics of the specialty, psychiatric nursing," this author stated the following:

> The nurse is the member of the mental health care team who has the responsibility for the continuity of patient care in in-patient settings and the

integration of a myriad of services in out-patient settings. Within hospitals, they diagnose and monitor the milieu in which patients are treated. They are responsible for the physical, as well as the psychosocial environment.

They are in charge of transitions. They orient patients upon admission, integrate their within-hospital shifts and changes, prepare them for discharge and follow them, frequently, into the community. Liaison nurses provide consultation to staff nurses on general hospital units and to public health nurses in communities about psychiatric and behavioral problems encountered by the nurses.

While all four of the mental health professions share roughly the same body of knowledge, the psychiatric nurse is unique in her:

1. use of biological as well as psychological theories in providing patient care;
2. providing continuity of patient care on all shifts and days;
3. planning, monitoring, and executing transitions for patients among modalities, services and settings; and
4. definition of the jurisdiction of her practice to be the diagnosis and treatment of human responses to actual or potential health problems. [Smoyak, 1985]

Nurses are close to their patients, both physically and emotionally. They frequently touch them in the course of providing care. The tremendous therapeutic impact of something so simple as touching has recently been documented by psychiatric nursing research (Duffy, 1982) which illustrates that patients who are touched more frequently by staff are less depressed, angry, and hostile than those who are touched less frequently. In summary, while psychiatric nurses who conduct psychotherapy work in ways similar to other mental health specialists, they also are unique in certain aspects (Flaskerud, 1984).

## STRENGTHS OF PSYCHIATRIC-MENTAL HEALTH NURSING

The clinical practice of psychiatric nurses is firmly rooted in theoretical frameworks and models. (See also Chapter 3.) Curricula in varied master's programs have a key element of this firm theoretical grounding, strengthened by an intense clinical supervisory process. Other areas of nursing, because of historical developments and the recently expanding technology, tend to be more pragmatic or guided by principles or techniques rather than theories. Psychiatric nurses are clearly committed to understanding the phenomena of disturbances in human behavior and to using applications of theory to guide intervention strategies. They are exceptional observers, recording these observations to make them accessible to others when multidisciplinary teams treat patients.

Since psychiatric nurses have a firm foundation in biological and somatic theories, research, and in the psychological and sociocultural dimensions, they are able to distinguish between organic and functional origins of behavioral disturbances. They do remember, in their day-to-day practice, that the head is connected to the body and that one influences the other greatly. A mentally healthy outlook is easier to achieve in an organically healthy body. Nurses remind their patients to pay attention to their physiological as well as psychological selves. It would not be unusual for a psychiatric nurse to monitor the blood pressure of a client who had sought her services to deal with unbearable stress at work or home, and who is at risk for hypertension because of such factors as age, weight, and family history.

Particularly in areas where access to comprehensive health care is unevenly distributed, psychiatric nurses provide a most needed, all-encompassing service to their patients. Because they are well-versed in the physiological as well as the psychological aspects of human body processes, they are looked upon as resources for information about nutrition, exercise, sleep, and other aspects of wellness. They provide assessments for both the family member under treatment, as well as others in the patient's system.

The secondary socialization to the nursing profession has historical roots of producing in its recruits a firm sense of responsibility to patients and families and a respect for life. Nurses need not be reminded constantly to "do no harm." They have internalized a sense of accountability for their actions within the scope of their clinical abilities, and they feel a responsibility to expand their knowledge and skills.

Other concomitants of their socialization to the profession include their resourcefulness, innovation, and creativity. They learn very early in their training to do without or to make use of what is available when resources are limited. Their experiences in public health environments and in the homes of patients of all social classes enhance their resourcefulness. Very often, in the middle of the night or on weekends, they are the only resource within hospitals and must, therefore, creatively and effectively handle the whole range of human behavior from violent outbursts to withdrawal and suicide attempts.

While well-prepared for their clinical work, psychiatric nurses do not characteristically leap ahead into territories that they do not know. They have a realistic sense of their limitations, based on the scope of their education. They are ready to say what they know, as well as what they do not know, and to consult, refer, cooperate, and collaborate appropriately in each situation.

Nurses are not likely to present themselves as omnipotent, thus being unlikely to endanger patients by experimental or ill-founded approaches to health care. Part of the reason that nurses are sued less often than other mental health practitioners rests in the felt assurance and comfort of their patients that the care that they have received has been safe and humane as well as effective.

Because nurses, in their generic preparation as generalists, have worked with patients whose illnesses or incapacities are of long duration or tending toward recidivism, nurses develop a patience and a respect for time. Nurses are able to judge when a patient in a rehabilitation program for a chronic condition needs a bit more time or a well-aimed push. Waiting for a patient to become ready is not seen as a waste of time, but as an opportunity to establish better rapport and trust.

Nurses frequently use a general systems approach and include all family members in their assessment and treatment plans. They are not likely to interpret symptoms as "belonging" to individual members, but rather to define symptoms as signals of system distress. This "no fault" approach increases the likelihood that the patient and family system will be more amenable to therapy and change.

In conducting their practice, nurses are more willing than the other core professionals to treat individuals and families in their own setting. This approach, which this author has described elsewhere (Smoyak, 1977), provides a far more accurate data base about pathological processes, especially in light of more recent theories. Its advantages far outweigh any associated costs.

## WEAKNESSES OF PSYCHIATRIC-MENTAL HEALTH NURSING

Most psychiatric nurses are women and, unfortunately, the positive effects of the women's movement have not yet erased many nurses' tendencies toward dependence, subservience, and obsequiousness that so badly hamper the profession (Hardin, Urbanus, & Green, 1986). While nurse psychotherapists and other nurse specialists in private practice may be less likely to downplay their skills and knowledge, other nurses still do. For example, many nurses still assume, to a large degree, that if they make a clinical discovery about a given patient or a generalized phenomenon, that this is not new and that someone else must have known it before. They tend to think that their uncommon findings are someone else's common knowledge.

Certainly nurses today are more assertive than they were twenty years ago, but damage to their collective self-esteem has been considerable. They are still rather reluctant to use their authority, based on education, license, and social mandate to act individually and collectively to create change.

Many nurses see what they do as "work" or a "job" rather than viewing themselves as career-oriented professionals. Of course, this perspective is less evident among nurse specialists who engage in private practice or in an academic or administrative career. Until recently, nurses were unlikely to seek a mentor relationship (Smoyak, 1985); instead they tended to seek the advice or consultation of non-nurses (e.g., psychiatrists, psychologists) rather than rely on the knowledge and expertise of other nurses. They tended to value the ideas and products of men rather than women. Happily, abundant evidence exists that a newly-found sense of professional self-worth is emerging. Private practice exemplifies this change.

In undervaluing themselves, psychiatric nurses have tended to produce a kind of deflation among all mental health professionals. If a nurse working in a community mental health clinic collects less than she is worth, the income of others will be affected. Patients will assume they have received second-rate care if they are charged bargain prices.

## THE NPT AS PRIVATE PRACTITIONER

Until recently, psychiatrists were by far the predominant mental health discipline in private practice. With changes in access to insurance reimbursement, stimulated primarily by clinical psychologists, psychiatric nurses have initiated nursing psychotherapy private practices in increasing numbers. Judging from dialogues and discussions at various conventions in the past few years, nurse psychotherapists seem to be distributed in a parallel way to the other professions, that is, clustering in urban settings and having appointments with the more "treatable" populations. Underrepresented in their practices are the elderly, poor, inner-city, and rural residents, chronic schizophrenics, and substance-abusers. Some optimistically projected that as more nurses entered private practice, they would continue to see the population that they traditionally had treated in hospitals and clinics—severely ill patients who needed supportive therapy and medications or other traditionally underserved groups.

There are, however, no data to support this speculation; indeed a study by Hardin and Durham (1985) found the opposite to be true.

Psychiatric nurses who engage in nursing psychotherapy practices do so for the same reasons as other mental health professionals. The advantages of private practice include maximal autonomy for patients and professionals alike with a minimum of bureaucratic red tape and interference with professional judgment. Patients, if they can afford it, or have insurance that will allow it, can freely select the practitioner of their choice, using such criteria as age, sex, race, credentials, style, location, availability, cost, educational background, and recommendation of others. Theoretically, this freedom to select the therapist may increase the probability that the treatment will be helpful. Similarly, the therapist's freedom to concentrate on specific treatments and kinds of patients should enhance their clinical skills.

A fee-for-service system, with practitioners earning income by hours spent in treating patients, tends to maximize productivity and minimize time spent on paperwork, meetings, and other nonincome functions. Private practice therapists spend less time worrying about filling out forms for regulatory bodies or agencies and can use a streamlined bookkeeping system of their own choosing. Therapists in private practice can set their own rules and standards for how much continuing education they need and decide which colleagues to seek out for advice and knowledge expansion.

NPTs in private practice are no more altruistic than the other core professionals; thus, they are subject to the same dangers or disadvantages. It is the tendency of the private practitioner to treat any patient who seeks services, with the methods that the therapist knows how to use, unless there is a glaring misfit between the need and the skills (Group for the Advancement of Psychiatry, 1985). Any single practitioner is usually more limited in potential treatment strategies or resources than a multidisciplinary group or agency. Factors that operate against a single therapist's admitting shortcomings include pride, an unwillingness to see one's practice as limited, deficient, or off-base, and economic fear. Economic motives of therapists who work solely in the private practice mode can threaten clients' receiving the most cost-effective or relevant treatment. Another danger in solo private practice is the absence of triage mechanisms, related to coherent and efficient referral processes, including hospitalization. In New Jersey, for example, litigation concerning the right of a master's-prepared nurse psychotherapist to follow her patient into a community hospital and to continue treatment is in progress (Wrable *v.* Community Memorial Hospital, 1985).

# SUMMARY

While psychiatric nursing is more than 100 years old, the trend of nurse psychotherapists in private practice is relatively new. Today, there is a general concensus that the private practice nurse is one who is at least master's-prepared in psychiatric-mental health nursing, so that her credentials approximate those of the other core mental health professionals. When psychiatric nurses engage in private practice, they do so for the same reasons that psychiatrists, psychologists, or social workers do—to be able to practice more autonomously, to give way to their entrepreneurial predilections, and to gain the freedom to develop their skills and practice as they like.

# REFERENCES

American Nurses' Association. (1965). *Standards for practice in psychiatric-mental health nursing.* Kansas City: American Nurses' Association.

American Nurses' Association. (1976). *Standards for practice in psychiatric-mental health nursing.* Kansas City: American Nurses' Association.

American Nurses' Association. (1981). *Inventory of registered nurses, 1977-78.* Kansas City: American Nurses' Association.

American Nurses' Association. (1982). *Standards for practice in psychiatric-mental health nursing.* Kansas City: American Nurses' Association.

Arnhoff, F., Rubinstein, E., Shriver, B., & Jones, D. (1969). The mental health fields: An overview of manpower growth and development. In P. Arnhoff, E. Rubinstein, & J. Speisman (Eds.), *Manpower for mental health* (pp. 1–38). Chicago: Aldine.

Committee on Governmental Agencies, Group for the Advancement of Psychiatry. (1985). *Changing roles of mental health professionals.* Manuscript in review. Washington, DC: Group for the Advancement of Psychiatry.

Duffy, E. (1982). *An exploratory study: The effects of touch on the elderly in a nursing home.* Unpublished master's thesis. New Jersey: Rutgers, the State University of NJ, New Brunswick.

Flaskerud, J. (1984). The distinctive character of nursing psychotherapy. *Issues in Mental Health Nursing, 6,* 1-19.

Hardin, S., Urbanus, P., & Green, D. (1986). The nursing class of 1963 revisited. *Journal of Nursing Education, 25*(4), 171-174.

Hardin, S., & Durham, J. (1985). First rate: The structure process and effectiveness of nurse psychotherapy. *Journal of Psychosocial Nursing and Mental Health Services, 23*(5), 8-15.

Mone, L. (1983). *Private practice: A professional business.* LaJolla CA: Elm Press.

National League for Nursing. (1978). *Some statistics on baccalaureate and higher degree education in nursing, 1965-1977.* New York: National League for Nursing.

Report of the task panel on mental health personnel. (1978). Submitted to the

President's Commission on Mental Health, February 15, 1978 in *Task Panel Reports, Vol. II, Appendix*. Washington, DC: U.S. Government Printing Office.

Smoyak, S. (1977). Homes: A natural environment for family therapy. In J. Hall & B. Weaver (Eds.), *Distributive nursing practice: A systems approach to community health* (pp. 369–380). New York: Lippincott.

Smoyak, S. (1985). Psychiatric-mental health nursing. In GAP report *Changing roles of mental health professionals*. Manuscript in review.

Taube, C., & Barrett, S. (Eds.). National Institutes of Mental Health. (1983). *Mental health, United States, 1983*. (DHHS Publication No. ADM 83-1275). Washington, DC: U.S. Government Printing Office.

U.S. Department of Health and Human Services, PHS., Division of Nursing. (1981). *Source book-nursing personnel*. (DHHS Publication No. HRA 81-21). Washington, DC: U.S. Government Printing Office.

Wrable *v.* Community Memorial Hospital. (1985). Superior Court of Monmouth County, NJ.

# Chapter 3
# Theoretical Models Underpinning Nursing Psychotherapy Practice

*Sally Brosz Hardin, Jerry D. Durham, Jan Pleak Spunt*

Psychiatric nursing has lacked a well-defined theoretical base in nursing science to guide advanced practice and instead has relied on models from psychology, medicine, sociology, and communication sciences. Psychiatric nursing curricula have often been portrayed as "eclectic," a term that may have become a euphemism for the absence of a unifying, nursing theoretical framework. To this end, Fitzpatrick, Whall, Johnston, and Floyd made a major contribution with their publication, *Nursing Models and Their Psychiatric Mental Health Applications* (1982). In emphasizing the need for this work, Peplau noted

> The profession of nursing is gradually moving away from the 'medical model' toward conceptual models that are more relevant to nursing practice . . . The development of nursing models . . . [represents] the intellectual ferment taking place during this transition from medically-oriented nursing care toward nurse-directed care. (p. vii)

Previous research by the authors identified the theoretical models and psychotherapeutic interventions nurse psychotherapists (NPTs) most often used in their practices (Spunt, Durham, & Hardin, 1984). Major theoretical bases used most frequently by these nurse specialists in 1983 included: dynamic (by far the most prevalent), systems, rational-cognitive, and behavioral models. Although nursing, humanistic, crisis, and developmental theories were also actualized by the NPTs, these were applied with much less frequency. Significantly, fewer than one-fourth of the 77 respondents in this study identified nursing theory as a foundation for their nursing practice.

Within these major theory categories NPTs applied more specific theoretical approaches. They most frequently used a psychoanalytic, Sullivanian, and ego-psychology approach within the dynamic category; a family, general, and communication approach within the systems framework; and a transactional, cognitive, reality-orientation, and rational-emotive perspective within the rational/cognitive model. For the minority of NPT subjects who based their practice on nursing theory, no one theorist was selected over others; Peplau, Rogers, Orem, Roy, and others were applied about equally. Most NPTs reported using several models of practice; only those within the psychoanalytic perspective had a tendency to restrict their theoretical bases to the psychoanalytic approach alone.

Some of the NPT respondents elaborated on how their perspectives were actualized when working with patients, and this amplification provided a better understanding of how NPTs combined various theories to guide an eclectic approach. One NPT, for example, explained that she used Martha Rogers' theory for a nursing perspective and the concept of "unitary man" for a nursing diagnosis. Another incorporated the work of Murray Bowen, including family genograms to obtain multigenerational data, with a transactional model to identify, clarify, or change patterns of communication. Still another nurse therapist blended problem-solving theory with Orem's self-care approach.

## EFFECTIVE NURSING INTERVENTIONS

In addition to examining the theoretical perspectives of the NPT subjects, the research also explored interventions that NPTs most frequently used and believed to be effective. NPT subjects described using nursing, psychodynamic, goal-setting, behavioral, and communication techniques. Specific interventions within the nursing category included, for example, education, use of self, providing empathy, focusing upon the here-and-now, increasing self-esteem, and using humor. Traditional techniques such as confronting, interpreting, and reframing were applied within a psychodynamic framework. Typical approaches such as behavior modification, relaxation exercises, limit-setting, and writing in diaries were included within the behaviorist framework.

While many of the interventions these NPTs use are general and characterize the work of all psychotherapists, others may be unique to the domain of psychiatric nursing. For example, under the major category "nursing approaches," education was an intervention reported by almost one-third of the NPTs. It is interesting that while so few nurses based their practice upon nursing theoretical models, many operationalized interventions that may be unique to nursing; and even more interesting, nursing interventions were the most frequent of all psychotherapeutic techniques used. Several NPTs provided specific examples of their interventions. For example, one NPT defined confrontation as working with the patient to clarify the "irrationality of her thinking and demonstrate how rational thinking will interrupt destructive feelings." Another NPT illustrated her use of empathy: "That must be painful—lonely. Thank you for letting me see some of your anger."

## Interventions that NPTs Wish to Add to Their Repertoires

Although many of the NPTs said they would rather improve the interventions they use than add additional techniques to their repertoires, the majority described potential interventions for their future practice. The interventions which NPTs planned for future use were categorized as psychodynamic, behavioral, holistic, family-oriented, cognitive-rational, or miscellaneous. Hypnosis received the largest number of responses as a technique NPTs would like to try. (Only two NPTs said they were currently using hypnotherapy.) Other psychodynamic techniques included paradoxical injunctions and confrontation. In the behavioral dimension, the NPTs said they would like to apply relaxation techniques, behavior modification, and role playing in their practices. In the holistic category nurses suggested biofeedback, gestalt, and exercise interventions. Even though the NPTs practiced individual therapy, several said they would like to include family-oriented techniques such as family therapy, sculpting, and home visits. Finally, NPTs listed cognitive-rational techniques such as cognitive therapy, imagery, and neurolinguistics; and several other interventions were noted, the most frequent being pharmacotherapy.

## THEORETICAL LINKAGES

It was difficult to see relationships between these subjects' purportedly effective interventions and theoretical bases for these interventions. Only a few relationships were observed. NPTs with a psychoanalytic approach, for example, identified interpretation as an effective intervention.

While NPTs from most theoretical perspectives intervened with education techniques, only two of the NPTs who identified nursing models as the theoretical underpinning to their practices also specifically reported education as an intervention. One might have predicted a closer relationship since the role of the nurse as patient educator is emphasized in nursing literature (Buckwalter, 1982; Bueker, 1966; Lego, 1973 & 1974).

# CONCLUSION

While most NPTs use theory as a basis for their practice, few rely on only one model and the minority who do so are from the psychoanalytic school. Rather, most NPTs use several models to direct their work with patients. What seems unique, if indeed one accepts the claim that nursing psychotherapy is unique, is as Sedgwick (1974) described—the way in which NPTs select, modify, and adapt theories to assess and treat total clients. Another distinguishing characteristic is the NPTs family orientation, even when treating individual patients. NPTs use psychotherapeutic approaches having verbal dialogue, rather than behavior rehearsal, altered states of consciousness, or chemical/physical interventions with the body. However, they indicate a willingness and interest in learning about these more dramatic and/or holistic approaches in the future.

Although nurse psychotherapists use interventions that might be described as unique to nursing, they do not report nursing theory as the basis of their practice. Rather, traditional psychological models such as psychoanalytic, Sullivanian or interpersonal theory, and systems theory are the most frequent bases of practice. One explanation for this finding may be that many NPTs studied psychotherapy at the graduate level when nursing theory was not an integrated part of the curriculum. As Lego reported in 1980, over half of the graduate psychiatric nursing programs at that time were strongly influenced by the psychoanalytic orientation. As an educational commitment to nursing models increases, so also might the utilization of nursing models by advanced practitioners. It is difficult to know if O'Toole (1981) is correct in her claim that psychiatric nurses tend to divorce theory from practice, or if other forces are operating. Perhaps it is too early in the era of nurse psychotherapy for practitioners to clearly articulate interventions and theoretical linkages; or perhaps NPTs are action-oriented and tend to use intuitively "what works."

NPTs tend to use general versus specific therapeutic interventions. Anderson (1983) argued that there are both advantages and disadvantages to this approach. An advantage of using general interventions is that they provide greater flexibility for the therapist and allow for individualization of interventions to meet specific patient needs. Alternately, Anderson pointed out that general interventions may decrease accountability in the therapeutic relationship or become so vague as to represent a trial-and-error approach to nursing treatment. If nurse psychotherapists used more specific interventions, the therapeutic relationship and the reformulation and evaluation of nursing therapy plans might be improved. More discrete descriptions could encourage NPTs to carefully examine and evaluate specific interventions and to modify them in a systematic manner. Continuity of care could also be improved, especially if more than one therapist were involved in treatment.

The study's findings corroborated Peplau's (1982) contention that psychiatric nursing is currently in a stage of transition from medically to nursing-based models of practice. According to Fitzpatrick et al. (1983), the tasks of this transition are "the reformulation of old theories within the nursing perspective" as well as the articulation of nursing theories. The former seems to characterize the practice of nurse psychotherapy at this time.

## REFERENCES

Anderson, M. (1983). Nursing interventions: What did you do that helped? *Perspectives in Psychiatric Care, 21,* 4–8.

Buckwalter, K. C., & Kerfoot, K. M. (1982). Teaching patients self-care. A critical aspect of psychiatric discharge planning. *Journal of Psychosocial Nursing and Mental Health Services, 12,* 15–22.

Bueker, K. (1966). The treatment role of the psychiatric nurse—one point of view. *Perspectives in Psychiatric Care, 4,* 15–19.

Fitzpatrick, J., Whall, A., Johnston, R., & Floyd, J. (1982). *Nursing models and their psychiatric-mental health applications.* Bowie, MD: Brady.

Lego, S. (1973). Nurse psychotherapists: How are we different? *Perspectives in Psychiatric Care, 11,* 144–147.

Lego, S. (1974). The one-to-one nurse-patient relationship. *Perspectives in Psychiatric Care, 18,* 67–89.

Lego, S. (1980). Theoretical Bases of Graduate Psychiatric Nursing Curricula. Paper presented at Perspectives in Psychiatric Care. Philadelphia, PA.

O'Toole, A. (1981). When the practical becomes theoretical. *Journal of Psychosocial Nursing and Mental Health Services, 19*(1), 11–19.

Peplau, H. (1982). In J. Fitzpatrick, A. Whall, R. Johnston, & J. Floyd (Eds.), *Nursing models and their psychiatric-mental health nursing applications* (p. vii). Bowie, MD: Brady.

Sedgwick, R. (1974). Nursing's Contribution to Social Psychiatry: A Holistic Approach to Personhood. Paper presented at the Fifth International Congress of Social Psychiatry, Athens, Greece.

Spunt, J., Hardin, S., & Durham, J. (1984). Theoretical models and interventions used by nurse psychotherapists. *Issues in Mental Health Nursing, 6,* 35–51.

# Chapter 4
# Elements of a Graduate Curriculum to Prepare Nurse Psychotherapists

*Anita Werner O'Toole*

The passage of the Mental Health Act in 1946 prompted the rapid development of graduate education programs in psychiatric nursing. As pointed out in Chapter 1, it was not until the mid 1950s, however, that graduate education in psychiatric nursing was devoted to preparation of the clinical specialist (Peplau, 1982; Rosenthal, 1984). These early programs prepared nurses to work intensively and therapeutically in one-to-one relationships and group therapy with patients, most of whom were residents of public mental hospitals. The content of the early programs focused upon interviewing skills and the therapeutic process as these related to individuals, groups, and social systems. Theoretical orientation was usually psychoanalytic, with a heavy emphasis on the interpersonal school within the psychoanalytic mainstream. At that time, it was not politically acceptable to call what graduate nursing students did "psychotherapy," although the resemblance was clear. Hence, individual psychotherapy was referred to as "one-to-one" and group psychotherapy as "group work."

It is interesting to note that as early as 1950 when psychiatric nursing leaders met at the University of Minnesota (see Chapter 1) they agreed that graduate education should prepare nurses as psychotherapists even though there was considerable resistance from other mental health professionals (Peplau, 1982). The participants concluded that the nurse was a therapeutic force in the treatment of patients; concepts of psychotherapy should be taught at the graduate level; and nurses should be participants in psychotherapeutic teams.

It was not until two decades later, however, with the publication of The American Nurses' Association's *Statement on Psychiatric Nursing Practice* (1967) that the term "psychotherapy" was used officially to describe the role of the psychiatric clinical specialist. At present a nurse who wishes to practice as a nurse psychotherapist should be minimally prepared with a master's degree in psychiatric-mental health nursing in order to meet the standards of the American Nurses' Association (1982). Currently, most psychiatric/mental-health graduate nursing programs that offer functional tracts in clinical specialization offer basic preparation for nurses wishing to assume the NPT role. This chapter focuses upon aspects of this curriculum and strategies for learning that should characterize graduate education to prepare nurse psychotherapists for private practice.

## CURRICULUM

Elements of the curriculum that prepare nurse psychotherapists for private practice are organized around four major content areas: clinical modalities; theory; research; and functional role development. Learning experiences that are specific to the practice of psychotherapy are described within each of the content areas.

### Clinical Modalities

The curriculum of most graduate programs is organized to include courses that address each clinical modality: individual psychotherapy, group psychotherapy, family psychotherapy, crisis intervention, and consultation (O'Toole & Morofka, 1984). The therapeutic process (or nursing process) is then addressed in relation to each clinical modality. Students learn how to assess patients in each of the three modalities: evaluate and diagnose phenomena of concern; plan and execute interventions to correct the phenomena; and evaluate the outcomes of interventions. Conceptualizing psychotherapy within the framework of the nursing process assists students to use their previous learning and clinical experience, thus easing the transition to the role of NPT.

Assessment of patients presupposes the ability to collect pertinent data. In psychotherapy, this means one must learn to conduct interviews that either directly or indirectly assess the patient's problems, personality, system characteristics, psychopathology, and ego strengths. Students are introduced to standard assessment formats and encouraged to modify these according to their own styles. The issue of whether to conduct assessments directly in the initial interview, or to do so more indirectly over a series of interviews, is presented; and students should be encouraged to experiment with both options.

Effective assessment requires skill in the basic techniques of interviewing. Often nurses acquire interviewing skills in undergraduate programs and/or in staff nurse positions. When these skills are missing or underdeveloped, review of content about interviewing should be encouraged or required.

Diagnosis or evaluation can be approached from two convergent perspectives. (See also Chapter 7.) The first is an introduction to the standard classification system used by most mental health professionals, the *Diagnostic and Statistical Manual of Mental Disorders* (APA, 1980), usually referred to as the *DSM III*. Development of proficiency in diagnosis using the *DSM III* is essential for the NPT since it is the code used to diagnose patients for purposes of third-party reimbursement; moreover, it is important for her to be able to use the same diagnostic language as other mental health professionals.

The second diagnostic perspective relates to the identification of phenomena of concern and generally involves recognition of behavioral phenomena of a more specific nature than the diagnostic categories in *DSM III*. For example, students are encouraged to identify such phenomena as anxiety, helplessness, and scapegoating. They are also directed to the literature on nursing diagnoses and encouraged to experiment with those categories that fit the problems at hand. A nursing diagnostic perspective is used to sensitize students to the profession's need to develop its own theories. Such practice-oriented theory begins with an identification of the phenomena of concern.

The intervention phase of the therapeutic process is often thought of as the most crucial, and hence the most difficult to learn. Intervention begins with assessment—and students learn that whatever they do or fail to do within the therapeutic process from the beginning is potentially an intervention. Theories and techniques of confrontation and interpretation are learned. Issues of transference and counter-transference and their relationship to the process of therapy are examined.

Students should be exposed to various styles and schools of therapy. Some graduate programs in psychiatric-mental health nursing emphasize only one style or school. Although this approach provides depth in one theory and creates a sense of confidence in the learner, its disadvantages are that the learner is deprived of the opportunity to experiment with several theoretical applications to discover those approaches that suit her personality and particular patient needs. Until research has established the efficacy of one therapeutic style or theory over another, the latter, more flexible approach is the most appropriate.

Evaluation of interventions involves the ability to examine critically one's work as a therapist. Students learn to base their evaluations on patients' behavioral changes. They must also learn to value patients' own direct evaluation of their progress and understand the importance of ongoing clinical supervision as an inherent part of therapy.

## Theory

Most theory taught in graduate programs that prepare nurse psychotherapists comes from disciplines other than nursing (O'Toole, 1973; Spunt, Durham, & Hardin, 1984). Psychiatric-mental health nursing is heavily indebted to psychiatry and psychology for theories of psychotherapy, personality development, and psychopathology. Students need at least a basic grounding in traditional psychological theories such as psychoanalytic (including interpersonal and ego analytic theories) and behavioral theories. Such understanding may be obtained in courses taken in other disciplines as cognates or in nursing courses. Regardless of the source for theoretical content, it is important that students have an opportunity to learn the clinical application of theory. Deductive use of theory in clinical practice requires careful instruction and close supervision.

In addition to using theories from other disciplines, psychiatric-mental health nursing has a long tradition of developing these conceptual frameworks for use within nursing. A notable example is Peplau's (1952) model for applying Sullivan's interpersonal theory to nursing practice, which has widely influenced graduate psychiatric nursing education. More recently Fitzpatrick, Whall, Johnston, and Floyd (1982) applied major nursing models to the field of psychiatric nursing.

In order to understand and apply nursing theory, aspiring NPTs need to study the current state of nursing theory in general and psychiatric/mental-health nursing theory in detail. Instruction in nursing theory should include basic education in the philosophy of science so that graduates are able to evaluate theory. Understanding theory development allows graduates to differentiate between a theory, concept, conceptual framework, and model, as well as to understand the way in which theories are developed inductively from one's own clinical data.

# Research

Nurses who enter graduate school with hopes of becoming nurse psychotherapists often wonder why they need to study research. Education in the design and methodology of scientific inquiry, including statistics, contributes essential knowledge to the psychotherapist. First, it prepares her to read research reports critically. Second, experience in conducting an investigation prepares her to evaluate her clinical practice and to test hypotheses about psychotherapy. Even if the NPT does not carry out a formal research project using her practice as a source of data, she will use the principles of research in her work. (See Chapter 5.) For example, formulating and testing hypotheses about the patient is part of the process of intervention, and bears a close resemblance to formal research. Likewise, understanding the processes of qualitative data analysis is invaluable in reviewing patient records. Knowledge of statistics also assists in keeping records.

# Functional Role Development

Students in graduate psychiatric/mental-health nursing programs generally choose to study a functional role such as clinical specialist, educator, or administrator. The private practice of nursing psychotherapy could be included within the functional role of clinical specialist or be offered as a separate course. Content might address: administrative and role aspects of private practice; professional issues, such as certification, specialty licensure, reimbursement, consultation, and supervision; and business aspects, such as legal and accounting requirements, referral systems, and record keeping. Interaction with NPTs who have established practices to explore their problems and successes would prove valuable.

# LEARNING STRATEGIES

## Clinical Practicum

The major learning strategies to prepare nurse psychotherapists involve the clinical practicum and include supervision of students' clinical work. Ideally, the student should be exposed to experiences with a wide variety of patients. Most of her clinical work should be in outpatient settings with patients similar to those who would be likely to seek private psychotherapy. She should also have experience in treating the chronically mentally ill since her practice may include such individuals.

She should have opportunities to practice all of the therapeutic modalities over a sufficient period of time to work beyond the orientation phase of the relationship. Making certain that students treat patients over a long enough time period to develop working relationships and experience termination may present problems in an educational program. Clinical experiences tend to be restricted by university calendars and are usually a semester, quarter, or academic year in length. Patients seldom proceed through therapy within these time constraints. It is ideal, however, to structure the clinical experience for the longest period of time possible (an academic year, for example) to permit students to experience the entire process of psychotherapy.

## Supervision

Clinical supervision is probably one of the most important learning experiences in educating the NPT. It provides the opportunity to examine the process of therapy in considerable detail, and through such scrutiny to validate and modify one's therapeutic approach. Critchley (1985) described the three major functions of clinical supervision as: "(1) to monitor the welfare of the client; (2) to promote the supervisee's professional growth; and (3) to evaluate the supervisory process and the resultant learning of the supervisee" (p. 498).

Supervision essentially involves a review with the student of her work with patients. The data presented by the student vary; the best source of data is videotape since this media allows analysis of both the verbal and nonverbal aspects of the therapeutic process. Such "public" interviews, however, may have an impact upon the nurse-patient relationship (Zinberg, 1985). Audio-recordings and process notes may also be used. Regardless of the type of data presented, the critical feature of supervision is collaborative review. Such collaboration requires an openness and willingness on the part of the supervisee to discuss all aspects of the psychotherapy situation. It likewise requires that the supervisor respond sensitively to the particular vulnerability such disclosure entails.

Supervision can be a painful process for the supervisee. Chessick (1971) described it as a chronically painful process in which the student must "mourn the loss of systematized and controlling . . . styles of relating . . . and must struggle to comprehend the unknown inside of himself as well as what is around him and his patients" (p. 273).

Friedlander, Dye, Costello, and Kobos (1984) proposed a model for supervision in which therapist growth is described in terms of four developmental crises. The first crisis occurs when the student realizes that psychotherapy demands a broad tolerance for the ambiguity that occurs because the student must function without the usual responses and gratifications found in other relationships. This crisis is resolved when the student learns personal flexibility by accepting values and behaviors that differ from her own. The second crisis occurs when the student becomes aware of her limited capacity to be therapeutic. During this crisis, the student learns how difficult it is to understand, establish rapport, and communicate. At the same time, she is made aware of the imperfections in the tools of psychotherapy. According to the authors, ". . . the third crisis concerns the discovery of therapy as communication in the deepest sense of the word, in contrast to a view of therapy as a sequential or repeated administration of techniques" (p. 195). The fourth crisis involves learning to use different models of therapeutic intervention and selecting those that fit the particular needs of a patient. Resolution of these crises turns a potentially painful process into one that facilitates the learning of psychotherapy and fosters personal growth.

## SUMMARY

The educational program to prepare nurse psychotherapists involves learning the therapeutic process in individual, group, and family psychotherapy. It is guided by a curriculum that provides content in theory, research, and functional role development. Students learn the process and techniques of psychotherapy through clinical practice that provides experiences with a variety of patients in both inpatient and outpatient settings. Clinical supervision of this therapeutic work is a critical aspect of the student's education to become an NPT.

## REFERENCES

American Nurses' Association. (1967). *Statement on psychiatric and mental health nursing practice.* Kansas City, MO: American Nurses' Association.

American Nurses' Association. (1982). *Standards of psychiatric and mental health nursing.* Kansas City, MO: American Nurses' Association.

American Psychiatric Association. (1980). *Diagnostic and statistical manual of mental disorders* (3rd ed.). Washington, DC: American Psychiatric Association.

Chessick, R. D. (1971). How the resident and the supervisor disappoint each other. *American Journal of Psychotherapy, 25,* 272–283.

Critchley, D. L. (1985). Clinical supervision. In D. L. Critchley and J. T. Maurin

(Eds.), *The clinical specialist in psychiatric mental health nursing* (pp. 495–510). New York: Wiley.

Fitzpatrick, J. J., Whall, A. L., Johnston, R. L., & Floyd, J. A. (1982). *Nursing models and their psychiatric mental health applications.* Bowie, MD: Brady.

Friedlander, S. R., Dye, N. W., Costello, R. M., & Kobos, J. C. (1984). A developmental model for teaching and learning in psychotherapy supervision. *Psychotherapy, 21,* 189–196.

O'Toole, A. W. (1973). Doctoral study for psychiatric nurses. *Perspectives in Psychiataric Care, 11,* 161–164.

O'Toole, A. W., & Morofka, V. (1984). Designing a graduate program in psychiatric nursing. In S. Lego (Ed.), *The American handbook of psychiatric nursing* (pp. 185–193). Philadelphia: Lippincott.

Peplau, H. E. (1952). *Interpersonal relationships in nursing: A conceptual frame of reference for psychodynamic nursing.* New York: Putnam.

Peplau, H. E. (1982). Historical development of psychiatric nursing: A preliminary statement of some facts and trends. In S. A. Smoyak and S. Rouslin (Eds.), *A collection of classics in psychiatric nursing literature* (pp. 10–46). Thorofare, NJ: Slack.

Rosenthal, T. (1984). University psychiatric nursing education in the United States: 1917–1956. *Issues in Mental Health Nursing, 6,* 21–33.

Spunt, J., Durham, J., and Hardin, S. B. (1984). Theoretical models and interventions used by nurse psychotherapists. *Issues in Mental Health Nursing, 6,* 35–51.

Zinberg, N. (1985). The private versus the public interview. *American Journal of Psychiatry, 142*(8), 889–894.

# Chapter 5
# Research Issues in Nursing Psychotherapy Practice

*Sally A. Hutchinson*

Both scholars and practitioners agree that a research perspective is vital to the art and science of nursing. Ideally, research should generate theory, theory should guide practice, and practice should modify theory. Dickoff and his associates (1968) emphasized the interdependence of Nursing theory, research, and practice: "Theory is born in practice, is refined in research, and must and can return to practice if research is to be other than a draining off of energy from the main business of nursing and theory more than idle speculation" (p. 415).

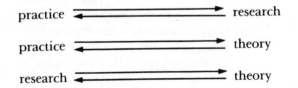

O'Toole (1981) warned that "psychiatric nursing without a theoretical base will not survive as a specialty within the profession" (p. 11). Without research to develop, refine, and test theory, psychiatric nursing must rely on traditional and intuitive ways of knowing.

In this chapter, existing literature directly addressing nursing psychotherapy is reviewed; philosophical and practical questions are examined; and a list of crucial considerations for NPTs interested in doing research are proposed.

## LITERATURE REVIEW

The literature relating to the practice of nursing psychotherapy falls into three major categories: descriptive articles explaining how psychiatric nurses have initiated private practices, including strategies for coping with financial, legal, managerial, personal, and professional issues (Blackburn, 1984; Geller, 1980; Hutchinson, 1972; Larkin & Crowdes, 1975; McShane & Smith, 1978; Randolf, 1975; Ricci & Hamera, 1981; Rouslin & Clark, 1978); theoretical articles dealing with such issues as autonomy (Dachelet & Sullivan, 1979), ethics (Hoeffer, 1983), professionalism (Gamer, 1979; Dachelet, 1978), conceptual frameworks (Clement & Boylon, 1982; Fitzpatrick et al., 1982; Hoeffer & Murphy, 1982; Lego, 1973; Meleis, 1975; O'Toole, 1981), and intervention (Anderson, 1983; Lego, 1980; Loomis, 1984); research articles describing models of therapy used by the NPT (Benton, 1984; Spunt, Durham, & Hardin, 1984), nurse psychotherapists' experiences in obtaining individual practice privileges (Durham & Hardin, 1985a), strategies used to promote advanced nursing practice (Durham & Hardin, 1985b), and the structure, process and effectiveness of nurse psychotherapy (Hardin & Durham, 1985).

An analysis of the existing and relatively scarce literature underscores that the development of nursing psychotherapy practices is an endeavor predominantly of the last decade. Descriptive articles prevail; such articles may provide guidelines for nurses interested in establishing their own nursing psychotherapy practice. The scarcity of theoretical articles is to be expected; these should increase as the private practitioner movement evolves and nurse scholars begin to analyze this new practice model. Existing research uses survey designs that are appropriate for this current level of knowledge. Fundamental questions concerning the nature of the practice of nursing psychotherapy underlie these exploratory, descriptive studies: What are the types of practice privileges? What are the strategies used to promote private practice? What conceptual models guide practice? What is the typical structure and the process of psychotherapy? How effective is it? These are good questions with which to begin; the answers may enable nurse psychotherapists (NPTs) to form a collective identity within the nursing profession.

# QUESTIONS PERTAINING TO RESEARCH ISSUES IN NURSING PSYCHOTHERAPY

*Who should do research on nursing psychotherapy?*

The competence of the NPT to also do research is a vital issue. Does an NPT necessarily have the competence, knowledge, and skills to do research? The answer resides in the education of each practitioner. Some nurse psychotherapists hold a clinical master's degree with a minimum of research preparation, while others (21% in Hardin & Durham's 1985 study) have doctoral education that requires a more rigorous research curriculum. The allocation of energy is related to the issue of competence. Good research takes a great amount of time and energy, as does good nursing practice. Both endeavors require scholarly knowledge, skill, creativity, flexibility, and commitment. Does a practicing NPT have the competence and energy to do both well, or does one role suffer at the expense of the other? In certain situations (i.e., academia) nurses are expected to meet many demands—teaching, research, and practice. Many nurses feel that they are being pulled in different directions and that the quality of their work suffers accordingly. It behooves NPTs to candidly and realistically evaluate their priorities. Their first priority should be their practice, since they are contracting with patients for a service. That service should not be compromised.

Another major issue concerns the ethics of the research. Different types of research raise different ethical issues. For example, the previously mentioned surveys of Durham and Hardin (1985, 1985a,b), Spunt, Durham & Hardin (1984), and Benton (1984) appear not to violate anyone's rights. The NPT who received the survey had the choice of responding. The patients/subjects were anonymous and the data were confidential. But, what if NPTs want to study their patients' responses to treatment or to them as NPTs? To whom are the patients giving consent—to their NPT or to a researcher? They may experience fear and/or anxiety, both about participating and not participating. Nurse/patient relationships are complex and intimate, frequently involving transference and counter-transference. Should they be further complicated by the NPT assuming the additional role of researcher, requesting that the patient not only be a client but a subject?

Nurse researchers and NPTs must always think first and foremost about human considerations. Consent ("To whom am I giving consent to do what?") cannot be taken at face value. Truly informed consent necessitates careful thought by the practitioner/researcher. Being a researcher ordinarily requires a differing degree of detachment than that of a practitioner. How the researcher/practitioner or practitioner/researcher views the subject/patient or patient/subject strongly influences that relationship. Can an NPT conduct research with patients without violating the therapeutic relationship? Or can the intimacy of the therapeutic encounter be examined by the NPT in a way that results in high quality research that is also beneficial to patients?

An additional ethical issue concerns experimental treatment. London and Klerman (1982) believed that any treatment modality that is not proven to be nonharmful is considered experimental treatment. For example, if a nurse uses alternative treatments with patients (such as rolfing or psychodrama) before they are studied, is the approach ethical? Or what is to prevent therapists from doing their own form of mini-research "to see what happens?"

Whereas some of these ethical issues may appear to be extreme, they should serve to alert NPTs to be acutely aware of their responsibilities to patients. By examining both existing and potential ethical issues, NPTs can more clearly define their multiple roles as they continue to evolve. It is the responsibility of NPTs as professionals to anticipate issues that will confront them if they choose to combine research with practice. As research increases, those conducting this research face new ethical dilemmas.

Bias is also a significant issue for practitioners involved in research. In Hardin and Durham's (1985) study on the structure, process, and effectiveness of nurse psychotherapy, NPTs mailed questionnaires to their patients regarding their perceptions of treatment. The patients who chose to respond remained anonymous, mailed their responses directly to the researchers rather than to their NPTs, and data were confidential. Hardin and Durham pointed out the sampling bias that is present because the patients were chosen by their therapists. How would patients not selected have responded to the survey? The sampling bias makes the validity of the data questionable, as Hardin and Durham recognized.

Research questions should be closely scrutinzed for possible bias. Studies that compare the patient outcomes of NPTs with patient outcomes of other therapists (psychiatrists, psychologists, social workers) could likely have built-in biases. Research in any profession that attempts to justify its existence or superiority should be carefully evaluated. In order to minimize bias, research could be done by an interdisciplinary team.

The issue of who should investigate the practice of nursing psychotherapy needs to be discussed and debated at nursing forums and in nursing journals. Considering that the role of the NPT is essentially new and somewhat fluid, most NPTs should invest their energy in pursing advanced clinical knowledge and skills. Perhaps the necessary research can be done by nurse academicians who are knowledgeable and interested in the field, or by NPTs and nurse academicians working together. An organization of interested nurse researchers and NPTs could be formed to address the research issues. NPTs have the expertise to propose significant and researchable problems; researchers can offer their expertise in research design and methods. Such fruitful collaboration will benefit nurse participants, patients, the specialty of psychiatric nursing, and the nursing profession as a whole. This approach will encourage NPTs to work with each other and with researchers, instead of in isolation, resulting in a more coherent body of knowledge.

Funding of research can be an additional aim of practitioner-academician collaborative groups. Locating funding sources, preparing research proposals, and actually receiving funding for doing research relevant to nursing psychotherapy practices is much more likely if there is a group effort. The pooling of resources should make each step of the process far easier than if practitioners and researchers work alone.

A final point concerns the publication of research findings. Researchers have an obligation to report the findings through presentations and/or publications. The research process is not complete until the findings are made public, since only by the dissemination of the results is knowledge generated or modified. Such dissemination can generate useful discussion, debate, and direction for future research. Completed research that is not reported benefits no one. Since publishing is an expected part of an academician's role, psychiatric nursing faculty can be especially useful in this phase of the research process. Selecting appropriate journals and audiences is a learned skill; appropriate collaboration among nurse practitioners and academicians can be beneficial in these endeavors.

*What types of research on nursing psychotherapy practices are needed?*

Brink and Wood's (1983) conceptualization of levels of nursing research offers a useful model for planning research in nursing psychotherapy. Level I studies are needed when information on a subject is minimal. The studies reported in this chapter are all Level I studies that use a survey design (Benton, 1984; Durham & Hardin, 1985a,b; Hardin & Durham, 1985; Spunt, Durham & Hardin, 1984). In each of these studies, the researchers explored and described certain defined variables (e.g., structure and process of nurse psychotherapy or theoretical models). Additional questions could be answered by a survey design: How do NPTs diagnose patients and how is the assessment used in treatment planning? Who refers patients to NPTs? For what reasons? What is the nature of the supervision NPTs desire? What are the ethical and/or legal issues NPTs face? These and many other such questions remain to be answered.

There are different types of surveys suitable for Level I studies—cross-sectional, longitudinal, descriptive, comparative, correlational, or evaluative (for elaboration see Wilson, 1985). Such surveys can be conducted by means of telephone, mailed questionnaires, or face-to-face structured interviews. The value of the survey is to gather basic data regarding the research question from as many NPTs as possible. While information gleaned from a survey is generally superficial, it may still lead to insights about private practice.

Case studies and case histories are other methods for doing a Level I study. Good case studies do not merely provide raw data (e.g., descriptions of a nurse-patient relationship), but also serve to generate theory to guide practice. In contrast, a case history uses exiting theory and applies it to the experience of a particular patient. These indepth approaches to research have much to offer NPTs. They both suggest interventions and illuminate the richness and complexity of the psychotherapeutic encounter. In this type of research, the practitioners are the researchers because only they have experienced the relationship. The practitioner becomes the instrument of the research and uses interpretive skills to analyze the empirical data. Whereas such studies yield vital knowledge, they also pose several quandaries for the NPT/Researcher as previously discussed.

Also needed are concept analysis studies that describe concepts relevant to NPT's practices (e.g., despair, loneliness, humor, empathy, anxiety) (see Forsythe, 1980; Hutchinson, 1976). Operational definitions and suggested nursing interventions are important aspects of this type of research.

Whereas Level I studies are designed to discover and explore variables relevant to NPTs, Level II studies search for significant relationships between two or more variables. Existing literature may suggest the relevance of the variables but does not propose the nature of the relationship. Evaluative and correlational surveys are examples of Level II studies. For example, does a significant relationship exist between NPTs' education and years of experience and patient outcomes? Is there a significant relationship between a particular conceptual framework and related nursing interventions in outcomes with patients with a specific illness (e.g., depression, panic reaction, middle-aged crisis)? Is there a significant relationship between patient outcomes and the professional credentials of the therapist (nurse *vs.* psychiatrist *vs.* social worker)? Understanding the relationships of such important variables has practical implications for NPTs.

Level III studies are derived from existing theoretical frameworks (from nursing theories or from borrowed theories such as feminist, psychoanalytic, family systems, behavioral, existential theories) and require the testing of hypotheses derived from these theories. According to Spunt, Durham, and Hardin (1984), many NPTs fail to connect their theoretical frameworks with specific interventions occurring in the nurse/patient encounter. If NPTs are "eclectic" (as many of them stated), then they need to be aware of how they make decisions to use specific interventions. Are their interventions dependent on such factors as patient diagnosis or patient behaviors? A clear connection between theory and practice is essential for good patient care.

Level III studies are causal models based on the underlying assumption that an independent variable directly affects a dependent variable. Experimental and quasi-experimental designs are used for Level III studies. For example, a nurse therapist who uses a gestalt approach with depressed patients can compare outcomes with those of a nurse therapist who uses a behaviorist approach or an approach based on nursing theory. This requires each NPT to clearly articulate the chosen conceptual model and the interventions that derive from that model. The researcher and the clinician derive hypotheses from the model and test them on the basis of selected patient outcome criteria. Lego (1980), in strongly supporting the need for research that generates new theory, stated "The nurse has empirically observed some conceptual arrangement of variables concerning the one-to-one relationship, hypothesized certain relationships between these variables, demonstrated the relationship and drawn conclusions which guide practice" (p. 81) (see Tudor, 1982).

A different category of research—methodological studies—develops data collection instruments to answer specific questions. Nurse researchers generally rely on existing instruments from other disciplines such as psychology or education. Examples of such instruments include the Myers Briggs Inventory, State and Trait Anxiety, and Rotter's Locus of Control. Methodological studies can be used to validate or evaluate these instruments and their relevance for NPTs or to design new instruments that more clearly answer research questions. Instrument development is a difficult, yet most necessary, form of research. It lends itself particularly well to group work.

Each level and type of research presented thus far has strengths and weaknesses. It is vitally important that the chosen design matches the research purpose. All research should aim for theoretical and methodological rigor. Well thought-out and relevant research questions followed by an appropriate research design will move NPTs out of the realm of intuition and into the realm of science. Scientifically based practice will ensure the credibility and effectiveness of nurse psychotherapists.

# CRUCIAL CONSIDERATIONS FOR NPTS DOING RESEARCH

Crucial considerations for NPTs conducting research include the following properties, problems, and strategies. Understanding these considerations should make it easier to NPTs to credibly and ethically combine practice and research.

## Properties

The following properties encompass both the assets (Items #1 through #3) and liabilities (Items #4 and #5) of research by NPTs.

1. *Access to rich research data.* NPTs see patients who are the source of data required for many types of research.
2. *Autonomy.* NPTs are not locked into highly structured formal bureaucracies. They have autonomy and the concomitant flexibility that permits them the freedom to balance research with their practice requirements
3. *Interest in research results.* Most NPTs wish to give the best treatment possible, and, therefore, are interested in the results of research in their field. Their interest also makes them a good source of research questions.
4. *Questionable research knowledge and skills.* Because of the clinical focus of many graduate nursing programs, many NPTs have little knowlege of the research process. Also, the practical aspects of research, the "how to's" necessary to carry out research, may not be in their repertoire of skills.
5. *Isolation.* NPTs often practice essentially in isolation from colleagues, which makes doing research more difficult. The sharing of ideas and problems and solutions is an asset at every step of the research process.

## Problems

Ethical and pragmatic problems are "given" because of the nature and structure of the NPT's work. As discussed earlier, NPTs may have a conflict of interest when they add the role of research to that of practitioner; thus, they must be certain that the research offers benefits for patients. Doing research without the support of a larger organization can be problematic. Information about funding sources, secretarial help, research assistants and associates, literature searches, and assistance with tasks (stamping envelopes, typing letters, and photocopying) is probably lacking. This can make the research process extremely tedious and time consuming. A research project may have hidden, as well as direct, costs. Unlike their nurse colleagues in institutional or academic settings, NPTs rarely have funding for such expenses. Since NPTs are not salaried, their research efforts are costly as they take place during unpaid time.

## Strategies

The following strategies are designed to help the NPT minimize the pragmatic problems encountered in doing research. First, the NPT might search for a joint appointment. Acquiring such an appointment at a college of nursing would permit the NPT to be both a clinical faculty member and a practitioner. Secondly, the NPT might collaborate with other academicians. Working with academicians can ameliorate the pragmatic problems involved in research. Both strategies provide built-in colleagues, a factor that decreases the NPT's isolation and facilitates a healthy exchange of knowledge and skills.

## SUMMARY

Because so few studies have been conducted on NPTs and their work, research priorities in this area should be determined. These priorities must take into consideration issues of feasibility, cost, ethics, and politics. NPTs must be as responsible in their research endeavors as they are in their clinical work. They must also be aware that their research is not done in isolation but rather under the scrutiny of their own profession as well as others. With organization and directed energy, NPTs can launch a much needed effort towards research in nursing psychotherapy. The results will be increasing credibility and clarity regarding practice.

## REFERENCES

Anderson, M. (1983). Nursing interventions: What did you do that helped? *Perspectives in Psychiatric Care, 21,* 4–8.

Benton, D. (1984). Models of therapy used by feminist nurse psychotherapists. Unpublished manuscript, University of Illinois, Chicago.

Blackburn, J. (1984). Perserverance and vision pays off: Psych mental health nurse tells of her success in private practice. *Tennessee Nurses' Association, 47,* 5–6.

Brink, P., & Woods, M. (1983). *Basic steps in planning nursing research, from question to proposal.* Monterey, CA: Wadsworth.

Clement, J., & Boylan, S. (1982). Actualizing theory in practice. *Perspectives in Psychiatric Care, 20*(3), 126–133.

Dachelet, C. (1978). Nursing's bid for increased status. *Nursing Forum, 17*(1), 18–45.

Dachelet, C., & Sullivan, J. (1979). Autonomy in practice. *Nurse Practitioner, 4*(2), 15–22.

Dickoff, J., James, P., & Wiedenbach, E. (1968). Theory in a practice discipline: Part I practice oriented theory. *Nursing Research, 17,* 415–435.

Durham, J., & Hardin, S. (1985a). Nurse psychotherapists' experiences in obtaining individual practice privileges. *Nurse Practitioner, 10*(11), 62–67.

Durham, J., & Hardin, S. (1985b). Promoting advanced nursing practice. *Nurse Practitioner, 10*(2), 59–62.

Fitzpatrick, J., Whall, A., Johnston, R., & Floyd, J. (1982). *Nursing models and their psychiatric mental health applications.* Bowie, MD: Brady.

Forsythe, G. (1980). Analysis of the concept of empathy: Illustrations of one approach. *Advances in Nursing Science, 2*(2), 33–42.

Gamer, M. (1979). The ideology of professionalism. *Nursing Outlook, 27,* 108–111.

Geller, J. (1980). Starting a private practice of psychotherapy. *Perspectives in Psychiatric Care, 18,* 106–111.

Hardin, S., & Durham, J. (1985). First rate: The structure, process and effectiveness of nurse psychotherapy. *Journal of Psychosocial Nursing and Mental Health Services, 23*(5), 8–15.

Hoeffer, B. (1983). The private practice model: An ethical perspective. *Journal of Psychosocial Nursing and Mental Health Services, 21*(7), 31–37.

Hoeffer, B., & Murphy, S. (1982). The unfinished task: Development of nursing theory for psychiatric and mental health nursing practice. *Journal of Psychosocial Nursing and Mental Health Services, 20*(12), 8–14.

Hutchinson, S. (1972). The psychiatric nurse therapist in private practice. *Journal of Psychiatric Nursing, 10*(4), 5–6.

Hutchinson, S. (1976). Humor: A link to life. In C. Kneisl and H. Wilson (Eds.), *Current perspectives in psychiatric nursing: Vol. 1* (pp. 201–210). St. Louis: Mosby.

Larkin, M., & Crowdes, N. (1975). A systems approach to private practice. *Journal of Psychiatric Nursing, 13*(2), 5–9.

Lego, S. (1973). Nurse psychotherapists: How are we different? *Perspectives in Psychiatric Care, 11*(4), 144–147.

Lego, S. (1980). The one-to-one nurse/patient relationship. *Perspectives in Psychiatric Care, 18*(2), 67–89.

London, P., & Klerman, G. (1982). Evaluating psychotherapy. *The American Journal of Psychiatry, 139,* 709–717.

Loomis, M. (1984). Phenomena of concern for psychiatric and mental health nursing. Unpublished manuscript, University of South Carolina, Columbia.

McShane, M., & Smith, E. (1978). Starting a private practice. *American Journal of Nursing, 78*, 2068-2070.

Meleis, A. (1975). Role insufficiency and role supplementations: A conceptual framework. *Nursing Research, 24*, 264-271.

O'Toole, A. (1981). When the practical becomes theoretical. *Journal of Psychosocial Nursing and Mental Health Services, 19*(12), 11-19.

Randolf, G. (1975). Experiences in private practice. *Journal of Psychiatric Nursing, 13*(6), 16-19.

Ricci, & Hamera, E. (1981). A nursing practice with a psychosocial focus. *Kansas Nurse, 56*, 7, 23.

Rouslin, S., & Clark, A. (1978). Commentary of professional parity. *Perspectives of Psychiatric Care, 16*(3), 115-117.

Spunt, J., Durham, J., & Hardin, S. B. (1984). Theoretical models and interventions used by nurse psychotherapists. *Issues in Mental Health Nursing, 6*, 35-51.

Tudor, G. (1982). A sociopsychiatric nursing approach to intervention in a problem of mutual withdrawal on a mental hospital ward. In S. Smoyak and S. Rouslin (Eds.) *A collection of classics in psychiatric nursing literature* (pp. 178-200). Thorofare, NJ: Slack.

Wilson, H. (1985). *Research in nursing.* Menlo Park, CA: Addison-Wesley.

# Chapter 6
# Legal Concepts for the Nurse Psychotherapist

*Diane Kjervik*

In view of today's litigious society, the best legal advice to offer nurse psychotherapists (NPTs) can be paraphrased from a famous United States President, Teddy Roosevelt: "Practice carefully and carry a big policy." Certainly, it is important that an inpatient nurse in any specialty area practice carefully and carry malpractice insurance. However, this caveat carries greater weight in private practice when the NPT is the only provider of mental health services to the patient and there is no sharing of liability with other providers such as a physician or hospital. The NPT must, therefore, be cognizant of legal concepts pertinent to her practice. A number of resources exist to aid her in understanding these concepts (Barton & Sanborn, 1978; Bullough, 1980; Cohen & Mariano, 1982; Klein & Onek, 1984; Sadoff, 1982; Simon, 1982; Ziegenfuss, 1983). Several journals (*Law and Psychology Review*; *Journal of Psychiatry and Law*; *International Journal of Law and Psychiatry*; *Law, Medicine and Health Care*) may also be helpful for the NPT in updating her knowledge in this area.

Careful practice in nursing psychotherapy can be discussed in terms of unintentional (negligence) and intentional wrongs inflicted on patients. Both criminal and civil penalties may be involved; thus, the NPT needs to be aware of how to avoid becoming a defendant in a lawsuit. This chapter provides an overview of the sources of law affecting psychiatric-mental health nursing practice, civil and criminal liability problems, malpractice insurance considerations, and methods of preventing malpractice complaints.

# SOURCES OF LAW

Law that is relevant to the practice of psychiatric-mental health nursing falls into four categories: (1) constitutional mandates; (2) statutory provisions; (3) judicial opinions; and (4) executive branch actions, such as agency rules and executive orders. Action by any of the four categories can direct, guide, influence, or preclude psychiatric-mental health nursing activities. Therefore, it behooves NPTs to be knowledgeable about these legal parameters.

## Constitutional Law

An example of constitutional law affecting psychiatric-mental health nursing practice is the Fourteenth Amendment to the United States Constitution, which states that no person shall be deprived of life, liberty, or property without due process of law. The liberty portion of this amendment is offended in some forms of commitment procedures that do not provide adequate notice and opportunity to be heard prior to the deprivation of liberty. NPTs may at some time need to recommend commitment of their patients and should be familiar with the commitment procedures followed within their jurisdictions.

## Statutory Provisions

Each state's Nurse Practice Act offers an example of statutory authority influencing the role of the NPT. This statute describes the authority of the nurse to diagnose and counsel independently; some nurse practice acts state whether the nurse can perform delegated medical functions. A nurse is not authorized to practice medicine and can be held legally liable for doing so. A commitment statute is another pertinent statute. Requirements regarding who may sign for the commitment of an individual, who must examine the potential patient, the type of evidence needed to commit the person, adequate notice, and timely hearings are explicated in the statute. Other examples of statutes that are relevant to the NPT are those that focus on the reporting of child and vulnerable adult abuse, the formation of and requirements for corporations, and income tax liabilities.

## Judicial Opinions

Judicial opinions interpret the meaning of statutory language and also articulate the precepts of common law. Judges have interpreted the meaning of nurse and medical practice acts, child-abuse reporting acts, as well as the meaning of Constitutional provisions such as the Bill of Rights and the Fourteenth Amendment. Precepts of common law such as those relating to negligence are also determined by courts.

## Executive Branch Actions

The executive branch carries out the law that is enacted by the legislative body. State Boards of Nursing and other licensure boards provide examples of agencies within the executive branch of government that create rules and regulations directly and indirectly affecting nursing practice.

The jurisdiction of the court, agency, constitution, or legislature also affects the nurse's practice within a given state. The federal courts are responsible for interpreting the United States Constitution and federal statutes. State courts can also interpret federal constitutional requirements, but ultimate authority rests with the United States Supreme Court. State courts and legislatures usually handle matters not specifically designated as federal concerns, such as divorce and negligence laws.

In order to ascertain the legal mandate for a given nursing practice function, one must seek out legal expertise in one's own jurisdiction. The intricacies of the interplay between legislative, judicial, and executive branch authority must be researched and articulated by an attorney. The general legal standards referred to in this chapter are provided to give NPTs an idea of potential areas for legal concern.

## CIVIL LIABILITY

Health care providers are commonly concerned with malpractice, i.e., professional negligence. Malpractice is the failure to meet an expected standard of care, this failure resulting in an injury to the patient. The standard of care that must be met is one of a reasonable prudent therapist in the same or similar circumstances (Beis, 1984). Specialty nurses are held to the standard of care held by other nurses in the specialty. Courts look to the expert testimony of specialty nurses, professional statements of standards about specialty practice, professional treatises, and professional codes of ethics in order to determine the legal standard. An error in professional judgment does not necessarily create legal liability. Only when the error falls outside the standard of care of the reasonable prudent caregiver does liability arise.

Standards can be thought of as duties owed to patients. One example of a court-created standard is the duty of a nurse psychotherapist to warn potential victims of homicidal outpatients (Kjervik, 1981). This duty arose from facts in a California case in which a young male patient in a psychotherapy clinic told his therapists that he was planning to kill a woman he knew. The patient was released without warning to the potential victim or her parents. The woman was subsequently killed by the former patient whose parents sued for relief. The court created the new duty and several states have followed this precedent. Another duty is to prevent the suicide of a patient. This duty falls more heavily on staff members of institutions in which a patient is hospitalized, but there are indications that outpatient therapists could be liable as well (Kjervik, 1984).

The fact that a legal duty exists does not mean that the duty is morally, ethically, politically, or therapeutically correct. The existence of the duty means that the court has weighed various factors and has determined that this duty is the most reasonable to expect without further evidence of arguments to the contrary.

NPTs must provide appropriate care based on the standards of their profession. However, few lawsuits against therapists have been based on the type of psychotherapy used because of the imprecision of verbal therapies. Cases are brought typically because of the patient's harm to self or because of violation of the patient's privacy and confidentiality. Recently, suits have been brought against therapists for engaging in sexual relationships with their patients. Courts have found this behavior to be malpractice, breach of contract, or criminal conduct (Beis, 1984).

Civil liability can also arise from intentional acts of the therapist that result in injury to the patient. These intentional acts are typically excluded from malpractice insurance policy coverage, unlike acts of negligence. Examples of intentional acts that may result in liability are false imprisonment, assault and battery, defamation, and fraud.

Entering into a therapeutic relationship with a patient results in the formation of a personal services contract (Nye, 1981). This is a mutual contract involving informed consent to treatment on the part of the patient. The patient should be informed about what he or she is being treated for, what the treatment alternatives are, what risks are foreseeable, and the nature of the possible benefits (Nye, 1981). Without adequate consent being given, the therapist potentially commits a battery upon the patient (Beis, 1984). If the patient lacks the capacity to consent, a relative or court appointed guardian may provide adequate consent.

As part of the contract between patient and therapist, expressed and implied warranties may be made, and a breach of these warranties may result in civil liability to the NPT. Expressed warranties include clear statements promising certain results to the patient (e.g., "psychotherapy for six months will end your depression"). Implied warranties include promises of confidentiality or adequacy of one's skills (Nye, 1981), so called because the therapist does not state them directly. Instead, the court interprets them to be part of the contract. Confidentiality requirements can also arise from statutes that provide for privileged communication between the patient and the NPT. Exceptions to this privileged communication exist in criminal situations, child abuse, peer review, and guardianship proceedings, to name a few (Beis, 1984).

Once a contract exists between patient and therapist, the NPT must be careful in ending the relationship. A wrongful termination of a relationship can result in what the law considers to be abandonment, another action that can result in civil liability. A therapist has a duty to continue treatment until a proper withdrawal occurs. The therapist must provide notice and an opportunity to find another therapist when ending the relationship and referral to another competent therapist during periods of absence (Beis, 1984).

If an employee is hired by the NPT to perform professional tasks, vicarious liability may fall upon the NPT for the negligence of the employee. Careful hiring and supervisory practices are thus necessary to reduce this risk.

## CRIMINAL LIABILITY

Criminal liability arises from the relationship between a person and the state, unlike civil liability, which arises from the relationship between two persons. In criminal law, the state or public at large has been offended, and the state prosecutes the alleged offender. Unlike civil liability, the convicted person can be imprisoned for the offense. Criminal acts by psychotherapists involve convictions for felonies and misdemeanors involving moral turpitude. As mentioned earlier, sex with a patient has been treated as a criminal offense in some states; aiding and abetting suicide is a crime in many states. Criminal acts, as is true with intentional acts involving civil liability, are typically not covered by insurance policies. Thus the NPT must pay all associated costs of a legal defense.

## INSURANCE CONSIDERATIONS

It is important for the NPT to carry an insurance policy with high limit coverage (see also Chapter 8). An "occurrence" policy is better than a "time period" policy because with the former the insurer is liable for all damages resulting from injuries caused during the policy period even if the damage does not show up until after the policy period ends. The time period coverage is limited to damages occurring only during the policy period (Beis, 1984).

Careful practice and a minimum number of successful lawsuits brought against nurses will keep malpractice rates down. This is another reason for the NPT to be aware of expected standards of professional conduct and to behave consistently with these standards. (See Appendix.)

# PREVENTION

In order to prevent being subject to a lawsuit, the NPT should keep careful written records of actions taken with each patient. If a patient does not show up for several appointments, a note should be placed in the record stating that phone calls were made or letters were sent to the patient. This will prepare the NPT for any charges of abandonment. If suicidal or homicidal threats are made by a patient, a note to this effect, along with actions taken to prevent the threatened harm, should be recorded.

The NPT should also be aware of professional standards in the specialty. Attending continuing education seminars, reading scholarly journals and books in the field, and reviewing standards that are published by professional organizations keep the NPT informed. Ongoing consultation from other psychiatric/mental-health nurses offers another way to keep abreast of the standards for experts in the field. The NPT must remember that ignorance of the law is no excuse; confronted with a legally questionable situation, she should consult a knowledgeable attorney.

# CONCLUSION

Legal obligations in the practice of psychiatric/mental-health nursing arise from constitutional, statutory, judicial, and executive mandates. NPTs can be subject to criminal and civil liability, which means that adequate measures to prevent lawsuits should be taken and adequate malpractice coverage should be carried in the event that a lawsuit occurs.

# REFERENCES

Barton, W., & Sanborn, C. (Eds.). (1978). *Law and the mental health professions: Friction at the interface.* New York: International Universities Press.

Beis, E. B. (1984). *Mental health and the law.* Rockville, MD: Aspen.

Bullough, B. (Ed.). (1980). *The law and the expanded nursing role.* New York: Appleton-Century-Crofts.

Cohen, R., & Mariano, W. (1982). *Legal guidebook in mental health.* New York: Free Press.

Kjervik, D. K. (1981). The psychiatric-mental health nurse's duty to warn potential victims of homicidal psychotherapy outpatients. *Law, Medicine & Health Care, 9*(6), pp. 11–39.

Kjervik, D. K. (1984). The psychotherapist's duty to act reasonably to prevent suicide: A proposal to allow rational suicide. *Behavioral Sciences & the Law, 2*(2), pp. 207–218.

Klein, J., & Onek, J. (1984). *Legal issues in the private practice of psychiatry.* Washington, DC: American Psychiatric Press.

Nye, S. (1981). Law in the everyday practice of psychotherapy. Unpublished speech, St. Paul, MN.

Sadoff, R. L. (1982). *Legal issues in the care of psychiatric patients.* New York: Springer.

Simon, R. (1982). *Psychiatric interventions and malpractice: A primer for malpractice prevention.* Springfield, IL: C. C. Thomas.

Ziegenfuss, J. T. (1983). *Patients' rights and professional practice.* New York: Van Nostrand.

# Chapter 7

# Assessing Patients in Nursing Psychotherapy Practice: A Comparison of *DSM III* and Nursing Diagnoses

*Maxine Loomis*

This chapter explores the utility of the diagnostic categories of the American Psychiatric Association's *Diagnostic and Statistical Manual III* (*DSM III*) (1980) and of the nursing diagnostic categories of the North American Nursing Diagnosis Association (Kim, McFarland, & McLane, 1984) in nursing psychotherapy practice. Nurse psychotherapists often feel compelled to choose between these two diagnostic systems. It is this author's contention that the two systems are compatible and can be utilized in a complementary manner.

The chapter opens by framing this author's ideas within the context of the American Nurses' Association's (ANA) Social Policy Statement (1980), followed by a definition of nursing psychotherapy practice phenomena, and then a discussion of these in relation to both the psychiatric and nursing diagnostic systems. Examples used in this discussion primarily reflect the young adult outpatient population, which comprises most of this author's practice. This approach was taken to ensure the clinical validity of the theoretical formulations proposed. Nurse psychotherapists working in other settings and with different populations may wish to further develop and expand these ideas for use in their own practice.

# DEVELOPMENT OF A MODEL FOR CLINICAL NURSING

Nursing has been defined by the ANA in its *Social Policy Statement* as "the diagnosis and treatment of human responses to actual or potential health problems" (1980, p. 8). While some have expressed concern about the inadequacy of this definition in addressing health promotion, the definition is being utilized by nurses at all levels of practice—from staff nurses to private practitioners to policy makers. This definition is meeting a need and is, to some extent, a useful, working definition of nursing.

One limitation of this definition, however, is its potential for a linear, cause-effect interpretation as illustrated in the following statement: "When an actual or potential health problem invades or 'comes over' patients they respond from one or several human response systems; the nurse diagnoses and treats the response(s)" (p. 4). Nursing practice, however, cannot really be defined or quantified in such equations. Despite the successful efforts of medical and basic science researchers to isolate and then treat causative factors, people still get sick. Therefore, the author and a colleague, D. Jean Wood, built upon the ANA definition of nursing, transforming it from a linear to a dynamic model.

This model purports that the domain of nursing is the diagnosis and treatment of human responses *as they interact with* actual or potential health problems. Indeed, nursing practice and research is multivariate; it must consider multiple variables that interact with and affect the health problems experienced by patients. According to Loomis and Wood (1983):

> In reality, any factor in the equation can affect any other. A human response called stress might be related to the onset of an acute illness episode. Conversely, the presence of a chronic health deviation might complicate a developmental life change as in the case of an adolescent with cystic fibrosis. It is even possible that the nursing treatment could induce or enhance/increase stress, illness, or health problems. What is required is a multivariate model in which all human response systems interact with all actual or potential human health problems as well as the clinical decision-making process. (p. 4)

The model in Figure 7.1 provides a schematic representation of the possible relationships among actual or potential health problems, human response systems, and clinical nursing decision-making. The model categorizes these problems into: (1) developmental life changes; (2) acute health deviations; (3) chronic health deviations; and (4) cul-

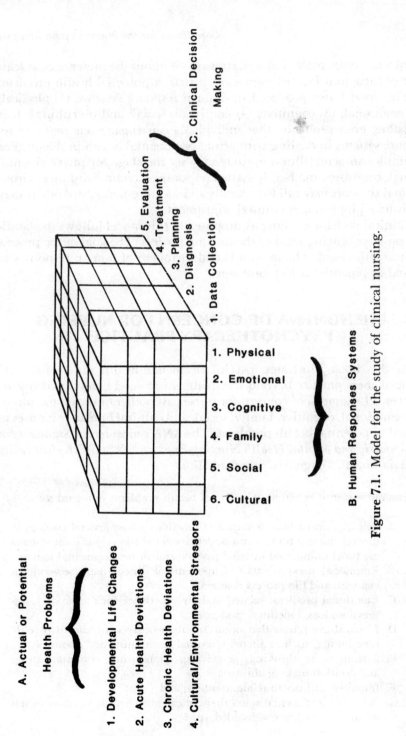

A. Actual or Potential Health Problems
1. Developmental Life Changes
2. Acute Health Deviations
3. Chronic Health Deviations
4. Cultural/Environmental Stressors

B. Human Responses Systems
1. Physical
2. Emotional
3. Cognitive
4. Family
5. Social
6. Cultural

C. Clinical Decision Making
1. Data Collection
2. Diagnosis
3. Planning
4. Treatment
5. Evaluation

**Figure 7.1.** Model for the study of clinical nursing.

tural/environmentally induced stressors. Without the presence of at least one of these four factors, there is no actual or potential health problem.

This model also proposed six human response systems: (1) physical; (2) emotional; (3) cognitive; (4) family; (5) social; and (6) cultural. It is possible, even probable, that individuals can engage one or more response systems in dealing with actual or potential health problems. For example, an acute illness episode may set the stage for physical, emotional, cognitive, and family system responses. Certain cultural/environmental stressors may call for a family and social response; still others may activate a physical and cultural adjustment.

Clinical decision-making as proposed in this model follows the familiar problem-solving steps of the nursing process. The goal of the process is straightforward: The diagnosis and treatment of human responses to actual or potential health problems.

## PHENOMENA OF CONCERN FOR NURSING PSYCHOTHERAPY PRACTICE

As this book illustrates, psychiatric/mental-health nurses have expanded their practice beyond the treatment of severe emotional disturbances. Phenomena of concern for nurse psychotherapists are the physical, emotional, cognitive, family, social, and cultural human responses to actual or potential health problems. The ANA's most recent *Standards of Psychiatric and Mental Health Nursing Practice* (1982) list the following criteria under "Diagnosis, Standard III":

The nurse identifies actual or potential health problems in regard to:

A. Self-care limitations or impaired functions whose general etiology is mental and emotional distress, deficits in the ways significant systems are functioning, and internal psychic and/or developmental issues;
B. Emotional stress or crisis components of illness, pain, self-concept changes, and life process changes;
C. Emotional problems related to daily experience such as anxiety, aggression, loss, loneliness, and grief;
D. Physical symptoms that occur simultaneously with altered psychic functioning, such as altered intestinal functioning and anorexia;
E. Alterations in thinking, perceiving, symbolizing, communicating, and decision-making abilities;
F. Impaired abilities to relate to others; and
G. Behaviors and mental states that indicate the client is a danger to self or others or is gravely disabled. (p. 5)

As illustrated in the above standard, psychiatric nursing practice includes the diagnosis and treatment of human responses to developmental life changes, acute health deviations, chronic health deviations, and cultural/environmental stressors.

## THE RELATIONSHIP BETWEEN DSM III AND PSYCHIATRIC NURSING'S PHENOMENA OF CONCERN

The *DSM III* (1980) presents an atheoretical approach to the definition of emotional disorders. It is structured according to differential diagnoses and diagnostic criteria and presents a set of diagnostic categories that are based on specific configurations of symptoms or behaviors. The *DSM III* classifications provide a relevant listing of commonly accepted and understood mental health problems. This system has the additional advantage of interdisciplinary acceptance and provides a common language among mental health professional and reimbursement agencies. Furthermore, the *DSM III* classifications are in keeping with the practice of nursing as the diagnosis and treatment of human responses to actual or potential health problems. Moreover, the diagnostic categories and behavioral criteria support the proposition that human responses and actual or potential health problems are interrelated. For example, generalized anxiety disorder is "manifested by symptoms from three of the following four categories: (1) motor tension; (2) autonomic hyperactivity; (3) apprehensive expectation; (4) vigilance and scanning" (pp. 134–135). An adult who has manifested this anxious mood continuously for at least one month without the problem being attributable to another mental disorder would be diagnosed as having a generalized anxiety disorder.

According to *DSM III*, ". . . each of the mental disorders is conceptualized as a clinically significant behavioral or psychological syndrome . . . that is typically associated with either a painful symptom (distress) or impairment in one or more areas of functioning (disability). . . . There is no assumption that each mental disorder is a discrete entity with sharp boundaries" (p. 6). For some diagnoses the etiology is known (i.e., organic disorder or adjustment disorder), but for most the etiology is unknown.

The *DSM III* diagnostic criteria are actually human responses that become patterns of behavior when they occur together in a specific configuration such as in generalized anxiety disorder. These *DSM III* behavioral patterns can be considered to be the phenomena of concern for nursing psychotherapy practice. All of the *DSM III* adult diagnostic classifications can be subsumed under the categories of actual or potential health problems presented in the proposed model for clinical nursing illustrated in Table 7.1.

The classification, "Conditions not attributable to a mental disorder," describes problems that are the result of developmental life changes. The classification, "Adjustment disorders," describes problems that result from cultural or environmental stressors. "Organic mental disorders" are generally regarded as chronic health deviations. The remainder of the diagnostic classifications can be categorized as either acute or chronic health deviations depending on the history of the problem and the patient's response to treatment. Three of the classifications (substance abuse disorders, affective disorders, and schizophrenic disorders) specifically allow for the coding of "in remission," which is determined by the frequency and intensity of past episodes, the need for continued evaluation and prophylactic treatment, and the period of time during which there have been no behavioral manifestations of the problem. Therefore, these classifications can be regarded as either acute or chronic health deviations.

The diagnosis and labeling of health problems in *DSM III* is based on a set of verbal, nonverbal, or affective behavioral manifestations. If NPTs

**Table 7.1 Actual or Potential Health Problem/*DSM III* Diagnosis**

1   Developmental life changes
     Conditions not attributable to a mental disorder
2   Acute health deviations
     Paranoid disorders
     Psychotic disorders not elsewhere classified
     Anxiety disorders
     Somatoform disorders
     Dissociative disorders
     Psychosexual disorders
     Factitious disorders
     Disorders of impulse control not elsewhere classified
     Psychological factors affecting physical condition
2.5  Acute or chronic deviations
     Substance abuse disorders
     Schizophrenic disorders
     Affective disorders
3   Chronic health deviations
     Organic mental disorders
     Personality disorders
4   Cultural/environmental stressors
     Adjustment disorders

treat these human responses and alter them in a healthy direction, then by definition they have cured the health problem.

The strength of *DSM III* for nursing psychotherapy practice lies in its behavioral definitions of acute and chronic health deviations. There is no need for NPTs to develop their own set of diagnostic labels to categorize actual health problems. If there are deficiencies in *DSM III* relating to *actual* health problems, it is likely they will be corrected within the process of revision. At the time of this writing, the ANA is attempting to insure that a psychiatric nurse advanced practitioner is on the American Psychiatric Association's committee charged to revise *DSM III*.

One major weakness of *DSM III* for nursing psychotherapy practice is its lack of specificity regarding potential health problems, particularly two categories of potential health problems with which nurses are concerned: developmental life changes and cultural/environmental stressors. Developmental life changes such as pregnancy, birth, going to school, adolescence, and marriage, can be distressing and/or growth producing. Timely nursing intervention can turn a potential health problem into a growth experience. For example, the family who learns to deal with the uncertainties of growing adolescents' decisions about drugs, sex, relationships, and careers has developed a resource for dealing with future problems such as divorce, retirement, illness, and aging together.

The same is true of cultural/environmental stressors such as rape, unemployment, relocation, racism, sexism, and natural disasters. NPTs who recognize such stressors as potential health problems are actively involved in facilitating coping and adjustment. While the prevention of actual health problems is difficult to document, there is enough evidence of the connection between stress and health problems to keep nurses, especially NPTs, active in preventing health disturbances related to these stressors. Several chapters in this book address developmental life changes and cultural/environmental stressors.

## RELATIONSHIPS AMONG *DSM III* CATEGORIES, NURSING DIAGNOSES, AND PSYCHIATRIC NURSING

To date the development of nursing diagnoses has been a clinically-based, inductive process, and the system of presentation is alphabetical. While presentations at the Fifth National Conference on the Classification of Nursing Diagnoses (Kim, McFarland, & McLane, 1984) in 1982 addressed the issue of building a conceptual taxonomy, there is currently no accepted conceptual system for organizing the North America Nursing Diagnosis Association's (NANDA) model.

In 1983, this author participated in an ANA survey to rank-order 50 diagnostic categories of NANDA according to their frequency of appearance in her practice. Table 7.2 contains this listing of 32 diagnoses (the remaining 18 were not seen within the practice, so were not ranked). In reflecting about these nursing diagnostic categories, it occurred to the author that: (1) they are all human responses; (2) it is not clear whether they are responses to actual or potential health problems; and (3) each of these responses has the potential for causing a health problem. It appeared that the nursing diagnostic categories could be used by nurse psychotherapists to augment the *DSM III* categories in providing a common nomenclature in the area of potential health problems.

One can tentatively conclude that the NANDA diagnoses are more useful for generic practice in psychiatric/mental-health practice than in practice as a nurse psychotherapist. In generic practice, beginning students and practitioners focus most of their attention on discrete behaviors, whereas advanced practitioners are concerned with behavior patterns and are often responsible for diagnoses. For example, although the nursing diagnosis of "anxiety" is generally useful, it is not specific enough for an advanced level of practice. Anxiety related to the threat of

### Table 7.2 Select Nursing Diagnoses

| | |
|---|---|
| 1. Anxiety | 19. Coping, ineffective family: disabling |
| 2. Self-concept, disturbance in | 20. Knowledge deficit |
| 3. Coping, ineffective individual | 21. Grieving, dysfunctional |
| 4. Injury, potential for | 22. Sexual dysfunctional |
| 5. Social isolation | 23. Grieving, anticipatory |
| 6. Thought processes, alterations in | 24. Nutrition, alterations in: more than body requirements |
| 7. Sensory perceptual alterations | 25. Nutrition, alterations in: potential for more than body requirements |
| 8. Violence, potential for | |
| 9. Powerlessness | |
| 10. Communication, impaired verbal | 26. Nutrition, alterations in: less than body requirements |
| 11. Fear | |
| 12. Sleep pattern disturbance | 27. Noncompliance |
| 13. Family process, alteration in | 28. Rape-trauma |
| 14. Parenting, alterations in: actual | 29. Self-care deficit |
| 15. Parenting, alterations in: potential | 30. Spiritual distress |
| 16. Diversional activity, deficit | 31. Comfort, alterations in: Pain |
| 17. Coping, family: potential growth | 32. Health maintenance, alterations in |
| 18. Coping, ineffective family: compromised | |

**Table 7.3  Health Care Prototypes**

Health problem(s) precede human response(s)
Human response(s) precede health problem(s)
Health problem(s) are defined by human response(s)
Health problem(s) interact with human response(s)

*Source:* Loomis, M. E., & Wood, D. J. (1983). Cure: The potential outcome of nursing care. *Image: The Journal of Nursing Scholarship, 15*(1), 4–7.

death is different from anxiety experienced by a schizophrenic and should be treated differently. Further, generalized anxiety disorder as defined in *DSM III* is a clinical syndrome, not a discrete affective human response.

To examine the relationships among *DSM III* categories, NANDA diagnoses, and psychiatric nursing phenomena of concern, the four "prototypes of health care" situations (see Table 7.3) developed by Loomis and Wood (1983) are helpful. This framework provided a means of structuring the complex exploration of these relationships.

## Prototype 1: Health Problem(s) Precede Human Response(s)

This prototype reflects a medical model perspective in which a disease, accident, or genetic defect affects a patient, and treatment efforts are mobilized to deter the invasive organism or repair the damage caused by trauma. The phenomena of concern to the nurse working in the general hospital are the emotional, family, and social human responses to illness or injury. These responses may include anxiety, fear, alterations in family process, and noncompliance to list only a few possibilities. Good emotional care may facilitate the physical healing process. Augmentation of individual and family strategies for coping with acute or chronic health problems will certainly prevent further disability and may even enhance future coping.

The *DSM III* diagnostic categories offer nurses no guidance in classifying their nursing interventions in this type of health care situation. Such practitioners would be well advised to utilize existing nursing diagnoses such as "Ineffective individual coping," "Fear," or "Alteration in family process" in structuring their interventions. They might also contribute additional diagnostic categories relevant to their practice to the work of NANDA.

## Prototype 2: Human Reponse(s) Precede Health Problem(s)

Developmental life changes and cultural/environmental stress are often precursers of physical or mental illness. For example, some adolescents respond to the developmental expectation of going away to college with anxiety, disturbance in self-concept, ineffective individual coping, or social isolation. For others, the unfamiliar university environment engenders a response of powerlessness, fear, sleep pattern disturbance, or an alteration in family processes. Any or all of these human responses may precede a case of mononucleosis, for example, or an accident that interferes with final examinations. Other distraught, unhappy students may resort to drug use, pregnancy, or suicide in an attempt to relieve their distress. The phenomena of concern to nurses in these situations are the human responses that can precede health problems. Support groups for college students, unemployed autoworkers, and professionals approaching retirement are all examples of efforts to help people deal with the human responses associated with stressful life changes to prevent health problems.

Again, nursing diagnoses appear to have more to offer clinicians in identifying problems and designing care in Prototype 2 situations than *DSM III*. However, *DSM III* categories such as "Conditions not attributable to a mental disorder" and "Adjustment disorders" can augment nursing diagnoses if appropriate.

## Prototype 3: Health Problem(s) are Defined by Human Response(s)

The diagnostic categories of *DSM III* are the best example of Prototype 3. This prototype refers specifically to acute or chronic health deviations; throughout *DSM III*, health deviations or problems are defined by their symptoms or human responses. Upon closer examination, it becomes apparent that the human responses listed as diagnostic criteria in *DSM III* are merely more specific statements of accepted nursing diagnoses. For example, the *DSM III* diagnosis of "Major affective disorders—Manic episode," lists diagnostic Criterion A as "One or more distinct periods with a predominantly elevated, expansive, or irritable mood. The elevated or irritable mood must be a prominent part of the illness and relatively persistent, although it may alternate or intermingle with depressive mood" (p. 208). While there are currently no accepted nursing diagnoses for alterations in mood or affect, these diagnoses are in keeping with the nursing diagnosis format; and with increased input from psychiatric/mental-health nurses, NANDA will undoubtedly develop and accept these diagnostic categories.

Referring once again to "Major affective disorders-Manic episode" in *DSM III*, Diagnostic Criterion B is even more illuminating: "Duration of at least one week (or any duration if hospitalization is necessary), during which, for most of the time, at least three of the following symptoms have persisted (four if the mood is only irritable) and have been present to a significant degree" (p. 208). Table 7.4 illustrates the *DSM III* diagnostic criteria along with the nursing diagnosis for each human response. It is clear from this comparison that the *DSM III* criteria are more specific versions of nursing diagnoses. The same type of comparison is possible across other *DSM III* diagnostic categories.

There need not be a conflict in utilizing both *DSM III* and nursing diagnoses. In fact, the human responses proposed in *DSM III* can assist in the development of additional nursing diagnoses and vice versa. This similarity and overlap in diagnostic systems should strengthen the ability of nurse psychotherapists to communicate with other mental health professionals as well as their nursing colleagues. This point is illustrated in Table 7.5, which compares nursing and *DSM III* diagnoses of "Major affective disorder-major depressive episode." Six accepted and four proposed nursing diagnoses match the *DSM III* diagnostic criteria.

**Table 7.4 Health Problem: Major Affective Disorder–Manic Episode**

| Human Response, *DSM III* | Nursing Diagnosis |
| --- | --- |
| Increase in activity or physical restlessness | Ineffective individual coping |
| More talkative than usual or pressure to keep talking | Impaired verbal communication |
| Flight of ideas or subjective experience that thoughts are racing | Alterations in thought processes |
| Inflated self-esteem (grandiosity) that may be delusional | Disturbance in self-concept |
| Decreased need for sleep | Sleep pattern disturbance |
| Distractibility | Alterations in thought processes |
| Excessive involvement in activities that have a high potential for painful consequences that are not recognized | Sensory perceptual alterations |

*Source:* Adapted from American Psychiatric Association. (1980). *Diagnostic and statistical manual of mental disorders* (3rd ed.) Washington, D.C. American Psychiatric Association.

**Table 7.5 Health Problem: Major Affective
Disorder–Major Depressive Episode**

| Human Response, *DSM III* | Nursing Diagnosis |
| --- | --- |
| Poor appetite or significant weight loss; or, increased appetite or significant weight gain | Alteration in nutrition more or less than body requirements |
| Insomnia or hypersomnia | Sleep pattern disturbance |
| Psychomotor agitation or retardation | Disturbance in psychomotor activity |
| Loss of interest or pleasure in usual activities (or) decrease in sexual drive | Alterations in usual activities[a] Alteration in sexual functioning[a] |
| Loss of energy, fatigue | Alteration in energy levels[a] |
| Feelings of worthlessness, self-reproach, or excessive or inappropriate guilt | Disturbance in self-concept |
| Diminished ability to think or concentrate | Alteration in thought processes |
| Recurrent thoughts of death, suicidal ideation, wishes to be dead, or suicide attempt | Potential for harm to self[a] |

[a]Proposed new Nursing Diagnosis.
*Source:* Adapted from American Psychiatric Association. (1980). *Diagnostic and statistical manual of mental disorders* (3rd ed.) Washington, D.C. American Psychiatric Association.

## Prototype 4: Health Problem(s) Interact with Human Response(s)

Some health problems cannot be cured. Chronic health deviations such as respiratory disease, diabetes, mental retardation, and organic mental disorders must be treated symptomatically. When the damage to the human organism has already been done, the focus of intervention is on maintaining functional abilities and preventing further deterioration.

However, other health problems, once thought incurable, can now be controlled or reversed through self-regulation. Exercise, biofeedback, mental imagery, and meditation are only a few of the techniques available for conscious control and regulation of the autonomic nervous system or various disease processes. Cousins (1979) claimed to have cured himself of ankylosing spondylitis by laughing. Simonton, Simonton, & Creighton (1978) reported extended life expectancy and remission in cancer patients who utilize relaxation and mental imagery. All of these techniques acknowledge the interaction between health problems and human responses. Green and Green (1977) stated that "Every change in the physiological state is accompanied by an appropriate change in the mental-emotional state, conscious or unconscious, and conversely, every change in the mental-emotional state, conscious or unconscious is accompanied by an appropriate change in the physiological state" (p. 33).

Whether or not the human problem is capable of cure, NPTs should focus upon human responses. An example from the author's private practice illustrates this point. The etiology of major affective disorders is unknown; competing theories attempt to explain its origins as genetic, biochemical, interpersonal, family scripting, or social reinforcement. *DSM III* allows for the possibility that affective disorders may be acute or chronic, or at least in remission. Whether the health problem (disease) causes the human response (behavior) or whether the behavior causes the disease remains an unanswered question. In the meantime, many patients with affective disorders seek treatment to ease their intrapersonal and interpersonal discomfort.

In the last two years of private practice in Michigan, the author treated two dozen patients with affective disorders. They were treated and cured by focusing attention (their and the author's) on the human responses listed in the *DSM III* diagnostic criteria (see Table 7.5). Work was directed toward self-monitoring and regulation of the agitation that correlated with their increase in activity and pressured talking. The patients used relaxation strategies and cognitive restructuring to deal with their mental and physical racing, and self-hypnosis programs to help them sleep. Each of these patients was willing and able to contract for social control or self-monitoring of potentially dangerous activities; the author checked their calendars regularly to assist them with time and activity planning. Eventually, these patients were able to contract for reparenting around the self-esteem issues involved with affective disorders. A common theme emerged: all of these patients believed, and acted as if, they could do anything in the world they set their minds to—but they would never do it well enough. The dichotomy between doing and not doing things, so prevelant in the affective disorders, was obvious (Loomis & Landsman, 1980).

Within the reparenting contract, these patients were able to take in new information and script messages about doing things successfully and realistically (Loomis & Landsman, 1981). They were able to reframe the competition they experienced internally in a way that made them comfortable and successful by social standards. Each has been able to experience a new intrapersonal and interpersonal comfort and grace as they move through life.

Are these patients permanently cured? It is impossible to know. Will they have problems in the future? Probably. That's part of being human, but these are all bright, sensitive people who will now recognize the early signs of distress and seek appropriate help. They all remain off medication and in touch with their feelings, dealing effectively with intimate and social relationships, and meeting their social and job responsibilities. By definition, they no longer have major affective disorders. In dealing with their human responses, they also dealt with their health problems.

## CONCLUSION

The phenomena of concern for nursing psychotherapy practice are the physical, emotional, cognitive, family, social, and cultural human responses to developmental life changes, acute health deviations, chronic health deviations, and cultural-environmental stressors. Nurse psychotherapists often identify these phenomena through patients' verbal, physical, and affective behavior. The strength of *DSM III* for nursing psychotherapy practice is in its clear definition of acute and chronic mental health problems. Unfortunately, *DSM III* offers little assistance in the area of potential mental health problems. The strength of the nursing diagnosis system for NPTs is in the areas of developmental life changes and cultural/environmental stressors.

As proposed previously in this chapter, *DSM III* with its emphasis on the diagnosis of syndromes or patterns of human responses is more likely to be useful to nurse psychotherapists than psychiatric nurses in beginning practice. The more general, behavioral NANDA diagnoses are likely to be most useful in generic practice and basic educational programs.

It is important that NPTs participate actively in the revision of *DSM III* and contribute vigorously to the addition of nursing diagnoses that will assist their practice. There is no inherent incompatability between *DSM III* and nursing diagnoses; they overlap in some cases and meet different needs in other cases. It is unnecessary to create a new system; rather, it is of greater importance to insure that the two current systems work for NPTs.

Finally, this author would like to encourage elaboration and extension of the ideas presented in this article. NPTs have daily opportunities to work with both nursing diagnoses and the *DSM III*. Their thoughts and refinements will contribute greatly to the phenomena of concern to the practice of nurse psychotherapists.

# REFERENCES

American Nurses' Association. (1980). *Nursing: A social policy statement.* Kansas City, MO: American Nurses' Association.

American Nurses' Association. (1982). *Standards of psychiatric and mental health nursing practice.* Kansas City, MO: American Nurses' Association.

American Psychiatric Association. (1980). *Diagnostic and statistical manual of mental disorders* (3rd ed.). Washington, DC: American Psychiatric Association.

Barnard, K. (1982). Determining the focus of nursing research. *Maternal Child Nursing, 7*(5), 299.

Cousins, N. (1979). *The anatomy of an illness.* New York: Norton.

Green, E., & Green, A. (1977). *Beyond biofeedback.* New York: Delta.

Kim, M. J., McFarland, G. K., & McLane, A. M. (1984). *Classification of nursing diagnoses.* New York: McGraw-Hill.

Loomis, M. E., & Landsman, S. G. (1981). Manic-depressive structure: Treatment strategies. *Transactional Analysis Journal, 11*(4), 346–351.

Loomis, M. E., & Landsman, S. G. (1980). Manic-depressive structure: Assessment and development. *Transactional Analysis Journal, 10*(4), 284–290.

Loomis, M. E., & Wood, D. J. (1983). Cure: The potential outcome of nursing care. *Image: The Journal of Nursing Scholarship, 15*(1), 4–7.

Simonton, O., Simonton, S. & Creighton, J. (1978). *Getting Well Again.* Los Angeles: Tarcher.

# Chapter 8
# Planning and Initiating a Private Practice in Nursing Psychotherapy

*Lynne Parsons*

## GETTING STARTED

As I review my experiences in developing a private nursing psychotherapy practice and read what other NPTs have said about their practices, two approaches seem to emerge. I call these the "hero" and the "politician" approaches. Some readers might question my use of these terms and think it more intellectual to call the first approach "developing expertise through specialization" and to refer to the second as "marketing." I prefer the former terms, however, because they have a multitude of associations—"hot" words in McLuhan's terminology (1964). Moreover, while the terms "specialization" and "marketing" convey the information you need to have, they do not require that you consider these approaches personally. Can you envision yourself performing heroically? Can you imagine yourself a politician who tells others about your work?

To be successful in initiating your private practice, you will probably need to be both a hero and a politician, in that order. The first concept focuses upon developing your expertise, and the second upon letting others know about it. These will both require a great deal of energy—thinking, planning, and doing will be continual. Also, heroes and politicians stand out and are comfortable in being with and being of use to people. The lonely quest for personal truth or knowledge probably won't get you into private practice!

# THE HERO APPROACH

In large urban areas, the process of specialization is amplified and often becomes the key to visibility as a professional. Additionally, from an ethical standpoint, a solo practitioner needs a special clarity about her/his capabilities and limitations. This clarity is more likely to emerge for those who specialize in a particular area of mental health service. Specialization helps you develop a sense of normal behavior for your clinical population and, hence, deviations that need consideration can be identified more readily. This adds to your strength as a clinician.

Following graduate school, I became involved with the humanistic-existential school of therapy called bioenergetics, which expands psychodynamic theory into the study of how our body structure correlates with behavioral tendencies. A social worker-colleague asked if I would see clients for bioenergetic therapy. I agreed and initiated my practice. I enjoyed the work but my practice was too small to produce an adequate income. I felt ready to see patients who sought me out, yet I felt unprepared to present myself as an experienced specialist. So I took several steps to develop more expertise.

First, I searched for a part-time job in a family service agency that would give me more experience working with the type of patient I would have in private practice. My second step was to enter a formal training program in bioenergetics. My commitment to the training program was a public statement of my intention to engage in private practice. A helpful aspect of the program was that my co-trainees were multidisciplinary and private practitioners. This allowed me to measure my skills against those of other professionals, gain confidence in my skills, and arrive at greater clarity about my weaknesses. My third step was to develop an organization of local professionals interested in learning more about bioenergetics. Through these workshops, I got to know many local professionals; my visibility grew along with my personal knowledge and experience.

These events took place over a four-year period. I was a "hero" in terms of developing clinical expertise and professional contacts. In concentrating on one area, I was counting on attracting a number of people in a large urban area that would have an interest in my skills. Also, bioenergetics was the "new baby" on the block, which elicited interest from patients and professionals alike.

In selecting an area of specialization, you'll need to think about the psychotherapeutic approach or psychological school that interests you. The three broad categories of treatment models in the Western World are psychodynamic, humanistic-existential, and behavioral. Each of these models is based on core assumptions that are neither provable nor disprovable. Both the psychodynamic and behavioral models assume a deterministic worldview; they share the belief that what has happened to us in our lives is crucial in predicting what will happen to us in the future. On the other hand, the humanistic-existential model emphasizes free will and a human, innate drive toward self-development. Traditionally, academic institutions have favored more deterministic approaches; and this preference is often reflected in hospitals, mental health centers, and public agencies. As you pursue your investigation of various schools as the foundation of your specialization, you'll need to examine their underlying assumptions and their relation to your personal philosophy.

Another avenue to selecting an area of specialization is to consider particular kinds of patients whom you would like to treat. You might choose developmental groups (e.g., children or elderly), various diagnostic categories, or a combination of these with particular treatment strategies. For instance, recent research has shown that group behavior modification is most effective in removing phobic symptoms. If you would choose this area of mental health service, you would combine an interest in a particular kind of problem with developing expertise in a school of treatment.

The success of the specialization route will be determined not only by your own competency but also by factors less under your control, such as interest in your specialty. There is now a growing market for services for the elderly, especially the care of people with Alzheimer's disease; another growth field is alcoholism treatment, particularly because private industry is increasing its commitment to employee rehabilitation. Eating disorders are drawing increasing professional attention, replacing sexual dysfunction and family therapy as new frontiers. Sexual dysfunction treatment and family therapy, meanwhile, have become respected specialties, still commanding important markets.

Henderson (1983) made the following analogy about marketing clinical skills: "The game of chess remains the same whether played by a novice or a grand master. The difference is not intelligence but in the ability to anticipate the eventual consequences of the specific moves in the present." Your clinical knowledge is what you have to sell. As in chess, your skills will lie dormant unless, as a strategist, you can foresee an area(s) in which they are in demand.

## THE POLITICIAN APPROACH

The politician approach, or marketing, centers around how well you understand consumers' needs and wants (Durham & Hardin, 1983; Hardin & Durham, 1985). Publishers sell ideas, not books; automobiles provide freedom, not transportation. A nurse psychotherapist sells increased satisfaction with self or alleviation of emotional pain, not therapy. Most people who begin therapy for the first time are genuinely bewildered about what is expected of them and how they will get better. Somehow you must learn about how therapy is viewed by different segments of the community where you want to practice, and how you can make your service meaningful to them. If you don't understand their wants and needs, you may offer a competent service that no one will buy. Private practice is a business and must be approached as objectively as any other business if you are to succeed. As you invest in a private practice, you need to look at trends in society that affect the market for therapists.

Some basic steps toward entering the private practice market are to: (1) investigate the marketplace; (2) use marketing strategies; and (3) assess mental health market trends. To investigate the marketplace, I recommend talking with key people in public agencies, school personnel, community nurses, other private practitioners, and personnel managers in local industry about the nature and structure of the therapy market in your community. It is important to explain to them that you are not seeking a job, but rather investigating the field to determine how you can best use your expertise in developing your own practice. If you persist in completing a broad survey of at least a dozen people, you will come away with a far better sense of your market. Being a nurse in this situation can give you a certain edge because you are a novelty as an independent entrepreneur. This fact may arouse some people's curiosity; others may find it appealing. A secondary benefit of your investigating the marketplace will be the practice you'll get in presenting yourself and your role to others. If you are like most nurses, you did not receive preparation on "selling yourself" in your nursing education. You will have to do so to become a successful private practitioner.

Your ability to develop referral sources will depend, to a large extent, upon others' perception of your competence—not actual competence which, although helpful, is not always congruent with reputation. Perception of your competence will be influenced by your professional visibility and by a more elusive quality—your charisma. A minister once showed me a remarkable assortment of documents that she and other ministers in the community had received from a new counselor who was opening a practice. My friend was much impressed with his presentation, which included several recommendations, statements of philosophy, and a resumé. This therapist went on to develop a financially successful practice through direct advertising in the local papers with ads that read, "If you think you have a problem, you probably do." His showmanship was perhaps not limited to the public arena, however, as several malpractice suits were later brought against him for sexual exploitation of clients. This man's marketing approach was effective initially; it wasn't enough, however, to make him permanently successful. Charisma can be likened to a fireworks display that is initially startling but soon over.

The second and probably more effective method of marketing yourself is by operationalizing others' reportedly successful marketing strategies. Durham and Hardin (1983; Hardin & Durham, 1985) found that private nurse psychotherapists reported that unique mental health services, third party payment, flexible scheduling, and meeting with physicians and other mental health professionals were most effective in building up a private caseload of patients. Tyron (1983), after surveying psychologists about their recommended marketing methods, reported that doing good work, being competent, giving speeches, displaying professional behavior toward referral sources, advertising, contacting physicians, and consulting were effective marketing strategies. Both groups of practitioners recommended providing services that meet local mental health needs, cultivating personal referral sources, and achieving professional visibility. Speaking to various community groups, giving workshops, publishing, and participating in professional activities can increase this visibility and remind your target audience about the product you seem to deliver competently.

Several nurses who were successful in achieving professional visibility to build a private practice used their own talents and good sense, rather than public relations gimmicks; they were also willing to take risks. One personal experience that I vividly recall was being unexpectedly invited to lead a small group in a professional workshop when I had just begun my private practice. The experience was somewhat unnerving, especially when I learned my former nursing research professor would be attending. Controlling my urge to retire to the restroom or develop a sudden illness, I simply accepted the fact that I was going to be extremely anxious and proceeded. The program went well and I was left with a stronger sense of my own skills, in addition to adding several new patients to my practice. Another colleague, who had never really been an effective public speaker, developed a local private practice association, a directory, and several helpful workshops. This enterprising nurse psychotherapist provided important services to private practitioners in the community while also dramatically increasing her own professional visibility.

The third step in entering the private practice market is to assess mental health trends. One nurse who analyzed local mental health needs realized that her community contained many professional women who were having their first child in their thirties. These women, who had once had a support network at work, now found themselves somewhat lonely and depressed as they were isolated with a new child. These women were dealing with typical issues with which a brief therapy model could be effectively put to use. The nurse, having experienced the same isolation and anxieties herself, had found ways of resolving them. She felt that as a nurse she could not only share her personal experiences, but also serve as an informational source for women dealing with the insecurities of new motherhood in later life. The nurse offered workshops to this group at a local college where she helped the women put names on their feelings and consider the reasons behind them. Several workshop participants requested her services as a private therapist; others became referral sources.

Two major mental health market trends will have major impacts on the general development of the role of the NPT. Widespread dissatisfaction with the segmented, chemically-oriented, and a symptom-centered Western health care system has led to an increasing appreciation of holistic health. The holistic health movement views psychotherapy as an essential medical tool, as a means to the end of better health, not just better mental health. Secondly, government and private corporations that are shouldering a large part of the financial burden of health care are exerting extreme pressure for cost containment. Joseph Califano, former Secretary of Health, Education, and Welfare, recently stated that Chrysler's total cost per employee averaged $57,000 per year, compared with an average of $815 per year for the same employee at Japan's Mitsubishi Motor Corporation (Kotulak, 1984). While this does not mean that nurses should step in and sell themselves cheaply, it does mean that our salary expectations are more reasonable than those of most physicians, and we can therefore deliver cost effective services and still be adequately.

The pressure for cost containment has also produced three major modifications in health care payment systems—Diagnostic Related Groups (DRGs), Health Maintenance Organizations (HMOs), and Preferred Provider Organizations (PPOs). These innovations will enhance the market for nurse psychotherapists because they mandate cost containment while providing effective referral sources. The DRG plan has meant government intervention in terms of fixing costs in a prospective payment system. Another government intervention, occurring quietly over the last decade, has been support of private HMOs, in which employees pay a fixed monthly fee in return for complete medical care, including specified psychiatric benefits. Government legislation has permitted HMOs to secure employee time within companies to educate them about HMO benefits as an alternative to regular fee-for-service coverage such as Blue Cross-Blue Shield. The PPO provides total coverage at a lower cost in return for substantial client referrals; an employee often receives a financial incentive to use a PPO organization.

As HMOs and PPOs provide a larger share of mental health services, the much-discussed issue of third-party payment will probably become less of a problem. Whereas psychiatrists and psychologists previously had the advantage of receiving third-party reimbursements, HMOs and PPOs are more interested in master's level personnel for both inhouse positions and referral purposes. Ordinarily, HMO staff make an initial assessment and quickly decide if a mental health problem is treatable within their time frame of twenty sessions per year. If the HMO therapist decides that the problem is not appropriate for time-limited intervention, the patient is referred out. Finding a competent and affordable therapist is the HMO therapist's task; therefore, the HMO staff is an excellent potential referral source, especially if you are willing to take cases at lower hourly rates. One is employed by a PPO by negotiating a contract with a company's Employee Assistance Program (EAP) to provide services for employees at a specific fee. This contract may be informal or formal and reflects the evaluation of the company's EAP officer that your clinical service is a cost-effective competent service that the company wishes their employees to use. Mental Health Service PPOs have evolved somewhat differently from strictly medical PPOs because of the history of EAPs (see Wrich, 1980).

In summary, new entrepreneurial opportunities exist for nurses today. Both government and private industry are seeking creative solutions to the delivery of cost-effective mental health services. Private industry is divesting from its past policy of direct cost reimbursement for psychiatric services. The advantage of receiving third-party payments from insurance that other mental health professionals have had over nurses is fast disappearing. New organizations like HMOs, PPOs, and EAPs recognize master's prepared nurses as key resources in delivering cost-effective services. Nurses need to demonstrate their interest and capacity to fill this market in competition with master's prepared social workers. It is important that graduate programs prepare nurses to work with disorders common in outpatient populations.

# PRACTICAL MATTERS

## The NPT's Office

A number of works exist to help the NPT initiate a private practice (Jacox & Norris, 1977; Kinlein, 1977; Kissel, 1983; Kaltz, 1979). One of the first considerations in initiating a private practice is office space. Many beginning practitioners consider converting a spare room into an office. The type of therapy you do will determine whether this is feasible. There is the question of how much the patient should know about your personal life style. Certain humanistic schools emphasize the value of the patient having realistic information about who you are as a person and as a role model. However, in more psychoanalytic schools this kind of information remains private so that the therapeutic process evolves out of a more neutral frame. Other important factors to consider are privacy and uninterrupted quiet. Robinson (1984) provides a review of issues in considering office design for psychotherapy.

An inexpensive office alternative is to sublet space from other private practitioners. The more established partner assumes the responsibility of a three- to five-year lease and rents out space to others. Unfortunately, in such an arrangement you cannot shape the office to your taste. The environment for psychological work is important because it expresses who you are to your patients. Also, if your office looks temporary, it does not convey the feeling that you will be there tomorrow. It is important to clarify with the major tenant your rights to receive or make phone calls and use the office at other times during the week for emergency appointments. Location of the office is becoming increasingly important. The rule used to be that for more conventional therapies, convenience was a prime consideration; whereas for esoteric approaches, patients would travel further. Because there are more private practitioners in the marketplace, however, convenience is probably going to become more important. Ultimately, you need to base your office location on whom your clientele will be and where they live or work.

## Fees

Several factors play a part in determining your fee scale (Blanck & Blanck, 1974). You will be looking at the market range for your community, for the kind of therapy you do, and for professionals with your type of education. You will be influenced by your personal and professional ethics; and there is the "bottom line"—how much money do you need to support yourself? Perhaps the hardest (but most crucial) question is how much do you think your services are worth? A major and complicated aspect of fee setting is the decision for a flat or sliding scale. If you feel your services are worth $60 an hour, but decide to charge $45 under extenuating circumstances, you may cause problems for yourself, depending on how important the money is to you both psychologically and economically. However, a successful beginning practitioner told me she accepted low-fee patients because if the therapeutic outcome was positive, they often referred others who could pay more. Because satisfied customers are the best referral source, she was making a sensible business decision. If you do adopt a sliding scale, you should avoid complying with what a patient feels she/he can afford; it is better for this patient to find another therapist since this makes a poor beginning to a good working relationship. Low-fee setting for beginning practitioners is not common. In a survey of one hundred and ninety-four psychologists in private practice, Inman and Busace (1984) found that fees were not different for experienced *versus* inexperienced psychologists; and level of educational preparation had only a moderate effect. In my experience, most patients ask about your fees when they first call you to discuss starting therapy. If they do not ask, it is appropriate to tell them. Nonphysician therapists often request payment at time of service, thereby avoiding billing. I have always followed this practice and found it very satisfactory. It keeps the money issue in a therapeutic light and missed sessions become immediate issues for discussion. Most therapists have specific cancellation policies. An NPT could, for example, request forty-eight hour cancellation notice; with extenuating circumstances, such as illness or financial problems, to be dealt with immediately.

## Insurance

Insurance is another important consideration. There are five kinds to decide on: professional liability, property damage and personal liability, overhead, disability, and personal health insurance. Professional liability insurance is usually secured through your professional organization; these policies may provide professional liability coverage for the NPT. Independent agencies may also provide this type of coverage. You might ask your local universities which insurance agency is providing malpractice insurance for their students in their practicum settings. This agency will also be likely to have a policy for the private practitioner. At the present time, nurses can still obtain extensive liability coverage for a minimal fee. This may change in the future, however, when larger numbers practice as entrepreneurs. Property damage and personal liability, which is the equivalent of your home owner policy, covers you if a patient is injured through an accident on your property. Overhead insurance and disability insurance are policies to consider if you are in full-time practice with sizable overhead investments. Also, think about self-insuring by putting some money aside into a separate office account on a regular basis. Health insurance costs, which have soared over the past five years, have become a major cost for the private practitioner. After investigating costs you will probably want to join a group that offers lower rates.

## Accounting

Keeping clear accounting records is a must. Not only does the IRS require it, but you will not have a W-2 payroll deduction tax form so you are more likely than others to be audited. Paying for the services of a tax accountant is money well spent. She/he can teach you how to set up your records to meet government requirements and advise you as to legitimate tax deductions. A self-employed person pays 2% more social security tax than a person in the institutional sector. In return, certain professional expenses such as supervision, educational activities, books, and journals are tax deductible. Like so many other aspects of any business today, tax accounting for the solo practitioner has become an area of special expertise. The tax laws change frequently and you need to have the counsel of someone who is aware of these changes. The best way to find a good accountant is to ask local colleagues in private practice for a recommendation or to seek out an accountant who specializes in small businesses.

## Third-Party Reimbursement

Although some inroads are being made into the problem of third-party reimbursement for private nurse practitioners (several states have now passed legislation mandating insurance companies to reimburse nurse specialists with specified experience), third-party reimbursement remains an obstacle to be overcome in many areas. Many NPTs have worked out an arrangement in which a supervising psychologist or psychiatrist signs insurance papers. While this is very common, there is pending legislation that may soon make it illegal for psychologists to have this arrangement. It is possible to have a private practice without benefit of patient health insurance reimbursement. It does mean that one's clientele is limited to employed persons, those with upper-level incomes, and persons who are willing to make an economic sacrifice to improve their mental health. A side benefit is that you may then treat patients who take their therapy very seriously. Others, however, may have to terminate therapy for economic reasons.

## Telephone Service

You will need a business phone; even if you are practicing out of your home you will want a second phone just for business calls. Listing your services in the phone directory can be complicated because directories usually list services under disciplines. However, many nurses have listed themselves as nurse-counselor. The directory often uses the generic category "psychotherapist," which you may want to consider.

Another decision is the choice of an answering machine or answering service. There is no doubt that most people probably prefer the human contact of an answering service. However, if an answering service is busy at certain times of the day, you may have difficulty retrieving calls and messages. An answering machine at least allows patients to hear your voice and permit you to hear the patients. People seem to be less intimidated by these machines than they used to be. The machines are quite reliable and have many different functions that allow you to be paged or to phone the machine to pick up your calls when you are away.

## PERSONAL DEVELOPMENT

### Supervision

The art of psychotherapy is perhaps best learned in the time honored way of all arts, apprenticeship. This is what supervision can be. As a professional you need to identify your professional resources. Hiring a good supervisor helps. You can work with the supervisor on the cases you find most difficult and in doing so, improve your clinical skill. Part of the joy of working in this field is the continuing process of development as a clinician. Doing psychotherapy has been called the impossible profession for good reason. Understanding and empathy can easily merge into identification. Supervision is a crucial check and balance system in delivering quality care. At its best, a good supervisory relationship will have some of the qualities of mentorship. You should enjoy and be challenged by your supervisor, and see the results of supervision in the increased effectiveness of your work.

Beyond the supervisory relationship, the best place to learn about the art of psychotherapy is in personal therapy. Human emotional distress is remarkably similar under its rainbow of defensive coverlets. Thus, when you touch a new place in yourself while looking at your own development with your therapist, and are responded to in a helpful way, you have acquired one more aspect of the emotional template within you. In the future, you can use this dimension to assist your patients.

### About Freedom

One of the most intriguing aspects of private practice is its potential for creativity. Most institutional jobs come with fixed priorities that force you to conform to standards set by others. Private practice forces you to be aware of your own development and skills more than institutional work; and to be solely accountable and responsible for your decisions (see also Chapter 9). Although private practice permits considerably more freedom, as a private practitioner you cannot lay the blame for a clinical shortcoming at the door of a controlling institution. You must make your best efforts and accept responsibility. Choosing to be more free and to take responsibility for yourself in a private practice setting is investing in yourself to benefit both self and others in a particularly conscious manner.

# REFERENCES

Blanck, B., & Blanck, R. (1974). *Ego psychology: Theory and practice.* New York: Columbia University Press.
Durham, J., & Hardin, S. (1983). Promoting independent practice in a competitive marketplace. *Nursing Economics, 1*(1), 24–28.
Hardin, S., & Durham, J. (1985). First rate: Structure, process, and effectiveness of nurse psychotherapy. *Journal of Psychosocial Nursing and Mental Health Services, 23*(5), 8–15.
Henderson, B. (1983). The anatomy of competition. *Journal of Marketing, 47*(2), 7–11.
Inman, D., & Busace, L. (1984). Fee policies of psychologists in private practice. *Psychotherapy in Private Practice, 2*(2), 3–7.
Jacox, A., & Norris, C. (1977). *Organizing for independent practice.* New York: Appleton-Century-Crofts.
Kaltz, C. (1979). *Private practice in nursing.* Germantown, MD: Aspen.
Kinlein, L. (1977). *Independent nursing practice with clients.* New York: Lippincott.
Kissel, S. (1983). *Private practice for the mental health clinician.* Germantown, MD: Aspen.
Kotulak, R. (1984, September 30). Employers attacking health costs. *Chicago Tribune,* p. 1.
McLuhan, M. (1964). *Understanding Media: The Extensions of Man.* NY: New American Library.
Robinson, O. (1984). *Office design for psychotherapy.* Springfield, IL: C. C. Thomas.
Tyron, J. S. (1983). How full-time practitioners market their services: A national survey. *Psychotherapy in Private Practice, 1*(1), 91–100.
Wrich, J. T. (1980). *Employee assistance programs: Updates for the 1980's.* New York: Hazelden.

# Chapter 9
# The Emotional Impact of Private Practice on the Nurse Psychotherapist

*Donna K. Ipema*

A good novel has the power to bring the reader into the emotional experience of its characters. To convey the emotional impact of private practice on a nurse psychotherapist, I shall attempt to share my feelings about this often demanding role within the confines of a few pages. (Readers may also profit by reading Balsam & Balsam, 1984; Burton, 1972; and Chessick, 1971.)

Take one particular day: As a nurse psychotherapist in private practice, I spent all day Thursday as usual in the office seeing patients. I was early as I walked up to the street level entrance of my office. It had continued snowing through the night and the unshoveled sidewalk was slippery where footsteps had packed the wet snow, forming a path to the elevated train station. For the hundredth time, I made a mental note to wear boots so I would not slip and slide the twenty feet from my parked car to the office door. By the time I had unlocked the door—balancing my briefcase, purse, and an armful of books on one arm and clenching a styrofoam cup of coffee between my teeth—I had already forgotten my resolve to wear boots once again.

Two years ago, I both loved and hated my private practice. I had been too busy to think—too busy, in fact, to care about my patients or to have any life of my own. I taught part-time at a university, was a full-time doctoral student, and saw twenty patients per week. Rushing from place

87

to place and juggling schedules, I was regularly late and began to wonder what I had been "trained" to do. As an overworked, irritable therapist with no time to be a real person, I felt stressed and unfulfilled, both personally and professionally. However, a flash of common sense held long enough to reorder my practice and daily routine. I decided to limit my patient load, reschedule my doctoral study program, and double the time set aside for myself, at the same time ignoring a sense of guilt and fears that I would never earn enough to pay the overhead.

My decision was the right one, though I still feel a jolt when I walk into the office and reflect back. But now I am happy to be in the office, eager to see my patients, and know I will enjoy the day. Once people seemed to abuse the hour and sessions would inevitably go overtime; I found myself using breaks to catch up on progress notes and to make telephone calls. Now I have time to bring closure to a session, take a short break, and be consciously ready and happy to see the next patient.

By the time I got upstairs this Thursday morning, I was aware of the day's schedule. Twenty minutes gave me time to turn up the thermostat, plug in the coffee, arrange the charts, and reflect on the marital dynamics of the nine o'clock appointment:

> Well-meaning friends had spent hours with each partner, separately, as conflict between the two festered and grew. Diane was seething with anger toward Peter who had talked about and not produced a windfall income for 17 years. Peter was baffled by Diane's angry outbursts, as she had previously been understanding and supportive toward him. Moreover, Diane's pregnancy with their seventh child (at age 39) was a shock for them both; it meant they would be destined to remain in a low-middle income life style just when their financial outlook had turned upward with Diane's full-time employment. Diane and Peter had many strengths and had operated with their often repeated motto, "We're in this together!" Neither had learned to express anger in a constructive manner and discredited or denied feeling angry. Five sessions had alleviated the crisis and both were engaged in therapy. A "working" marital pair was a nice way to start out the day.

My private practice had started ten years ago when I received a master's degree in psychiatric nursing. Not knowing if I wanted to teach or practice, I taught full-time and continued to see patients at an agency used for my graduate clinical experiences. The private agency permitted me to determine my caseload and earn 80% of the paid fees. Under ongoing supervision, my caseload slowly grew and I recognized that referrals came from former patients. Changing to an agency closer to home brought an even larger clientele, thus enabling me to start a small savings. The idea of private practice became a reality four years ago when two other nurses wanted to set up a practice as partners with separate profit motives.

My strongest assets were an established clientele and my confidence as a psychotherapist. Certification from the American Nurses' Association in adult psychiatric and mental health nursing provided official endorsement of my clinical expertise. The greatest uncertainty was, and continues to be, whether or not other professionals will recognize my expertise and credentials. The message from some of the professionals in the local area was clear: "Nurses are not qualified to do therapy and should not receive third-party payment." Others thought, rather patronizingly, that nursing was "a good field for a woman," as if a nurse were an overpriced mother. Some nurses felt I had escaped into the private practice of nursing psychotherapy because the demands were few and the money was easily earned.

Actually, private practice is difficult to begin and maintain; psychotherapy is no easier than other nursing practice. Psychiatric nursing appeals to me because of its scope—I am not confined to one type of problem or person. Psychotherapy involves rethinking, restructuring, and discovering the freedom to feel and express emotions. This ranges from marital pairs who are surprised they need a therapist after seventeen years of marriage; teenagers who are honor students and suicidal; a 50-year-old man newly unemployed; or a deserted 55-year-old lesbian. Psychotherapy is a fascinating field with diverse people who are changed during therapy and who change the therapist.

A sense of pride helps turn the key in the lock on a snowy January Thursday morning and swells when Diane and Peter saunter in the room with filled coffee cups. Surreptitiously, I studied their facial expression, shoulder tension, and gait. My heart lifted as they smiled easily at each other and returned my smile. I could anticipate their report that they had had good talks this week. As anticipated, the talks were useful and had included sharing some of their earlier life histories that they could see affecting the marital relationship. I loved my patients and the problems they posed—from the delicacy of heated anger to the challenge of bringing insight to highly guarded information. Each hour through the day brought new challenges and new rewards. One Thursday hardly ended, when it was time to begin again. The sense of accomplishment is a mainstay, but is it enough to carry one through all the weeks of the year? While the autonomy inherent in setting one's own time, fees, and workload has the attraction of freedom, these benefits are counterbalanced by a sometimes gnawing sense of loneliness.

# HOW MUCH AUTONOMY DO YOU WANT?

The reality of a private practice for many NPTs is isolation. Even though colleagues may know you have a private practice and ask about it, and your supervision is regular and beneficial, when you are in session, you are the sole professional. While the acquired skills, theoretical knowledge, experience, and successes bolster you as "expert," you are ultimately the professional upon whom patients rely at critical moments. Some of these moments illustrate this factor of isolation.

The first contact, usually by telephone, marks the beginning therapeutic relationship; a receptionist or intake worker does not provide notes or schedule an appointment as in the institutional setting. Several vital decisions need to be made and questions answered during this first contact. Do I have time to see this person? Can I work with this person? What makes me think I can or cannot? What are the advantages/disadvantages for us to work with each other? How do I feel about what this person is saying—and not saying? These questions and decisions require immediate responses that you make, alone. No colleague is present for a quick consultation. Just you and the patient.

This feeling of isolation can be illustrated from a set of messages from my telephone-answering tape:

> Seven messages from the same person placed within ten minutes were on the tape. The caller identified himself as a prospective patient's boyfriend and insisted "Susan needs help!" With my help, Paul was sure she would "come to her senses" and understand how much she needed him! A variety of telephone numbers were given for returning the call to Paul or Susan. Feeling annoyed, I debated. Don't call—Paul's insistence and request to persuade Susan to meet his wishes is not therapy. Return the call—explore what is going on as someone may really need to talk. But who? Am I putting myself into a hornet's nest, or is this the way someone asks for help? Who do I suggest come in? Paul, Susan, or both? At that moment, a supervisor or colleague was desirable but unavailable and I was tired after seeing several patients that day. To have a colleague return the call for me or to have someone to talk with about the taped messages preoccupied my thoughts. Still feeling restless and annoyed, I called Susan only out of a commitment to return all calls.
>
> The case was complicated and a series of calls took up the next hour. Susan did want to come in, but without Paul's knowledge. Paul was informed that I had to maintain strict confidentiality and would not be able to let him know whether or not I saw Susan or what we might talk about in therapy. Paul understood but argued that he had a right to know something since he was paying for the sessions. Payment was arranged from Susan, and she scheduled an appointment for the next day.

My sense of isolation increased for several weeks thereafter. Paul had a criminal record and had served a two and one-half year jail sentence for assault and battery. Susan, a divorcée and mother of three girls, had attempted to end the relationship, which enraged Paul and caused him to physically threaten her and her daughters. Francis, another male friend with whom Susan was living, bought and carried a handgun, allegedly to protect himself, Susan, and her daughters. Throughout the next weeks, arrangements were made for Susan and her daughters to return to her home state without Paul's knowledge. During the first three weeks of therapy, my emotional responses ranged from fear to calm as Susan's move was planned and carried out. Francis registered and later sold his handgun. Paul decided to forget about Susan for a "new chick." Although supervision and legal counsel were used extensively throughout this period, the loneliness was acutely felt during several sessions.

The isolation was felt most intensely with this case and produced an awareness of how alone a therapist can be in decision-making and during sessions. The isolation is not limited to complicated cases; there are other times one wants to consult briefly with another familiar therapist. Spouses, friends, and colleagues provide support to some degree, but they may not be available or able to understand the dimensions of being alone in a practice.

Crisis calls elicit another set of emotional responses and an awareness of isolation. People call because they have seen the name of the practice, been referred by another, are currently in therapy, or know you personally. In general, the timing of the calls is manageable, but at times they interrupt sleep, social engagements, holidays, weekends, or study. Such calls can be brief or extended, but all share the commonality of interruption.

Interruptions elicit several responses, one of which is anger. It is sometimes irritating to be interrupted; however, this anger is also counterbalanced by pleasure because the person sought you for help. These emotional responses, with various levels of intensity, need no apology and are part of the repertoire of the therapist's normal reactions.

During the course of therapy, patients may call for additional support, while others attempt to abuse your time. To some extent, these calls can be anticipated and become part of the agenda in subsequent sessions. However, patients (or their family members) can easily usurp your time. While you feel affirmed by their calls, you may also feel abused or manipulated in spending time on the telephone rather than in sessions.

The progress made during therapy carries its own rewards. A 35-year-old woman emancipates herself from home and is no longer depressed after thirteen months of therapy. A high school senior graduates and enters college—no longer suicidal. These are the people who become part of the success of private practice and help reopen the doors for another day of therapy sessions.

However, other patients move slowly. Ann, 37, says she is feeling better, but continues to ignore her household tasks, borders on losing her job, and fails to develop new interests. Progress for Ann is marked by an absence of day-long crying, sleeping through the night, and, for the first time in her life, holding a job for one year. Ann has been in therapy for two years, and although her performance has improved, her ability to gain and use insight is limited. Or Mark, 29 and successful in his law practice, is plagued with doubts about his interpersonal relationships. Mark's latest accomplishment is in dating the same woman for six weeks (his terms) and staying with the same therapist for eight months (my terms). Trusting what he feels is new and frightening to him.

The rate of patient progress and the therapist's emotional responses to patients are the crux of therapy. Emotions, ranging from warmth to fear, are stimulated by a variety of events. From the unexpected, untimely telephone calls to the routine of patients every Thursday, the therapist experiences anger, love, irritation, amusement, fear, hope, sadness, and laughter as single or combined emotional responses: fearful but hopeful, saddened and yet amused, angry and afraid. Regardless of the emotional response, the work of the NPT requires that emotions are attended, sorted, and managed.

## ATTENDING, SORTING, AND MANAGING

The processing of emotional responses can be described as attending and sorting. This is an ongoing process that may occur during or after a session, after a day of work, or at a specified time set aside for an emotional inventory. Although attending and sorting can become spontaneous activities, specific focusing upon emotional reactions can easily be taken for granted. It needs to be a deliberately planned activity.

"Attending" is the label chosen for the process in which I ask: What am I feeling? My clues to let me know I have some unattended feelings are a jittery sensation in my legs and continued thinking about a person or event. It is signalled by my saying, "I'm obsessing over this." Am I feeling anger, irritation or a mixture of different feelings?

"Sorting" is the label chosen for the process in which I ask: What am I thinking about as I feel a particular emotion? Who or what is this related to? Does it occur every time I'm with a particular person, working with a specific dynamic? Is it related to the business of private practice, professional issues, patients, or to my personal life? In short, in what pigeonhole does this feeling belong?

"Management" of emotions is deciding what to do with what you are feeling. Emotional reactions are complex and not always known. To systematically attend to our emotions and sort them out is a means to identify what is happening within ourselves. Once identified and known, the next step is to decide how we are going to manage these emotions.

The irritation over a bank error or broken equipment, anxiety over a suicidal patient, anger about the stepparent who sexually abuses a child, sadness related to your parent's illness, or frustration with cynicism toward NPTs are experienced in varying degrees and can be experienced over several weeks or in one day. The important question to ask is: What do I do with what I feel? Is it enough to recognize, "Ah, this is how I feel!" Or do I need a workout on the racquetball court? Who do I need to talk to? About what? How will I do that constructively?

Private practice has changed what I want out of life. I do not want the biggest, busiest, richest practice, with a big group of my own. I want time for my patients and time for myself. I feel mixed emotions in response to a variety of experiences and people, and I am obligated to attend to these feelings.

Brushing an eight-hour accumulation of snow off of the car on Thursday evening was a time for reflection. Some of the sessions were hard work: Lee was especially anxious and the session moved slowly. Carol had decided to file for a divorce and was ambivalent about her decision. The quarrels between Linda and Ed were not new, and their details demanded tedious listening. The dependency of Jeannie was heavy. In a very real way John had made progress when he called his father this week. Myriad thoughts triggered feelings that would require some processing at a later time. For the moment, the idea of a short jaunt on cross-country skis was appealing—a fantastic way to cope with the accumulated tension. After that I could refocus on specific patients and the practice. I felt confident and secure about myself and the practice. People were getting help and I was helping them with enough time for myself.

# REFERENCES

Balsam, R., & Balsam, A. (1984). *Becoming a psychotherapist.* Chicago: University of Chicago.

Burton, A. (1972). *Twelve therapists: How they live and actualize their lives.* San Francisco: Jossey-Bass.

Chessick, R. (1971). *Why psychotherapists fail.* New York: Science House.

# Part II
## Patients of Unique Concern to the Nurse Psychotherapist

# Chapter 10
# The Nurse as Patient

*D. Jean Wood*

Conducting psychotherapy with peers is not unusual, although it is not well reported in the literature. In the author's experience, the problems that bring nurses to therapy are not remarkably different from those of other patients. However, treatment relationships and the course of treatment can suffer or be enhanced because of commonalities in the backgrounds of nurse psychotherapists and nurse-patients. Psychotherapy is inevitably influenced by unresolved personal issues of therapists as well as patients. Nurse-patients and nurse-psychotherapists bring to a therapeutic relationship unique attributes and problems embedded in a common matrix. Nurses are predominantly women and members of a profession that embodies the traditional and stereotypical feminine goals of nurturing and caretaking. Regardless of the presenting problem of the patient, therapy will be influenced by the orientation and adjustment of both the NPT and patient to their sexual and professional roles.

For several years, the author provided individual and group therapy services in a university medical center setting. During that time, she treated a number of nurse-patients and developed the premises that are shared in this chapter. Over half of the author's caseload were nurses, with only one nurse being male. The issues and examples described in this chapter reflect the eclectic therapeutic orientation of the author and the fact that her caseload consisted primarily of adults in short-term therapy.

# GENERAL TREATMENT ISSUES

The author's experience suggests that nurses seek out NPTs for psychotherapy because they are women and because they are nurses. The author's nurse-patients often expressed concern that male therapists, particularly psychiatrists, might respond to them in terms of traditional sex-role or work-role stereotypes. They wanted someone who would understand them as women and would constructively respond to their desire for personal change. Additionally, role conflict and other career performance issues were major struggles for many of these women and they perceived the NPT as comfortingly familiar with these issues. Because these patients purposefully chose to enter treatment with an NPT, therapy of necessity dealt with both the realities and fantasies of their expectations.

## Patient Issues

The nurse-patients in the author's caseload varied considerably in their levels of preparation and in the kind of problems or issues that brought them into treatment. These ranged from the licensed practical nurse struggling with the sequelae of early incestual experiences, to the doctoral student dealing with a disintegrating marriage. Despite these differences, recurring themes arose in treatment. These themes related to the shared nursing background of the patient and NPT and to their common gender.

# THE PATIENT AS A NURSE

## Idealization of the NPT

One theme that arose with some regularity in the treatment of nurse-patients was the fantasy that the NPT was somehow a special and superior nurse. Features of this fantasy included the attribution of superior intelligence, mental health, knowledge and/or skills to the NPT. Another aspect of this fantasy was the assumption that private practice was the ultimate achievement for a nurse. For most patients this fantasy clearly reflected their dissatisfaction with themselves and their work situation. The assumption that the NPT and her situation were ideal served several purposes.

With many patients, the idealization of the NPT perpetuated their sense of personal inadequacy: "I can't possibly measure up to you and your achievements." The fantasied superiority of the NPT maintained those nurses' identification of themselves as helpless victims of the vicissitudes of life. By overestimtaing the attributes of the NPT, they reaffirmed their underestimation of their own adequacy and excused themselves from attempting to change. Intervention in the situation included identifying this polarity response, confronting the distortion involved, and affirming the realities of the patient's abilities. The technique of *Reductio ad Absurdum* (Jones, 1984, p. 232) was often used successfully here to highlight the symptoms and point out that the patients were not as inadequate as they believed; nor were their situations immutable to change.

For other nurse-patients, the idealization of the NPT, and her practice reflected dissatisfactions with their work situations that were not being dealt with effectively. Private practice became an idealized solution in the absence of realistic and effective problem-solving about work-related (or other) problems.

One patient, a clinical specialist in a large public hospital, persisted in her complaints that she was not able to do what she wanted to do and was prepared to do in her work role. She believed that "the system" was the problem, citing its inflexibility, constant sex- and work-role stereotyping, and persistent challenges to her autonomy and expertise. She fantasized that she was fated to struggle unsuccessfully while the NPT obviously never had to confront such problems. Initial interventions with this patient were focused on the development of more realistic and effective problem-solving skills, beginning with a careful examination of her expectations of herself and the work environment. It quickly became clear that this patient had unrealistic expectations that derived from early childhood experiences in which she learned that even though one could not expect things to go right, one should keep trying. The problems at work then became a metaphor for this distorted life view that was addressed in subsequent treatment sessions.

For other nurse-patients the work situation was genuinely problematic and the treatment issue for them was to learn more effective personal and political strategies for dealing with an unfair and restrictive system. Some needed permission not to suffer or feel guilty and responsible, but to take care of themselves by finding new, more rewarding work situations.

Finally, a few patients perceived the NPT's "success" as a direct challenge and engaged in overt discounting and distancing maneuvers such as: "How could you possibly understand, you have had it so much better (i.e., easier)"; or "You're an exception; you had to leave nursing to advance." Because the defensiveness of these patients was so overt, it was often simple to deal with, especially if the NPT maintained her sense of humor. With one nurse-patient the author remained quiet and thought-ful for some time after an episode in which the patient insisted the NPT's success was irrelevant and unrelated to her being a nurse. The patient finally said "Well?" The author responded, "I was just thinking about how to explain this to my mother!" With this the patient broke into a grin and, with her defensiveness interrupted in a nonthreatening way, was able to productively examine her need to protect herself in this situation.

## Rejection of the Therapist as Nurse

Another theme that appeared in the treatment of nurse-patients was some patients' insistence upon denying or distorting the fact that their therapist was a nurse. While the author perceives no specific need to highlight the fact that she is a nurse, ignoring or denying that fact calls for attention. The rejection of the NPT's "nursehood" most often ap-peared when patients related how they identified their therapist to family or friends. The therapist, who has a doctorate, would be referred to as a doctor or psychologist, and the fact that she was a nurse would be avoided. When the behavior was explored, it usually reflected ambiva-lence about or rejection of their *own* nursehood. Many nurses consciously or unconsciously perceive nursing as a second class, women's profession. More overt denial or rejection of the NPT as a nurse can be confronted directly by asking the patient to consider personal and professional potency issues. Role-modeling confidence and forthright consideration of sensitive issues is an effective strategy here. With a few patients, there was a more unconscious distortion or denial process involved. In such cases, the therapist may need to attend to more basic examples of distor-tion and redefinition of reality before reasonably dealing with this issue.

The self-esteem of some nurse-patients was so vulnerable that they had to reject, at least initially, the nursehood of the NPT. These women had great difficulty with assertiveness and competitiveness. They were so used to receiving rewards for nurturing and placating others as nurses that it was very threatening for them to acknowledge that there were other, perhaps more effective, ways to be a nurse. To acknowledge that the NPT was also a nurse was to feel anxious and guilty about the difficulty they experienced taking themselves or their careers seriously. In the author's experience, these patients were more likely to benefit from group therapy until they felt more empowered and personally directed. Within this kind of group they were able to experience both the support of other women who had similar feelings, and the diffusion of the anxiety they expe-rienced with the potency of the NPT. Perhaps the greatest contribution of the group experience for these women was the opportunity to understand how their sense of themselves had been shaped by their social environment and that it was possible for them to grow and change.

## Avoidance of Professional-Related Issues

A few nurse-patients stood out in their omission of professionally-related concerns or issues. With one patient this took the form of being clearly uncomfortable when the NPT commented on the patient's presenting a paper at an upcoming state nurses' association convention. The patient flushed and stammered, mumbled a few words, then changed the subject. When the NPT returned to this issue, what emerged was the patient's concern that the NPT would not value what she was doing. Somehow she had compartmentalized her therapy experience as separate from and unrelated to her practice experience. The therapy experience was where the "good stuff" went on, while her nursing practice was less valuable. She assumed that the NPT also would not value her practice. The exploration of this issue led to some useful consideration of this patient's tendency to compartmentalize rather than integrate selected life experiences.

With another patient, avoidance of issues related to nursing was a way to escape dealing with unresolved adolescent struggles for autonomy. As long as she kept that area of her life private from the NPT, she felt she was in control. When she began to experience an increased sense of personal empowerment, she was able to consider nursing issues more directly and comfortably.

## THE PATIENT AS WOMAN

### The Therapist as Mother

There are a variety of issues that arise in the psychotherapy of women, but none so pervasive and significant as those relating to the mother-daughter bond (Goz, 1981). Conflicts over the desire for the exclusive attention of a dependably nurturing, idealized mother appear in many forms.

Some nurse-patients have developed an adapted, accommodating approach to others as a way of trying to please. For these women, their sense of self has been defined in terms of others' expectations; being a "good girl" has been one dependable, if not fully satisfying, way to gain attention and affirmation. When therapy focuses on their over-adapted mode

of adjustment there are predictable outcomes. Initially, there is an inten-
sification of efforts to please the NPT. However, what usually ensues is
anger followed by depression.

For example, Ann was unusually articulate about this dilemma. She
found it hard to acknowledge her anger at the NPT, but her dreams were
increasingly clear, even to her: "I have had several dreams about you
having an accident and, with the last one, I had to admit that I was
creating those situations myself—and it really scared me!" As treatment
progressed, Ann was able to acknowledge the anger she felt at both
parents, her mother in particular, for fostering her adapted mode of
adjustment. After anger came sadness upon her realization that there was
no way to achieve longed-for symbiosis, and that she was on her own in
the world. Giving up the fantasied nurturing mother is a very significant
step in treatment. At this point the patient is now free to begin living in
the world on new terms—her own—in the here and now.

In contrast to the patient with an over-determined need to please the
fantasied parent is the patient whose adaptation takes the form of rebellion against the mother's wishes. Adaptation is still the major treatment
issue, but the therapist's strategies must address the patient's need to
oppose, deny, or refute any perceived attempts to influence her. The
author maintained a consistent, caring, but firm stance with one nurse-
patient who was sexually involved with a physically abusive former
patient and was herself abusing alcohol and drugs. The patient was
angry and unhappy about her relationship with her mother, whom she
perceived as critical and uncaring; and she readily over-reacted to the
NPT's attempts to focus on her handling of herself. Her verbal and
nonverbal behavior communicated her almost desperate desire for maternal nurturing and protection, coupled with an equally desperate need to
react against this desire.

The NPT gave clear and consistent messages that: (1) she expected the
patient to take care of herself and not get involved in unsafe situations; (2)
the patient was in charge of how to do this; and (3) the NPT would
intervene only if the patient did not accept responsibility for taking care
of herself. A treatment contract with specific behavioral outcomes was
very useful in this situation. When this patient was able to perceive her
behavior as a reflection of her need to evoke/reject a caring response from
her mother, she could then look at the over-adapted nature of her response and begin the process of separating fantasy from reality.

Many developmental markers of a woman's life can present a reawak-
ening of issues relating to the mother-daughter bond. Marriage, pregnancy, child-rearing, sexual functioning, divorce, menopause, and illness

or disability all carry the potential for a resurgence of concerns about unresolved issues in the patient's relationship with her mother. If the NPT is sensitive to and comfortable with the mother-daughter context of treatment issues, without over-reacting to it, her patients will be free to work through their conflicts and pursue their goals for change.

Incest, rape, and wife-battering also present special cases that heighten the mother-daughter context of treatment. The author's caseload had limited numbers of patients confronting these situations, primarily because of the availability of crisis intervention programs for rape and abuse victims. However, for several patients, the long-term effects of incest and rape were such that they were still working on issues of shame, guilt, impotent rage, and vulnerability. It was important not to over-nurture these patients while affirming them and supporting their change efforts.

## THE THERAPIST AS ROLE MODEL

Bernstein and Warner (1984) commented on women's "almost ubiquitous defect in self-esteem" (p. 177). The author's nurse-patients were all in some way attempting to improve their estimation of themselves and clear away obstacles to growth and change. Some patients admitted to purposefully seeking out an NPT with a reputation as a competent woman in order to have an effective role model for personal and career change. For others, the mentoring dimension of the therapist's role evolved over time. Aside from the need to deal with the heroine worship that can be part of the early stages of mentoring or role-modeling, there are other issues to be considered.

Women have had less experience with mentors than have men. While this situation is changing, the facts are that there are still too few competent nurses to provide mentoring. This means that the nurse-patient may perceive the NPT as the only available example of a suitable mentor, and there may be some basis in fact for this perception. It is a disadvantage to have only one mentor as it can limit awareness of the richness and diversity of options for obtaining goals. Both the patient and NPT need to be alert to the tendency to over-invest in the NPT's contribution as role model or mentor.

Nurses confronting developmental life changes may benefit from the NPT's experience and counsel once they have accepted the NPT as a significant resource. In this therapist's opinion, the NPT should feel free to share whatever experiences she believes will be helpful, so long as she deals with possible "fallout" and encourages the patient to explore additional resources. Mary, for example, was attempting to change the way she related to her parents. In particular, she was trying to decrease her sense of guilt about not wanting to spend as much time with them as they wanted. The NPT willingly shared her experiences with her own parents in this regard. Mary commented that it was hard for her to imagine the NPT experiencing the same feelings as she did. She both wanted and did not want to believe this was possible. This led to a very useful consideration of Mary's fantasies about what it meant to be an adult woman with respect to one's parents. In the author's experience, women, and especially nurses, have considerable difficulty defining themselves as mature, independent adults because of their investment in nurturing and accepting responsibility for others' well being.

## HOMOSEXUALITY

Goz (1981) suggested that one major reason patients may request women therapists is that they hope, consciously or unconsciously, to talk about some of their struggles with sexual feelings for other women. The author agrees with Herron and Rouslin (1982) that the therapist's values and beliefs are always at issue in good therapy. Nowhere is this more evident than when the NPT and nurse-patient deal with homosexual issues.

One nurse-patient made it clear that she would not go to a male therapist because she expected personal and social rejection of her lesbianism from men. She and her nurse-partner were experiencing conflicts in their relationship and she wanted help changing responses that were contributing to their problems. She did not want to change her sexual orientation and sought a woman therapist who would treat her on these terms.

With another nurse-patient, the emergence of her sexual feelings toward women was an outgrowth of years of bitterness and despair in an unsatisfying relationship with an abusive alcoholic husband. Libidinal wishes and fantasies began to be transferred toward the NPT, who was perceived as consistent, nurturing, and affirming. This patient spent several months struggling with her feelings before being willing to deal with this issue in therapy. She felt extremely vulnerable in her relationship with the NPT and needed encouragement to have and deal with her feelings. Most of all, she needed to feel safe to explore her feelings without having to act on them or have the NPT respond negatively or sexually to her.

In the author's experience, it is not unusual for women in therapy, who become more open and caring in their relationships with other women, to question whether this feeling reflects emerging homosexuality. Being able to be open and loving with others is a human capacity that is only generally related to sexuality; that is, the capacity to experience others fully. It is not tied to a specific sexual orientation and this was the discovery of the author's patients.

## THE THERAPIST AS NURSE

The author was fortunate to be practicing in an environment where there were other NPTs. Some of the issues identified in this section are from the experiences of colleagues or peers. Others were universal to our collective experience.

## Protection of the Profession

One of the most unsettling issues for the author was her impulse to protect the profession from nurse-patients who were practicing unethically or unsafely. This was an issue the author often sought supervision for because her own values made it difficult not to reject these nurse-patients. Over time, the author became more comfortable taking a strong and clear stance about these issues without rejecting the patient. It is important for the patient who is an unsafe nurse practitioner to hear that unsafe practice is not acceptable, and that the NPT and the patient will immediately plan for alternatives if the patient is unable to change her behavior.

One patient who was experiencing considerable anxiety and depression over a disintegrating marriage was going to work on the night shift fatigued and preoccupied. She was making medication errors and ignoring patient needs because she was so distressed. Because of her unsafe behavior and because she was the only R.N. on the shift, an alternative plan was considered essential to protect both her and her patients. She transferred to another shift where she had more supervision and she was able to stablize her sleep pattern more effectively.

Unethical or unsafe practice on the part of nurse-patients calls for a clear and immediate response from the NPT. At the heart of nursing is the nurse's obligation to care for those in her charge. To ignore or diminish the importance of unethical or unsafe practice is to discredit the common humanistic commitment of the patient and NPT.

## Rejection of the Profession

For some NPTs, their identification as a nurse carries with it a lingering sense of being second-class. They prefer to identify with human service workers they perceive as having more social status: social workers, psychologists, or marriage and family therapists. Rightly or wrongly, these NPTs believe their marketability and economic success as a psychotherapist would be diminished by their being identified specifically as a nurse. They withdraw from professional involvement with nursing, preferring to attend meetings and interact with others they believe are more directly supportive of their practice goals. These NPTs have chosen to reject their nursehood; and this rejection is conveyed to their nurse-patients in the course of therapy.

Other NPTs are ambivalent about their nursehood and swing between rejection and acceptance. One NPT told me she was concerned about the message she was giving her nurse-patients about nursing. She was aware she was "down" on nursing at the time and feeling like some professional issues would never change.

Conflict about professional identification with nursing is not new. Some time ago Kramer (1974) identified that rejecting nursing was one solution to nurses' conflicts between their expectations and the reality of nursing practice. NPTs and prospective nurse-patients need to consider the potential significance of the NPT's identification with nursing to the patient's change goals.

## Avoidance of Professional Issues

It is tempting for some NPTs to avoid professional issues so as not to get involved in the patient's idealization or rejection of the NPT's nursehood. As mentioned earlier, women in general have little experience with mentoring. If the NPT feels awkward in the role, she may avoid professionally related issues. Additionally, incorporating a mentoring dimension into the therapeutic relationship may pose an insoluable problem for some NPTs. Under these circumstances, it is better for the NPT and the patient to identify other successful women, even non-nurses, with whom the patient can meet these needs. Where the avoidance is a function of awkwardness and/or inexperience, the NPT may want to seek supervision from others who have more experience and comfort with mentoring.

The author found that patients' mentoring needs are more likely to arise near the end of treatment or after termination, although some patients enter treatment with this as one of their expressed needs. The challenge to the NPT is to determine the appropriateness of these needs in relation to the patient's change goals and evaluate whether they serve legitimate or dysfunctional purposes. One patient, a clinical specialist who worked with oncology patients, contacted the NPT, asking that she act as a sounding board about ethical concerns the patient had with one of her own patients. The nurse was clear about her need and growing awareness of the NPT as a mentoring resource. Some guidelines for the mentoring were readily and mutually established, which provided a clue to whether dependency needs were contaminating the mentoring request. In another situation, a nurse-patient's request for the NPT to mediate a work-related conflict was more related to her desire to have "mother fix it" than it was for her to receive mentoring.

## THE THERAPIST AS WOMAN

### Nurturing/Over-Protection of Patient

Bernstein and Warner (1984) noted that the most common counter-transference issue with women therapists is the tendency to be too maternal or over-protective instead of recognizing and treating regression as a defense. An NPT may be even more tempted to nurture nurse-patients because of the double common bond they share. In addition to her direct experience as an NPT, the author has supervised the therapeutic work of graduate nursing students for many years. These students' needs to take care of patients often made it difficult for them to communicate expectations clearly, identify and deal with sensitive issues directly, and set limits effectively. The author believes that the NPT's effectiveness is comprised if she is not able to define the same behaviors as both therapeutic and caring.

### Rejection of Feminine Patients

Nurse-patients who manifest stereotypical feminine sex-role characteristics such as vanity about personal appearance, passive-dependent relationships with men, extreme emotional reactions, and intuitive versus logical approaches to problem-solving may present problems for some NPTs. The NPT who has rejected a stereotypical sex-role definition for herself and has worked hard at raising her own consciousness about being a woman may find herself impatient with and critical of nurse-patients who have not. Some women do not define their problems in these terms. Rather than set up mutually unsatisfying therapeutic situations, the NPT needs to be clear about her own values in this regard and whether these values should be imposed on others who do not espouse them. This is a particularly sensitive issue for feminist therapists who have a keen investment in liberating women from oppressive or stereotypical roles.

The patient may evoke conscious or unconscious feelings of competition and rivalry in the NPT who then finds it difficult to respond to the patient's distress. One particularly attractive young nurse-patient was reflecting on her relationships with men and commented that she got along better with men than women and did not understand why. The NPT stifled her first inclination to respond critically, but instead used her awareness of her jealousy of this woman's youth and sexual attractiveness to good advantage in subsequent explorations of this issue. The patient was genuinely taken aback that other women might be jealous of her and even reject her, and this led to fruitful discussions of how to deal with this issue as she attempted to improve her relationships with women.

## Avoidance of Sexuality Issues

The NPT may avoid sexually laden issues for several reasons. She may consciously or unconsciously believe that sexual issues are private, embarrassing, frightening, or nasty. Under those circumstances, avoidance serves the purpose of protecting both the NPT and the patient from having to confront disagreeable issues. Since many nurses come from very conventional, middle-class backgrounds, it is not uncommon for them to be reticent about dealing with sexual issues. This may be especially true for older NPTs or nurse-patients who did not take part in the sexual revolution. Supervision for this issue, participation in sexuality and sex-therapy conferences, and acquainting oneself with current literature can be very helpful in freeing the NPT to respond naturally and effectively to sexual issues.

Some NPTs are troubled about their own sexuality and are unwilling or reluctant to do anything about it for fear of disrupting the precarious balance they have obtained. One NPT friend spent most of a year struggling with her growing sexual attraction to another man before she was willing to confront the dissatisfaction she experienced in her marital relationship. Another NPT found it very difficult to confront a lesbian patient about sexual acting out because of her own homosexuality, which she was unwilling to acknowledge. Supervision and/or personal therapy are the most viable means of addressing issues that present obstacles to effective functioning as a therapist.

# TREATMENT ISSUES WITH SPECIFIC GROUPS

## Nursing Undergraduate Students

Most undergraduate nursing students are late adolescent, middle-class young women who are still actively dealing with developmental issues related to autonomy and social and sex-role identity formation. The undergraduate nursing curriculum is demanding and stressful, and many students become depressed as they attempt to meet the expectations of parents and faculty (Haack, 1985).

One of the author's student-patients set impossibly high standards for herself and was, at one point, on the verge of suicide because she could not measure up to what she expected of herself and thought others expected of her. Fortunately, the depth of her despair frightened her into seeking help. She was able to become more realistic and accepting of herself with support and a reality-oriented therapeutic approach. Another student was referred for treatment when her psychiatric nursing instructor became aware of her growing apathy, preoccupation, and difficulty attending. This student had deferred grieving over the death of a close friend in a questionably intentional automobile accident. The two had made a pact in high school to always be friends and the student-patient was disturbed and confused about how to deal with her feelings. The friend had been eccentric and discounting of conventional standards for achievement, whereas the student-patient was very successful by conventional standards. The friend's possible suicide interrupted and challenged the student-patient's movement toward more conventional standards for role development. With support for grieving her loss and realistically re-examining her goals, she became more comfortable with her choice and was able to move on with her own life.

In the author's experience, it was uncommon to see student nurses who sought therapy because of their concern about their acting out of sexual or aggressive impulses. Most of these students were achievement oriented and accepting of, or at least adapting to, conventional standards of behavior. However, one student-patient entered treatment because her procrastination about completing assignments was threatening her ability to finish course expectations and graduate. In her therapy sessions, her striving for autonomy from demanding and critical parents emerged as the key factor in her procrastination. Witholding action on expectations had become a way of exercising control over demanding adults. As she came closer to graduation, her procrastination became an obvious problem, so much so that her friends urged her to see someone about it. When the student-patient was able to redefine receiving her nursing degree as something she wanted for herself, she readily agreed to a structured, behaviorally oriented program for accomplishing her assignments.

## Nursing Graduate Students

The decision to enter graduate school is an overtly self-affirming decision; she decides to return to school after setting goals for personal and professional development that she believes are attainable and desirable. Since this decision is usually made after a period of practice, graduate students in nursing are older and are often married and/or mothers. The decision to pursue graduate studies can disrupt previously stable marriages in which the nurse deferred to the husband's needs and goals. Some nurses make this decision in anticipation of or after divorce to prepare themselves economically and professionally to be a single parent.

The issue of needing to negotiate multiple demands placed great stress on two graduate student nurses in the author's caseload. One sought counseling to deal with her anxiety and depression about not being able to meet anyone's expectations: hers, her husband's, her children's, or her instructor's. She had hoped her husband would support her decision to return to school by altering his expectation that all household and childcare tasks continue to be accomplished by her. Although he overtly supported her decision initially, his subsequent behavior demonstrated his ambivalence about her attaining her goals by his passive resistance to any change in family routines. This patient barely managed to complete her first semester requirements, and did this only with extraordinary effort and little sleep.

When the NPT helped the patient identify her priorities, she placed graduate education near the top of her list, along with being a good wife and mother. This student acknowledged she had not demanded that changes be negotiated because she felt guilty about asking for something for herself. She was accustomed to taking care of her husband and children and they had grown to depend on her doing that. She felt it was not "fair" to ask them to change just to accommodate her. The author asked if her children had asked her permission to grow and change, and she was able to see the point. She was entitled to grow and change too and to expect to work that out with those who loved her. Within a few sessions this nurse was ready to more directly and assertively negotiate with her husband and children. She found them more willing to accommodate when she was clearer and more assertive about what she wanted and needed.

Another graduate student-patient had relocated to be with her fiancé, whom she planned to marry when they both finished graduate school. The university setting presented her with a world of possibilities she had never experienced before and she was delighted at the opportunity to grow and change. She and her fiancé soon began to have serious conflicts and she became very troubled about the disruption she was experiencing in her life. She sought counseling to "get my head straight." Within a few sessions, she was able to identify that she was growing and changing in this new setting but her fiancé was not. His expectation that she remain committed to their earlier goals for a traditional marriage relationship was no longer acceptable. There was no going back for her. In fact, she wanted to go on, but she recognized she probably would have to go on without her fiancé. She expressed her sadness and loss of what had been and then was able to deal with how to break her engagement and start anew.

## Practicing Nurses

Nurses practicing in hospitals confront problematic issues every day. Most feel reasonably prepared to deal with them. For several nurses in the author's practice, some issues generated stress, difficulty making ethical decisions, burnout, and even abuse of drugs.

Ann worked in the ICU of a local hospital. She had entered group therapy with the NPT during a painful divorce to help stabilize her life and facilitate effective problem-solving. Before the divorce was final, she began an affair with a married physician who was unhappy in his marriage and was drinking heavily. She was unusually quiet during one session and, when this was commented on, she reluctantly shared that she was uncomfortable about something that was going on, but didn't know what to do about it. Her lover had asked her to cover for him several times when he was too drunk to come in during nights he was on call. Initially that had meant making excuses for him, but more recently she had found herself making decisions in patient situations that she knew were beyond her legal scope of practice. The NPT gave her a lot of support for taking a stand with her lover that she would not cover for him again. Additionally, the NPT suggested that she examine how this situation exemplified the basic problem that she had in establishing and maintaining effective relationships. The risk and need for secrecy heightened the gamelike quality of her involvement, while the excitement and affirmation she derived from the affair highlighted her need for stimulation and diversion. The childlike and irresponsible quality of these needs was addressed in subsequent sessions, as was the responsibility all adult women, especially nurses, have for ethical decision-making in their lives.

For another patient, entering treatment with the NPT served as a means to deal with her growing sense of burnout. She had worked in a Veterans Administration hospital for some time and was making a good salary; but gradually she had become discouraged about changing the system or policies that inhibited a rewarding work environment and better patient care. She felt stuck—too burned out to stay, but unwilling to leave her salary and accrued benefits. "I've become like some of my patients, who have learned there are more rewards from the system if you stay sick than if you get well," she explained.

Personal and professional empowerment issues were the crux of change for this patient. She had become apathetic about being able to change anything, including herself. When she was able to clarify and "own" her growth and change goals, she was able to identify a variety of action alternatives, including remaining in the system but taking a different, more challenging position. She eventually went on for graduate study, returning to the Veterans Administration system in a role she had helped to define.

One nurse-patient was referred by the state board of nursing as part of the probationary process following the suspension of her license for drug abuse. This woman was a loner who handled chronic pain from a back injury by taking pain medications prescribed for her patients. Her suspension came when her abuse was detected by coworkers. She was ashamed, depressed, and frightened enough by what had happened that she was eager to have help.

The biggest challenge to treatment with this nurse-patient was her isolated lifestyle. Over the course of several months she was able to see how working permanent nights had gradually become an excuse for withdrawing from involvement with others. Treatment focused on developing strategies for: (1) dealing more constructively with her back pain; (2) strengthening her involvement with others; (3) stabilizing her work and licensure situation; and most importantly, (4) accepting the need to actively deal with her depression. Over the period of one year she made remarkable changes. Swimming and yoga had relieved her back pain; she regularly socialized with friends from work and was steadily dating; and she had worked on changing thoughts and behavior that reinforced depression. Her license was reinstated and she felt like, and was, a new woman.

# GENERAL GUIDELINES

The guidelines suggested here are not new; they may apply to any therapy situation. However, the author found them particularly relevant to therapy with nurse-patients. They are not exhaustive by any means, but they are important issues that NPTs encounter in the treatment of nurse-patients. [See Appendix "A" for a working draft of "Guidelines for Private Practice" (1985) proposed by the American Nurses' Association Council on Psychiatric and Mental-Health Nursing.]

## Clear Treatment Contracts

Clear and behaviorally-specific treatment contracts clarify expectations about the treatment process and roles of the patient and therapist. Particularly when the NPT is known to the patient, a clear treatment contract can effectively initiate the process of separating fantasy from reality. Expectations about attendance at sessions and handling of fees should also be clear at the outset. The author has had several nurse-patients comment on the ease with which the author dealt with those issues, adding that they appreciated a clear and forthright approach.

## Firm Standards for Confidentiality

Confidentiality becomes an even more important issue than usual when dealing with nurse-patients who know each other, work together, and/or have key positions in local health care institutions. It is reassuring to patients when this issue is affirmed clearly in treatment. It has also been the author's practice to make clear that she would always respond in the patient's interest if there were a question about the patient harming themselves or others, even if that meant contacting family, friends, or the police. While confidentiality is a most important standard to adhere to, it does not take precedence over the protection of the patient from harming herself or others.

## Need for Supervision

All therapists need supervision to effectively deal with obstacles to therapeutic progress that are a function of their own background and personality. It is best if this is structured on a regular basis, although the author's experience is that many therapists only seek supervision periodically or when they are aware of a problem. The NPT developing her practice is most vulnerable to transference and counter-transference problems with nurse-patients because of her limited experience identifying and dealing with these issues. Ongoing supervision from a more experienced NPT would be ideal, but it is most important that the fledgling NPT find an experienced and competent supervisor to facilitate the growth of her skills. No therapist outgrows the need for supervision.

## Socializing with Patients

It is not unusual for nurse-patients terminating treatment to want to become a friend of the NPT whom they have come to respect and whose attention they have come to value. The patient's interest in being friends with the NPT may stem from (1) unresolved dependency needs; (2) the desire to maintain and develop a relationship with someone who has become important to her; or (3) the natural reluctance of the terminating client to separate and go her own way. The NPT should be clear that this is not likely to be growth-producing for the patient. There is likely to be continuing contact with many patients because of the common backgrounds and professional associations of the NPT and her nurse-patients. In the author's experience, it is easier to maintain friendly contact with former patients when this issue has been dealt with forthrightly when it arises and when the NPT has a well-established and satisfying network of friends.

## Professional Contacts with Patients

Professional contacts with patients are inevitable and, in the author's experience, remarkably free from problems. When the issue of socializing with a former patient has been dealt with successfully, the NPT and former patients are able to relate more naturally. Also, mentoring requests from nurse-patients who have completed treatment are not uncommon. In these instances, patients should be clear about what they want and the NPT clear about her willingness or ability to meet the need.

## The "Old Girl" Referral System

Nurse colleagues and former patients readily become part of the NPT's referral network, particularly if the NPT has been in practice for a while. Increasing numbers of nurses are pleased to have competent NPTs to whom they may refer troubled friends or family members. Satisfied patients are a major resource for referrals. The NPT can increase her visibility generally, and particularly with nurses, by being active in relevant committee work (e.g., local, state, or national nursing association interest groups for psychiatric/mental-health nursing practice); by providing consultation or continuing education services to community mental health agencies; and by generally making her skills and services known. Acceptance by and recommendations from colleagues and former patients are highly desirable, but most NPTs will want to appeal to a broad clientele. Effective marketing of one's services is a challenge for all therapists in private practice (see Chapter 8).

## CONCLUSION

Hardin and Durham's research (1985) suggested that the number of nurses in this author's caseload was not unusual. While the experience of the author has unique features that derive from her characteristics and those of her patients, this chapter has focused on themes and issues that have seemed of general relevance to NPTs and their nurse-patients. Particular attention has been paid to the therapeutic impact of their common gender and nursing background. Case examples, altered to assure patients' anonymity, were used to elaborate upon issues along with treatment approaches for handling them.

Many of the author's nurse-patients were psychiatric/mental-health nurses striving to improve their personal and professional functioning. To them in particular, and to all her former and future nurse-patients, the author expresses her affection and appreciation for the opportunities they presented for us to grow and change together.

## REFERENCES

American Nurses' Association Council on Psychiatric and Mental Health Nursing. (1985). Guidelines for private practice. *Pacesetter, 12*(1), p. 3.

Bernstein, A., & Warner, G. (1984). *Women treating women.* New York: International Universities Press.

Coche, J. (1984). Psychotherapy with women therapists. In F. Kaslow (Ed.), *Psychotherapy with psychotherapists* (pp. 151–169). New York: Haworth.

Goz, R. (1981). Women patients and women therapists: Some issues that come up in psychotherapy. In E. Howell & M. Bayes (Eds.), *Women and mental health* (pp. 509–542). New York: Basic Books.

Haack, M. (1985). Antecedents of the impaired nurse: Burnout, depression and substance use among student nurses. Unpublished doctoral dissertation, University of Illinois, Chicago.

Hardin, S., & Durham, J. (1985). First rate: Structure, process and effectiveness of nurse psychotherapy. *Journal of Psychosocial Nursing and Mental Health Services, 23*(5), 8–15.

Herron, W., & Rouslin, S. (1982). *Issues in psychotherapy.* Bowie, MD: Brady.
Jones, S. (1984). Family therapy. In S. Lego (Ed.), *The American handbook of psychiatric nursing* (pp. 224–234). Philadelphia: Lippincott.
Kramer, M. (1974). *Reality shock: Why nurses leave nursing.* St. Louis: Mosby.

# Chapter 11
# The Oppressed Client

*Denise Webster*

Oppression is a harsh word. It conjures up images as disparate as ridicule or concentration camps. It is an uncomfortable concept. To see oneself either as oppressed or as an oppressor is a self-image that few would wish to embrace. And yet, recognition of oppression in clients'[1] lives is essential for the nurse psychotherapist (NPT) to assist them in the necessary task of accurately evaluating their own experiences and defining options for change. To ignore such realities, in fact, is to utilize the therapeutic relationship in a potentially oppressive manner (Schaffer, 1980).

## DEFINITIONS OF OPPRESSION

Definitions of oppression vary and are closely related to concepts of power and powerlessness, helplessness and subordination. Anthropologists point out that no universal set of criteria constitutes oppression from one society to another (Brown, 1981). Many, if not most, psychological theories focus on intrapsychic or individual dynamics; oppression as a concept is rarely addressed in the professional literature. The relative invisibility of explanatory concepts that are social in nature is curious, particularly in light of the relationship between depression and oppression.

---

[1] While the author recognizes the Editors' preference for the term "patient," this chapter retains the use of the term "client" to reflect the belief that the NPT has been contracted to provide services. The term "client" is also preferred by those women in the author's private practice.

All persons are oppressed to some extent. Small children, by virtue of their dependency, experience frustration of their immediate demands. Adolescents remind adults to treat them like grownups when limits are placed on their experimental behaviors. The elderly may be denied the option to continue working or to live as independently as they would wish because of losses of an economic, physical, or social nature. Yet, to imply that all groups experience the same kinds and degree of oppression is to dilute the concept to ultimate meaninglessness (Frye, 1983).

Since the social movements of the 1960s, oppressed groups are increasingly referred to as victims of "isms:" racism, sexism, ablism, heterosexism, classism, ageism. All are forms of elitism—ways in which certain groups define other groups as inferior in order to assert their own superiority. Such assertion of superiority must, however, be constantly reinforced in order to be effective. Usually the reinforcements are so ingrained in the dominant group as to be invisible (at least to the dominant group). Everyone "knows" that Jews are tight with money, that Poles are stupid, that Blacks are lazy, that the poor are looking for a handout, and that women are jealous of each other, vain, and more emotional than men.

Prejudiced beliefs about groups constitute a form of oppression. The forms may vary from jokes to job discrimination, and from unequal protection under the law to overt violence against those who dare to step out of their "place." Probably the most pervasive and invisible form of oppression is realized in group stereotyping.

This chapter examines the oppression of women as a group and the implications of such oppression for NPTs who are counseling them. It is intended to be representative of the general experience of oppression, while recognizing that individual and group experiences may differ. It is further acknowledged that information about groups experiencing multiple oppressions (e.g., poverty, racism, sexism, and ageism) is often contradictory or nonexistent.

Two decades before *The Feminine Mystique* (Friedan, 1963), sociologists had begun to identify parallels between Blacks and women (Hacker, 1951; Myrdal, 1944). High social visibility (i.e., skin color, secondary sex characteristics, clothing) made the groups easily identifiable. "Passing" was difficult. Both groups were ascribed such psychological characteristics as having inferior intelligence, being emotional, childlike, and sexually dangerous. General belief in the innate inferiority of each group was supported by biological models that explained each group's "natural" predisposition for certain roles and functions that were necessary to the survival of the dominant group but that were devalued within the society's reward structure. Both groups were characterized as using such coping behaviors as deferential manners, feigned helplessness, and attempts to outwit the dominant group through stealth and guile. The inferior status of Blacks and women was rationalized by the common knowledge that, given a choice, each would not want greater freedom or the burden of responsibility. In the middle class White suburbs it was often asserted that the "good coloreds" didn't want integration anymore than the Whites did. They knew their place and had enough to worry about without causing trouble. Similarly, working women were, by definition, selfish, rejecting wives and mothers, and, perhaps worst of all, "unnatural." In an era of postwar marital togetherness, to question the concept of separate spheres was unconscionable. It followed that since women and Blacks were inferior and would not want a different life, limited educational opportunities and low-level occupations were appropriate. Any other alternatives would only set them up for disappointment.

## PSYCHOLOGICAL THEORIES AND THE OPPRESSION OF WOMEN

Most persons utilize social as well as psychological explanatory frameworks to explain mental health and other everyday phenomena. Assumptions about the inevitability and/or desirability of the existing social structure are often masked with psychological theories about the causes of psychopathology and psychotherapeutic interventions. Undoubtedly, the most vocal criticism of theories about women's psychological development has been launched against Freudian psychoanalytic theory. Recent critics charge that psychoanalytic theory presents women as morally, intellectually, and sexually inferior, and that such inferiority is biologic in origin, and, therefore, inevitable. Some authors argue that theories that address only behavior, and make no judgment about its meaning, are the only nonsexist theories in use (Tennov, 1976). Others believe that ignoring the social significance of behavior is naïve, and quite possibly supports the existing social structure by not exploring its importance in the development of behaviors.

Proponents of humanistic/existential approaches to therapy focus on the importance of choice and responsibility in considering change in an individual's life. Critics of these humanistic/existential assumptions point out that such a framework does not adequately acknowledge that some choices are more realistic for some people than they are for others. Clearly the consequences for choosing certain behaviors are not the same across all groups in society (Greenspan, 1983).

Social learning theories and cognitive theories have also been seen as inadequate concerning women's psychology; they have been criticized for recognizing the social pressures that affect the range of models of female behavior that are available and the sources and political consequences of ideas accepted as truths. Stereotypes and social myths are examples of ideas that may mediate between a developmental capacity to organize and structure information, and the value placed on the information. Until recently, few therapists questioned whether their psychological theoretical assumptions were appropriate for use with all client groups. Even fewer therapists are aware of or make explicit to their clients the social explanatory framework from which they operate.

## SOCIAL PERSPECTIVES ABOUT THE OPPRESSION OF WOMEN

Contemporary theorists who explain the oppression of women have identified several different sources of oppression and, therefore, beliefs about steps necessary to address this oppression. These may be categorized as conservative, liberal, Marxist/Socialist, and radical critiques. The conservative belief explains the oppression of women as universal, natural, and unchangeable. Biologic and/or evolutionary explanations are seen as sufficient explanation for male dominance. The liberal analysis holds that individuals should have equal rights to the opportunities a society has to offer, based on the individual's abilities without regard to race, sex, or other inherent characteristics. The uneven distribution of power, wealth, and position are not questioned; and there is a belief that the proper reward for demonstrated abilities ought to be determined by a market economy. Where the source for discrimination is legal, the liberal often engages in activities to change such laws.

Marxist/socialist critics vary in extent to which they address "the woman problem" separate from the problems of class discrimination. They reject biologic and liberal beliefs that equality is possible within any society in which "the pursuit of profit by the ruling class determines all aspects of life." According to this philosophy, only a redistribution of the means of production would create a society in which an individual, male or female, could have the work they do valued appropriately.

The radical critique is the least developed of the philosophies and tends to be process-oriented, in continuous revision, and embracing a multitude of beliefs. For this group, the belief is that the oppression of women is fundamental and exists in socialist, as well as capitalist, societies. Many assert that the oppression of women has existed longer than any other form of oppression. These groups protest violence against women, including pornography, and have often developed alternative support systems for women such as consciousness-raising groups (Jaggar & Struhl, 1978).

A social explanatory framework helps to guide the NPT in interpreting women's problems and selecting therapeutic approaches. For example, it is commonly believed that mental health consists of adapting to reality; the NPT with a socialist or radical belief system would be less likely to see adaptation as either a therapy goal or a sign of mental health, than might the conservative or liberal therapist.

## SIGNS AND SYMPTOMS OF OPPRESSION

Various characteristics have been observed among members of oppressed groups. These can include the internalization of stereotypes, which may lead to low self-esteem and feelings of helplessness and powerlessness. The concept of "learned helplessness" (Seligman, 1975) in women is one example of this internalization and also demonstrates oppressed groups' tendencies to escape dominant group punishment by avoiding any appearance of coveting their power. Henley (1977), in comparing the nonverbal behaviors of status equals and unequals, noted that women's behaviors around men are consistent with those shown by subordinates around superiors. These include being circumspect and polite, averting eyes, watching, and smiling. Another response of oppressed groups is identification with the aggressor (Allport, 1954). This identification may be seen among women who are flattered to hear that they "think like a man." Burgess and LaZarre (1976) point out that this type of identification tends to reduce anxiety and alleviate feelings of helplessness. In current parlance, the "Queen Bee" is the woman who perceives herself to have made it to the top without any help from anyone (Staines, Tavris, & Jayaratne, 1974). She finds all the talk about women's networks and sisterhood irrelevant to her success. Often the token woman in a setting, the Queen Bee is unlikely to extend opportunities to other women.

The Queen Bee syndrome is also related to the phenomenon of denial and rejection of one's own group. If one on some level believes stereotypes about women but does not apply them to oneself, then association with other women may create anxiety. Having close relationships with other women may either threaten the stereotype or incite the fear that others may see all women as equally inferior. This woman tends to be very isolated and perhaps more comfortable in the company of men.

Among this group, the tendency for women to distrust other women is presumed to be associated with their competition for the attentions of a superior—the male.

Clearly there are also those who handle oppression by developing strong in-group ties and rejecting the values of the dominant group. While this phenomenon is perhaps more common in ethnic or religious subgroups, it is less likely in the case of women since many, at the present point in time, are psychologically and/or financially dependent on men. Miller (1976) contends that this leads to survival behaviors intended to avoid direct responses to ill-treatment. "Hidden defiance," disguised as pleasing and accommodating behavior, may be indirect responses to the situation. Women become very adept, as do members of any minority, at knowing and understanding the behavior of the dominant group. Fostering the growth of men and children may be seen as the most valuable roles available since the woman's inherent sense of value is limited (Penfold & Walker, 1983).

## POWER AND OPPRESSION/NURTURANCE AND ANGER

Power is usually defined as the ability to carry out one's own wishes and/or to influence others. Legitimate power is that attached to real authority, while coercive power is that associated with the ability to punish. Expert power is based on personal knowledge and expertise. Women are probably more familiar with the use of reward power (particularly as they may use it in raising children) and with referent power, which is based on one's identification with a more powerful person (Morrison, 1982).

Powerlessness associated with oppression may contribute to the high rate of depression among women. Several researchers and theorists have noted that interpersonal relationships appear to be more important to women than to men and that disruption of attachment bonds are particularly stressful for women (Weissman & Klerman, 1979). Others have noted that depression is a likely outcome for anyone who feels powerless, regardless of the reality of the situation (Collier, 1982).

While the ability to nurture others is perhaps a woman's most powerful strategy to control others (and the sine-qua-non of valued stereotypic female characteristics), it is also the potential source of her despair. If a woman sees her only value to be her ability to meet other peoples' needs, then she has been set up to fail. First, the judgment about the adequacy of her attempts is left to those whom she serves. Should she have either highly critical evaluators or nurturees who are "bottomless pits," she will always fail. Secondly, if she is basing her own value upon the successes of those whom she nurtures, her self-value derives from their success. If nurturees are involved in time-consuming competitive efforts, that quest for success may be a source of loneliness for this "cheerleader" who has developed few resources on her own behalf. In addition, particularly in the case of children, the outcome of successful nurturing involves working oneself out of a job as the child becomes confident and independent. Should this success, confidence, and independence not come to fruition, then the nurturer has also failed at her job. An inability to control important reinforcements is at the base of feeling powerless (Johnson, 1976).

Nurturing, to the extent that it is required of women, is perhaps the essence of oppression within the female experience. It is demanded, but must be given freely. It is not necessarily expected to be reciprocated in kind (Eichenbaum & Orbach, 1982; Flax, 1981). It is this element of a double-bind that characterizes oppression (Frye, 1983). No matter what women do, it may not be enough or right. To refuse doing it is to court punishment either by others, or if the expectation has been predictably internalized, by one's own guilt. It would be naïve, however, to presume that simply teaching women to be more discriminating in their decisions to nurture and teaching them to be assertive would undo this double-bind. Both anecdotal and research evidence suggests that assertive behavior in women is evaluated much more negatively than is identical behavior in men (Kelly, Kern, Kirkley, Patterson, & Deane, 1980). The *piece de resistance* of this dilemma is that this double-bind, socially constructed and consistently reinforced by self and others, has been interpreted by some within psychiatry as evidence that women's core characteristics include passivity and masochism (Deutsch, 1944).

Feelings of powerlessness, helplessness, and guilt are frequently accompanied by feelings of anger. Since anger is not only seen as unfeminine, but may also be experienced as dangerous, women very often deny such feelings. Women may describe their anger with such euphemisms as "upset," "disappointed," "frustrated," "irritated," and "I don't know how I feel about that."

## THE NPT WHO WORKS WITH WOMEN

For all of the above reasons, the NPT who frequently works with women clients must explore the internalized psychological constraints as well as the real and perceived social limitations on women's options. Foremost among the assumptions to explore is the obligation to nurture others, to the exclusion of meeting one's own needs; and, secondly, the taboo against feeling or expressing anger. These factors frequently co-exist with the stress of balancing work and family, having low-paying, low-status jobs, carrying the majority of childcare and household respon-sibilities, and having few rewards built into the kinds of repetitious tasks that typify the female experience (Gove, 1980; Weissman & Klerman, 1979). Studies by Broverman et al. (1970) demonstrated that female as well as male therapists harbor sex-role stereotypic assumptions within their definitions of healthy behavior in men and in women. Some have pointed out, in fact, that many presumed characteristics of females (such as dependence, submissiveness, and lack of aggressiveness) are consistent with symptoms of depression (Rothblum, 1983). To the extent that these stereotypes restrict life options for all of us, as men or women, as clients or therapists, they must be challenged directly.

Guidelines for working with women from a nonsexist perspective have been developed by the American Psychological Association Task Force on Sex Bias and Sex Role Stereotyping in Psychotherapeutic Practice (1978). These guidelines remind therapists to avoid sex-role assumptions about their clients' experiences, life options, or behavior in the context of the therapeutic situation. Therapists are cautioned against attributing to the individual those problems that are at least in part related to social and cultural pressures.

## THE CLIENT-NPT RELATIONSHIP

Chesler (1972), Tennov (1976), and others have commented extensively on the potential for the psychotherapy situation to reproduce and rein-force the oppressive circumstances in a client's life. Chesler maintained that most outpatient private clients are women who seek male therapists to interpret their situation and guide their decisions, thereby recreating the unequal status relationship between men and women. However, to suggest that women should not see male therapists would make no more sense than to suggest that women could change their lives positively by simply refusing to nurture others. Since one goal of all therapy is to seek a corrective emotional experience, there are certain aspects of the tradi-tional therapeutic model that NPTs need to consider carefully. Among these are the issues of modeling, interpretation, transparency, and profes-sional "objectivity."

Research suggests that many Black, Hispanic, and female clients prefer to see and have more confidence in White male therapists (Acosta & Sheehan, 1976; Howell & Bayes, 1981). This may be evidence of identification with the aggressor; it may also reflect low esteem for one's own group. If only for this reason, exposure to a model of a competent, risk-taking, and nurturing member of one's own group can provide a powerful corrective emotional experience.

On the other hand, if an NPT adopts a model in which he or she is required to appear "neutral" or to assume control in the relationship, then the client is potentially reexperiencing an uncomfortable state of unequal power. To know nothing about the NPT's life, while being expected to reveal the most intimate or painful details of one's own life, is not necessarily therapeutic. While it is certainly inappropriate to create a situation in which the client feels obligated to listen to the NPT's problems, a rationally considered transparency (or self-disclosure) can help clients know that the NPT is human; that her own problems are not unique or irresolvable; and that many of her experiences are not a result of personal failure.

For this reason, many believe that the ideal modality for working with women is group therapy (Rawlings & Carter, 1977). However, most clients seek individual therapy; therefore, one way to decrease a sense of isolation and personal ineffectiveness is for female NPTs to create some sense of universality by revealing some of their own experiences when treating females. Transparency can also dilute the inherent power hierarchy in the therapy experience.

Teaching clients the process of therapy is equally important. When interpretations seem to come from a nondiscernable background, they may take on an aura of magic and the fantasy that the NPT knows more about the client than the client does. Clients have a right to know and understand the NPT's theoretical perspectives and to have interpretations made clearly in context. This requires helping the client to make connections between what she has said, felt, and done in the past, how this connects with what is being said, felt, and done now, and how the NPT tries to understand what is going on. In this way, both the client and the nurse can sort out social and psychological assumptions and work with them directly. This process of modeling direct communication and unearthing of invisible assumptions is perhaps the most important aspect of the therapeutic process.

## TECHNIQUES FOR THE NPT TO CONSIDER

The process of identifying, confronting, and re-evaluating internalized beliefs and perceptions of external expectations is essentially a process of values clarification. The process of consciousness-raising, which was used in group settings during the early Women's Movement, provides a useful format for exploring assumptions about women and their life options. Questions about what women clients learned about what it meant to be a woman, from whom, and what models they saw are a beginning. The NPT might also assess how clients learned about female sexuality and in what context. What was it like for their friends, sisters, and brothers? What messages were they given about their life options? Who is in their support network? From whom do they receive nurturance? What is a "good woman?" How does the therapist's experiences compare with the client's? In what ways are they similar and why might they differ?

This process is an ongoing one that is explored in relation to current situations, problems, or relationships. Encouraging the client to begin a journal of memories, thoughts, and insights can help her begin to focus on who she is, how she got to be that way, and how she might like to change. Many women feel they have no control over their destinies or their pasts, the result of inadequate problem-solving skills. Teaching women how to identify problems, consider alternatives, weigh consequences, and evaluate outcomes can be powerful tools. For many women, connecting feelings with events may be a necessary precursor to identifying problems.

One of the best ways to decrease anxiety and help clients identify connections between thoughts, feelings, circumstances, and behaviors is to encourage them to audiotape therapy sessions. This strategy has several advantages. Clients learn that they can have access to data in the therapeutic process and that they, as well as the NPT, can seek clarification about points. They can learn, by replaying tapes, to check out the reality of what they recalled from an interaction; moreover, they can also practice assertive risk-taking by learning to confront the NPT with questions about sessions. Taping also helps clients to work on issues between sessions.

The NPT may wish to consider providing clients with several self-evaluation sheets for physical, nutritional, stress, and other pertinent psychosocial areas. These remain the property of the client, who also has complete access to her records and may, if she chooses, keep her own progress notes as well. Also, during the initial evaluation session, the NPT may give clients printed information on how to choose a therapist, client rights, and questions they might consider asking a therapist (Fishel, 1979; Women in Transition, 1975).

Goals for working with women must include empowerment as well as insight. This goal can take many forms. The first should be the NPT's declaration that her expertise is in understanding theories and having had experience with dealing with other's problems. It must be stressed, however, that the client brings to therapy the most important expertise—knowledge of her own experiences and ways she has learned to cope with difficult situations. By sharing expertise, the therapy process can be successful and credit can be appropriately apportioned.

NPTs working primarily with women clients may wish to develop a list of readings and books about therapy and about women. This reading list can be shared with clients. This form of bibliotherapy contributes to the process of values clarification and consciousness-raising, and promotes personal empowerment through information and knowledge (Sanders & Steward, 1977).

Consciousness-raising is a painful as well as empowering process. There are several responses that can be predicted and, if anticipated and discussed openly, can help a woman feel more in control of the process. Initial curiosity about what their personal problems have to do with women's issues usually leads to some identification with other women and recognition of the similarities in their conditions. This awareness is almost inevitably followed by a period of mounting anger, which may be focused on parents, family, friends, husbands, lovers, and oneself for having been "victimized." Only after this anger is experienced and expressed can the woman begin to explore the ways in which she has consciously or unconsciously collaborated in the "victimization" by limiting her own options and/or avoiding taking responsibility. After exploring the external and internal sources of her oppression, as well as her conflicts about personal power, she can then begin to channel her anger into energy for creating change. For some women this change may lead only to personal redefinition of self; others, however, may decide to become involved in ongoing efforts to change some of the social institutions that have contributed to women's oppression (Rosenthal, 1984).

## THE NURSE AS OPPRESSED WOMAN

Few people are aware that Florence Nightingale (1979) wrote a passionate protest against the oppression of women. This fact is particularly ironic in view of the public stereotype of nurses as subservient to physicians and as either endlessly nurturing or consumed by the desire to boss patients around. There is even a script described in transactional analysis (Steiner, 1974) called "Nurse," in which the expectation of caring for others first, never asking for what one wants, and being a hard worker are foremost characteristics.

Studies show that while those women who tend to go into nursing are likely to hold very traditional values (Schwirian, 1978), there is also evidence that nurses in psychiatry and nurses in private practice may be less traditional than other nurses (Mlott, 1976; White, 1975). It seems unlikely that many nurses could work in an institutional setting without having some ambivalence about responsibility, authority, and the limits of one's capacity to nurture in the absence of personal power and respect for one's efforts.

NPTs' decision to become private practitioners may have been precipitated by such ambivalence. The tendency then to identify with the aggressor may require that NPTs remain vigilant about exploring and exposing their own biases to avoid accepting too enthusiastically the role of the "expert." In seeking to control the work environment, the NPT must take care not to exploit the considerable power associated with taking the role of therapist. For it is only through continuing efforts at self-awareness and respect for the potential of the therapeutic process to oppress clients that NPTs can expand the external horizons of both their clients and themselves.

# REFERENCES

Acosta, F., & Sheehan, J. (1976). Preferences toward Mexican-American and Anglo-American psychotherapists. *Journal of Consulting and Clinical Psychology, 44*, 272–279.

Allport, G. (1954). *The nature of prejudice.* Cambridge, MA: Addison-Wesley.

American Psychological Association. Task Force on Sex Bias and Sex Role Stereotyping in Psychotherapeutic Practice. (1978). Guidelines for therapy with women. *American Psychologist, 33*, 1122–1123.

Brodsky, A., & Hare-Mustin, R. (Eds.). (1980). *Women and psychotherapy: An assessment of research and practice.* New York: Guilford Press.

Broverman, I., Broverman, D., Clarkson, R., Rosenkrantz, P., & Vogel, S. (1970). Sex role stereotypes and clinical judgments of mental health. *Journal of Consulting and Clinical Psychology, 34*, 1–7.

Brown, P. (1981). Universals and particulars in the position of women. In The Cambridge women's studies group (Eds.), *Women and society* (pp. 242–254). London: Virago Press.

Burgess, A., & Lazare, A. (1976). *Psychiatric nursing in the hospital and the community* (2nd ed.). Englewood Cliffs, NJ: Prentice-Hall.

Chater, S. (1967). Differential characteristics of graduate students of nursing. *Nursing Research, 16*(2), 146–153.

Chesler, P. (1972). *Women and madness.* New York: Avon.

Collier, H. (1982). *Counseling women: A guide for therapists.* New York: Free Press.

Deutsch, H. (1944). *The psychology of women.* New York: Grune & Stratton.
Eichenbaum, L., & Orbach, S. (1982). *Understanding women: A feminist psycho-analytic approach.* New York: Basic Books.
Fishel, A. (1979, June). What is a feminist therapist and how to find one. *Ms.,* 79–81.
Flax, J. (1981). The conflict between nurturance and autonomy in mother-daughter relationships and within feminism. In E. Howell & M. Bayes (Eds.), *Women and mental health* (pp. 51–69). New York: Basic Books.
Franks, V., & Burtle, V. (1974). *Women in therapy.* New York: Brunner/Mazel.
Friedan, B. (1963). *The feminine mystique.* New York: Norton.
Frieze, I., Parson, J., Johnson, P., Ruble, D., & Zellman, G. (1978). *Women and sex roles: A social psychological perspective.* New York: Norton.
Frye, M. (1983). *The politics of reality.* Trumansberg, NY: Crossing Press.
Gove, W. (1980). Mental illness and psychiatric treatment among women. *Psychology of Women Quarterly, 4*(3), 345–376.
Greenspan, M. (1983). *A new approach to women and therapy.* New York: McGraw-Hill.
Hacker, H. (1951). Women as a minority group. *Social Forces, 30,* 60–69.
Henley, N. (1977). *Body politics.* Englewood Cliffs: Prentice-Hall.
Howell, E., & Bayes, M. (1981). *Women and mental health.* New York: Basic Books.
Jaggar, A., & Struhl, P. (1978). *Feminist frameworks: Alternative theoretical accounts of the relations between women and men.* New York: McGraw-Hill.
Johnson, P. (1976). Women and power: Toward a theory of effectiveness. *Journal of Social Issues, 32*(3), 99–110.
Kelly, J., Kern, J., Kirkley, B., Patterson, J., & Keane, T. (1980). Reactions to assertive versus nonassertive behavior: Differential effects for males and females and implications for assertiveness training. *Behavior Therapy, 11,* 670–682.
Miller, J. B. (1976). *Toward a new psychology of women.* Boston: Beacon Books.
Mlott, S. (1976). Personality correlates of a psychiatric nurse. *Journal of Psychiatric Nursing, 14*(2), 19–22.
Morrison, E. (1982). Power and nonverbal behavior. In J. Muff (Ed.), *Socialization, sexism, and stereotyping: Women's issues in nursing.* St. Louis: Mosby.
Myrdal, G. (1944). *An American dilemma* (pp. 1073–1078). New York: Harper and Row.
Nightingale, F. (1979). *Cassandra.* Old Westbury, New York: Feminist Press.
Penfold, P., & Walker, G. (1983). *Women and the psychiatric paradox.* Montreal: Eden Press.
Rawlings, E., & Carter, D. (Eds.). (1977). *Psychotherapy for women: Treatment toward equality.* Springfield, IL: C. C. Thomas.
Rich, A. (1978). *The dream of a common language.* New York: Norton.
Rosenthal, N. (1984). Consciousness raising: From revolution to re-evaluation. *Psychology of Women Quarterly, 8*(4), 309–326.
Rothblum, E. (1983). Sex-role stereotypes and depression in women. In V. Franks & E. Rothblum (Eds.), *The stereotyping of women: Its effects on mental health* (pp. 83–111). New York: Springer.

Sanders, J., & Steward, D. (1977). Feminist bibliotherapy—prescriptions for change. In E. Rawling and D. Carter (Eds.), *Psychotherapy for women: Treatment toward equality* (pp. 328–344). Springfield, IL: C. C. Thomas.

Schaffer, K. (1980). *Sex-role issues in mental health.* Reading, MA: Addison-Wesley.

Schwirian, P. (1978). Prediction of successful nursing performance (DHEW Publication No. HRA 77–27). Washington, DC: U.S. Government Printing Office.

Seligman, M. (1975). *Helplessness.* San Francisco: Freeman.

Staines, G., Tavris, C., & Jayaratne, T. (1974). The queen bee syndrome. *Psychology Today, 7*(8), 55.

Stein, J. (Ed.). (1967). *Random House Dictionary.* New York: Random House.

Steiner, C. (1974). *Scripts people play.* New York: Grove Press.

Tennov, D. (1976). *Psychology: The hazardous cure.* Garden City: Anchor Books.

Weissman, M., & Klerman, G. (1979). Sex differences and the epidemiology of depression. In E. Gomberg & V. Frans (Eds.), *Gender and disordered behavior: Sex difference in psychopathology* (pp. 381–425). New York: Brunner/Mazel.

White, M. (1975). Psychological characteristics of the nurse practitioner. *Nursing Outlook, 23*(3), 160–166.

Women in Transition, Inc. (1975). *Women in Transition.* New York: Scribner.

# Chapter 12
# The Worried-Well Patient

*Lois Sullivan-Taylor*

Anxiety is basic to all nonadjustive behavior. Anxiety and worry are frequently the byproducts of individuals' attempts to adapt to the stresses of an uncertain and, in the view of some, hostile world. The *Diagnostic and Statistical Manual III* (1980) classification of anxiety disorders includes the subcategories of agoraphobia (with or without panic attacks), phobias (social or simple), panic disorders, generalized anxiety disorders, post-traumatic stress disorders (acute or chronic), and atypical anxiety disorders. The "worried-well" individual to be discussed in this chapter harbors a pervasive sense of anxiety about the world but is less incapacitated than persons with traditional psychoneurotic labels. He has a broader spectrum of coping mechanisms and does not limit anxiety-reducing methods to one or two defense mechanisms (as seen, for example, in the overuse of displacement and repression in the phobic patient). Moreover, the worried-well individual's projected image differs dramatically from his self-view, an inconsistency that results in internal conflict, anxiety, and the inability to function effectively in daily living.

According to Fox (1977), the "worried-well" label was coined to describe those persons "who seem to have some need of [physicians'] therapeutic services, but who technically cannot be considered ill" (p. 10). Worried-well patients are likely to seek treatment with the nurse psychotherapist (NPT) for such problems as generalized anxiety or depression, low self-esteem, insecurity regarding control over their own lives, and/or difficulties with interpersonal relationships. None of these problems are so intense as to be functionally debilitating. By external standards many among the worried-well function quite adequately in work and social spheres. Internally, however, they are plagued by feelings of inferiority, inadequacy, role conflict, and a continual fear that others will discover that they are "fakes," reflecting a belief that their projected image of competency is a facade. Their struggles with inconsistencies between the external and internal evaluation of self cause intrapsychic conflict and an inability to attain a realistic sense of self. The worried-well require excessive personal energy to maintain a stable intrapsychic equilibrium and a cohesive identity. Their search for satisfying love and work sometimes creates new problems because, before all else, they must hide the discrepancy between their public self-image and their secret perception of an inadequate self.

According to Harvey (1984), who has written about the "imposter phenomenon," an inner sense that one is really a fake may be prevalent in as many as two of every five successful people in all walks of life. Ironically, for those who mask their sense of inadequacy, the more they accomplish, the more troubling become their feelings of fraudulence. Additional successes are not seen as evidence of their own competence; rather, they view each success as either a fluke or the result of Herculean efforts, reinforcing a pattern of self-doubt instead of self-confidence.

The worried-well patient's cognitive style is one of worry. This worry assumes the form of continuous preoccupation with an unsolved conflict. Worriers think over their predicament again and again, but not constructively (Shaffer & Shoben, 1956). It is an ineffective form of trial-and-error without a well-defined goal. At times worriers speak their meditations aloud and gain some tension reduction by sharing them with others; usually, however, they mull difficulties over in implicit speech, talking only to themselves, thereby reinforcing a circular reaction that aggravates the persistent nonadjustive response. Thus fear arouses worry, and worry in turn arouses more fear, the negative psychological state being constantly stimulated anew.

The NPT will recognize in this description the common phenomenon of rumination, for example, problem-solving that goes nowhere. Rumination is an anxiety response that generates futile problem-solving activity, but relieves the patient of the added burden of passivity in the face of intense pain. It differs from signal anxiety, wherein anxiety serves its survival-oriented function of alerting the person to danger and goal directed problem-solving. It also differs from catastrophic anxiety, which is so overwhelming that the person is unable to mobilize defenses against it, but rather surrenders to some form of psychosis.

Feelings of fraudulence and resultant worry about being discovered were originally thought to be more prominent among women than men. Later research (Clance, 1978), however, showed it to be equally prevalent in both sexes. Interestingly, men are often likely to view this as an isolated problem with their career, focusing their energy upon solving circumscribed problems in their external world. In doing so, they may develop a new compensatory skill or reinforce an area in which they fear discovery as an impostor with even greater (and energy consuming) hypervigilance.

Women, by contrast, experience this as a pervasive sense of internal inadequacy, possibly because they are more sensitive to their own emotions or are more likely to seek internal versus external solutions to problems. Moreover, these traits, coupled with emerging and changing cultural expectations, may cause women to be the most likely to be designated as the worried-well and to seek treatment for its associated cluster of problems. This is particularly true of women entering new roles traditionally assigned to men or assuming positions of power and influence. As nurses (many of whom come from middle and lower-middle socioeconomic backgrounds) gain increasing prestige in academic and clinical settings, they will also be quite vulnerable to this dilemma.

The worried-well female patient often seeks a female therapist who can relate on an experiential level to this world of worry. The NPT may be seen as an excellent choice of therapists because she presents, via her professional identity, a model of contradictory cultural demands for toughness and tenderness. Thus the NPT can be idealized initially as possessing the stereotypic masculine qualities of being successful in a career, as well as the stereotypic feminine qualities of caretaker associated with nursing in our society. Before examining ways in which an NPT can assist worried-well men and women, it may be useful to review the socialization process and its importance to self-esteem and solid identity as prerequisites to good mental health.

## IDENTITY AND SELF-ESTEEM OF MEN AND WOMEN

It would be a serious error to think of gender-related socialization and identity development as a superficial matter. Maleness or femaleness becomes one of the primary ingredients of self-identity and is probably of more importance in determining the future of a child than his race, intelligence, or social class. Sex role development refers not only to sex or reproduction but also to the whole constellation of behaviors considered appropriate for each sex by society (Smitherman, 1981). In the recent past, both men and women rated men as more worthwhile than women; and both men and women preferred to have male children (Dinitz, Dynes, & Clark, 1954; McGee & Sheriffs, 1957). One might conclude that women are socialized into a role of low self-esteem and/or negative self-concept from birth. Although some traits connote good mental health in either sex, the overall list of traits for a mentally healthy person in our society are those stereotypically attributed to men (Broverman, Broverman, Clarkson, Rosenkrantz & Vogel, 1970). On this basis, females exhibiting typical female behaviors could be thought of as mentally unhealthy (Lips & Colwill, 1978). In their landmark study, Broverman et al. (1970) showed that clinicians actually held different ideals for healthy, fully functioning males and females. The ideal healthy woman was described as being:

> . . . more submissive, less independent, less adventurous, more easily influenced, less aggressive, less competitive, more easily excitable in minor crises, more easily hurt, more emotional, more conceited about (her) appearance, less objective, and less interested in math and science. (p. 6)

Clinicians' ideal of a healthy man was similar to that of a healthy mature adult, but their ideal of a healthy woman was quite different from both. Or in other words, male is the norm; female is the emotionally unhealthy male (see also Chapter 11). This overstatement emphasizes how sensitive the NPT must be to gender issues. The NPT does well to recognize that socialization biases do not escape therapists. The typical NPT is a woman and thus subject to inaccurate assumptions about her own identity which, left unexamined, can lead to subtle devaluations of her and of other women's identity. For example, in treating the less frequently seen but equally suffering worried-well male patient who seeks her help, the NPT needs to dispel quickly his possible expectation that she will have endless maternal or feminine sympathy—but very little insight about how the "real world" operates. Such a patient sometimes unconsciously hopes that the NPT will fulfill the expectation of tender-hearted and unending forbearance so that the hard choices and changes needed in his life can be avoided.

The NPT heals the worried-well male patient primarily by demonstrating to him that clarity of thought, toughness of spirit, patient persistence, even street-wiseness, are not gender related. By such modeling, the NPT can free some worried-well men from the culturally idealized yet identity-destroying, male-stereotypic traits of impulsivity, aggression, arrogance, and insensitivity. The separation of positively characterized traits from gender connotation can heal both the worried-well female and male. Gender related biases are a significant enemy to therapeutic progress, whether existing in the patient or the therapist, and whether the patient is male or female. At the most insidious level (for example, in the use of negatively-toned, sex-linked connotative language) the myth might be promulgated that for women to be mentally healthy, they must fall short of mental health standards for the general population or that mentally healthy males must reflect the cultural male stereotype of domination and subjugation of their personal and impersonal world.

## Identity and Self-Esteem: General Considerations

Although cultural forces shape gender-related aspects of socialization, and hence identity, other important characteristics of identity formation hold true for both men and women. The word "identity" has the mixed connotations of a solid structure (closely akin to the concept of "ego") and a fluid malleable structure (similar to memories of "what I am like"). The concept "identity" is not as static and rigid as the concept "ego;" it is not as elusive to define as "self-concept," but lies between the two, as a stable, organized, and organic structure. In ideal child development, this spontaneous and expressive potential of the child unfolds in the context of an accepting and affirming environment, encouraging the child to anticipate that most events and reactions in life are likely to be "good," if not "downright wonderful." Children who later develop authentic versus pseudo-identities were usually motivated through love and absorbed parental confidence; conversely, persons with pseudo-identities were motivated by fear and terror. Insofar as there is not adequate affirmation or receptivity, energy spent maintaining dynamic, fluid, and naturally adaptive reactions to life is used instead to defend studied, nonspontaneous reactions. Pseudo-identity has solid and rigid features, as in a mask; authentic identity is unpredictable, complex, and has the alive, breathing, and dynamic characteristics of a face.

To the extent that a person lacks self-esteem, life is lived negatively and defensively. Particular values and goals are chosen, not to afford positive enjoyment of existence, but to defend against painful feelings of anxiety, inadequacy, and self-doubt. Pseudo self-esteem is maintained through evasion, repression, rationalization, and denial of ideas and feelings that could affect self-appraisal adversely. Individuals with pseudo self-esteem derive a sense of worth by adopting externally approved values or goals such as being financially successful, career oriented, or sexually attractive. Developing such facades is experienced as less demanding—or perhaps all that is possible—for patients with the imposter identity. From what has been said one could agree with Branden (1969) that a person is psychologically healthy to the extent that there is no internal clash between perceiving reality and preserving self-esteem.

## THERAPY WITH THE WORRIED-WELL

To achieve ideal mental health the worried-well person must establish an equilibrium between perceived reality and preserved self-esteem. A way to conceptualize the central issues of the worried-well is to focus upon their fragile identity and self-esteem and their development of a pseudo, rather than authentic, self. The primary work of the NPT and patient is to dismantle the pseudo selves and to discover the authentic self.

The tension state between public and private self-images sets the stage for rigidity and defensiveness in meeting the personal and impersonal demands of living. The sense of a coherent and stable identity eludes this patient because he does not know whether to act as his public (often pseudo) self or his private (usually more authentic) self. Subsequently, self-esteem precipitously crumbles in the face of negative or highly stressful external life events.

In initial therapy sessions, the NPT needs to assess levels of anxiety and stress along with the patient's coping mechanisms. A precipitating stressful event usually prompts the patient to seek treatment; a sense of disequilibrium has usually broken through the patient's usual defensive style. Circumstances surrounding the event, the significant people involved, and, most particularly, how the patient perceived the event, need to be explored. The relationship between precipitating events, past life, and the stresses of the patient's developmental stage of life also needs to be established (Erikson, 1963). The therapist must be very cognizant of how various developmental issues are manifested in the adult; this is especially true of the worried-well patient.

By paying particular attention to the characteristic ways in which patients express themselves, the NPT may understand how they perceive and understand the world. For example, with the worried-well patient, the NPT listens carefully for expressions of "shoulds" that do not support the individual's growth, but are aimed at defending their precarious sense of worth. She listens for the most important identity-enlivening emotions in the patient, i.e., how the patient finds expression of love and hate, anger and joy, trust and distrust, hope and despair, embitterment and fulfillment. To assess identity stability and authenticity, the NPT examines how the individual copes with the "shoulds" of life as well as the demands of the primitive emotions. When, and if, worried-well patients are moving toward identity breakdown or diffusion, their panic can rival that associated with the schizophrenic's break in terms of the pain it produces, even though the ego and cognitive processes do not surrender to severe regression.

After the initial sessions, the NPT can make a more in-depth analysis of the patient's ego functioning and defenses. Bellak and Small (1978) have devised a clinical scale for rating ego functions that includes the following elements: reality testing; judgment; sense of reality; regulation and control of drives; affects and impulses; object relations; thought processes; adaptive regression in the service of the ego (appropriate relaxation of inhibitions); defensive functioning; autonomous functioning; synthetic-integrative functioning; and sense of mastery and competence. The NPT should at least have a working familiarity with patients' strengths and deficits in these areas.

The actual nature of therapeutic action with the worried-well is, to some extent, shrouded by ambiguity, as is all verbal psychotherapy. Basic to the NPT's approach is the notion that patients need an incentive to change maladaptive patterns in living (from which they derive at least a modicum of familiarity and comfort). This incentive is provided by the openness and acceptance of the NPT to a wide spectrum of values and human experiences. This openness in the therapeutic relationship may itself initially confuse and frighten the patient in that it implies that a new synthesis of the identity will be the eventual solution. In psychodynamically-oriented, as well as other forms of therapy, the therapist's refusal to prematurely give advice may provoke even more anxiety in the patient. Indeed, if the patient is already highly anxious, a more directive approach may be indicated until the patient is better able to rely upon natural coping strategies. The NPT can then subtly take up a more neutral, nondirective position as the patient's own authentic identity begins to organize and direct itself toward the genuine opportunities for fulfillment that exist in his real world.

As a general rule, the healthier the patient, the more the NPT can remain neutral, allowing the patient's natural coping mechanisms to emerge. In this way, unspoken, untested, and often unrealistic assumptions about life and living are eventually subject to conscious analysis. Psychodynamically-oriented therapists think that an entirely new synthesis is the best solution to this dilemma. Behaviorists maintain that reconditioning of ideas is a sufficient and less time-consuming treatment. Each approach will have a proper place, depending upon the patient's personality and the NPT's theoretical preference.

Whichever theoretical approach is applied, the goal is to increase the patient's self-understanding, self-comfort, and self-acceptance. In this process, the patient discovers previously unknown, often unacceptable, aspects of the self. New complexities in human relationships and in the perception of the self and others are less likely to come as shocking surprises. Such recognition facilitates greater understanding of how unacknowledged parts of the self may have contributed to distortions in relationships and life goal formations. Besides obtaining a new and broader understanding that healthy human relationships are based upon honestly and mutuality, the patient also learns to minimize self-protective distortions. The NPT teaches the patient to modify stereotypical thinking such as "All men are arrogant" or "All women are opportunistic" into more realistic guidelines for interpersonal involvement: "Joe gets arrogant when he is under pressure" or "When Jill claims the only reason she stays engaged to Jim is his family name, she may really mean (but cannot admit) that she loves him."

Acquisition of new knowledge about the self contributes to change. This understanding in turn reduces anxiety and provides a sense of control over one's life. Resistance is generally encountered initially because patients have not yet learned to give free expression to thoughts and feelings that threaten their defended self-image. But as complexity of understanding increases through interpretations, clarifications, and other therapeutic approaches, resistance to understanding gives way to exploration of the self and the world. The patient's pain can thus be explained, understood, and brought under control.

Increased self-awareness almost automatically helps patients develop new solutions to their problems. As therapy proceeds, patients test the validity of their assumptions about the world by trying out new attitudes and behaviors. As they experiment with these new behaviors, old assumptions about the world are contrasted with new hypotheses discovered through therapy. As they begin to perceive the world and themselves as more controllable, they feel and act more in keeping with these newly adopted hypotheses about themselves and others.

Brief examples of clinical cases in which patients' self-acceptance, self-comfort, and development of an authentic, dynamic identity were therapeutic goals follow. These cases illustrate a behavioral-cognitive and a psychodynamic approach respectively:

J. P. was the only female lawyer in her firm consisting of five partners. She continually dreaded that her work would be evaluated as less competent than that of her peers and that any flaw would be viewed as proof of what "illogical thinkers" women were. She devoted enormous amounts of time to preparation of briefs, depositions, and court appearances—frantically worrying about the next project being the big failure that would cost her her job.

With this worried-well young woman, the NPT employed cognitive methods to help the patient analyze her ruminations and change anxiety producing self-statements to authentic and self-affirming statements. To change nonproductive self-talk, the NPT challenged the accuracy of J. P.'s self-defeating statements and encouraged her to change the focus from self to the task at hand. J. P.'s self-defeating statements assumed two forms—worrying about performing adequately and obsessing about gaining approval from others. J. P. demanded perfection of herself and wanted very much for her male colleagues to respect her and approve of her work. Instead of allowing J. P. to devalue herself with such statements as, "Maybe I'm not as smart as my peers," the NPT reminded her to say to herself that she graduated fifth in her law school class. Encouraging her to concentrate upon doing her best in preparing depositions also reduced anxiety, rather than magnifying and generalizing self-doubts to all aspects of her law practice.

The NPT suggested J. P. check herself on whether she was exaggerating the actual importance of a situation. J. P. was asked what she thought would happen if she made an error; whether her law partners were correct to attribute her errors to the fact that she is a woman; or whether they held the distorted belief that women are illogical thinkers. In addition, methods of "thought stopping" were used to counteract self-defeating thoughts.

A psychodynamic approach was applied in working with S. V.:

> S. V. entered therapy with complaints of anxiety, guilt, and depression. She was the first in her family of five to receive a college degree; no one in her blue-collar family had gone beyond high school and most of them worked at mechanical or factory jobs. Because no one in her family had the same experiences she was going through, she felt she didn't have anyone close who could advise her on how to handle her new role in business. Most of her coworkers came from more privileged families with business backgrounds and she assumed that they knew exactly how to behave and what to do in their roles. She was afraid of failing and causing shame to her family, but at the same time feared success would alienate her from them. Moreover, she had always been the "good, nice girl" in her family, and she feared that she could not compete in the aggressive, competitive business world.

Within the neutral, safe atmosphere of therapy, S. V. was able to disclose deep feelings of inadequacy by recounting numerous childhood memories of conditional love from her parents. She learned that achievements would win her parents' approval and thus directed all of her energies in this manner. Her success-failure conflict unfolded as a fear of competitive rivalry with her parents' lower status in life. An unconscious desire for failure had evolved that she believed would keep her close to her parents.

Allowing S. V.'s catharsis of previously unacknowledged fear, anger, and sadness helped reduce the tension she experienced at work. Through the process of confronting repressed positive and negative feelings and memories, she came to be more aware of her authentic aspirations and limitations in life. Rather than searching for success as a means to obtain parental love, or fleeing from success to avoid parental rejection, she separated the issues of "loveability" and work success. She engaged her parents in more intimate conversations that clarified her doubts and fears about their relationship. Freed from this unconscious preoccupation, her work life became more conflict-free. S. V. obtained and began to read as much literature as possible on corporate operations. Knowledge of her parents and of the objective corporate world gave her a beginning sense of mastery in her roles. The NPT helped her to develop assertiveness skills; to effectively state her points, even in conflicting situations; and to know that this behavior enhanced, rather than diminished, her as a person.

## CONCLUSION

Regardless of the NPT's theoretical framework, she helps worried-well patients integrate and "like" their inner and outer selves; to live by a series of self (rather than other) choices; and to abandon nonproductive gender/stereotypical personality traits and behaviors. These changes can lead to decreased worry and improved mental health for the worried-well. Conducting therapy with the worried-well can be a most rewarding experience for the NPT insofar as it involves patients who are not merely trying to rid themselves of crippling conditions, but rather seeking to govern their lives increasingly by principles of self-expression and freedom from anxiety. Therapy with the worried-well usually unfolds with a great variety of unexpected turns. In working with them, the NPT has the privilege of being the catalyst to a host of creative and sometimes very surprising solutions to life events.

## REFERENCES

American Psychiatric Association. (1980). *Diagnostic and statistic manual of mental disorders* (3rd ed.). Washington, D.C.: American Psychiatric Association.

Beck, A., Rush, A., Shaw, B., and Emery, G. (1979). *Cognitive therapy of depression*. New York: Guilford.

Bellak, L., & Small, L. (1978). *Emergency psychotherapy and brief psychotherapy* (2nd ed.). San Francisco: Grune and Stratton.

Branden, N. (1969). *Psychology of self-esteem.* Los Angeles: Nash.

Broverman, I., Broverman, D., Clarkson, F., Rosenkrantz, P., & Vogel, S., (1970). Sex role stereotypes and clinical judgements of mental health. *Journal of Consulting and Clinical Psychology, 34*(1), 1-7.

Clance, P., & Imes, S. (1978). The imposter phenomenon in high achieving women: Dynamics and therapeutic intervention. *Psychotherapy: Theory, Research and Practice, 15*(3), 241-247.

Davanlao, H. (1980). *Short-term dynamic psychotherapy.* New York: Jason Aronson.

Deutsch, H. (1944). *The psychology of women.* New York: Grune and Stratton.

Dinitz, S., Dynes, R. R., & Clark, C. (1954). Preferences for male or female children: Traditional or affectional. *Marriage and Family Living, 16,* 128.

Ellis, A., & Harper, R. (1961). *A guide to rational living.* Hollywood: Wilshire.

Erikson, E. (1963). *Childhood and Society.* New York: Norton.

Fox, R. (1977). The medicalization and demedicalization of American society. In J. Knowles (Ed.), *Doing better and feeling worse* (pp. 9-22). New York: Norton.

Gilligan, C. (1982). *In a different voice: Psychological theory and women's development.* Cambridge: Harvard.

Goffman, E. (1959). *The presentation of self in everyday life.* Garden City, NY: Doubleday.

Hagerty, B. K. (1984). *Psychiatric-mental health assessment.* St Louis: Mosby.

Harvey, J. with Katz, C. (1984). *If I'm so successful, why do I feel like a fake: The imposter phenomenon.* New York: St. Martin.

Horney, K. (1950). *Neurosis and human growth.* New York: Norton.

Horney, K. (1967). *Feminine psychology.* New York: W. W. Norton and Co.

Hutton, A., & Clayton, B. (1984). The process of psychotherapy. In C. Beck, R. Rawlins, & S. Williams (Eds.). *Mental health-psychiatric nursing: A holistic life cycle approach* (pp. 337-383). St. Louis: Mosby.

Kaplan, A. (1985). Female or male therapists for women patients: New formulations. *Psychiatry, 48*(8), 111-121.

Kerr, N. (1984). The tyranny of the should's. *Perspectives in Psychiatric Care, 22*(1), 16-17.

Lips, H., & Colwill, N. (1978). *The psychology of sex differences.* Englewood Cliffs, NJ: Prentice-Hall.

McGee, J. P., & Sheriffs, A. C. (1957). The differential evaluation of males and females. *Journal Perspectives, 25,* 356.

Millman, H., Huber, J., & Diggins, D. (1982). *Therapies for adults: Depressive anxiety and personality disorders.* San Francisco: Jossey-Bass.

Seligman, M. (1975). *Helplessness: On depression, development, and death.* San Francisco: Freeman.

Shaffer, L., & Shoben, E. (1956). *Psychology of adjustment.* Boston: Riverside.

Smitherman, C. (1981). *Nursing actions for health promotion.* Philadelphia: Davis.

# Chapter 13
# The Patient with Premenstrual Syndrome

*Alice J. Dan, Janet Konat, Linda L. Lewis*

Premenstrual syndrome (PMS) has been written about in sensational and exaggerated terms. Exploitative PMS clinics claim to diagnose and treat this disorder, in the absence of credible diagnostic tests or demonstrated effective treatments. A recent advertisement for one of these clinics asked, "Are you anxious or depressed? You probably have PMS." Despite these overstatements, many women do experience premenstrual changes. Because they may seek guidance in managing the distressing aspects of premenstrual symptoms, nurse psychotherapists (NPTs) need to be knowledgeable about PMS. In addition to supporting patients who are trying to cope with PMS, NPTs should recognize the potential impact of premenstrual changes upon the women they treat and upon the therapeutic situation.

PMS is a complex and puzzling problem. Approaches that view causation in purely physiological or purely psychological terms are unlikely to promote women's health as much as approaches that examine the interactions among biological and psychosocial variables. Nurse psychotherapists are well-suited to provide holistic care, recognizing that any illness usually stems from multiple factors and has multiple effects. An explosion of research on PMS is currently examining physiological, dietary, emotional, behavioral, environmental, pharmacological, and psychiatric aspects of the syndrome. Many conflicting statements about etiology and treatment appear, especially in popular literature; thus, it is important to recognize that there is no consensus among experts on the nature of PMS.

This chapter provides an overview of current thinking about PMS, with a focus on how therapists can help women to manage their premenstrual experiences.

## OVERVIEW OF PREMENSTRUAL SYNDROME

### Definition

PMS can be defined as a set of symptoms that begins during the premenstrual phase of the menstrual cycle (anywhere from ovulation to the beginning of menstruation) and is relieved or greatly diminished within the first few days of the menstrual flow. This generally accepted definition is not specific about the nature of the symptoms, but rather emphasizes timing in the cycle. According to Abplanalp (1983b), no one set of symptoms is the hallmark or standard criterion for defining PMS. In fact, the number and variety of symptoms vary widely from one woman to another, and even from one cycle to another in the same woman. The same symptoms do occur at other times in the cycle, since many are common symptoms for the worried-well woman, such as depression, low self-esteem, insecurity regarding control over her own life, and difficulties with interpersonal relationships.

One controversy about defining PMS concerns women whose symptoms do not disappear during the rest of the menstrual cycle. Harrison (1985) provided a term for this group—"premenstrual magnification." Many psychiatric patients would fit this category better than the general definition of PMS because their symptoms seem to be exacerbated premenstrually. Each woman's PMS profile is different, and management strategies should be based on an individual's specific set of symptoms (Fritz & Speroff, 1983; Shangold, 1982).

Attempts to classify PMS into sub-categories, thus aiding in the discovery of a variety of causal pathways, have not yet resulted in consensus about etiology or definition (Abraham, 1983; Endicott & Halbreich, 1982; Hamilton et al., 1984). A 1983 conference sponsored by the National Institutes of Mental Health concluded that the attempt to establish PMS as a psychiatric classification was premature, and such a step is being resisted by women's groups who feel this would be a move backward, to the "it's-all-in-your-head" school of thought. Despite all the discussion, understanding of PMS is still rudimentary. It is unknown, for example, if the extreme changes experienced by some women are exaggerations of the normal changes experienced by most women or if some other pathological process is operating.

In the current atmosphere of controversy and rapid change in theories of PMS, the authors propose that NPTs subscribe to the following definition in providing support for women coping with PMS: Premenstrual Syndrome is a chronic, recurrent disorder that can be seen as a vulnerability associated with physiological changes over the menstrual cycle. Approaching PMS as an ongoing condition of vulnerability suggests that a woman has some control over the severity of her distress and that many interacting factors need to be considered within the context of each woman's life situation.

## Symptoms

The most common PMS physical symptoms include breast tenderness, abdominal bloating, a perception of weight gain, craving for sugar (for some women, craving for alcohol), swelling of hands/feet, aching joints, constipation, allergy flare-ups, headaches, and fatigue (Abplanalp, 1983a). For most women, the physical symptoms are relatively tolerable; it is the change in sensitivity or responsivity to her environment during the premenstruum that provokes the greatest concern. It is as if the PMS patient's reactions to the world around her are different during the symptom days. Women have described their experience of PMS as "devastating," "lousy," and living with "a sense of being out of control" (unpublished interview comments). Relationships with family, co-workers, and friends are frequently affected by the cyclical changes in emotional reactions experienced by women with PMS (Hurt, Friedman, Clarkin, Corn, & Aranoff, 1982).

Although these psychosocial symptoms must be individually assessed, most women with PMS experience one or more of the following problems: feelings of loss of control, anxiety, irritability, hostility, poor body image, decreased sense of sexual attractiveness, low energy, and depression. The symptoms ebb and flow with the menstrual cycle, compounding a woman's difficulty in dealing with them. Almost every woman with PMS demonstrates a profound loss of self-esteem.

## Prevalence/Incidence

Because no laboratory tests or universally agreed-upon diagnostic criteria exist, any effort to determine the actual incidence of PMS is extremely difficult. Many women have some physical and/or mood changes premenstrually during some of their cycles. Thus the presence of sporadic symptoms does not mean that a woman has PMS. Only by daily assessment of symptoms over several menstrual cycles can a diagnosis of PMS be postulated. It is likely that a very small percent of PMS patients (approximately 5%) have severe PMS; many more probably have a mild to moderate form of PMS (Speroff, 1983).

## Etiological Theories

Scientists do not know what causes PMS. Research has not supported lay beliefs in currently popular treatment approaches such as natural progesterone drug therapy. Neither a lack of progesterone nor the efficacy of progesterone therapy has ever been demonstrated in double-blind controlled studies (Keith, 1985). Other types of hormonal imbalance have also been investigated, including estrogen/progesterone ratios, and pro-lactin; but so far no consistent results have been found. Other theories of PMS include fluid retention, vitamin deficiency, allergic reaction, and neuroendocrine mechanisms (Reid & Yen, 1981). Although each of these factors probably plays a role in precipitating symptoms, none alone has been shown to cause PMS.

One interesting aspect of PMS studies is the high rate of placebo response (Abplanalp, 1983a). Almost any treatment helps to diminish symptomatic distress for several cycles, with decreasing effectiveness over time. This phenomenon suggests that some sort of organizing effect may occur when people pay attention to premenstrual symptoms. One possi-bility that the authors are currently investigating is that PMS represents a vulnerability to circadian desynchrony (disruption of the 24-hour biolog-ical rhythms), hypothesizing that "hormonal imbalance" is hard to iden-tify because it is not a matter of hormonal levels, but rather of hormonal timing (Dan & Chatterton, 1985). Other researchers are currently looking at the effects of estrogen and progesterone on the monoamine oxidase system in the brain, a system that exerts changes in the arousal (or responsivity) threshold. Another leading theory proposes that changes in endorphin levels trigger physiological events resulting in PMS symptoms (Reid & Yen, 1981). Psychosocial researchers are examining cultural conditioning and contextual issues in the lives of women suffering from PMS. It is most likely that both physiological and psychosocial/environ-mental elements contribute to PMS (Koeske, 1983).

## DIAGNOSTIC ISSUES

Because PMS has received so much publicity, women are likely to ask a health professional whether some or all of their distress may be PMS-related. However, the issue of PMS often arises after a therapeutic relationship is well-established, when a woman begins to feel better some of the time but still has difficult times that may be associated with some menstrual cycle change. Sometimes the question of PMS is first raised by the NPT who has noticed some cyclicity of symptoms or emotional changes.

In whatever way the possibility of PMS comes to an NPT's attention, the single most significant tool in diagnosing and managing PMS is daily charting. Retrospective questionnaires, in which a woman is asked about her usual symptoms, or even about her most recent cycles, have not been found to reliably differentiate PMS from other problems. Moreover, several of the questionnaires widely used in research have been based on questionable or inadequate theories (Rubinow & Roy-Byrne, 1984).

The authors use the factor-analytically based Premenstrual Assessment Form (PAF: Endicott et al., 1982) during the first session with a prospective PMS patient. This questionnaire is well-constructed and contains an extensive catalogue of previously stated PMS symptoms. It has a complex scoring system (available for computer use) however, its division of PMS into sub-syndromes has not yet been validated. Although the PAF is not recommended for valid diagnosing of PMS patients, filling out the form is useful for sensitizing patients to all the various changes that may occur over the cycle.

This assessment procedure requires two sessions, scheduled about 4–6 weeks apart. During the first session, the patient is presented an overview of PMS, and the NPT explores the patient's complaints or problems related to the menstrual cycle, obtains a brief health history, and administers the PAF. It is important to keep track of symptoms daily for at least one cycle, and preferably several. This can be done on a simple calendar or on forms available for this purpose (i.e. Harrison, 1985; Lark, 1984). There are forms with standardized items (Endicott & Halbreich, 1982), and some patients also keep track of basal body temperature, since it is useful to know when and whether ovulation is occurring. However, the simplest and most important step is for the patient to keep track of when distressing symptoms occur. It is a good idea to use at least a simple rating of severity as well.

After receiving symptom charts for at least one full cycle, the patient is scheduled for a second session. In the second session the NPT examines the relationship of the charted symptoms to the menstrual cycle and discusses with the patient a plan for managing her symptoms. It is remarkable how often the symptoms show *no* relationship to *time* in the menstrual cycle. This is a most important point since many false attributions about the causes of symptoms are related to time. When problems occur premenstrually, symptoms are often attributed to "time of month";

but when they occur at other times, their relationship to menstruation is frequently missed (Koeske, 1980). This is why it is so important to look not only at the premenstrual time, but at the entire cycle to form a sense of the changes typical for a woman.

Negative findings for one cycle do not indicate the complete absence of premenstrual symptoms because a major characteristic of PMS is its variation from one cycle to another. In order to best assess the nature of premenstrual changes, several cycles should be charted. It is likely, however, that a woman without premenstrual symptoms during the first screening cycle does not have severe PMS. The relative lack of symptoms premenstrually indicates that she certainly has "good cycles," as well as possibly some bad ones, and continued charting can help to sort out what the differences are. Thus, charting is also an important aid to managing PMS.

The distinction between PMS and dysmenorrhea is also important to understand. Dysmenorrhea, or menstrual distress, is a more limited and specific symptom pattern, usually consisting of abdominal cramps lasting less than 48 hours around the onset of menstruation. Research in the last ten years has demonstrated that these cramps are associated with high levels of uterine prostaglandins, and they can be relieved by the use of prostaglandin synthetase inhibitors (such as ibuprofen) available either by prescription or over-the-counter. Other symptoms sometimes associated with prostaglandin release include headache, GI upset, chills, weakness or dizziness, and fatigue. If these symptoms occur within 24 hours of menstrual onset, they are more likely related to dysmenorrhea than PMS.

## PREMENSTRUAL SYNDROME AND PSYCHIATRIC SYMPTOMATOLOGY

Since NPTs may be involved in treating patients with varying presenting problems, an awareness of how psychiatric symptoms interact with premenstrual problems is needed. In particular, affective disorders and neurotic symptoms have been studied in relation to PMS. NPTs who see women with a diagnosed affective disorder should be especially attuned to cyclic variations in psychiatric symptoms. According to Endicott, Halbreich, Schacht, and Nee (1981) and Clare (1983), a majority of women diagnosed as having major affective disorders exhibit premenstrual symptoms, as compared with women who do not show evidence of a disorder. Depression is the major symptom that is exacerbated premenstrually in clinical populations. Psychotic and manic episodes have also been documented as increasing premenstrually in some patients (Endo, Daiguji, & Asano, 1978).

The relationship of neurotic symptoms to the menstrual cycle has also been studied, but early studies linking PMS with neuroticism have been questioned (Coppen & Kessel, 1963; Rees, 1953). Methodological issues plagued the earlier research that associated psychiatric symptoms with PMS; the use of retrospective questionnaires to assess PMS was particularly questionable. There have also been reports of an increased incidence of suicide attempts and psychiatric admissions premenstrually, but procedures for recording these phenomena may lack reliability and validity (Rubinow & Roy-Byrne, 1984).

PMS and psychiatric disorders, although co-existing in some cases, are separable and distinct problems. One cannot assume that women with psychiatric symptoms will suffer premenstrual exacerbations, nor do women with PMS necessarily need psychiatric help. NPTs who suspect premenstrual problems should ask their patient to keep a daily symptom chart in order to determine cyclical variation. Hamilton, Parry, Alagna, Blumenthal, & Herz (1984) recommended that women who initially present with premenstrual complaints be evaluated for psychiatric problems that might contribute to the symptoms presented. However, since many women with PMS are leary of being treated as "crazy," it is best to keep this evaluation minimal until serious psychiatric symptoms are suspected.

## APPROACHES TO MANAGEMENT OF PMS

Because there is no definitive therapy for PMS, the standard medical model does not fit the PMS treatment process. A self-care approach, designed around an individual woman's symptom profile, resources, and support systems, is better suited to managing distressing aspects of premenstrual change. In the authors' self-management model, the NPT acts as a consultant in the development of this self-care plan and provides support for the woman to implement her plan.

Some conceptualizations of PMS foster the notion that women are victims of their biological make-up and cannot control their negative emotional states. Thus, some women feel helpless and seek an expert to remedy their "hormonal imbalance." The explicit sharing of responsibility for a self-management plan provides an opportunity for increasing a woman's sense of self-efficacy, a therapeutic benefit. Abplanalp (1983b) also noted the importance of researchers and clinicians recognizing the impact of PMS on patients and of having their complaints taken seriously by the health care provider.

With the information provided by daily symptom charting, the NPT and patient together can identify points of vulnerability by reviewing diet, sleep, physical activity, and stress patterns, and discussing ways to minimize their disruptiveness during the premenstrual time. The issues that arise premenstrually should not be discounted; although the reaction may be more intense than the woman feels comfortable with, the content may be valid. A self-management plan may include any of the following components: education/increasing awareness, diet, vitamins, exercise, turning negatives to positives, stress management, therapeutic support, or medical approaches.

## Education/Awareness

Historically, women have either hidden PMS symptoms or have been humiliated for discussing them. Disclosing their symptoms, taking steps to determine whether PMS is present, and learning those treatments that are available are affirming first steps for most women. Being able to attach a name to their experience and receiving support legitimizes it and reduces the toll on their self-esteem. Workshops on PMS are available in many areas, support groups can be helpful for sharing information, and articles written for lay readers are accessible (Abplanalp, 1983b; Angier, 1982; Henig, 1982).

Another method of increasing awareness is to "tune in" to one's body and focus on occurring changes. Keeping a daily calendar of symptoms and their severity helps to identify a woman's individual concerns. It is wise to also record events (both good and bad) in a woman's daily environment in order to determine whether other factors are influencing her symptoms. Comments on eating and sleeping, health problems, and general stress levels should also be recorded (Hamilton et al., 1984).

## Diet

Many women are helped by changing their eating habits. Lark (1984) offered suggestions for these changes, including recipes and menus. While it may be easy to state some of these rules, actually changing how and when one eats requires time and effort to figure out and apply.

Eliminating caffeine is an important first step to try. Women have reported that this one step has made a great difference in their premenstrual problems. Cutting back should be done gradually (1/2 cup per day) to avoid withdrawal headaches, remembering that tea, chocolate, and cola or certain other soft drinks also contain caffeine and should be eliminated.

Another suggestion that has helped many women is to reduce or eliminate simple sugars from their diets, including white sugar, candy, cake, or processed foods. Instead, the patient should eat proteins and complex carbohydrates in small amounts over the entire day. Women may have low blood glucose during symptom days. Simple sugars (like chocolates) serve only to create a sudden glucose spike in the blood, which the body responds to with an outpouring of insulin, sending the glucose level back down. Some researchers believe that this low blood sugar level is related to the woman's irritability, rage, and out of control perceptions (Jung, Khurana, Corredor, Hastillo, Lain, Patrick, Turkel-taub, & Danowski, 1971). Creating a complicated diet formula for a woman to follow is not helpful. The logic behind eating complex foods, and not fasting, but spreading small meals over the day, is to maintain a relatively steady, adequate blood glucose level.

## Vitamins

The effectiveness of vitamins for relieving PMS symptoms has not been substantiated. However, vitamin B complex and vitamin B6 make a special contribution (as chemical cofactors) to the synthesis of important brain chemicals. The use of these vitamins in PMS is generally accepted as a reasonable addition to self-care efforts. In doses of 100–400 mg per day, these vitamins appear to reduce irritability and agitation in many women (Reid & Yen, 1981). Reports of neuropathy following excessive vitamin B6 usage applies to dosages in the 2000 mg range (Schaumberg, Kaplan, Windebank, Vick, Rasmus, Pleasure, & Brown, 1983). Other vitamin regimens, even those specifically designed for PMS (such as Optivite), are of unproven value in its treatment. An individual woman's belief in vitamin therapy should be considered in recommending the use of vitamins.

## Exercise

The key to an exercise plan is to find one that a woman can stay with. Some recommend aerobic exercise for the tension release; others recommend stretching exercise (such as yoga) for the relaxation. While no particular exercise has been found especially effective for relieving PMS, women who experience a restless energy may find it more soothing to move around than to try to sit still or to relax. Here again, the need is to individualize.

## Turning Negatives to Positives

For some women, PMS symptom days can become their most creative days. If they are more sensitive to their environment premenstrually, creative expression in writing or art may result in positive and satisfying outcomes in what is otherwise a very negative time.

It may also be revealing to examine carefully the feelings that are expressed during PMS days. Are these "inappropriate" or is it possible that some important issues are surfacing that are avoided at other times? Writing about perceptions and incidents during symptom days, and reading or discussing what has been written at a later nonsymptom time, may prove to be a useful experiment for a woman.

Women in therapy have reported that premenstrual days can be times for important therapeutic work to be done, in part because conflicts seem closer to the surface or because there is less tolerance for conflict. For this reason, it is important not to discount the issues that come up, even when the patient may wish to moderate her reactions. Intentionally coming back to examine these issues during nonsymptom days can be a way for NPTs to gain insight regarding the symptom's impact. "Turning negatives to positives" does not mean "it's all in your head," or if the PMS patient simply changes her attitudes that her PMS will disappear. It means recognizing that PMS is real and that some of its effects can, under certain circumstances, be useful in helping a woman to understand what is going on in her life.

## Stress Management

Although research associating PMS with stressful life events is still in its early stages, studies have indicated that women with PMS have experienced a high level of negative stressful life events (Seigel, Johnson, & Sarason, 1979; Wilcoxen, Shraeder, & Sherif, 1976; Woods, Dery, & Most, 1982). It remains unclear, however, whether stress causes or exacerbates premenstrual symptoms, and whether PMS results in more stressful events due to symptoms or to ineffective coping strategies.

Stress management techniques have been used with patients having a variety of physical complaints (Charlesworth, 1982), and show promise in aiding PMS self-management. Increasing rest is the first priority followed by the scheduling of relaxation times. Learning to use progressive relaxation techniques and relaxing imagery is a good way to maximize resting in the time available.

Cognitive strategies include time management and reviewing one's support system to locate resources to help in controlling stress. Planning ahead can help the patient avoid scheduling difficult projects during probable PMS days, but stressful situations cannot always be avoided. Providing for extra time alone or engaging in social activities can also be nourishing. Finding ways to make the environment more pleasant can help.

## Therapeutic Support for the Woman with PMS

Professional counseling is something many women with PMS avoid. They are sensitive to the invalidation of their experience suggested by an approach of "it's all in your head." Women can be encouraged to seek counseling by viewing it as another tool in their efforts to deal with a poorly understood syndrome that has no definitive therapy readily available to lessen its impact. It is a struggle to live with PMS. Finding help in the struggle should be an important goal in the self-care plan.

Sources of help include support groups and family members, as well as the NPT. Involvement in a group with other women who experience PMS can also be beneficial for many patients. An NPT might consider starting such a support group. Often these groups serve primarily an information-sharing function and meet only a few times. Some groups also set up a buddy telephone system, thus encouraging women to feel free in reaching out whenever they are in need.

Nursing therapy can also support a woman to accomplish the changes in lifestyle and habit patterns called for by her self-management plan. In the process of attempting to carry out the plan, changes may need to be made, as both patient and therapist monitor progress and problems. Another area to address is that of behavioral reactions during the premenstrual time and alternative expressions for powerful feelings. It is crucial for NPTs to realize that cyclical variations in problems or a diagnosis of PMS does not diminish the validity of the problems that are expressed by women premenstrually. Significant problems may exist in interpersonal relationships, but a woman may be more apt to express her emotions about these concerns premenstrually. It may be easy for mates or significant others to dismiss a woman's emotions as being due to PMS and to diminish the validity of the woman's concerns. NPTs should be aware of this tendency, and include significant others in the treatment process where this would be beneficial to addressing the patient's concerns.

## Medical Approaches

As in any other situation, ruling out medical problems is important. Part of general self-care is having up-to-date physical examinations with the health provider of the patient's choice. Most physicians, however, have little in the way of demonstrated therapies to offer women with PMS. If a woman is interested in experimenting with a pharmacologic treatment, she should definitely consult with an appropriate practitioner (e.g., a gynecologist for progesterone or a psychiatrist for psychoactive drugs). Reviewed below is research on various drug therapies that should provide NPTs with an objective overview of the possible benefits and risks of drug therapy approaches.

Treatment with drugs is not generally indicated, as none has proven effective in double-blind controlled studies, including various prescription drugs, natural progesterone, vitamin products, diuretics, oil of evening primrose, or tranquilizers (Chakmakjian, 1983; Greene, 1982). The high placebo response rate further indicates that drug therapy may not be the most appropriate treatment (Speroff, 1983). Over-the-counter drugs and ineffective prescription drugs only serve to financially exploit women with PMS. In some cases, when symptoms are limited and well-defined (such as fluid retention or breast pain), women can find relief through medication; but these results do not seem to hold for all women or for all symptoms. Harrison (1985) considered all drug treatments experimental. If a woman wishes to try progesterone, for example, she should sign an informed consent form, clearly identifying the known risks.

Natural progesterone is expensive and is not scientifically supported as effective (Keith, 1985; Sampson, 1979). It is also a depressant (Bardin, Milgrom, & Mauvais-Jarvis, 1983). It should be avoided in a woman whose individual profile is dominated by depression. Long-term side effects are unknown, but short-term side effects include headaches, euphoria followed by depression, changes in menstrual cycle timing, changes in amount of menstrual blood, changes in libido, and irritation or infection of vaginal or rectal tissue (due to the route of administration used for natural progesterone). Oral progestagens have also not been shown to be effective and some are possibly carcinogenic (Frank, 1979).

Psychoactive or mood-altering drugs have also not proven effective in PMS and can make some women feel worse. The fact that some women feel better when they take diazepam, progesterone, or spironolactone (a diuretic) may indicate that there are sub-types of PMS relieved by drugs or may be attributed to a placebo effect. Ultimately the individual woman decides whether she wants to try a drug regimen. The NPT can support her with information, referrals, and advocacy.

# CONCLUSION

In the face of a problem as puzzling as PMS, health practitioners and patients alike feel a sense of inadequacy. In systematic observation and attention to the unique experience of each individual, NPTs can provide significant help to women in sorting out factors that are most salient in their own situations. Also, research on PMS would benefit from NPTs' participation.

# REFERENCES

Abplanalp, J. (1983a). Psychologic components of the premenstrual syndrome: Evaluating the research and choosing the treatment. *Journal of Reproductive Medicine, 28*(8), 517–524.

Abplanalp, J. (1983b). Premenstrual syndrome: A selective review. *Women and Health, 8,* 107–123.

Abraham, G. (1983). Nutritional factors in the etiology of the premenstrual tension syndromes. *Journal of Reproductive Medicine, 28*(7), 446–464.

Angier, N. (1982). Dr. Jekyll and Ms. Hyde. *Discovery Magazine,* November, 1982, 28–34.

Bardin, C., Milgrom, E., & Mauvais-Jarvis, P. (Eds.). (1983). *Progesterone and progestins.* New York: Raven Press.

Chakmakjian, Z. (1983). A critical assessment of therapy for the premenstrual tension syndrome. *Journal of Reproductive Medicine, 28*(8), 532–538.

Charlesworth, E. (1982). *Stress management.* Houston: Biobehavioral Press.

Clare, A. (1983). Psychiatric and social aspects of premenstrual complaints. *Psychological Medicine,* Monograph Supplement 4, 1–58.

Coppen, A., & Kessel, N. (1963). Menstruation and personality. *British Journal of Psychiatry, 109,* 711–721.

Dan, A., & Chatterton, R. (1985). Rationale and evidence for the role of circadian desynchrony in premenstrual symptoms. Presented to the Meetings of the Society for Menstrual Cycle Research, Galveston, TX. May, 1985.

Endicott, J., & Halbreich, U. (1982). Retrospective report of premenstrual depressive changes: Factors affecting confirmation by daily ratings. *Psychopharmacology Bulletin, 18*(3), 109–112.

Endicott, J., Halbreich, U., Schacht, S., & Nee, J. (1981). Premenstrual changes and affective disorders. *Psychosomatic Medicine, 43*(6), 519–529.

Endo, M., Daiguji, M., & Asano, Y. (1978). Periodic psychosis recurring in association with the menstrual cycle. *Journal of Clinical Psychiatry, 39,* 456–466.

Frank, D. (1979). Mammary tumors and serum hormones in the bitch treated with medroxyprogesterone acetate or progesterone for four years. *Fertility and Sterility, 31,* 340–346.

Fritz, M., & Speroff, L. (1983). Current concepts of the endocrine characteristics of normal menstrual function: The key to diagnosis and management of disorders. *Clinical Obstetrics and Gynecology, 26*(3), 647–689.

Greene, J. (1982). Recent trends in the treatment of PMS: A critical review. In

R. Friedman (Ed.), *Behavior and the menstrual cycle* (pp. 367–395). New York: Marcel Dekker.

Hamilton, J., Parry, B., Alagna, B., Blumenthal, S., & Herz, E. (1984). Premenstrual mood changes: A guide to evaluation and treatment. *Psychiatric Annals, 14*(6), 426–435.

Harrison, M. (1985). *Self-help for premenstrual syndrome* (2nd ed.). New York: Random House.

Henig, R. (1982). Dispelling menstrual myths. *New York Times Magazine,* March 7, 1982, 64ff.

Hurt, S., Friedman, R., Clarkin, J., Corn, R., & Aranoff, M. (1982). Psychopathology and the menstrual cycle. In R. Friedman (Ed.), *Behavior and the menstrual cycle* (pp. 299–316). New York: Marcel Dekker.

Jung, Y., Khurana, R., Corredor, D., Hastillo, A., Lain, R., Patrick, D., Turkeltaub, P., & Danowski, T. (1971). Reactive hypoglycemia in women. *Diabetes, 20,* 428–434.

Keith, G. (1985). A study of the premenstrual syndrome and progesterone/placebo therapy. Unpublished doctoral dissertation, Walden University, San Diego, California.

Koeske, R. (1983). Lifting the curse of menstruation: Toward a feminist perspective on the menstrual cycle. *Women and Health, 8*(2–3), 1–16.

Koeske, R. (1980). Theoretical perspectives on menstrual cycle research: The relevance of attributional approaches. In A. Dan, E. Graham, & C. Beecher (Eds.), *The menstrual cycle: An interdisciplinary synthesis of research.* New York: Springer.

Lark, S. (1984). *PMS self-help book.* Los Angeles: Forman Publishing.

Rees, L. (1953). Psychosomatic aspects of the premenstrual tension syndrome. *British Journal of Psychiatry, 99,* 63–73.

Reid, R., & Yen, S. (1981). Premenstrual syndrome. *American Journal of Obstetrics and Gynecology, 139*(1), 85–104.

Rubinow, D., & Roy-Byrne, P. (1984). Premenstrual syndromes: Overview from a methodologic perspective. *The American Journal of Psychiatry, 141*(2), 163–172.

Sampson, G. (1979). Premenstrual syndrome: A double-blind controlled trial of progesterone and placebo. *British Journal of Psychiatry, 135,* 209–215.

Schaumberg, H., Kaplan, J., Windebank, A., Vick, N., Rasmus, S., Pleasure, D., & Brown, M. (1983). Sensory neuropathy from pyridoxine use. *The New England Journal of Medicine, 309*(8), 445–448.

Shangold, M. (1982). PMS is real, but what can you do about it? *Contemporary Obstetrics/Gynecology, 19,* 251–256.

Seigel, J., Johnson, J., & Sarason, I. (1979). Life changes and menstrual discomfort. *Journal of Human Stress, 5,* 41–46.

Speroff, L. (1983). PMS—looking for new answers to an old problem. *Contemporary Obstetrics/Gynecology, 20,* 102–128.

Wilcoxen, L., Shraeder, S., & Sherif, C. (1976). Daily self-reports on activities, life events, moods, and somatic changes during the menstrual cycle. *Psychosomatic Medicine, 38,* 399–417.

Woods, N., Dery, G., & Most, A. (1982). Stressful life events and perimenstrual symptoms. *Journal of Human Stress, 8*(2), 23–31.

# Chapter 14
# The Patient with an Eating Disorder

*Jane H. White*

Because of their holistic approach to patients, their knowledge of physiologic as well as psychological problems, and their present emphasis on women's health care, nurse psychotherapists (NPTs) can uniquely contribute to the treatment of patients with eating disorders. Most of these patients have complex health problems requiring NPTs to apply their knowledge not only of psychiatric nursing, but also of nutrition and physiology. The NPT must employ a variety of assessment and intervention strategies in their treatment.

The patient with an eating disorder, usually female, seems to prefer women therapists—and most NPTs are women. Additionally, the psychopathology of this patient usually involves identity issues. For example, a distorted gender identity is central to the psychopathology of the female with anorexia nervosa; thus female therapists may be more successful in treating these patients than male therapists (Frankenburg, 1984).

## DEFINITION AND SCOPE

By definition, Eating Disorders are those psychological syndromes in which a profound disturbance in eating predominates as the primary symptom. Although the *Diagnostic and Statistical Manual (DSM III)* (1980) does not consider obesity in its classification of eating disorders, this condition can be grouped with these disorders if the underlying etiology is psychological in nature. In addition to obesity, anorexia nervosa and bulimia are considered in this chapter as the "classic" eating disorders. Some eating disorders classified in the *DSM III* involve children (e.g., pica). This chapter does not focus on eating disorders specific to children but rather explores the "classic" eating disorders more commonly associated with adolescents and adults.

The NPT may also encounter other eating problems. For example, a patient may present with a complaint of compulsive eating or binge eating, exclusive of other symptoms. These behaviors alone do not necessarily mean that the patient has one of the classic eating disorders. However, careful assessment will help to identify: (1) if other symptoms exist that might form a significant cluster necessary for a diagnosis of an eating disorder; and (2) the presence of the significant underlying issues.

## GENERAL TREATMENT ISSUES

One of the major difficulties in working with these patients in private practice is the decision about the mode and the type of treatment to be undertaken. Since they may present with both physiological and emotional problems, the selection of treatment modalities and the priority of these treatments may present a dilemma. Bruch (1982), in discussing a case study of a patient with anorexia nervosa, maintained that without first attending to the weight of the patient (particularly because it may be life-threatening), attempts to work with underlying psychodynamic issues may be useless. Patients who are nutritionally deficient are often irritable and unable to concentrate in therapy sessions.

The decision to focus upon physical needs or psychological issues depends upon the specific patient, the type of eating disorder, and the severity of symptoms. Attending to physical needs may require hospitalization, including tube feeding and a structured behavioral program; this treatment decision delays resolution of the psychodynamic issues for awhile. Thus an early treatment priority involves assessment to determine severity of symptoms and priority of interventions. Since symptoms of eating disorders differ, treatment approaches may also differ.

Behavioral approaches have been used to treat bingeing in patients with bulimia and to foster weight reduction and maintenance in the obese. Many hospital units designed to treat patients with an eating disorder use a variety of behavioral approaches. These programs may be similar to token-economy programs in which privileges are earned for weight gains for the patient with anorexia nervosa. Although effective in symptom relief, underlying psychodynamic issues still require treatment with individual, family, or group psychotherapy.

The choice of modes of therapy depends upon the patient's living situation, age, and problems, as well as the NPT's philosophical and theoretical approaches. Patients with bulimia and anorexia nervosa often live with their nuclear families because the age of onset is in adolescence or young adulthood; thus families are often involved in the treatment of these patients.

## THE PRIVATE PRACTICE MODEL

The private practice model for working with these patients involves a multi-modal as well as a multi-treatment approach as shown in Figure 14.1. Both behavioral and psychodynamic work through individual and/or family therapy are usually necessary. In addition, some patients may benefit from group therapy at some later point in their treatment. The private practice model also frequently includes physician support for medication or hospitalization and dietary consultation as necessary.

This NPT has found the multi-modal/multi-treatment approach to be more effective than single approaches (White, 1984, 1985). Few patients with an eating disorder respond well to only one approach since their underlying issues and physiologic problems are multifaceted and often stem from or involve family dynamics (White, 1985; Swartz, 1982).

## THE PATIENT WITH BULIMIA

Bulimia—the binge-purge syndrome—literally means "ox hunger." It has also been called bulimia nervosa (Casper, 1983) and bulimarexia (Boskind-White & White, 1983). It has most frequently been defined as an uncontrollable ingestion of large amounts of food over a short period of time, terminated by physical discomfort, social interruption, sleep, or induced vomiting. The patient who presents with bulimia is usually female and in late adolescence or early adulthood. Her weight is generally within normal range but can fluctuate 10-15 pounds.

### Diagnosis

The *DSM III* (1980) has specifically outlined the criteria for diagnosis of bulimia as shown in Table 14.1. In spite of these detailed criteria, it is not at all clear whether bulimia is a sign, symptom, or entity (Vincent &

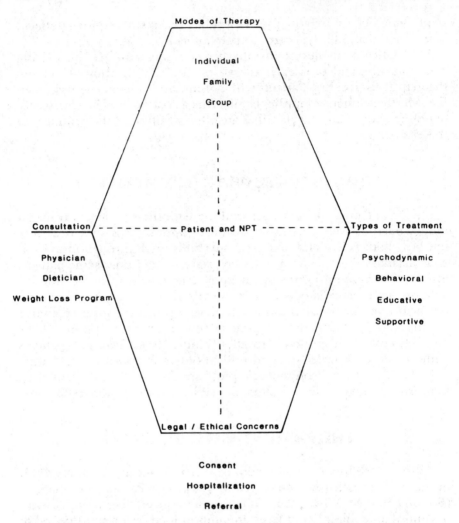

Individual

Family

Group

Consultation - - - - - - - Patient and NPT - - - - - - - Types of Treatment

**Figure 14.1** Private practice model: The patient with an eating disorder.

Kaczkowski, 1984). On college campuses, the percentage of students who binge-eat has been reported as high (Katzman, Wolchik, & Brauer, 1984). However, whether this is purely a habit unaccompanied by other criteria necessary for a *DSM III* diagnosis, or true bulimia, has not been determined. Nevertheless, these criteria provide the NPT with clear assessment parameters for diagnosis and treatment; binge eating alone does not warrant a diagnosis of bulimia. The underlying issues with which the

## Table 14.1 Diagnostic Criteria for Bulimia

Recurrent episodes of binge eating (rapid consumption of a large amount of food in a discrete period of time, usually less than 2 hr)

At least three of the following:
(1) consumption of high-caloric, easily ingested food during a binge
(2) inconspicuous eating during a binge
(3) termination of such eating episodes by abdominal pain, sleep, social interruption, or self-induced vomiting
(4) repeated attempts to lose weight by severely restrictive diets, self-induced vomiting, or use of cathartics or diuretics
(5) frequent weight fluctuations greater than ten pounds due to alternating binges and fasts

Awareness that the eating pattern is abnormal and fear of not being able to stop eating voluntarily

Depressed mood and self-deprecating thoughts following eating binges

The bulimic episodes are not due to anorexia nervosa or any known physical disorder

*Source:* American Psychiatric Association. (1980). *Diagnostic and Statistical Manual,* 3rd Ed. Washington, D.C.: APA, pp. 70–71.

bulimic patient presents may warrant an additional diagnosis such as depression, identity disorder, or adjustment reaction. Careful history and intake sessions will determine this.

## Psychodynamics

Outpatient therapy with the NPT focuses primarily upon the psychodynamic issues underlying the bulimia. However, some therapists include a behavioral component to interrupt the binge-purge cycle (Johnson, Schlundt, Kelley, & Ruggiero, 1984).

This patient's underlying issue involves separation/individuation; some clinicians see bulimia as a symptom of family disorder rather than individual pathology alone (Swartz, 1982). The patient is often confused about her values vis-à-vis her parents and has had strict parental upbringing. She struggles with becoming independent and leaving home, generally expressing feelings of worthlessness, shame, and guilt. Often the central theme is fear of failing or a sense of failure. Gandour (1984) summarized one view of the bulimic as an individual having "a high need for achievement and recognition, whose affective and cognitive characteristics would make achievement of her goals particularly difficult" (p. 17).

The family of this patient is often dysfunctional with the patient feeling responsible for problems between parents, thus the spousal system often needs assessment and intervention. Many mothers of bulimic patients become overly involved in their daughters' lives because of conflict in their own marriages (Minuchin, 1974; Swartz, 1982; White, 1984). The NPT, after careful assessment, may want to arrange to treat the patient and her family. Without family intervention, it may be difficult to resolve many of the family issues that contribute to the patient's disorder, particularly if she lives at home.

## Goals and Outcome Criteria

The goals of individual and family work with one bulimic patient treated by this author appear in Table 14.2. The outcome criteria used for evaluation of the treatment are based on these goals. Helping the patient to develop insight into her anger and to work through these feelings can facilitate reaching such goals as an increase in self esteem; improved relationships with peers (especially with males); the establishment of her own value system; and an increased sense of independence and emotional separation. Achievement of these goals should lead to a decrease in binge-purge behavior.

Outcome criteria for family work depends upon the family's problems. Improvement of the spousal relationship and clearer boundaries between family subsystems should be evident. Such areas as improved communication and establishment of appropriate family roles could also be specific outcomes measured.

## Private Practice Issues

Private practice with patients who have bulimia has some unique aspects. The NPT should monitor the number of times the patient vomits (self-report), not only as an objective criterion of improvement, but also because of the potential risk of physical problems. If frequent and severe enough, vomiting can cause serious, even life-threatening, electrolyte imbalances. These imbalances may be compounded by gastrointestinal problems related to laxative abuse. Careful identification of the presence of these signs and symptoms and the availability of medical support, if required, are thus recommended.

If diet or intake is significantly impaired because of the restriction of food, fasting, or bingeing, a dietician may be consulted. Helping the patient with a structured eating program (food to be eaten, amounts, and

## Table 14.2 Treatment Goals for the Client with Bulimia

| Individual therapy | Family therapy |
| --- | --- |
| *To facilitate separation and individuation:* | *To strengthen boundaries and improve transactional patterns:* |
| Explore the self-system with patient. | Strengthen spousal system's boundaries. |
| Reinforce positive aspects of self. | |
| Identify feelings associated with bingeing/purging | Strengthen parental system's boundaries. |
| Help patient connect feelings and behavior of bingeing/purging. | Discourage patient's involvement in the spousal system. |
| Identify anxiety and intervene with fears of failing. | Refocus the mother's attention on the spousal system. |
| Encourage peer relationships. | Encourage a parental focus for father with patient. |
| Support independent functioning around job and peer issues. | Later, explore the sibling system vis-à-vis the parental system. |
| Facilitate patient problem-solving around career and values. | Improve transactional patterns in sibling system where needed. |
| Format: Weekly sessions until most of goals met. | Format: Sessions every two weeks, while individual work continues. Begin when most of individual goals have been met. Work with patient and parents only, not siblings. |

*Source:* Adapted from White, J. H. (1985). Behavioral intervention with the obese client. *The Nurse Practitioner*, p. 25.

times) represents a part of a behavioral approach to the bingeing and purging. Involvement of significant others in these efforts is often necessary to achieve therapeutic goals.

Educating patients about their eating may also be a part of the role of the NPT. However, she may choose, because of her limited knowledge in this area or because of her theoretical orientation to therapy, to refer this aspect of care to a dietician. However, coordinating the patient's care with these professionals—physician and dietician—is the responsibility of the primary care provider, the NPT.

# THE PATIENT WITH ANOREXIA NERVOSA

Anorexia Nervosa was cited in the literature as early as 1689 when Richard Morton described a "nervous consumption," using the description of a patient as "a skeleton only clad with skin" (Bruch, 1978). It is seldom a disease of the poor and has not been reported in underdeveloped countries. It, like bulimia, is most often seen in adolescent girls whose families are in the upper-middle to upper socioeconomic position.

Currently this disease is on the increase in this country. It is estimated that one out of every 250 females between the age of 12 and 18 may develop this disorder. While the bulimic patient's weight fluctuations are usually not life-threatening, in individuals with anorexia nervosa weight loss is significant, at least 25% below ideal weight for diagnostic purposes.

## Diagnosis

The *DSM III* (1980) describes anorexia nervosa as a disorder in which the essential features are an intense fear of becoming obese, disturbance of body image, significant weight loss, refusal to maintain a minimum body weight, and amenorrhea in females. Some current research on anorexia nervosa has focused upon sorting out such differential diagnoses as obsessive-compulsive disorder and phobia (Solyom, Freeman, Thomas, & Miles, 1983), which are often features of the anorexic; psychodynamic conceptualizations (Swift & Stern, 1982); psychodiagnostic evaluation issues (Small, 1984); and various treatment approaches. This research is incorporated in this chapter (see also Darby, Garfinkel, Garner, & Coscina, 1983).

## Psychodynamics

The literature dealing with the psychodynamics of anorexia is voluminous and diverse. Each NPT's theoretical orientation will dictate the conceptualization of these dynamics. Earlier psychoanalytic theorists viewed anorexia nervosa as a defensive adaptation to highly instinctualized, unconscious fantasies in which eating was equated with the wish/fear of oral impregnation by the father (Swift & Stern, 1982); this theory has been challenged in the literature.

Bruch's (1973, 1978) interpersonal theory has been useful in understanding the dynamics of this disorder. She viewed this patient as having major ego deficiencies resulting from chronically disturbed mother-child interactions. In her formulation she outlined three specific issues: (1) failure to develop autonomy from parents—especially the mother because of over control; (2) the elaboration of a highly compliant self deficient in individualized thoughts, feelings, and body sensations; and (3) ego-vulnerability.

Other clinicians have utilized object relations theory to further explain the dynamics of anorexia (Masterson, 1977). It has been conjectured that the mother emotionally abandons the child if she demonstrates signs of independence, while on the other hand rewarding the child for clinging, infantile behavior. Masterson further claimed that the symptoms of anorexia nervosa represent the need on the part of the patient to remain childish for fear of confronting an abandonment depression that might occur if individuation were attempted. These writings maintain that separation/individuation represent the key dynamic issues for these patients (Lamb, 1978).

## Goals and Outcome Criteria

The patient with anorexia must first be treated for her weight loss. Without adequate nutrition, concentration in therapy will be difficult and the patient will not be psychologically responsive (Bruch, 1982). Some patients may be near death because of their starvation, requiring inpatient treatments, including tube feeding or other forms of feeding. The number of inpatient units specifically developed to treat patients with eating disorders has increased. The NPT should be familiar with these programs to facilitate referral when appropriate. Attempts to bolster the patient's weight should not be undertaken in an outpatient setting if the patient's weight is dangerously low. Therapy can be initiated during hospitalization with close supervision and reinforced in private practice upon discharge.

It has been said that anorexic patients are among the most difficult to treat. Some authors have viewed the symptomatology of the anorexic along a continuum—at one end the more "borderline" individuals, and at the other, the more "neurotic" ones (Swift & Stern, 1982). Since failure of the task of separation/individuation is the central issue, the more autonomous patient is less ill; thus the goals of therapy derive from an assessment of the patient's level of separation/individuation. Both individual and family therapy are usually necessary. Families of these patients are often enmeshed; since many of these patients live at home, individual therapy alone may not prove adequate treatment (Minuchin, Rosman, & Baker, 1978).

With the more borderline patient with anorexia nervosa, the goals focus on object relations—or a more cohesive view of self and others since these patients have failed to achieve object constancy. The NPT helps the more neurotic patient cope with anger underlying her compliance, confusion about identity, and dysfunctional interpersonal relationships—the ultimate goal being separation/individuation. Family therapy focuses upon restructuring, defining, and strengthening the boundaries of family subsystems (Minuchin et al., 1978). Group therapy may also be initiated to help the patient with social adaptation and peer relationships.

Outcome criteria should take into account the goals of the treatment—resolved identity confusion, improved peer relationships, independence, decreased rebellion, weight stabilization and a family system with stronger boundaries between parental and spousal subsystems, more healthy interaction patterns, and less enmeshment.

## Private Practice Issues

Specific private practice guidelines for working with the patient with anorexia nervosa are numerous. Many administrative issues can be delineated from the therapeutic ones when the patient is an inpatient. However, in private practice, the NPT must deal with both. Foremost is the necessity to monitor the patient's weight since anorexia nervosa is a potentially lethal disorder. Therefore, physician and hospital back-up are necessary if weight drops below an established minimum. The NPT should strongly consider contracting with patients in the first session about the possible need for hospitalization. The patient should also be weighed on (at least) a weekly basis.

If the patient is a minor, depending on each state's age of adulthood (consenting adult), parental consent to treat may be necessary. These patients are generally younger than bulimic patients at onset of the disorder. If parents consent and are not involved in therapy, the adolescent's progress should be reviewed with them frequently. In some cases, these patients may be deemed incompetent to make judgments about their own care (e.g., refusing hospitalization). Therefore, both legal and parental aid may be necessary in their treatment (Dresser, 1984).

The use of some behavioral techniques may also be an important consideration with these patients. Anorexics often do not accurately perceive stimuli arising in the body, especially around nutritional needs. Additionally, because of their obsessive natures, these patients may over exercise, depleting their bodies of needed calories. Since increasing food intake to compensate for exercise is difficult for the anorexic, monitoring and contracting around exercise is also important. If the patient begins to lose weight, dietary consultation will be important. Many dieticians have worked with such patients and can provide them with structured meal plans for weight increase if hospitalization is not necessary.

Critical to the success of any of these contracts or plans with this patient is the therapeutic alliance. Because rebellion and control are predominant themes in the relationships of these patients, so too will these be a focus in the therapy relationship. However, the author has found that the therapy sessions can be fertile ground for working through these control issues (representative of earlier unresolved struggles) as they arise.

## THE PATIENT WITH BULIMIA AND ANOREXIA NERVOSA

It is important to note that some patients will meet the criteria for both anorexia nervosa and bulimia (*DSM III*, 1980). The psychodynamics of these disorders were explored earlier. The focus of the NPT will depend upon the patient's symptoms and their severity. Again, a dangerously low body weight often requires hospitalization and artificial feeding. Work in a private practice setting assumes that the patient is not in a life-threatening situation because of weight loss.

## THE OBESE PATIENT

Obesity is a chronic condition affecting a large percentage of Americans. Obesity can be defined as a bodily weight 20% or more above ideal weight. It has been estimated that 14% of men and 24% of women between the ages of 20 and 74 are overweight (Bray, 1980). Some have estimated that as many as 80 million Americans can be classified as obese.

### Diagnosis

The *DSM III* (1980) does not consider obesity, per se, as a psychological problem. However, many clinicians and researchers believe that this condition, particularly if developed in childhood or adolescence, has a psychogenic component. Unfortunately, the absence of uniform psychological features in this condition makes a psychological diagnosis complicated.

The NPT may want to use the diagnosis "Psychological Factors Affecting Physical Condition" (*DSM III*, 1980, p. 303) when there is evidence that psychological factors are of importance in the etiology of a particular case of obesity. Patients do not usually present with complaints of obesity in private psychotherapy practice settings; rather, depression is a common complaint of these patients. Their negative body images, poor self-concepts, and often dependent behaviors accompanied by feelings of helplessness bring them into treatment. Because of their negative self-view, these patients are usually nonassertive and have impaired interpersonal relationships. This is not to imply that depression is the only psychiatric disorder accompanying obesity. Character pathology, as well as some psychotic states, may also exist (Wolman, 1982). On the other hand, many obese persons function normally without evidence of psychiatric problems.

## Psychodynamics

Psychoanalytic formulations of obesity have posited the existence of emotional problems at the oral stage of psychosexual development because of unresolved dependency needs. Obesity as a symptom, therefore, has been viewed as fixation at, or regression to, this stage. Symptom removal (decrease in weight) alone will not resolve underlying conflictual issues. It should be noted, however, that few clinicians today ascribe to this viewpoint of the origin of obesity.

Bruch's (1973) interpersonal theory postulated that obesity is caused by a fundamental feeling of rejection from the mother. The mother may overcompensate for this feeling with overprotective behaviors toward the infant or child, sometimes resulting in excessive feeding. Therefore, as the child develops, he cannot cope with felt needs or disappointment and is unable to distinguish various bodily sensations or urges. The child develops a disturbed body image and feelings of inferiority. He may feel as if he does not own his body. These feelings may be reinforced by society because the obese are often stigmatized.

The learning theorists or behaviorists view eating as an overlearned habit that has been generalized to a variety of environmental cues and states of arousal. They believe that bringing eating under the control of stimuli that are more appropriate for weight loss and maintenance of that loss should be the goal of treatment (Stuart & Davis, 1972).

Other theories including biologic/biochemical ones have also attempted to explain obesity. Since obesity is a complex phenomenon, especially if developed early in life, a single explanation seems inadequate for determining treatment. It must be noted that not all obesity is psychogenic. A careful assessment of the patient's development of obesity, interpersonal relationships, and psychosocial development, along with presenting complaints and symptoms, will help to outline the modes and types of treatment necessary.

## Goals and Outcome Criteria

The NPT should assist the obese patient with weight loss as well as the emotional problems accompanying this disorder. Unlike the patient with anorexia nervosa, these individuals are not usually at life-threatening stages, although some suffer from morbid obesity. Therefore, both the physical and emotional aspects can be treated simultaneously. Behavioral interventions, along with calorie reducing diets, are often effective for weight reduction and maintenance. Some of the key components of a behavioral program are contracting, monitoring, reinforcement techniques, cue elimination, and alternate response development (White, 1985).

In individual therapy, the patient's helplessness, dependence, and overly compliant behavior are central themes. Their disturbed mother-child relationships have interfered with the formation of healthy self-concept. Uncovering these feelings and helping patients move toward independence, effective ways of dealing with disappointment, and improved interpersonal relationships are important.

Although weight loss would be a simple objective criterion for treatment outcome, maintaining lost weight over a period of time (1–3 years) is more important. Outcome often depends upon an accurate assessment of psychological and physical aspects and upon the appropriate selection of types of treatment.

## Private Practice Issues

All patients who are obese do not benefit from the same types of treatment. The NPT must determine if the patient's obesity is accompanied by emotional problems. If there are no emotional issues, referral to an appropriate weight control center may be appropriate. However, the NPT herself may choose to intervene by using an educative/supportive/behavioral approach. Consultation with a dietician may also be useful in working with the obese patient (see Figure 14.1). Some obese patients may also have serious medical problems (e.g., hypertension, diabetes, or cardiovascular disease) requiring medical supervision; referral or consultation with a physician will be necessary in these cases.

Using both a psychodynamic and behavioral approach for these patients can be very effective. If only a psychodynamic approach is undertaken, the patient may develop insight into his/her behavior but will still need to learn new habits related to eating and exercise. If the patient engages in only behavioral treatment and has some underlying emotional issues, weight may be reduced; but these unresolved issues often exacerbate regaining of lost weight.

# FUTURE DIRECTIONS FOR THE NPT

Three areas—education, research, and clinical accountability—are important considerations for the future of NPTs who work with patients having eating disorders. The formal education of psychiatric nurses in the area of eating disorders is almost nonexistent. Yet current epidemiological data suggest that these disorders are on the increase as evidenced by the opening of inpatient facilities to treat these patients. They often need referral to private practitioners for long-term therapy after hospital discharge. Without formal education in this area, the NPT may be reluctant to include such individuals in her caseload. Influencing educational institutions, particularly graduate programs in psychiatric-mental health nursing, to include some content in this area can be one way to prepare NPTs. Additionally, NPTs can take advantage of the various workshops given throughout the country on these disorders and their treatment in private practice.

The nursing research literature contains very few studies on eating disorders, especially anorexia nervosa and bulimia. Intervention-oriented studies are needed to guide nursing practice. Lists of approved nursing diagnoses do not, as yet, include one on eating disorders. NPTs could contribute to the development of such diagnostic nomenclature by describing their work with these patients; these anecdotal reports would outline responses to these disorders that are part of nursing practice, thereby expanding the body of nursing knowledge in this area.

In private practice accountability is paramount and central to the psychiatric nurse's work. In treating patients with eating disorders, such accountability includes obtaining the prescribed licensure, certification, education, supervision, and documentation criteria. However, because of the unique aspects of these disorders (weight loss, medication needs, dietary complications), accountability also includes medical and dietary consultation. Because of the limits of some NPT's expertise, they should also consider developing consultative relationships, outlining roles for each discipline, and collaborating in treating these patients.

# REFERENCES

American Psychiatric Association. (1980). *Diagnostic and Statistical Manual*, 3rd Ed. Washington, DC: American Psychiatric Association.

Boskind-White, M., & White, W. (1983). *Bulimarexia: The binge/purge cycle.* New York: Norton.

Bray, G. (1980). *Obesity in America.* NIH Publication No. 80-359, Washington, DC: U.S. Government Printing Office.

Bruch, H. (1973). *Eating disorders: Obesity, anorexia nervosa and the person within.* New York: Basic Books.

Bruch, H. (1978). *The golden cage: The enigma of anorexia nervosa.* Cambridge: Harvard University Press.

Bruch, H. (1982). Psychotherapy in anorexia nervosa. *International Journal of Eating Disorders, 1*(4), 3–14.

Casper, R. (1983). On the emergence of bulimia nervosa as a syndrome. *International Journal of Eating Disorders, 2*(3), 3–16.

Darby, P., Garfinkel, P., Garner, D., & Coscina, D. (1983). *Anorexia nervosa: Recent developments in research.* New York: Alan Liss.

Dresser, R. (1984). Legal and policy considerations in treatment of anorexia nervosa patients. *International Journal of Eating Disorders, 3*(4), 43–51.

Frankenburg, F. (1984). Female-therapists in the management of anorexia nervosa. *International Journal of Eating Disorders, 3*(4), 25–33.

Gandour, M. J. (1984). Bulimia: Clinical description, assessment, etiology and treatment. *International Journal of Eating Disorders, 3*(3), 3–38.

Hardin, S. B., & Durham, J. D. (1985). First rate: The structure, process and effectiveness of nurse psychotherapy. *Journal of Psychiatric Nursing and Mental Health Services, 23*(5), 8–15.

Johnson, W., Schlundt, D., Kelley, M. S., & Ruggiero, L. (1984). Exposure with response prevention and energy regulation in the treatment of bulimia. *International Journal of Eating Disorders, 3*(2), 37–46.

Katzman, M., Wolchik, S., & Brauer, S. (1984). The prevalence of frequent binge eating and bulimia in a nonclinical college sample. *International Journal of Eating Disorders, 3*(3), 53–62.

Lamb, D. (1978). *Psychotherapy with adolescent girls.* San Francisco: Jossey-Bass.

Masterson, J. (1977). Primary anorexia nervosa. In P. Hartocolis (Ed.), *Borderline personality disorders* (pp. 475–494). New York: International Universities Press.

Minuchin, S. (1974). *Families and family therapy.* Cambridge: Harvard University Press.

Minuchin, S., Rosman, B. L., & Baker, L. (1978). *Psychosomatic families.* Cambridge: Harvard Unversity Press.

Small, A. (1984). The contribution of psychodiagnostic test results toward understanding anorexia nervosa. *International Journal of Eating Disorders, 3*(2), 47–59.

Solyom, L., Freeman, R., Thomas, C., & Miles, J. (1983). The comparative psychopathology of anorexia nervosa: Obsessive compulsive disorder or phobia. *International Journal of Eating Disorders, 3*(1), 3–14.

Stuart, R., & Davis, B. (1972). *Slim chance in a fat world.* Champaign, IL: Research Press.

Swartz, R. (1982). Bulimia and family therapy: A case study. *International Journal of Eating Disorders, 2*(1), 75–82.

Swift, W., & Stern, S. (1982). The psychodynamic diversity of anorexia nervosa. *International Journal of Eating Disorders, 2*(1), 17–35.

White, J. H. (1984). Bulimia: A case study utilizing individual and family therapy. *Journal of Psychosocial Nursing and Mental Health Services, 22*(4), 22–28.

White, J. H. (1985). Behavioral intervention with the obese client. *The Nurse Practitioner.*

Wolman, B. (1982). Depression and obesity. In B. Wolman (Ed.), *Psychological aspects of obesity*, (pp. 88-103), New York: Van Nostrand Reinhold.

Vincent, S., & Kaczkowski, H. (1984). Bulimia, sign, symptom or entity, a survey of three professional populations. *International Journal of Eating Disorders*, *3*(2), 81-96.

# Chapter 15
# The Patient with a Chemical Addiction

*Mary R. Haack*

Traditionally, patients with addictive disorders have been considered undesirable patients by most nurses; moreover, even though chemical dependency is a major health problem in most of the world today, most nurse psychotherapists (NPTs) avoid treating this illness (Hardin & Durham, 1985). This attitude is the consequence of inadequate education about addictive disorders and, possibly, painful past experiences with addicted patients or family members. Many nurses feel, either consciously or unconsciously, that addictions are not treatable health problems, but rather issues of morality.

Large numbers of addicted patients are seen daily in health care facilities; thus it is essential that professional nurses overcome detrimental attitudes. Often the client enters the system with a health problem other than chemical dependency. Typically nursing care is directed toward the presenting problem, and this orientation prevents accurate assessment and, ultimately, adequate treatment.

Although NPTs often lack knowledge of appropriate counseling techniques for treating the addicted patient, they have a unique background that is particularly useful given the patient's physical and emotional problems, which often precede and/or follow chemical dependency. If appropriately trained in addiction counseling, nurse therapists are particularly qualified because of their biopsychosocial orientation when compared to other disciplines which are active in the chemical dependency field. The purpose of this chapter is to discuss selected philosophical and treatment issues related to nursing psychotherapy and chemical dependency.

## BARRIERS TO THE TREATMENT OF CHEMICALLY DEPENDENT PATIENTS

The traditional models that currently dominate most treatment programs in the United States present a major obstacle to the involvement of NPTs in the care of chemically dependent patients. NPTs often perceive these traditional models as anti-intellectual or anti-professional. For this reason, obtaining appropriate counseling skills for treating chemically dependent patients can be difficult for the NPT. Also, it is not always clear where nurses fit into treatment models. Finally, paraprofessionals who are very powerful in alcohol treatment programs and the professional disciplines frequently fight territorial battles over who should properly treat these patients.

Nurses need to claim their legitimate role within the field. In doing so they must address the issue of craft versus scientific models of practice and establish nursing practice in relation to the care of patients with psychiatric disorders concurrent with chemical dependency. Nurses need to define nursing practice appropriate to that of chemotherapy in the presence of chemical dependency. Doing so involves developing nursing practice that describes suitable individual and group psychotherapy for the chemically dependent patient. These goals require nursing supervision for all nurse psychotherapists in the field.

In addition to the intellectual and territorial disputes that block nursing's therapeutic involvement with chemically dependent patients, philosophical barriers also exist. Until the late 1960s and early 1970s, chemical dependency treatment was largely in the hands of paraprofessionals and a few professionals who managed detoxification problems and medical complications. Counseling was structured on a craft model as opposed to the scientific model that structures nursing practice. According to Kalb and Propper (1976), a craftsman gains knowledge and skill through direct observation and experience under the tutelage of a master craftsman. In the field of chemical dependency, the master craftsman was most often a paraprofessional who was himself a recovering addict. The test of the apprentice's learning is the ability to consistently replicate the master teacher's performance. Critical analysis of the overall traditions of the craft are actively discouraged. Mutual agreement is the basis on which loyalty is established among the membership of a craft organization.

On the other hand, nurses as scientist-professionals learn skills not only experientially but also within a research-based context. The education of the scientist-professional consists of exposure to a broad variety of competing viewpoints and the encouragement of an autonomous conceptualization of issues. Although there are craft-like aspects within the scientist-professional model, professionals demonstrate the ability to engage in unique, independent thinking and to evaluate teachers and peers. This is the critical difference between the two models.

Recovering chemically addicted persons who treat patients are frequently resistant to research—and understandably so. If an individual has a deep conviction that his or her recovery rests solely on the acceptance of techniques and philosophy of Alcoholics Anonymous (AA) or a therapeutic community such as Synanon, then it can be very threatening to gain information that may bring these principles into question. The Rand Report (Polich, Armor, & Braiker, 1981) and research on controlled drinking conducted by Sobell and Sobell (1979) offer two examples of such information. On the other hand, professionals expect to challenge traditional beliefs.

Kalb and Propper (1976) contend that the professional has three options in facing the conflicts within the field of chemical dependency. The first option is to reduce the cognitive dissonance by subscribing to traditonal views, or "going native" in sociological terms. This process is necessary for a time for every professional entering the field. In learning about an unknown condition, it is beneficial for the clinician to learn from the person who is afflicted. Visits to AA groups and therapeutic community treatment programs provide valuable experiential learning. The recovering addicts in these programs have much to teach about the recovery process. However, to adhere rigidly to the traditional views of this model suppresses scientific principles of the nursing process, forcing nurses to relinquish power as professionals who have something unique to offer the field.

The second option, according to Kalb and Propper (1976), is to use the professional's scientific perspective. The NPT working with chemically dependent patients will inevitably be caught in conflict when, for example, psychiatric disorders such as schizophrenia emerge after detoxification; the patient may still be subject to a rigid treatment plan that is only appropriate for the uncomplicated addicted patient. Conflicts with the manner in which the group therapy is conducted within a therapeutic community model (Synanon) can also be troublesome to the nurse who is skilled in group dynamics (e.g., when a patient with schizophrenic tendencies is subject to intensive confrontation). Conflicts over medication are also common since models such as AA reject the use of antidepressants or neuroleptics. The resolution of these conflicts requires that the NPT become bicultural; to become as competent and effective in the new subculture chemical treatment milieu as in the old without feeling torn (Kramer & Schmalenberg, 1977). The process of becoming bicultural usually demands supervision by a nurse therapist who has already adopted a bicultural perspective.

A third problem also results in nontreatment of chemically dependent patients. It is estimated that 12–20% of all private office patients, 30–35% of all emergency room patients and at least 30% of all medical and psychiatric patients have an addictive disorder (NIAAA, 1978). Frequently the addiction is simply ignored and other health problems, such as depression, are focused upon. Unfortunately, this approach results in inadequate care for the patient and frustration for therapists. According to the *Diagnostic & Statistical Manual III* (1980), substance abuse disorders are primary conditions that require a primary treatment plan. While it is true that other conditions may co-exist, the treatment of these accompanying disorders does not necessarily also constitute treatment of the addiction.

The final barrier interfering with the NPT's positive attitude toward treating addicted patients is the personal history an NPT may bring into the therapeutic situation. Work by Black (1981) and Pilat and Jones (1985) indicated that many individuals who choose to become professional caretakers do so because they have learned how to take care of others as a function of their role in their family of origin. A typical example is the oldest child of an alcoholic parent who takes on the role of caretaker to compensate for the dysfunction of the ill parent and who simultaneously becomes a high achiever to demonstrate that the family is all right. These skills then are translated into a career.

While these children may become very good at being caretakers, it cannot be assumed that as professionals they know how to deal with their own feelings about growing up in such a situation. Unresolved emotions may interfere with the therapeutic relationship. Given that most nursing school curricula do not include the treatment of addictive disorders, there is very little to help the NPT through these difficulties. Competent supervision from a supervisor familiar with these issues offers the best means for an NPT to overcome this obstacle.

Overcoming the barriers to effective treatment of chemically dependent persons is worthwhile for the nurse psychotherapist. Chemical dependency is a complex illness that manifests itself in several different forms and arises from a variety of factors that are not clearly understood. For this reason, the chemically dependent patient can be challenging and frustrating; but recovery can also be a dramatic and satisfying experience for the NPT with the knowledge and skills to facilitate it.

# THERAPY WITH THE ADDICTED PATIENT

The most important step in treating any patient is to accurately assess the problem. Thus all history taking should include information about when the person first began to drink or take drugs (this includes prescription drugs as well as recreational drugs) and the pattern of usage throughout the person's life. This is true regardless of the presenting problem.

## Early Treatment—Assessment

Pattison (1985) proposed an initial set of factors that can be used in a Lickert-type fashion to assess chemical dependency: *Alcohol and Drug Consumption.* This factor refers to the quantity, frequency, and volume of alcohol consumed over time. The NPT should ask about specific drugs: "Have you ever used marijuana? How many times? Did you smoke in the past month? Did you smoke in the past week? How many joints do you smoke in a day?" If she feels confident that the patient has an addiction problem, the question can be phrased in a way that gives permission to divulge large quantities: "Have you ever drunk a case of beer?"

*Drinking Behavior.* This factor refers to preoccupation with obtaining alcohol or drugs, the need or craving for alcohol or drugs, the inability to control chemical use, attempts to control drinking, and the pursuit of chemicals in the face of high physical, interpersonal, social, vocational, or psychological costs.

*Psychic Dependence.* This factor relates to the dependence on chemicals to achieve desired psychic change, observed personality change when drinking, and self-experienced change in self-operation. This assessment may require the observations of significant others.

*Physical Dependence.* Physical dependence refers to the pharmacologic actions and effects of alcohol and drug consumption. It involves two clinical dimensions: development of tolerance and occurrence of withdrawal symptoms. Tolerance is the condition in which an increased amount of drug is necessary to produce the same effect or in which less effect is produced by the same dose of drug. Withdrawal is defined as the physiological disturbances that occur after sudden cessation of large amounts of addictive substances that have been used over a long period of time. Symptoms of withdrawal depend upon the chemical involved.

*Physical Consequences.* The physical consequences of alcohol consumption can be categorized: (1) as acute consequences of drinking (intoxication syndrome); and (2) chronic organic damage due to direct or indirect effects of chemical use.

*Psychological Consequences.* The use of mood altering chemicals can affect psychic operations and produce paranoid ideation, sexual fantasy or anxiety, shame, guilt, altered reality testing, anxiety attacks, panic states, grandiosity, and depression. These states should be assessed while the patient is drinking, after drinking, and as a chronic state apart from drinking. Accurate reporting of these psychological states may require the observations of significant others.

*Interpersonal Consequences.* Effects of drinking on interpersonal relations include problems in maintaining intimate relationships with spouse, children, friends, and relatives. Changes in social network affiliations from nondrinking to deviant drinking are also related to this factor.

*Vocational Consequences.* This factor includes failure to achieve competence, decrement in performance, and a loss of competency. Accurate assessment of these behaviors usually requires the observation of the employer since denial may prohibit the individual from seeing his/her work accurately.

*Social Consequences.* This factor relates to socially deviant behavior attendant to obtaining or consuming alcohol or drugs, resulting in adverse consequences on social relations, for example, the disruption of social role expectations and social role performance. These role changes are frequently seen in the family when a spouse or child takes over the role of the addicted individual.

*Legal Consequences.* Legal consequences of the chemical use include arrests, investigations, accidents, and criminal and/or civil litigation or allegation.

## Early Treatment—Overall Treatment Plan

The assessment phase of treatment provides a data base upon which to develop an individualized, overall treatment plan. At this time the NPT can provide the patient with immediate feedback about alcohol- and drug-generated problems and can also verbalize the problem, thus making the problem more real and acceptable to the patient and significant others. The early phase also provides a basis for evaluation of goal attainment at the end of treatment.

During the early phase, the NPT must make a decision about the need for inpatient detoxification if the patient is actively using chemicals. Counseling intervention with an intoxicated person is fruitless. Available research indicates that many detoxification problems can be handled on an outpatient basis (Pattison, 1985); this decision rests upon each patient's unique circumstances. The need for inpatient treatment is based upon the duration of the chemical dependency problem, the type and extent of chemicals involved, and the history of previous convulsions or delirium tremens.

If an NPT refers the client for inpatient treatment, careful consideration should be given to the program. A treatment program should provide continuity of care through every phase of rehabilitation; or, if necessary, should provide careful transfer of the patient from phase to phase and to different facilities. Programs that provide only one phase of treatment without specific linkages are likely to be ineffective. Occupation, sex, race, age, and social class must also be considered.

Patients who are functioning well in social, vocational, and physical areas of life but are nonetheless using chemicals in an abusive manner are not likely to accept psychological treatment. Such individuals may be good candidates for hospital or freestanding programs that stress medical and disease aspects of chemical dependency. Patients who are functioning reasonably well in psychological, social, vocational, and physical areas of life but who are also experiencing some self-defined emotional distress are likely to accept various forms of psychotherapy.

Patients who have a past history of reasonable life functioning but who are seriously impaired at present in their ability to be self-sustaining are likely to need vocational assistance, halfway housing, and/or long-term treatment. The "Skid Row" type individual often requires supportive care over a long period of time. Psychotherapy, aversive conditioning, disulfiram (Antabuse), antidepressants, and behavior modification approaches are not usually appropriate for this alcoholic.

Disulfiram treatment may be appropriate for individuals who are socially stable, somewhat psychologically dependent, and positively oriented toward authority figures (Pattison, 1985). Methadone maintenance may be useful for patients who are motivated to improve social or emotional functioning but not to be abstinent.

## Mid-Treatment—NPT Interventions

The overall goal of nursing psychotherapy for the first two years of recovery is to guide the patient in learning to live life comfortably without the use of chemicals. This task often overwhelms the patient. Serious life problems have usually developed during the course of chemical use; and unless these are worked through, more chemical use will take place. Techniques of reassurance, active assistance, and enhancement of problem-solving will help the patient during this period.

Denial is the primary defense mechanism employed by the addicted person and significant others. The function of denial is to maintain the addiction. Every effort is put forth by the patient and the family members to protect themselves from the negative label of "addict." Denial can take many forms: minimizing the seriousness of the problems; attributing the chemical use to factors no longer present; or blaming others. The strength of the denial system is directly related to the duration of the addiction. Those addicts who are in the beginning stages are usually more open and capable of seeing the impact of the chemical use upon their lives.

Breaking through denial is an important therapeutic task of the mid-stage; it involves the establishment of trust, the use of confrontation and support, and, frequently, the help of significant others. The purpose of breaking down the denial is to assist the patient to see the reality and consequences of chemical use. In achieving this goal, the patient often experiences emotional pain, often responding with anger or tears. This process may also be very uncomfortable for the NPT. However, confrontation is a skill that must be mastered if the NPT is to work effectively with the addicted patient.

Chaney and colleagues (1981) tested a cognitive-behavioral model of addictive treatment characterized as "relapse prevention" because of its focus on identifying situations that place the patient at risk for addictive relapse. Patients given skills training had less severe (though no less frequent) relapse episodes, were more likely to be employed, and attended aftercare more regularly than control groups. A replication with alcoholic subjects of higher socioeconomic status than the population originally studied found both skill training and discussion groups to be superior to minimal-treatment groups, but otherwise not different from each other (Jones, Kanfer, & Lanyon, 1982).

It is sometimes possible to conduct individual psychotherapy with patients who are not consistently abstinent, but the NPT must be careful to control the degree of uncovering so as not to increase anxiety that could precipitate relapse. Therapy during this period is predominantly supportive and educative. The NPT helps the patient to seek new interests to replace the chemicals and to evaluate old facets of life that are still valid and workable.

Some clinicians have argued against the use of psychotherapy in the early stages of recovery on the grounds that it may strip patients of defense mechanisms that could be used in the service of abstinence (Wallace, 1978), and that it makes demands that addicted individuals are not ready to meet (Vaillant, 1981). Nevertheless, some evidence exists that psychodynamically oriented group therapy may be preferred for certain subgroups of addicted individuals (Kissin, 1977).

## Termination

Termination should occur when the patient is able to take charge of his/her life without resorting to the use of mood altering chemicals. However, it may occur at other times as well. If a patient is unable to achieve any abstinence and comes to the sessions under the influence of chemicals, treatment is not being effective. The NPT runs the risk of becoming an enabler and reinforcer of chemical use. Under such circumstances, the patient should be terminated and referred to inpatient treatment.

Estes and colleagues (1980) suggest certain questions to help establish whether a patient is ready for termination. Has the patient achieved significant progress toward goals? Can the patient communicate nondefensively most of the time? Can the patient handle the activities and demands of life without recourse to chemicals? To what extent is the patient involved in a well-rounded life? Is the patient making use of more internal resources, showing consistent, constructive involvement with work, and meaningful interpersonal relationships? Finally, how is the patient reacting to and handling problems?

## Concurrent Alcoholics Anonymous and Narcotics Anonymous Involvement

When working with chemically dependent patients, many therapists insist that patients concurrently attend Alcoholics Anonymous (AA) or Narcotics Anonymous (NA) meetings. Alcoholics Anonymous and Narcotics Anonymous are based upon twelve steps that guide the individual through the process of admitting powerlessness over alcohol, asking God (as the concept of God is understood) for guidance, reflecting on one's assets and shortcomings, making amends, and carrying the message of AA and NA to others. These self-help groups provide a community-based social support system for abstinence. Attendance to these meetings can be an effective single treatment or an adjunct to other therapies. There are no dues and the only requirement for membership is the desire to stop using chemicals.

## Pharmacotherapy

Depression is a common side effect of chemical dependency during early and/or active recovery stages. These depressions may last several months and require pharmacotherapy. Any administration of anti-depressant medication should be carefully monitored by the NPT and a physician.

Research findings on the use of lithium with recovering addicts have been inconclusive. In one study, depressed patients taking lithium had fewer drinking episodes compared with placebo-control patients, but without greater alleviation of the depression (Kline, Wren, Cooper, Varga, & Canal, 1974). In other studies, however, depressed patients did not consume less alcohol while undergoing lithium therapy (Pond, Becker, Vandervoot, Phillips, Bowler, & Peck, 1981). Fawcett and colleagues (1984) found that high lithium levels (greater than or equal to 0.4 milliequivalent per liter) and medication compliance were found to be related to higher abstinence rates, but not directly related to depressive severity or social functioning.

Ciraulo and Jaffe (1981) reviewed the use of tricyclic antidepressants in alcoholics. They reported success in treating initial symptoms of withdrawal such as anxiety, depression, and somatic complaints, but only within the first 2 to 3 weeks after cessation of drinking. In a subsequent study, however, they demonstrated that alcoholics show greater clearance and lower plasma levels of imipramine than nonalcoholics, suggesting that previous studies which found persistent restlessness and malaise may have utilized dosages that were inadequate for alcoholics (Ciraulo and Jaffe, 1982).

The value of pharamcological agents such as disulfiram (Antabuse) as a deterrent to drinking is of continuing research interest. A study on the effect of disulfiram use in an industrial setting showed that improved compliance was achieved and absenteeism reduced during the treatment period (Robichaud, Strickler, Bigelow, & Liebson, 1979). The NPT should consider the use of disulfiram only if she has daily contact with the patient.

## Family Therapy

Chemical dependency is an extremely stressful illness that disturbs the functioning of the entire family. Family members can no longer expect the affected member to behave in a predictable manner or to meet the demands of his/her role. Other members often take on the responsibilities and roles of the chemically dependent member. The family becomes crisis-oriented in response to the unpredictability of the chemically dependent member. This situation leads to a dysfunctional family.

Booz, Allen, and Hamilton (1974) noted specific patterns of adaptation among children of chemically dependent parents. Flight, fight, or being "super good" are common ways a child copes with an addicted parent. Young children may hide under the furniture and older children may stay away from home as much as possible. Other children may escape emotionally and withdraw into themselves or block out the painful experiences. Fight, which is characterized by rebellion, physical and verbal aggression, and acting-out in socially unacceptable ways is another way of adapting to the problem at home. Super good children are those who never do anything wrong, are excellent students, and obey authority figures. They usually do for others rather than themselves. Adaptation of the super good children is not without problems. Children who cope by over-achievement and caretaking for others frequently have problems as adults with relationships, depression, and chemical dependency. A high proportion of children of alcoholics marry chemically dependent people. Following such marriages they may require treatment for their own problems in living or for stress caused by the spouse's drinking. Chemical dependency is also frequently a generational problem that can be treated effectively with family therapy (Stanton & Todd et al., 1982). For this reason, skills in family therapy are often very useful to the NPT.

Kauffman and Pattison (1982) classified families of alcoholics into four groups that may remain discrete entities or change from one stage to another. The "homeostatic family" has drinking only outside the family, which does not affect its functioning. All family members effectively deny the existence of a problem. Such families neither require nor are able to utilize family therapy. They respond best to educational approaches that include parent function and communication skills.

The "neurotic enmeshed" family responds rapidly and with great intensity to alcoholic behavior. Other members assume the alcoholic's parental and spousal roles but are repeatedly critical of the alcoholic's behavior. Alcoholics have constant power struggles with their spouses, which they feel they always lose; however, the spouses also feel like losers. These families require intensive long-term family therapy to work toward sweeping changes in the family system through structural, strategic, or behavioral approaches.

The "disintegrated alcoholic" family has been "burned" repeatedly by attempts at rehabilitation and sobriety. They are resentful and, if brought to therapy too early, will only reject and punish the alcoholic. These family members will benefit from individual therapy, which allows expression of feelings and encourages self-care and improved self-image.

The "isolated alcoholic" has severed all family ties, leaving no family members to join in the therapy. Often these people do have connections with supportive networks in social agencies that may be helpful in therapy.

Coleman and Stanton (1978) indicated that a high proportion of alcoholic families have experienced traumatic, untimely, or unexpected loss of a family member. This phenomenon has led to the hypothesis that the high rate of death, suicide, and self-destruction among addicts simply reflects a family phenomenon in which the addict's role is to die or to come close to death as part of the family's attempt to work through trauma and loss. Alexander and Dibb (1975) and Vaillant (1981) reported a high rate of addiction for offspring of people who have immigrated from another country or different sections of the United States. What appears to happen is that many immigrant parents tend to depend on their children for emotional support, clinging to them and becoming terrified when the offspring begin to separate from them during adolescence (Coleman & Stanton, 1978). The children then seek relief through chemicals. The task of the NPT is then to help these families separate and grieve their loss.

# CONCLUSION

In the past decade much progress has been made in addiction research and treatment. Even more progress in these areas can be expected in the future. Some of the current issues in the field have been reviewed in this chapter. Each step toward greater understanding of treatment of addiction raises more questions and invites further investigation. NPT's can keep informed about the developments in the field of addiction by requesting literature searches, research monographs, and educational materials from the National Clearinghouse for Alcohol Information (NCALI) and the Clearinghouse for the National Institute for Drug Abuse (NIDA), Rockville, Maryland.

It would be a mistake to encourage NPTs to treat addicted patients without some specialized training, but nurses who are prepared in this area can participate in a stimulating and rewarding experience. Certification in this area requires formal education and clinical supervision with addicted patients. Most of this training is currently provided within a craft model by large treatment agencies. Only a few graduate programs in nursing have components in this area. Rather than avoiding addicted patients, NPTs should demand and seek appropriate training in the treatment of this very prevalent health problem.

# REFERENCES

Alexander, B., & Dibb, G. (1975). Opiate addicts and their parents. *Family Progress, 14*, 499–514.
American Psychiatric Association. (1980). *Diagnostic and statistical manual of*

*mental disorders*, 3rd ed. Washington, D.C.: American Psychiatric Association.

Black, C. (1981). *It will never happen to me*. Denver: MAC.

Booz, Allen, & Hamilton, Inc. (1974). An assessment of the needs of and resources for children of alcoholic parents. Final report. Submitted to National Institute on Alcohol Abuse and Alcoholism.

Chaney, E., O'Leary, M., & Marlatt, G. (1981). Skill training with alcoholics. *Journal of Consulting and Clinical Psychology, 46*, 1092-1104.

Ciraulo, D., & Jaffe, J. (1981). Tricyclic antidepressants in the treatment of depression associated with alcoholism. *Journal of Clinical Psychopharmacology, 1*(3), 146-150.

Coleman, S. B., & Stanton, M. D. (1978). The role of death in the addict family. *Journal of Marriage and Family Counseling, 4*, 79-91.

Estes, N., Smith-DiJulio, K., & Heineman, M. (1980). *Nursing diagnosis of the alcoholic person*. St. Louis: Mosby.

Fawcett, J., Clark, D. C., & Gibbons, R. D. (1984). Evaluation of lithium therapy for alcoholism. *Journal of Clinical Psychiatry, 45*(12), 494-499.

Hardin, S., & Durham, J. (1985). First rate: Structure process and effectiveness of nurse psychotherapy. *Journal of Psychosocial Nursing and Mental Health Services, 23*(5), 8-15.

Jones, S., Kanfer, R., & Lanyon, R. (1982). Skill training with alcoholics: A clinical extension. *Addictive Behaviors, 7*(3), 285-290.

Kalb, M. & Propper, M. (1976). The future of alcohology: Craft or science. *American Journal Psychiatry, 133*(6), 641-645.

Kaufman, E., & Pattison, E. (1982). Differential approaches to family therapy in the treatment of alcoholism. *Journal of Studies on Alcohol, 41*, 951-971.

Kissin, B. (1977). Theory and practice in the treatment of alcoholism. In B. Kissin & H. Begleiter (Eds.). *The biology of alcoholism*, Vol. 5: *Treatment and rehabilitation of the chronic alcoholic*, New York: Plenum Press p. 36.

Kline, N., Wren, J., Cooper, T., Varga, E., & Canal, D. (1974). Evaluation of lithium therapy in chronic and periodic alcoholism. *American Journal of the Medical Sciences, 268*(1), 15-22.

Kramer, M. & Schmalenberg, C. (1977). *Path to biculturalism*. Wakefield, MA: Contemporary Publishing.

National Institute on Alcohol Abuse and Alcoholism (NIAAA). (1978). *Third special report to the U.S. Congress on alcohol and health from the Secretary of Health, Education and Welfare*. (DHEW Pub No. (ADM) 78-569). Washington, D.C.: U.S. Government Printing Office.

Pattison, E. M. (1985). New directions in alcoholism treatment goals. In B. S. McCrady, N. E. Noel, and T. D. Nirenberg (Eds.), *Future directions in alcohol abuse treatment research*. (DHHS Pub. No. ADM1322). Washington, D.C.: U.S. Government Printing Office, p. 13-14.

Pilat, J. & Jones, J. (1985). Identification of children of alcoholics: Two empirical studies. *Alcohol, Health and Research World, 9*(2), 27-36.

Polich, J., Armor, D. & Braiker, H. B. (1981). *The course of alcoholism: Four years after treatment*. New York: Wiley.

Pond, S., Becker, C., Vandervoot, R., Phillips, M., Bowler, R. & Peck, C. (1981). An evaluation of the effects of lithium in the treatment of chronic alcoholism: Clinical results. *Alcoholism Clinical and Experimental Research, 5*(2), 247-251.

Robichaud, C., Strickler, D., Bigelow, G., & Liebson, I. (1979). Disulfiram maintenance employee alcoholism treatment. A three phase evaluation. *Behavior Research and Therapy, 17*(6), 628–631.

Sobell, M. & Sobell, L. (1979). *Behavioral treatment of alcohol problems.* New York: Plenum.

Stanton, D., Todd, T. & Associates (1982). *The family therapy of drug abuse and addiction.* New York: Guilford.

Vaillant, G. (1981). Dangers of psychotherapy in the treatment of alcoholism. In M. H. Bean and N. E. Zinberg (Eds.), *Dynamic approaches to the understanding and treatment of alcoholism.* New York: Free Press, p. 40.

Wallace, J. (1978). Working with the preferred defense structure of the recovering alcoholic. In S. Zimberg, J. Wallace and S. B. Blume (Eds.), *Practical approaches to alcoholism psychotherapy.* New York: Plenum, p. 29.

# Chapter 16
# The Aging Patient

*Marguerite A. Dixon*

The proportion of persons over 65 has been increasing since 1900. Of the total American population in 1980, more than 25,000,000 (11%, or 1 in 9) were over 65. By comparison, in 1900 the aged comprised only about 4% (or 1 in 25) of the population; in 1970, 20 million Americans (10% or 1 in 10) were over age 65. The over-65 age group is projected to double between the years 1976 and 2020 (Siegel, 1979).

In 1980, the states of California, New York, Florida, Pennsylvania, Texas, Illinois, Ohio, Michigan, New Jersey, and Massachusetts—listed from most to least—had the greatest populations aged 65 and older (U.S. Senate Special Committee on Aging, 1981). The greatest concentrations were in urban areas, then small cities, followed by rural or farm areas. The impact of this social phenomenon is reflected in increased media attention, proliferation of studies, modification of health and social services, and the clamor in institutions of higher learning to develop course content focused upon the older population. Nurses and other providers of health-related services are challenged to keep abreast of unique and changing needs of these "senior citizens" and to competently attend to their health requirements. In light of this shift in the composition of the population, psychiatric-mental health nurses are being called upon more frequently to teach and to consult in geriatric mental health, as well as to provide services to senior adults.

## WHO IS THE AGING PATIENT?

Aging is an inextricable part of the life process that begins at the moment of conception. The word "aging," however, is typically used to describe people who are at or beyond the age of retirement. In the United States, the age 65 is strongly associated with retirement because it is the cutoff used by the Social Security Administration, various retirement programs, and income tax tables, and is widely regarded as the transition from older middle years to "aged" or "old."

Aging is a complex process encompassing more than simply calendar time. Many invisible physical changes occur within the body, including visible indicants (such as behavior and appearance) and subjective evidence accessible through self-reports of older adults. Objective or observable signs include: sagging and wrinkled facial skin, stooped torso, and graying hair. Slowed and/or unsteady gait, tremor of the extremities, change in pitch of the voice, and diminishing vision also may be age-related phenomena. The aging adult may report that, compared with earlier ages, he or she experiences joint or muscle pain, has difficulty walking or using the arms and hands, does not feel well, or is more forgetful. Such changes may be perceived as losses by the aging. Although there are some similarities in the aging process for all persons, this experience is also unique for each person.

## AGE-RELATED CHANGES

The nurse psychotherapist (NPT) treating elderly patients must be knowledgeable about their age-related psychobiological changes, general health status, and lifestyle in order to conduct a thorough assessment and develop a holistic treatment plan. The NPT should consider the whole individual when completing a health assessment, since data from the physical examination can augment therapeutic intervention. While advancing age is accompanied by physical alterations in almost every body system (as discussed in greater depth by others such as Ebersole & Hess, 1981, Chap. 4; Gioiella & Bevil, 1985, Chap. 5; and Yurich, Spier, Robb, & Ebert, 1984), the following overview will alert the NPT to general physical changes.

### Skin

The combined effect of loss of subcutaneous fat below the dermis, cellular changes, and changes in collagen and elastin cause the skin to become less pliable, less resilient, more friable, and wrinkled. Pigmentation ("brown spots") is not uncommon. Heat and cold are less tolerated. Distribution of body hair may change, with the hair becoming gray and thin.

## Musculoskeletal

Muscle mass decreases and bony prominences are accentuated. Demineralization causes bones to become more porous with greater risk of fractures. Range of motion becomes limited and arthritis and rheumatism are common.

## Cardiovascular

Arteriosclerosis (progressive deposition of fatty deposits between the lining layer and middle layer of the blood vessel) causes loss of elasticity and contributes to vascular diseases. Changes in elastin, collagen, and smooth muscle affect the overall functioning of the cardiovascular system.

## Respiratory

Loss of tissue elasticity causes air to move in and out of the lungs less efficiently than in younger persons. Respiratory muscles and their epithelial lining atrophy. Secretions accumulate as ciliary action (which moves secretions along) declines. Emphysema, tuberculosis, and cancer are common.

## Gastrointestinal

Changes occur throughout the gastrointestinal tract, beginning in the mouth. As taste buds atrophy, taste sensation diminishes. Periodontal disease (associated wtih inflammation and atrophy of gingival tissue), advancing reabsorption of alveolar bone, and loosening of the teeth is common. Tooth loss impairs mastication and, therefore, strongly influences the individual's choice of foods. Decrease in saliva production slows digestion and passage of food to the stomach. Throughout the digestive tract—the mouth, esophagus, stomach, and intestines—epithelial cells undergo structural change. There is cell loss accompanied by hyposecretion of normal fluids and enzymes, and hypoabsorption of nutrients. Peristalsis or motility decreases with age.

## Endocrine and Reproductive

Structural changes occur in the pituitary gland. In general, change in level of hormone production is not consistent or symmetrical for units of the endocrine system. Gradually, intra- and intercellular structures change and secretory function decreases.

## Neurosensory

As voluntary reflexes slow, there is diminished ability to respond to multiple stimuli. Hand tremors may occur. The aging person may experience fatigue earlier with less exertion. Insomnia may become an annoyance, Stage IV sleep is reduced, and there is an increase in spontaneous awakening. The voice may become higher pitched while its range, duration, and intensity diminish. The aged can hear high frequency better than low frequency tones. Diminished vascular and cellular structure and function in all visual structures causes decreased visual acuity and sensitivity to color. Older adults tend to see bright colors better than dark and/ or subdued colors. Changes in cerebral weight and cellular structure are reflected in slower comprehension and retention of new material, increased difficulty in recall, and decreased speed in performance.

## Genitourinary

Changes may include loss of protein from the kidneys due to decreased cardiac output, reduced filtration rate, and diminished renal efficiency. Prostatic enlargement may cause urinary frequency in men; decreased perineal muscle tone may cause urgency and stress incontinence in women. Nocturia and polyuria are not uncommon.

Cellular changes in the reproductive organs of both male and female are reflected, respectively, by corresponding decreases in testosterone and estrogen. In the male, testes decrease in size, the sperm count decreases, and viscosity of seminal fluid diminishes. In the female, breast tissue diminishes, vaginal epithelial lining atrophies, and vaginal secretions become less acidic. There are also alterations in sex drive and performance in both sexes.

Physical, mental, and social functioning and well-being are interrelated. Like individuals of other age groups, older adults differ in their responses to actual or perceived loss and change in these areas, and are influenced by coping patterns accumulated and molded through the years. Self-initiated strategies that rechannel or refocus interest and energies in ways that improve the parameters of the senior adult's life should be identified, encouraged, and supported. Responses may signal psychological distress and/or problems and the need for psychotherapeutic intervention include: memory loss, sudden decreased energy and drive, sustained grief, depression, regression to child-like behavior, exaggerated fantasy, disorientation, delusions, and hallucinations.

In summary, physical aging reflects cellular, structural, and secretory alterations throughout the body. The aging process and one's response to this process are influenced by genetic, physical, environmental, and life style factors, and is unique for each individual. Physical, mental, social, and health dimensions are interrelated.

## IMPLICATIONS FOR THE NURSE PSYCHOTHERAPIST

Nurse psychotherapists who treat patients can expect to be called upon more frequently than in the past to consult about, and have contact with, senior adults as the senior population increases. In addition to the patient's presenting problem or identified need (the need may be to "maintain a healthy existence") and demographic data, the assessment should include information about the person's general health status, level of intellectual and physical functioning, and disability or special problems. Providers of health and social services fail in their responsibility when the residential environment and lifestyle are given only cursory attention or are ignored. Attention to this aspect is especially relevant to assessment and planning for service to the aging patient. This information will help to minimize errors in planning intervention(s) and maximize opportunities for patient-therapist collaboration and cooperation. The NPT should not ignore the physical component of the patient in providing a credible mental health service. For example, the patient who has a hearing deficit should have the problem evaluated. Based upon evaluation of the deficit, the NPT can adopt interventions—how loud the NPT's voice must be to be heard by the patient, in what proximity or in what (body) positions the patient and therapist should be during an individual or group therapy situation, and whether to use flash cards or similar devices for emphasis or explanatory purposes. (The NPT should use large lettering on written or printed materials that will be used by older clients.) Problems of hearing and vision, urinary incontinence, ambulation, and cognition are some factors the NPT may need to consider in planning for therapy sessions. In general, the NPT should incorporate all the psychosocial and biological information about the patient to promote health. The NPT who is mindful of the patient as a unique person demonstrates acceptance and regard for the patient.

## PSYCHOSOCIAL FACTORS ASSOCIATED WITH AGING

Intellectual and adaptive ability, family and interpersonal relationships (or lack thereof), medication and treatment regimens associated with illness states, and moral/ethical/spiritual aspects of life are among the psychosocial factors that affect, and are affected by, aging.

## Intellectual and Adaptive Ability

One's level of intellectual functioning is a determinant of what one can do with information—one's capacity to learn. The capacity for learning, defined by Kalish (1977, p. 54) as "the relatively permanent modification of behavior as the result of experience" is thought to be unaffected by chronological age. Studies suggest that, rather than diminishing intellectual function, there is a generational effect, that is, an age-related decline in performance (speed and reaction time) (Schaie & Strogher, 1968; Zarit, 1980). It remains unclear whether recent versus remote memory is more frequently impaired in the elderly (Zarit, 1980). Because much of the NPT's service to the patient includes teaching, assessing the patient's intellectual ability is prerequisite to developing patient-appropriate educational and other types of interventions. Techniques used for the assessment will vary, depending upon a wide range of patient-relevant factors (e.g., family history, work history, educational level, interests).

Intellect is required to adjust to gradual or abrupt changes in one's role, body, or environment, to stimulate awareness of one's present and potential circumstances, to weigh attendant advantages and difficulties, and to initiate (mental) assimilation and accommodation processes.

Adaptation, defined as "the process of adjusting ourselves to fit a situation or environment" can be routine and automatic or precipitous and forced (Atchley, 1985). Adaptation to internal processes (for example, change in body tissues and secretions) and external forces (such as living arrangement or subsisting on a lower, fixed income) are concomitant with the gradual aging process. Throughout life one experiences expected and recurring events (e.g., birthdays or receiving bills) but also encounters new and perhaps unanticipated circumstances (e.g., losing jobs, meeting new persons, becoming ill, or having accidents). New experiences are perceptually modified to fit already existing ideas, a process known as *assimilation*. For example, the retired adult who eagerly prepared for this phase of life, expecting a different but desirable adjustment, has reconciled the inner experience to fit reality. Still other individuals reluctantly accept the status of being "retired." The latter situation illustrates *accommodation*, or the process of altering one's behavior to more nearly conform to external demands (Atchley, 1985, p. 238). Assimilation and accommodation are integral to overall adjustment to expectations, surprises, and realities of life at any age. Senior adults differ from earlier generations only in that they have had more time—and supposedly more practice—in using these processes to manage transition and change.

## Family and Interpersonal Relationships

Family members are usually counted among a person's continuing social and adaptive support network. When individuals have no biologic relatives, or there is loss of or separation from relatives by death, physical distance, or estrangement, it is not unusual for individuals to develop a substitute family composed of friends and associates. Ideally, relationships within the family are reciprocal and partially serve to sustain and nurture its members. Coping abilities are enhanced and fortified. Through these relationships members feel better prepared to "face the world."

It is not unusual for persons who are growing older to renew, and/or reinforce, their family and friend ties. Although relationships that have endured through the years are especially meaningful, the aged are generally receptive to sincere, kind attention from persons who are new to their circle of family and friends.

Senior adults who have managed to remain more or less independent several years past retirement, perhaps well into their late 70s or early 80s, may become dependent as they move into the old-old (80+) years. Others may become more dependent in young-old (65-70 or 72) years. Although no specific age marks the transition from independent to dependent patterns, physical and/or mental disorders often necessitate assistance with aspects of daily care, such as bathing one's self, dressing, walking, shopping, cooking, making and keeping appointments, and managing one's home, income, and bills.

It is commonly believed that the retired, if given a choice, would choose to live with, or in close proximity to, their children and grandchildren. Recently this author and a nurse colleague surveyed one-third of the independent elderly residents of a 164-unit apartment building (Dixon & Barge, 1985). Although responses have yet to be completely analyzed, a preliminary review suggests that a majority of the residents prefer to live alone or with their mates, and desire to limit visits with their children and (especially) their grandchildren to about once per week. Although culture and family size may be related to this outcome (the residents in this study are of a minority population and tend to have three or more children), these preliminary findings suggest that stereotypical beliefs should be questioned. Because each individual is unique, the NPT should investigate the patient's personal customs, beliefs, and preferences. These may differ little or greatly from those of her/his cultural, family, or work group.

## Illness and Medication

Acute infections and chronic illnesses are associated with advancing years. Most older persons have at least one chronic condition and many have multiple conditions. The most frequently occurring include arthritis, hypertension, hearing impairments, cardiac disorders, sinusitis, visual and orthopedic impairments, arteriosclerosis, and diabetes (Health and Health Care, 1984). Since medications are part of the treatment of both acute and chronic diseases, this group is a major consumer of prescription and over-the-counter (OTC) drugs. It is estimated that senior adults, who constitute about 11% of the population, consume 25 to 28% of prescription drugs and an even greater percentage of nonprescription drugs (Gioiella & Bevil, 1985, pp. 402–404; Mullen & Granholm, 1981). The combination of physiologic changes in the elderly, their sensitivity, or altered response to medications, and the likelihood that many among them are taking an assortment of drugs (in some cases unprescribed and unsupervised) makes the risk and danger of drug toxicity, drug interactions, and untoward effects real and probable.

It is generally acknowledged within medical circles that some medications useful for treating pain and certain physiologic disorders should be carefully monitored when prescribed for the elderly. Side effects may include confusion, disorientation, depression, and idiosyncratic reactions (Ban, 1984). Apparent signs of dementia may, in fact, be attributable to drug toxicity or untoward reactions.

## Moral, Ethical, and Spiritual Aspects

To live to age 65 or beyond is somewhat miraculous in view of such dangers and risks as infection, illness, accidents, and stress, which threaten longevity. When a person reaches age 100 or more, the question is often asked, "How did you live so long?" or "What did you do to live to (*age*)?" Typically, respondents reveal a sample of their moral, ethical, and spiritual beliefs and values. They talk about their "good" and their "unhealthy" dietary—and other—habits, and make statements about their moral or spiritual views. All persons are guided by beliefs and values that originate in childhood and are subsequently modified by varied and innumerable experiences. The NPT who is careful to explore this facet of the patient obtains a wealth of data that, when appropriately used, can facilitate therapeutic processes. To engage the patient with techniques that contradict her/his philosophy is folly.

## THE NURSE PSYCHOTHERAPIST AND THE AGING PATIENT

Elderly persons tend to endure rather than report symptoms of illness. In a study about unreported symptoms, Brody and Kleban (1981) found that 40 to 50% of elderly persons did not tell anyone about experiences of dizziness, feeling blue, headaches, leg cramps, or shortness of breath and, of the reported symptoms, 56% were not reported to health professionals. Older adults commonly are self-medicators who under-utilize health services except in acute or emergency situations. Information about the health and mental health of this population points to the need for health education. The NPT can ably address this need.

Estimates of mental illness in the older adult population range from 9% (Atchley, 1985) to about 15% (Butler & Lewis, 1983). In general, the mental disorders of later life are classified as either organic, which have an identifiable physical or chemical cause, or functional, which appear to be more related to personality and life experiences. Distinctions between these categories are becoming clearer. Current research in the biological sciences suggests biochemical correlations with functional disorders, while social and psychological integrants have been associated with organic disorders (Butler & Lewis, 1983). Features of organic brain syndrome include impairment of memory, intellect, judgment, and orientation, and lability and shallowness of affect. Organic brain disorders include the following conditions: delirium, dementia ("chronic" or "irreversible" brain syndrome), primary degenerative dementia with senile onset (senile dementia of the Alzheimer type), reversible delirium or dementia, presenile dementia, Alzheimer's disease, Pick's disease, Binswanger's disease, Creutzfeldt-Jakob disease, and Huntington's disease (DSM III, 1980).

Functional disorders include schizophrenia, paranoid states and affective disorders (DSM III, 1980; Butler & Lewis, 1983; Whanger & Meyers, 1984). Schizophrenia, a severe emotional disturbance, is primarily characterized by thought disorganization. Other features of schizophrenia are mood and behavior disorders, delusions, and hallucinations. Butler and Lewis (1983) noted that the condition labeled "senile schiozophrenia" or "paraphrenia" in other countries may be other names for the American label "paranoid states."

The presence of persistent (usually persecutory) delusions is a core feature of a paranoid disorder (DSM III, 1980). Other diagnostic criteria include illness duration of a minimum of one week and absence of major hallucinations. Paranoid, acute paranoid disorder, shared paranoid disorder (*folie a deux*), and atypical paranoid disorder are subcategories of the umbrella term "paranoid disorders."

Among the elderly, affective disorders are the most common psychiatric disorders. Mood is the primary feature that distinguishes these disorders from schizophrenia. Three categories of affective disorders are (1) major affective disorders (bipolar: mixed, manic or depressed; major: single episode or recurrent); (2) other specific affective disorders (cyclothymic, dysthymic); and (3) atypical affective disorders (atypical bipolar disease and atypical depression) (DSM III, 1980).

## Assessment and Planning

The circumstances that initiate NPT-patient contact provide the first assessment data. Did the patient find the NPT or did the NPT find the patient? If someone referred the patient for care, who made the referral? What is the relationship of the referring person(s) or agency/institution to the patient? Why is the patient seeking help or why is the patient being referred for treatment?

The NPT should observe the patient's appearance, behavior, attitude body movement, speech, mood, and affect as part of a comprehensive examination including a health history. Nursing diagnoses are based upon a compilation of data from: (1) the health history; (2) the client's view of the presenting problem; (3) ethnic, cultural, and environmental/ life-style factors; (4) medical; and (5) other relevant data (Blake, 1980). In exploring the patient's current lifestyle, the NPT should ask about the patient's living arrangement. Does the client have a physical or mental disability? If yes, what is the overall effect of the disability? Assessment and planning recur throughout the therapeutic process. Further information about the assessment of the aged is provided by Blake (1980); Butler and Lewis (1983); and Zarit (1980); Whanger and Myers (1984) give additional information about mental health assessment of the aging patient. If there is indication that the patient needs a physical examination, the NPT may perform the examination or encourage the client to obtain one elsewhere.

The NPT should ask what the patient does to keep healthy. (The patient may share information about use of home remedies or other practices.) The NPT should inquire about a typical day's meals, what foods are liked and disliked, and what is eaten (ill-fitting dentures or having no teeth may be a hindrance to proper nutrition). The NPT needs to know about the medicines the patient is taking and which are prescribed or are over-the-counter drugs. It is helpful for the NPT to actually see all the medicines the patient is taking. The NPT should evaluate recent losses (What kind of losses have occurred? How is the patient adapting to these?) What are the patient's activities?

## The Patient-Nurse Psychotherapist Contract

When the patient and NPT agree to work together, the NPT should develop a verbal and/or written agreement, stipulating the purpose and guidelines or rules for the relationship. It is helpful to have the agreement in writing. Senior adults can then refer to the agreement at will should they forget what was said. The patient's participation in developing the contract should be encouraged for at least two reasons: (1) a collaborative relationship is more likely to succeed than a directive one; and (2) the process is one way for the therapist to acknowledge the patient's value and role as a partner.

The contract should identify the focus and set the organizational parameter for the patient-NPT relationship, including times and dates for therapy sessions. The specified location of therapy sessions should be a comfortable and bright place with little or no distractions. (Older adults tend to like bright colors.) The chair should be of height and construction that permits the patient to sit and to rise with minimum difficulty.

The NPT should provide support by assisting the patient to reinforce existing social support systems or to build a support system; teach when teaching is indicated; and involve professionals from other disciplines such as nutrition, occupational therapy, and social work. (The patient may need and require the skill and attention of more than one professional health worker.)

# CONCLUSION

The older population—persons aged 65 and older—represented about 11.3% (about 25.5 million persons) of the American population in 1980. This age group is projected to become about 20.9% (51.6 million persons) in the year 2030. Associated needs and demands for health and mental health services will have an impact upon psychiatric-mental health nurses. NPT's then, are obligated to expand their knowledge base to become familiar with the physical changes in older adults that influence, and are influenced by, mental status. Retirement, loss of mate and/or friends, role alteration, relocation, and gradual or abrupt change in health status are examples of events and circumstances commonly experienced by older adults.

These alterations can have profound and stressful effects upon one's health, especially when changes occur unexpectedly or when several undesirable events occur within a brief time span. Comprehensive assessment and planning based upon a range of biopsychosocial data should facilitate successful therapeutic intervention(s). In general, the NPT should incorporate all the psychosocial and biological information about the patient to help promote health—mental health and comfort. The NPT who is mindful of the patient as a unique person, demonstrates acceptance and regard for the patient.

# REFERENCES

American Psychiatric Association. (1980). *Diagnostic and statistical manual of mental disorders*, 3rd ed. Washington, D.C.: American Psychiatric Association.

Atchley, R. C. (1985). *Social forces and aging: An introduction to social gerontology*, 4th ed. Belmont, CA: Wadsworth.

Ban, T. (1984). Chronic disease and depression in the geriatric population. *Journal of Clinical Psychiatry, 45*(3, Sec. 2), 18–23.

Blake, D. R. (1980). Psychosocial assessment of elderly clients. In I. M. Burnside (Ed.), *Psychosocial nursing care of the aged* (pp. 73–86). New York: McGraw-Hill.

Brody, E. M., & Kleban, M. H. (1981). Physical and mental health symptoms of older people: Who do they tell? *Journal of the American Geriatrics Society, 29*, 442–449.

Butler, R. N., & Lewis, M. I. (1983). *Aging and mental health*. St. Louis: Mosby.

Dixon, M. A., & Barge, F. C. (1985). Perceptions of aging black adults about living arrangements and health. Unpublished manuscript, University of Illinois, Chicago.

Ebersole, P., & Hess, P. (1981). *Toward healthy aging: Human needs and nursing response*. St. Louis: Mosby.

Gioiella, E. C., & Bevil, C. W. (1985). *Nursing care of the aging client: Promoting healthy adaptation*. Norwalk, CT: Appleton-Century-Crofts.

Health and Health Care. (1984). *A profile of older Americans*. Washington, D.C.: American Association of Retired Persons.

Kalish, R. A. (Ed.). (1977). *The later years: Social applications of gerontology*. Monterey, CA: Brooks/Cole.

Mullen, E. M., & Granholm, M. (1981). Drugs and the elderly patient. *Journal of Gerontological Nursing, 7*(2), 108–113.

Schaie, K. W., & Strogher, C. R. (1968). A cross sequential study of age changes on cognitive behavior. *Psychological Bulletin, 70*, 671–680.

Siegal, J. D. (1979). *Prospective trends in the size and structure of the elderly population, impact of mortality trends, and some implications*. Current

Population Reports, Special Studies Series, p. 23, No. 78. Washington, D.C.: U.S. Department of Commerce, Bureau of the Census.

U.S. Senate Special Committee on Aging. (1981). Washington, D.C., 32.

Whanger, A. D., & Myers, A. C. (1984). *Mental health assessment and therapeutic intervention with older adults.* Rockville, MD: Aspen-Systems.

Yurick, A., Spier, B., Robb, S., & Ebert, N. (1984). *The aged person and the nursing process.* Norwalk, CT: Appleton-Century-Crofts.

Zarit, S. H. (1980). *Aging and mental disorders: Psychological approaches to assessment and treatment.* New York: Free Press.

# Chapter 17
# The Grieving Patient

*Sherry Johnson*

Grief is complex and has the potential to become a destructive process. When a loved one dies, grief allows for the expression of great loss and emptiness. If not expressed or experienced in a healthy manner, grief may develop longitudinally into physical and/or emotional problems (Friedman, 1973; Johnson, 1983; Parkes, 1965; Worden, 1982). The nurse psychotherapist's goals in grief therapy are to guide the patient/family in the healthy expression of grief; to correct mourning complications that may have developed; to prevent potential grief problems (since it is easier to prevent pathology than to undo it); and to assist survivor(s) to make a healthy detachment or decathesis from the dead person and reattachment to another relationship or goal(s).

This chapter explores two major grief practice models in addition to the author's own model of Family Themes that developed from personal research, practice, and literature review (Johnson, in preparation). A Grounded-Theory approach (Glaser & Strauss, 1967; Johnson-Soderberg, 1982) was utilized to develop theory arising from practice, then validated, and returned to patient care. Following this discussion of theoretical models, the chapter explores factors that may contribute to complicate mourning. It is important for the NPT to be aware of these complicating factors so prevention and/or interventions can be accomplished before destructive processes occur. Several interventions are then explored. Finally, factors that relate to the termination of the mourning are presented.

The terms "grief," "mourning," and "bereavement" are often used interchangeably. However, their meanings are different. Grief relates to the physical, emotional, and behavioral reactions to, and feelings about the loss. Bereavement is an all-encompassing term that includes physical, emotional, social, and cultural responses to the pain of loss. Mourning, then, is the process of readjustment to one's life with the loss.

## MODELS OF GRIEF THERAPY

Elizabeth Kübler-Ross is a recognized authority on reactions of adults who are faced with death, their own or that of a loved one (1969). Her five stages of grief—denial, anger, bargaining, depression, and acceptance— have provided a model for assessing the behaviors of dying patients and their families. These stages, however, are just a model. All persons do not experience these stages; and certainly these do not necessarily occur in sequence, as many people mistakenly believe.

Worden's (1982) model dealt primarily with survivor bereavement. Instead of stages, he developed four primary tasks of mourning: (1) to accept the reality of the loss; (2) to experience the pain of grief; (3) to adjust to an environment in which the deceased is missing; and (4) to withdraw emotional energy and reinvest it in another relationship.

Many others have researched the process of grief, bereavement, and mourning (Bowlby, 1980; Parkes, 1970; Schoenberg, Carr, Kutscher, Austin, Peretz, David, & Goldberg, 1974; Westberg, 1961) and have presented important data relevant to practice. Although these grief models are helpful, the author wished to develop a model to include the individual, family and history, and the reactions, feelings, and tasks of mourning (Johnson-Soderberg, 1982). From this need, the author's model of Family Themes emerged.

Family Themes offers a structure by which to consider the themes which are reoccurring subjects or motifs throughout the history of a family without apparent resolution. Themes are labels which can be used to describe family behavior during a crisis situation. Additional purposes of the family themes are to provide: (1) an historical perspective of key family dynamics that may influence the coping mechanisms at the time of death; (2) a broader understanding of Kübler-Ross's, Worden's and other stages or process of mourning; and (3) a basic understanding of family coping, so that necessary interventions can occur.

## A FAMILY THEME MODEL FOR GRIEF THERAPY

The family theme model for grief therapy indicates that the most common family themes are scapegoating, conspiracy of silence, detachment, guilt, and symptom formation (Johnson-Soderberg, 1981, 1982;

Johnson, 1983, in preparation). Each of these important concepts will be considered.

## Scapegoating

Scapegoating is a process of singling out one or more persons to bear the brunt of a family or group's dissatisfaction or anxiety. A scapegoating situation always requires the existence of an individual or group who is threatened. In grief therapy, death or potential death is the threat that triggers the scapegoating process.

Scapegoating may have been a means of coping with threatening situations in the past. Scapegoating occurs in varying degrees, ranging from a short-term displacement of anger from a terminally ill family member onto a nurse or physician to a very destructive, long-term process (Bermann, 1973; Johnson-Soderberg, 1981; Johnson, in preparation).

For example, a young woman, Mary, who had been in grief therapy for several years because of a terminal illness exhibited low self-esteem, schizophrenic qualities, alcohol abuse, and self-destructive behaviors. Her family history revealed that her father consistently made her the scapegoat for a tragic accident (he had run over a child) that occurred in his early adulthood. He never sought therapy and defended against his pain by scapegoating Mary. The scapegoating process was supported by other family members for different reasons.

## Conspiracy of Silence

A conspiracy of silence occurs when no one will talk about "IT," "IT" being death and aspects of death (such as illness or funeral planning and survivor issues, including remarriage, managing money and property, and future decisions and goals). This conspiracy derives primarily from cultural and social taboos against discussing death issues, even within one's own family. The conspiracy of silence does not include the silent response of the patient's family upon initially hearing tragic diagnostic information, although this may initiate the conspiracy. The conspiracy of silence usually develops over time; it may continue for years, causing pathological and destructive family relationships.

The author has been treating a client, Wes, whose daughter died three years ago, followed by his wife committing suicide a year later. After the death of their daughter, the wife, Sue, had refused to speak of her, thus developing a conspiracy of silence. Wes attempted many times to break this conspiracy, but his wife would not allow this to happen. Sue buried her grief pain and it was translated into depression.

Sue's symptoms became pervasive and Wes finally persuaded her to see a psychiatrist, although she denied that her depression was related to her daughter's death. Anti-depressants were prescribed. The evening of her first appointment, Sue complained that "therapy was a waste of time and money." The couple made love; the next morning she committed suicide by over-dosing with the anti-depressants.

The conspiracy of silence was never broken between Wes and Sue, leaving Wes feeling very alone and guilt-ridden. He attempted to get through his grief, but it was not until he met a woman whom he really cared about that he realized the results of the conspiracy. He became impotent because of his association of lovemaking with Sue's suicide. He felt he never had the chance to know the torture his wife must have been feeling inside, and his sense of helplessness and guilt contributed to his impotence.

Breaking the conspiracy of silence is difficult, especially if it concerns the loved one who is dead. In the above example, the therapist asked Wes to write Sue a letter and then write a reply from her. In a planned visit to her grave he verbally told her all his plans and said goodbye, thus indirectly confronting the conspiracy of silence.

The conspiracy of silence serves as an umbrella to shield the client/ family from psychic pain. By not talking about the loved one, feelings, or reactions, denial is exhibited. There is often extreme and inappropriate anger, which is usually aimed indirectly toward people and/or issues. Since feelings are not directed toward the triggering source, depression frequently develops. Often bargaining occurs: "I'll be good, God, and then this will never happen again." Guilt develops since acts cannot be undone: "If only I could have gotten Sue to talk; maybe she wouldn't have killed herself."

A conspiracy often affects children as well. It is usually initiated by a parent who is experiencing difficulty with grief. Such was the case with 2½ year old Billy whose grandmother had died. She had been a primary caretaker for him, but the parents never told him where "Nannie" had gone. Billy's mother was having an extremely difficult time accepting her mother's death and projected her need for conspiracy onto Billy. He was confused, but knew something "terrible" had happened to Nannie. The conspiracy resulted in his regression: he would not be alone in his room, had to have the windows shut (even though it was summer) because a "ghost" might get him, would not let mom and dad out of his sight, forgot his numbers and letters, and protested violently about attending pre-school.

Patients often comment that even if they want to break the silence others will not allow them to do so and treat them as though they have "leprosy." The conspiracy of silence is never helpful; it is always destructive. Grief needs direct expression. The conspiracy of silence leaves people feeling alone, lonely, isolated, and guilty.

## Detachment

Detachment is a process in which people pull away from each other because of their own or significant other's bereavement pain. Detachment usually occurs between people who have had a close bonding prior to the death of a loved one. Detachment can occur over a short period of time or extend over a prolonged period. It is a normal process, and if it does not last too long, it can be healthy because it relieves the pressure of listening and giving support. These behaviors are very difficult when one has little energy to give to others. Detachment is common with parents who have had a child die, but also occurs in many other relationships.

There are several reasons why detachment occurs. At the time of death, the mourner is usually in shock and often tends to process information silently. Also, detachment is used to protect oneself or spouse; survivors often think that if they detach, their loss won't hurt as much. Others are too pained to give support. Detachment may also occur as a defensive maneuver in which the unstated fear is "Will you go away and leave me too?" Moreover, when a marriage or relationship may have been unstable or detached before death, the death potentiates the detachment.

One sad example of detachment occurred with a couple who had had a child die of Sudden Infant Death Syndrome (SIDS). Each was grieving differently. Ann talked and cried and Fred worked hard and stayed away from home. Ann was too upset to give any support and Fred did not know how to support her. Fred had had many previous losses in his life (his father and sibling died when Fred was young), with which he had never dealt; he did not see any connection between these past losses and his present grief. This detachment continued until there was a separation and divorce, an all too common family response to a child's death.

Usually parents end detachment by developing new goals either together and/or separately. This often occurs near the end of the first or beginning of the second year of mourning. A mutual decision-making process tends to be the turning point in helping individuals reattach to the relationship (Johnson-Soderberg, 1981; Johnson, in preparation).

## Guilt

Guilt is probably the most powerful concept in the themes model of grief. Often guilt holds the key to the destruction of physical and emotional health of the survivor. Guilt is a feeling of culpability with offenses of commission or omission (Johnson-Soderberg, 1982). As with other themes, guilt may have been used previously as a means of coping. Although not everyone will necessarily experience guilt (some may feel shame or intimidation), it is a normal feeling and theme in the grieving process.

Guilt is one means of structuring an answer to a question that has no answer. Patients have expressed two primary reasons for experiencing guilt as part of the grief process. The first is often the legitimate reason: "My child got hit by a car. If I had only held his hand tighter, he couldn't have darted into the street." The second cause of guilt is usually kept secret, and often a torturing secret, which reflects past "sins": "My child died because I had an affair and now I am being punished." In therapy, it is important to uncover any secret guilts. Once the person can understand and verbalize these secrets, there is an opportunity to become aware of their invalidity, which is followed by a great sense of relief.

Guilt instillers are people who attempt to or actually induce guilt in the bereaved. Patients are often victimized by direct guilt-instilling statements (e.g., "Why didn't you know something was wrong? You are a bad mother!"). In another case, a minister told a patient that both the death of her daughter and her arthritis were the result of her unforgivable sins. Also, comments that indirectly instill guilt may be expressed by more distant friends or family, such as, "If my children ever go astray, become disobedient or go far away from what I desire for them, I pray to God to 'take' them."

Guilt movies are repetitive, compulsive flashbacks of the person's most intense guilt feeling. They are usually in color and sometimes occur hundreds or thousands of times a day. People associate this with hallucinations and fear they are going "crazy." One father's movie dealt with him coming upon the accident scene where his son had been run over by a car: "The most troublesome image I have is coming on him at the scene. That is emblazed (sic) on my mind!"

People cope with their guilt in different ways. Some work hard, some repress it, and still others turn to drugs or alcohol. The healthiest mechanism for coping with guilt is to discuss it, conduct reality-testing, attempt to understand its roots, and channel it into altruistic behaviors (Johnson, in preparation). For example, one patient said, "Because of my guilt over my son's death, I am going to start a day-care center for children whose parents work. I know I can take good care of them."

## GRIEF SYMPTOMS

In addition to the above themes, another important area for the therapist to consider is one of grief symptoms. Symptom formation is a normal and healthy component of grief because it is a means of expressing directly the pain of grief. If expression is repressed or discouraged, it may be re-expressed in psychological and/or pathological forms such as ulcers, ulcerative colitis, asthma, depression, phobias, and/or compulsions. According to Parkes (1972),

> if it is necessary for the bereaved person to go through the pain of grief in order to get the grief work done, then anything that continually allows the person to avoid or suppress this pain can be expected to prolong the course of mourning. (p. 173)

This author's research (Johnson-Soderberg, 1982) indicates that expression of the type and degree of the symptoms, their potency, and their duration are affected by many variables: women express more symptoms than men, as do those with a strong attachment to the dead person; there are individual personality differences; contagious family effects; length of preparation time for death; cultural, social, economic, and spiritual influences; the lack or existence of a helpful support system; multiple crises and life changes during the last year prior to the death and/or during the first year of bereavement; and the preventability of the death.

Research suggests that a wide variety of grief symptoms can emerge (Johnson, 1983, in preparation; Westberg, 1962; Worden, 1982). It is important for the NPT to assess which symptoms are being expressed and how they change over time. Many of the symptoms are extremely frightening to the patient who often keeps them secret, fearing admission to a psychiatric unit. Patients are greatly relieved to know their symptoms are normal and to be expected.

In complicated grief, although the person may be in therapy, grief symptoms usually start to decrease after the first three months, increase at six months, twelve months, and eighteen months (Johnson-Soderberg, 1982; Johnson, 1983, 1984). Symptoms also tend to increase at anniversary times, birthdays, holidays, and special occasions. Most grief symptoms should be resolved prior to or during the second year of bereavement. If by the third or fourth year, multiple symptoms remain, redevelop, or accelerate, complicated or pathological mourning should be considered as a diagnosis. Table 17.1 displays the most common feelings, physical and psychological responses, and reactions and behaviors of those experiencing grief process.

Medication should be prescribed in limited circumstances and in small quantities; for example, if grief symptoms are exaggerated or life threatening, medication should be used. Medication that is used for symptom regression only adds to the list of variables that may complicate mourn-

**Table 17.1 Common Symptoms of Persons Experiencing a Grief Process**

| Feelings | Psychological and physical responses | Reactions and behavior |
|---|---|---|
| Shock | Vacant or hollow feeling inside | Depersonalization |
|   hysterical | Backaches | Time confusion |
|   tranquil | Aching arms | Difficulty concentrating |
| Anger | Anorexia or weight gain | Suicidal ideation and/or |
| Guilt | Xerostomia |   plans |
| Sadness | Dyspnea | Increased accidents |
| Powerlessness | Hyperventilation | Social withdrawal |
| Helplessness | Signing | Preoccupation with |
| Hopelessness | Lump in one's throat |   dead person |
| Relief | Migraine headaches | Storytelling |
| Emancipation | Sleep disturbances | Secret behaviors and/or |
| Pining | Nightmares |   thoughts |
| Anxiety | Cyring or total inability to cry | Hallucinations |
| Fatigue | General malaise | Phobias |
| Loneliness | Nasal congestion | Compulsions |
| Depression | Scratchy eyes | Flight behaviors |
| Self-hatred | Food does not taste right, if it does |   alcohol abuse |
| |   have taste at all |   drug abuse |
| | Uncontrollable shaking |   affairs |
| | Overactivity | Running away |
| | Oversensitivity to noise and/or light | |
| | Muscle weakness | |
| | Lack of strength | |
| | Weight pulling from back of neck, | |
| |   down arms and shoulders | |
| | Multiple somatic symptoms | |

ing. Psychotherapy is potentially healthier and more beneficial than prescribing medications.

It is easier to prevent grief problems than to undo them. If problems are not anticipated, prevented, or corrected before death, then it is helpful for the health care professional to encourage survivors to consider treatment soon after the death. It is often difficult to convince survivors, as well as health care providers, that help is needed. Usually the person begins to realize that there are problems only after severe psychological pain affects them and their relationships. When complicated grief is present, therapy usually takes longer and the interventions are often more painful and difficult for both the therapist and the patient/family.

## FACTORS AFFECTING COMPLICATED MOURNING

After any death, complicated mourning may develop. Many studies have attempted to predict which survivors will develop complicated mourning (Johnson-Soderberg, 1982; Parkes, 1972, 1975; Raphael, 1977). Parkes found that widows with personality characteristics, such as being young, having children, being dependent or non-expressive of feelings, and having a history of depression, were significantly at risk. Raphael (1977) examined general rather than personality characteristics and reported that survivors who perceive that they had little support during the bereavement or crisis experienced a traumatic death, had ambivalent marital relationships, and the presence of multiple life crises and were at risk for complicated grief reactions.

Johnson-Soderberg (1982, 1983, 1984) found that those who are at high risk for complicated grieving are the following: parents, especially women, who have had a child die; young children whose parent(s) have died; those who experience large amounts or no guilt or grief symptoms; those whose relative's death was traumatic, preventable, or sudden; those who have had multiple or unresolved deaths in the past; those who consistently utilized inadequate family themes and coping mechanisms; and those who tend to be dependent, masochistic, or had a highly ambivalent relationship with the dead person. Although women present themselves for treatment more frequently, this should not be interpreted to mean that men do not experience grieving problems. Men tend to channel their symptoms by working hard or developing physical symptoms such as ulcers or heart problems.

## INTERVENTIONS

All NPT interventions are based upon the presentation and assessment of themes. The interventions are helpful to the therapist, as well as the patient, because grief therapy is often very sad and depressing. The interventions become a creative area in which one can respond to the needs of the patient. It is very gratifying to watch wholeness and health develop out of deep and torturing pain. This section will review specific interventions used by the NPT in grief therapy including issues of story-telling, journals, use of pictures, saying goodbye, and dream work.

## Storytelling

When the therapist initially sees a patient/family, it is important to hear and assess their "story." Stories tend to be a memorized script of the who, what, when, where, and how aspects of death. For the therapist, stories are a means of assessing areas that are a prelude to complicated grief. For the patient, it is a way to structure the situation. By telling the story over and over, it becomes a means to work through grief. A completed story will eventually bring relief and peace. Patients may either write or tape-record their story so that in the future, when memories are fading, they will always have a record of what happened: who the dead person was, what they miss about that person, who were the special and helpful people during their crisis, and their own grief and how it has changed over time.

## Journals

Journaling is another very helpful tool for patients if they enjoy writing or talking into the tape recorder. It offers a means by which they can track their feelings and reactions. With the permission of the patient, the therapist may review the journal to discover both problems and positive aspects. The journal is a private document but patients are usually willing to share it. Some patients have used the journal to later write short articles for newspapers, church journals, and magazines.

## Pictures

In an early session, patients bring in family pictures; this helps the therapist learn about the grieved person and it is an excellent opportunity to assess clues about family dynamics and history. For the patient, it is another way to express grief about that person's death and its impact on the family.

## Saying Goodbye

One of the major issues in survivors' stories, movies, and journals is that they never were able, or allowed, to say goodbye to their loved one. Sometimes circumstances dictated this (e.g., the body was burned beyond recognition). Other times, it was the insensitivity or lack of knowledge of health care providers in understanding the need to see, touch, and verbalize goodbyes at the time of death. "Seeing is believing," as proven by the families of the missing servicemen from Vietnam who still believe their sons are alive. In a traumatic death, it may only be the little finger that they are able to see, but they will know that little finger belongs to "my mother." This prevents a great many future problems (e.g., "Is that really her in the casket?;" "What did he look like?;" "I don't believe he's dead."). Not seeing and saying goodbye leaves unfinished business.

If the person is unable to say his goodbyes, it is necessary to accomplish this in therapy. One technique that can be useful is talking to an empty chair in order to say what needs to be said. Writing a letter to the dead person and then pretending they are that person and writing a reply letter may be used. These are often helpful ways to verbalize the unsaid and to discuss future issues such as remarriage. Other farewell techniques are to draw pictures, create stories, or utilize puppets and/or dolls with children (For more specific details with these techniques, see Johnson, in preparation).

## Dream Work

It often takes a great deal of convincing that dreams and nightmares are "friends" and not "enemies." Dreams serve as a means to work out issues at a symbolic and unconscious level. The themes that arise in grieving patients' dreams are usually unresolved conflicts concerning issues that occur in daily living in conjunction with grief pain. One patient described, "In my dream I kept seeing Bill (son) driving up the driveway and walking on the street. I can't believe he is dead even in my dreams." Patients are encouraged to keep a pad of paper and pencil by their bed and upon awakening, write down the dream in as much detail as possible. Grieving patients can be taught how to interpret their dreams, using a methodology such as Gestalt (Perles, 1969). Patients can also draw the dream. This gives reality to the dream, as well as allowing the therapist to obtain more specific details about troubling issues. In certain instances, drawings from the nondominant hand, as well as dominant, can bring forth more detail and subconscious issues (Edwards, 1979; Johnson, in preparation).

## TERMINATION OF MOURNING

A person does not necessarily finish mourning when she/he completes therapy. In therapy, the grief goals should be fulfilled so that patients leave with a good understanding of the source of their pain and are able to cope and take care of themselves. Such persons should not experience actual or potential psychological hazards. Some patients may reach a plateau, function without therapy for a time, and then return to therapy, often at the anniversary of the death or at the time of an additional loss. Patients should be well aware of the danger signals that should encourage their return to treatment (symptoms increasing for no apparent reason, relationship problems, new beginnings, or another loss).

Mourning is never truly finished. Survivors will always be bereaved to some extent, although pain changes from a torturing hurt to what may be described as a "sweet sadness." The steps toward healthy mourning are very gradual; they come slowly and quietly. Patients may notice they become able to tell their story without "falling apart"; slowly begin to reorganize their life without their loved one; are ready to clean out closets; have the courage to go to a dinner party; or sing hymns in church without crying through each one. In assessing this process, the tasks of mourning are an excellent guide to completion of grief.

There is no timetable for grief. There are too many variables to say specifically when it will end. However, an important turning point occurs when the survivor is able to make a decision to go on living. This decision is always accompanied by a new goal or the regeneration of an old goal (e.g., "I'm going to school to develop my career.").

## SUMMARY

This chapter has explored three models of mourning; factors contributing to complicated mourning; interventions for NPTs to use with grieving persons; and issues regarding the termination of mourning. Grief, mourning, and bereavement are complicated issues. It was not the intent of this chapter to train grief therapists; however, this information may be helpful in giving form to the issues of grieving and complicated mourning so the NPT may become more aware of this important topic in her own practice. The NPT has a special opportunity to offer preventative interventions so the mental and physical health of the survivors, as well as that of the dying person, are maintained at their optimum level.

## REFERENCES

Bermann, E. (1973). *Scapegoat: The impact of death-fear on an American family.* Ann Arbor: The University of Michigan Press.

Bowlby, J. (1980). *Attachment and loss: Loss, sadness, and depression* (Vol. III). New York: Basic Books.

Edwards, B. (1979). *Drawing on the right side of the brain.* Los Angeles: J. F. Tarchu, Inc.

Friedman, J. J. (1973). Depression, failure, and guilt. *N.Y. State J. Med.,* 1700–1704.

Glaser, B. & Strauss, A. (1967). *The discovery of grounded theory: Strategies for qualitative research.* Chicago: Aldine Publishing.

Johnson-Soderberg, S. (1981). Grief themes. *Advances in Nursing Science, 3,* 15–26.

Johnson-Soderberg, S. *The ethos of parental bereavement and guilt.* Unpublished doctoral dissertation, University of Michigan, University Microfilm, Ann Arbor, Michigan, 1982.

Johnson, S. (1983). Giving emotional support to families after a patient dies. *Nursing Life,* 34–39.

Johnson, S. (1984). Counseling families experiencing guilt. *DCCN, 3,* 238–244.

Johnson, S. (in preparation). *Give sorrow words: Counseling the dying and bereaved.* New York: Springer Publishing Co.

Kübler-Ross, E. (1969). *On death and dying.* New York: The Macmillan Company.

Parkes, C. M. (1965). Bereavement and mental illnesses: Part I. A clinical study of the grief of bereaved psychiatric patients. *Br. J. Med. Psychol., 38,* 1–12.

Parkes, C. M. (1970). "Seeking" and "finding" a lost object: Evidence from recent studies of the reaction to bereavement. *Social Science and Medicine, 4,* 187–201.

Parkes, C. M. (1972). *Bereavement studies of grief in adult life.* New York: International Universities Press.

Parkes, C. M. (1975). Determinants of outcome following bereavement. *Omega, 6,* 303–323.

Perles, F. (1969). Compiled and edited by John D. Stevens. *Gestalt therapy verbatim.* Lafayette, California: Real People Press.

Raphael, B. (1977). Preventive intervention with the recently bereaved. *Archives of General Psychiatry, 34,* 1450–1454.

Schoenberg, B., Carr, A. C., Kutscher, A. H., Peretz, D., & Goldberg, I. K. (Eds.). (1974). *Anticipatory grief.* New York: Columbia University Press.

Westberg, G. E. (1962). *Good grief—A constructive approach to the problem of loss.* Philadelphia: Fortress Press.

Worden, J. W. (1982). *Grief counseling and grief therapy.* New York: Springer Publishing Company.

# Chapter 18
# The Depressed Patient

*Ruth Dailey Knowles*

Depression is the most common psychiatric condition. It also occurs normally in many physical illnesses. Depression is the expression of perceived loss, varying from the "Monday morning blahs" to immobilizing psychotic depression. It can be brought on by either hormonal/chemical changes or by reactions to significant life changes. This altered mood state is characterized by a feeling of sadness, lowered self-esteem, inactivity, and self-deprecation. Distortion in thinking is present in all degrees of depression, reflecting hopelessness and despair.

Psychodynamically, depression has been interpreted as resulting from anger that is turned inwardly to the self, rather than being expressed openly. Other psychodynamic interpretations view depression as learned helplessness, a signal that the individual needs to make some life change, or the absence of reinforcement. As the nurse psychotherapist (NPT) sees the depressed patient, she may use one or more explanations of depression to structure interventions.

Physical characteristics associated with depression include a sad expression, crying, bowed posture, psychomotor retardation, slowed speech, disturbed sleep patterns (usually early morning awakening), constipation, eating disturbances (much more or less than usual), headaches, poor concentration with slow thinking, malaise, and anxiety. One or more of these characteristics/symptoms are usually seen with depression, with sleeplessness and agitation interfering most with functioning; hence interventions are focused first on relief of these symptoms.

Emotional characteristics of depression include distorted thinking leading to the cognitive triad of depression—hopelessness about the self, hopelessness about the world in general, and hopelessness about the future (Beck, 1967). Unrealistic attending to negative detail, searching for negative rather than realistic interpretations, and suspicious or outright paranoid ideation may occur. Feelings of sadness, pessimism, guilt and self-blaming, worthlessness, isolation, and depersonalization may exist. As depression deepens (or after a very deep depression has started to resolve and the patient is feeling better with diminished psychomotor retardation) suicide becomes a real and present danger.

Lethality of suicidal ideation/behavior must be assessed in the very first interview. Those most prone to suicide present one or more aspects of the following profile: elderly; white; male living alone; recently divorced; widowed, or suffering from overwhelming loss; chronically ill; approaching important holidays or anniversaries; previously attempted suicide; parents or close friends committed suicide; extremely hopeless; and recently released from psychiatric hospitalization (either on pass or discharge) (Pokorny, 1966). Behaviors that are highly lethal include selection of and accessibility to irreversible methods, for example: jumping; auto accidents; shooting; sleep disturbances; impaired nutrition; drug or alcohol intoxication; giving away prized possessions; suicide note left or mailed; psychotic, injurious, or threatening hallucinations with impulsivity; and sudden euphoria as the patient is coming out of deep depression with tidying up of life matters. If distortion of thinking with highly lethal behavior exists, the NPT is obligated to intervene for the physical safety of the patient, whether by hospitalization, involvement of responsible family members or social service agencies, or other immediate means by which the patient's safety is assured.

## NPT ASSESSMENT

During the first interview with a patient who is depressed, answers to the following questions should be obtained directly or indirectly:

1. What is the depth of depression?
2. How much is the patient able to function normally?
3. What depressed symptoms (physical and/or emotional) are present?
4. How well is the patient sleeping?
5. To what degree is the patient reporting negative ideation?
6. What external situations signify real or potential loss?
7. What might the patient be angry about that is being expressed through the depression?

8. What have been the patterns of previous depression, i.e., incidence, duration, symptoms, precipitating events, helpful interventions, and outcome?
9. To what degree is there suicidal ideation? What is the selected method? How lethal or irreversible is the method or agent? Is the patient impulsive or impaired in thinking so seriously as to irrationally act on suicidal ideation?
10. What is the patient's supportive network of family, friends, co-workers, and others?
11. What amount of psychomotor retardation exists and how much physical exercise (sports, strenuous activity) does the patient engage in regularly?
12. Are there life changes needed that this depression may be signaling?
13. What is the previous and/or current use of psychotropic medications, particularly anti-depressants, dosage, course of treatment, therapeutic effect, side effects, etc.?

# INTERVENTIONS

The NPT must be knowledgeable of the appropriate use of both medical and nonmedical interventions for the depressed patient. Following are some current interventions that have proven useful in the management of the depressed patient.

## Pace and Lead

Because the depressed patient is experiencing emotional pain, motivation for relief or modification of the symptoms is usually high; and because this responsivity to intervention is present, the immediate establishing and maintenance of rapport is highly important. To accomplish this, the NPT should avoid initial cheerfulness, and instead pace sad or pessimistic ideation until rapport has been established soundly enough to lead the patient to more realistic interpretation of events and outcomes. Pacing and leading is exemplified when the NPT initially speaks in a soft, slow voice; attends intently but patiently to answers being elicited; refrains from positive interpretation of events or situations; and seeks, rather than gives, information. After rapport is established, the NPT can then vary voice tone and tempo, alter her body position to one that is less compatible with depression, and begin to explore the inevitable distorted, negative thinking. If, during any session, the patient and therapist lose rapport, the NPT can return to these initial pacing behaviors to once again establish rapport.

## Identification of Anger

Since depression may be seen as the turning inward of anger that is not expressed in other ways, it is useful for the NPT to inquire about frustrating situations of loss, grieving, or blocked goals. "What am I angry about?" has been illuminating to many patients, particularly to those in whom depression is a signal that all is not right, and to those needing to "do something" about a life situation. When uncomfortable feelings arise, the NPT might appropriately suggest that the body/mind is attempting to give the patient a signal that some life situation needs to be changed. Frequently, just the identification of the event to which the patient is reacting, or the realization that changes need to be made, starts the cognitive process leading to diminution of the depression.

## Distorted Thinking

Where there is depression, there is distorted thinking. The cognitive triad of depression exists: hopelessness about the self, about the world in general, and about the future. Pessimism reigns to varying degrees, and self-talk is invariably not useful, resulting in negative rather than realistic interpretations of events. The patient rationally questions the thought disturbance associated with depression only upon realizing it is time-limited, inevitably carries with it distortion of perception and thinking, and is actually a temporary belief pattern. Depressed patients who can acknowledge that their thinking is distorted may alter negative self-talk, which in turn alters thinking (hence feelings), and may come to believe that the depression will be time-limited. Thus, they will be able to interpret this mood state in a much more realistic light.

## Negative Self-Talk

Statements made and believed within the self about the self determine one's self-esteem. As the depressed patient engages in negative self-talk, feelings of worthlessness and sadness accelerate. Since feelings arise from either the words the patient says in the mind, or the pictures/images made, controlling the words and/or pictures can to a large extent control the consequent feelings. The patient should be reminded, particularly when positive ideation and its subsequent lightening of mood is observed by the NPT, that feelings are altered by either negative or realistic thoughts.

Identifying negative self-statements, writing them down for examination, intentionally using "thought-stopping" to decrease their frequency, and replacing them either with rationally predetermined arguments or with opposite thoughts, proves highly useful in mild to moderate depression. By listing and reviewing positive attributes, characteristics, accomplishments, and qualities, the patient fills more minutes per day with realistic thinking rather than with depressed negative ideation. This literally bombards the unconscious mind with realistic self-talk as a substitute for negative and depressed self-talk and its consequent depressed feelings.

## Imagery

Some highly visual individuals can use imagery to replace negative ideation. They may imagine themselves one month, six months, or one year into the future at a time when they are not depressed, using all senses to construct this imagery. This can be coupled with imagery utilized as anxiety management, for example, "going on a mini-vacation" in the mind. Sometimes a depressed patient has difficulty actually engaging in activities until vividly imagining what she might look like, sound like, and feel like when engaging in the positive activity.

## Diversion

Since the depressed patient usually focuses on how sad her feelings are, the NPT may choose not to discuss it beyond the initial assessment, thereby eliminating one source of depression reinforcement. Patients should be encouraged to not talk about their depression to family members and friends, as this encourages more depressed ideation and negative self-talk, and can even temporarily impair relationships if significant others become overwhelmed by the patient's negative attitude.

Depressed individuals should spend time with "comfortable others" who will neither reinforce the depression nor provide an overly sympathetic ear. To act "as if" one is not depressed can be a powerful tool, and realization (in the mildly to moderately depressed patient) that thoughts and self-talk can determine feelings may lead the patient to alter some of the distorted thinking so characteristic of depression. Having activities to engage in that are not depressing to the patient temporarily aids in the lightening of depression, because of altered thinking while engaging in them. These activities could range from a favored hobby (knitting, woodworking, plant care) to a solitary pastime (shopping, strolling through a park, reading a magazine) to strenuous activity such as surfing, skiing, or playing tennis.

## Exercise

There is evidence that as individuals increase their exercise, and engage in strenuous activity, hormones and chemicals are created that are essentially natural anti-depressants ( Appenzeller, Standefer, Appenzeller, & Atkinson, 1980). Jogging, running, and strenuous sports have been used recently as powerful self-management strategies to decrease or even eliminate depression (Greist, Klein, Eischens, Farris, Gurman, & Morgan, 1978; Sachs, 1981). If possible, this method of treatment should be instituted early in therapy, ranging from brisk walks around the block twice per day to tennis, running, or other strenuous activity of the patient's choice. For those individuals who resist outside sports, one can work up quite a sweat vigorously scrubbing kitchen and bathroom floors or enthusiastically weeding the garden.

The depressed patient will not usually engage in strenuous group activities, so should be encouraged to begin with solitary activities, progress to activities with one other, and then ultimately with groups. Depression seems to lift quicker when the strenuous activities/sports have a striking motion (e.g., golf, tennis, volleyball, bowling). The striking motions release some of the energy associated with internalized anger, consequently diminishing the angry energy whose internalization causes the depression.

## Suicide Prevention

Because suicide is a real and present danger with moderately depressed patients (the mildly depressed generally lack the distortion of thinking for suicide, and the severely depressed are frequently prevented solely by psychomotor retardation), the NPT must directly or indirectly assess suicidal potential at the first interview. The author has never allowed a depressed patient to leave the office after the first session without first inquiring about suicidal ideation. To date, only three out of approximately 300 clinically-depressed patients have stated that they did not have suicidal ideation when depressed, leading to the conclusion that suicidal ideation is a naturally-occurring phenomenon to be expected in the depressed patient. Sometimes the reassurance that the depressed patient is not "going crazy" because of these thoughts is relief enough to free him/her to alter perceptions about the depression. Of course, if the patient is at risk for suicide, the NPT is obliged to intervene physically by such means as hospitalization, release only to responsible family members, or contracting.

## Medication

There is probably more variability among NPTs on the use of medication than on any other factor. Although some NPTs institute the use of anti-depressants with the initiation of psychotherapy—tricyclics are effective in 60 to 65% of depressives (Beck, 1967)—the author believes that psychotropics should be used only after patients have been given an opportunity to affect their depression through cognitive/behavioral means. If, however, a patient remains depressed or is suicidal after initiation of psychotherapy, anti-depressant medications should be instituted. One of the drawbacks to the use of anti-depressants is that almost immediately the patient experiences side effects (dryness of mouth, sleepiness, "strange" internal feelings), but it may be 5 to 14 days until a therapeutic effect is experienced. Many patients discontinue their anti-depressant medications long before they can truly evaluate their effectiveness. On the other hand, anti-depressants are powerful tools in reversing depression and allowing the patient to be more amenable to psychotherapy.

## Teaching/Anticipatory Guidance

Depression is usually a lifestyle, a behavior pattern, or a solution to difficult situations; it can be expected to return with either stress, physical illness, or loss situations. To plan, in advance, what one will do in future depressions is to help prevent the serious deterioration that frequently comes with untreated depression.

To prevent future serious depressions is the ultimate therapeutic goal. The NPT can teach patients to be assertive, stand up for their own rights, not keep strong feelings inside (which leads to resentment and depression), to physically exercise to create their own anti-depressants within the brain, and to recognize life situations that might precipitate depression. Psychodynamic psychotherapy, family therapy, and strategic therapy may be used to assist in the prevention of serious depressions in the future.

## REFERENCES

Appenzeller, O., Standefer, J., Appenzeller, J., & Atkinson, R. (1980). Neurology of endurance training: V. Endorphins. *Neurology, 30*(4), 418–419.

Beck, A. (1967). *Depression: Causes and treatment*. Philadelphia: University of Pennsylvania Press.

Greist, J., Klein, M., Eischens, R., Farris, J., Gurman, A., & Morgan, W. (1978). Running through your mind. *Journal of Psychosomatic Research, 22,* 259–294.

Pokorny, A. (1966). A follow-up study of 618 suicidal patients. *American Journal of Psychiatry, 122,* 1109–1116.

Sachs, M. (1981). Running therapy for the depressed client. *Topics in Clinical Nursing, 3*(2), 77–86.

# Chapter 19

# The Patient Needing Long-Term Supportive Therapy

*Laina M. Gerace*

The purpose of this chapter is to explore the role of the NPT in providing long-term, supportive care for chronically ill patients. The chapter focuses on how changes in the health care system have led to problems and gaps in care for the chronically ill that can potentially be addressed by the nurse psychotherapist (NPT). The role of the nurse in supportive therapy is explored, with special emphasis upon supportive care of chronic schizophrenics because they comprise the largest percentage of the chronically mentally ill population. Ways of developing a practice to help these patients and their families are suggested. However, many of the issues and strategies discussed here can apply to all chronically ill persons and their families.

## GAPS IN CARE FOR THE CHRONICALLY ILL

Changes in public attitude and revisions in health care policies have led to changes in health care delivery as well as to unanticipated problems and gaps in care for the chronically ill. One such change is the shortened hospital stay for patients. With the development of cost-con-

A special thanks for sharing their clinical "know-how" goes to Mary Haack, Joan Rosner, and Terry Ryan.

tainment policies, patients are now hospitalized only during the acute phase of their illnesses. Early discharge renews the focus on home health care of an earlier era. However, many of the traditional supports, such as church, extended family, schools, and community are not as strong as they were in earlier times. Moreover, while a team of experts takes care of the ill person in the hospital, family members without any training are expected to assume this job upon his discharge, using only brief phone calls to the attending physician as back-up. Emotional support for both the ill person and the family are frequently missing or inadequate.

Similarly, changes have taken place in the care for the mentally ill. In the 1960s, public belief that individuals have the right to be treated in the least restrictive environment and that community-based care is more cost effective than institutional care led to the deinstitutionalization of the mentally ill. As a result of these changes, chronically mentally ill patients are often discharged to their families while still exhibiting symptoms. In a review of literature on family coping subsequent to these changes, Kane (1984) found that while families try to accept and understand the behavior of the chronically mentally ill member, they report that mental health services are not adequate to help them deal with the ill member at home. The many social problems incurred by having a family member with a chronic psychiatric illness are frequently not acknowledged by mental health professionals; nor is the need for supportive care assessed or provided (Bassuk & Gerson, 1978). Furthermore, community support services have yet to be developed to meet the needs of the chronically mentally ill.

Thus, these changes in the health care system have provided the NPT with a potentially large, albeit challenging, field for practice. Within this domain of practice are patients and families needing long-term supportive therapy to help them deal with problems incurred by chronic illnesses. These are patients with diagnoses marked by frequent symptom recurrence over time or by slowly progressing seriousness, the effects of which create additional family and social problems. The chronic schizophrenic can be considered a prototype of such patients. Many health care workers find these patients undesirable for a variety of reasons; nurses, however, are uniquely prepared to provide services to them.

## THE ROLE OF THE NPT
## IN SUPPORTIVE THERAPY

Rowan (1980) maintained that nurses can provide valuable health services to long-term emotionally distressed patients (e.g., patients with chronic schizophrenia, depression, or personality disorders, as well as those with such disabling medical conditions as quadriplegia, cystic fibrosis, muscular dystrophy, and stroke). These patients and their families live within every community, receiving little attention until confronted with a crisis. Then they often require emergency or hospital care in order to regain their equilibrium; otherwise many go unsupported in their efforts to cope with their illnesses.

Nurses are most qualified to intervene on a long-term supportive basis with such patients largely because of their educational preparation as well as the value placed by the profession on nurturance. The broad theoretical background of nurses is pertinent to this population, allowing them to use their knowledge of disease processes, physical assessment, and pharmacology from the physiological sciences. Theory about family dynamics, the therapeutic relationship, and community networks from the sociological and psychological sciences gives the NPT a unique ability to be a first-line health advisor and supportive counselor to the patient and family.

Many NPTs can evaluate the patient's condition over an extended time, observing and responding to subtle physiological and psychosocial cues. For example, they are skilled in determining which signs and symptoms need medical attention, which complaints are somatic expressions of anxiety, and when the dosage of medication needs adjustment.

Nurses are also accustomed to longer and daily clinical contacts with patients than are members of other health care professions. Nurses, therefore, have a more realistic sense of what patients and their families experience throughout the illness process. Moreover, much of the contact with patients centers around activities of daily living. Because nurses are accustomed to assessing the difficulties patients encounter in both the physical and social realms, they have a kind of "staying power," an ability to stick by a patient even when progress is slow or the prognosis is unknown or poor.

These skills of the nurse fit nicely with the concept of long-term supportive therapy (i.e., giving assistance primarily to help the patient and family deal with the problems incurred by the illness). Personality change or family structural change is not the main focus. Rather, behaviors of the patient and family are evaluated to identify, develop, and reinforce more positive ways of coping. Through this supportive process, the individual and the family are affirmed and motivated to view limitations as challenges. Encouragement and empathy are given. The nurse stays available to the patient and educates him about his illness. Linkages with appropriate community networks are facilitated.

In order for the NPT to engage chronically mentally ill patients in private therapy, inpatient psychiatric experience is essential. Unless one fully understands the acute phase of schizophrenia and its current medical management, for example, the risk for judgment errors during case management is increased. This inpatient clinical experience provides the NPT with a background that enables decision-making about when hospitalization should be recommended, when consultation from another discipline is necessary, and when stressors in the patient's life need further assessment. It also helps the NPT to appreciate what the patient has experienced in the acute phase of illness and, most important, the kinds of management problems the family might encounter when the patient returns home.

# NURSING THERAPY WITH CHRONIC SCHIZOPHRENICS

## General Considerations

Schizophrenia, given its prevalence and severity (it strikes about one of every one hundred Americans), has low priority in mental health care. Schizophrenia may rank second only to aclcoholism as one of this nation's most neglected diseases. This may be due in part to the denial, stigma, and myths that accompany this condition.

Denial accompanies most psychiatric conditions but seems especially pronounced in the case of schizophrenia. Generally one does not hear the term "schizophrenic" used when persons refer to a family member or neighbor with the illness. Rather, that member "moved away" or "went to the hospital for a rest." Denial of any problem leads to avoiding its identification and its scope and, unfortunately, results in a lack of resources to deal with it.

Schizophrenia carries with it a stigma that adds to the burden individuals with this disease and their families must bear. Furthermore, this stigma devalues the disease within our society which, in turn, leads to lack of professional interest and lack of funding for research and treatment. In the clinical setting, for example, many patients and their families still are not being told of their exact diagnosis or being educated about the disease. At one time a diagnosis of cancer also carried a stigma; when that diagnosis was given, it was shrouded in secrecy and shame. Fortunately, patients demanded to know about cancer and its treatment options. The same should be true for schizophrenia. Indeed, the consumer movement for mental illness is having an impact in this regard. How can a family deal with a problem when it is viewed by others as a shameful secret?

Beyond denial and stigma, certain myths have served to confuse both the public and health care professional about the reality of schizophrenia. One such myth is that persons with schizophrenia are creative romantics who simply see the world differently than do ordinary people. In actuality, there is nothing productively creative about schizophrenia. While some persons with the disease may be creative, the disease causes great anguish for them and disrupts their ability to work and to express themselves. Another myth holds that schizophrenic patients are dangerously unpredictable. While there are occasional incidents of violence that may be publicized in the media, most schizophrenic patients are not aggressive and simply appear to behave irrationally to outside observers. These seemingly irrational and unpredictable behaviors become quite rational and predictable once one understands their origin and knows the patient as an individual.

Other myths about schizophrenia support the view that schizophrenia is produced from adverse family dynamics and/or communication patterns; that the patient is merely responding rationally to an irrational world; or that schizophrenic patients are societal or family scapegoats. While aspects of such theories may have merit, too often these theories are taught in nursing and other mental health programs without critical examination. Certainly it is acknowledged that familial and environmental factors exert an influence upon individuals' vulnerability to schizophrenia. However, research indicates strong genetic and biochemical components for the disease. Increasingly, schizophrenia is being seen as a brain disease or a group of brain diseases ( Torrey, 1983). Studies indicate that schizophrenia is primarily a deficiency in the central integrative systems of the patient (Schmolling, 1983) and that such a system breakdown leads to many disorganized thoughts and behaviors. Information processing is inadequate. These findings are less often included in psychiatric nursing texts and in nursing curricula. Yet, to hold an uncritical view of psychosocial theories of schizophrenia risks creating harmful effects on the patient and his family, as will be discussed later in this chapter.

Many NPTs are reluctant to treat either alcoholics or schizophrenics. In a survey of patients treated by nurse psychotherapists, for example, only one patient reported experiencing psychotic symptoms, whereas most sought therapy for depression, low self-esteem, and problems in coping (Hardin & Durham, 1985). The NPT needs to move beyond the denial, stigma, and myths surrounding schizophrenia and maintain a realistic picture about its course. In particular, the NPT should understand these patients' abilities and limitations and become familiar with the problems they and their families experience. The NPT helps the patient and family adapt to these problems and limitations. The nurse appreciates how difficult interpersonal experiences and life problems can be for the schizophrenic patient and provides support to guide him. The nurse monitors the patient's illness and helps the family cope with the problems incurred by the illness.

## A Systems Perspective

A systems model provides one method of organizing and categorizing the vast amount of literature on schizophrenia, including psychotherapy with the schizophrenic patient. Schmolling (1983) reviewed and synthesized biochemical, genetic, cognitive, familial, and sociocultural findings on schizophrenia and reported that central integrative, as opposed to peripheral, systems are primarily affected in schizophrenia. A central system is one that receives input from all other subsystems, in turn, processing, coordinating, and transmitting the outputs that regulate the system. In terms of the schizophrenic patient, Torrey (1983) suggests that evidence points to the limbic system in the brain as the site of pathology. The limbic system, found deeply below the peripheral surfaces of the brain, serves as a central integrating system, the gateway through which most incoming stimuli must pass. Impairment within this system affects the unifying functions by which raw experiences are made congruent with reality and coordinated with behavior that is goal directed and organized. From a systems perspective, the breakdown of the central integrative system allows individuated, segmented subsystems to function independently, resulting in incongruent and disorganized responses. Subsequently, most schizophrenic symptoms can be understood as information processing problems.

Information processing consists of input (external and internal stimuli), throughput (the central processing of such stimuli), and output (the information provided from the central system upon which the person subsequently bases thinking, feeling, and behavior). It also follows that if throughput is impaired, output will be faulty; this, in turn, results in distortions of thinking, behavior, and emotion, which are observable to others. It also follows that, since output is disordered, thoughts, behaviors, and feelings, while appearing illogical or "crazy" to others, may seem perfectly logical to the patient.

Some of the specific identified problems in central integrating functions are an inability to: factor out minor or irrelevant internal and external stimuli; integrate conceptual and perceptual activities; deal with complexity; and register feedback on errors (Schmolling, 1983). Symptoms commonly experienced by schizophrenics flow from these system impairments. These are sensory flooding, excessive attention to minor environment details, distortions in thinking and perception, altered sense of self, boundary problems, lack of goal direction, inability to make decisions, withdrawal, and regression.

Overall, the personality undergoes a shift from relative order to disorder, from predictability to increased random activity. These changes reflect a central systems breakdown that produces altered system boundaries, internal disorder, and semi-autonomous subsystem activities. Thus after the acute phase of care, much of the work with patients requiring long-term supportive care is focused on helping them and their families compensate for system deficiencies and deal with problems created by such a systems breakdown.

## The NPT-Patient Relationship

In addition to major disturbances with the central, integrating system, patients requiring long-term supportive therapy also present a dilemma in relationships. For the schizophrenic patient, a relationship, by its very nature, creates stress. Kahn (1984) noted that "rigid, primitive coping strategies and labile emotions leave little latitude or flexibility to deal with the stress relationships impose" (p. 20). The patient longs for a relationship but at the same time fears it; he fears self-destruction and/or that the NPT might be destroyed. Therefore, safety is an issue in the therapeutic relationship.

Because the patient's personality has healthy as well as disturbed aspects, a therapeutic relationship, although difficult, is possible. Kahn (1984) explained that the therapist can develop the alliance with the healthy portion, and, through this, reach out to the regressed portion. The NPT should strive to appreciate how difficult a relationship is for the patient, disregard preconceptions about what persons "should be," and accept the limitations a disorder like schizophrenia imposes. Patience is essential. Assessment of anxiety needs to be ongoing as the relationship develops because of the intensity of emotions and distrust such patients experience. The NPT must gauge the relationship carefully, providing leadership and structure. This will contribute to the patient's feelings of safety and trust.

While many texts on therapy interpret thereapeutic relationships in terms of transference and countertransference, examination of relationships with schizophrenic or other psychotic patients in terms of Sullivan's (1953) "parataxic distortion" may be more useful. Parataxic distortions are psychotic or unrealistic perceptions about people in the patient's life, including the therapist. Such distortions are the basis for misunderstanding and misconceptions that characterize the patient's relationships. They also reflect the personality disturbance of the patient and may represent an obscure attempt to communicate something important to the therapist. For example, a patient, in observing that the nurse has slightly prominent teeth may wonder out loud if the nurse is "Dracula."

Because supportive therapy is focused on what is occurring here and now, both in the patient's life and between the NPT and the patient, attention to such distortions as they arise is most important. In the above example, the NPT would assess this distortion. The NPT would first determine if the patient were becoming psychotic. Further, the NPT would also determine whether the therapeutic relationship was becoming too intense for the patient, the patient was afraid of the nurse, or the discussion just prior to this observation too frightening for the patient. The NPT might respond in several ways, including reducing anxiety by changing to a safer topic and assessing whether she was too intrusive or the sessions too long. The NPT would also assess whether the patient experiences other psychotic symptoms. Finally, verbal interventions that clarify reality, such as, "My teeth do stick out a bit because I never had braces as a child, but I am not Dracula," could be initiated.

In a traditional, psychoanalytic approach to therapy, the patient's strong feelings towards the therapist are allowed to develop in order for interpretation of these feelings to take place. This process allows the patient to learn about self through experiencing the self in relation to the neutral therapist. However, this kind of a therapeutic process is not appropriate for chronic schizophrenic patients because the anxiety of such an experience is too intense. Nevertheless, strong feelings evolve within any relationship and it is helpful for the NPT to be aware of these so that she can attempt to gauge and control the relationship.

In any helping relationship, the patient is by definition dependent; and all patients test their dependency on the therapist. Chronic schizophrenic patients experience strong dependency feelings. Kahn (1984) noted that such feelings can be managed by differentiating which needs, if met, will strengthen the relationship, and which needs, if met, will interfere with patient growth and autonomy. Clarity about what the nurse can and cannot do for the patient is necessary. For example, under what circumstances can the patient telephone the nurse between visits? What is the agreement about the patient's responsibility for taking prescribed medications?

Contract-setting is a specific way to help structure the relationship so that boundaries stay clear and intense dependency feelings are not fostered. A treatment contract was defined by Loomis (1985) as an openly negotiated, clearly stated, written set of mutual expectations that indicate what the nurse and patient can expect of each other. It includes a clear understanding of the structure and process of arriving at mutually determined outcomes.

Together, the NPT and patient assess patient and family resources and how the nurse may be helpful in providing support. Then a written contract is made. To illustrate, consider the chronic schizophrenic patient who complains of boredom and loneliness, lives alone, remains isolated from others, and perfunctorily performs a technical job. The contract with this patient might include: (1) the commitment to regularly attend a designated number of treatment sessions; (2) the amount and method of paying a predetermined fee; (3) the patient's agreement to take prescribed medication; and (4) assessment of the loneliness and boredom the patient feels. As therapy progresses, the contract may be revised to focus more specifically on how feelings of boredom and loneliness could be decreased, perhaps outlining ways the patient could improve social skills, broaden social contact comfortably, and schedule his days more creatively.

In addition to feelings of dependency being frightening to chronic schizophrenic patients, feelings of anger are also likely to surface in the therapeutic relationship. Anger is a frightening emotion for most people and is especially so for chronic schizophrenic patients who may distort their anger by projecting it onto others. Anger directed at the NPT may be related to authority issues arising from earlier experiences with parents (Kahn, 1984). In traditional therapy the patient might be encouraged to freely ventilate the anger and then to explore sources of the anger. However, this process is not advisable for more psychotic patients. It is more helpful to acknowledge the anger while simultaneously setting firm limits on its expression. For example, consider the patient who becomes angry and starts pacing around the room soon after the NPT discloses that she is going on vacation. The NPT might say, "You feel angry that I am not going to be here for the next two weeks. It is hard when someone you count on regularly won't be here for you. But right now it would be better for you to sit down so we can talk about how you will manage things while I am gone."

Sexuality is another concern that may emerge within the therapeutic relationship. Confusion about sexuality and sexual characteristics is fairly common in schizophrenic patients. The fact that most schizophrenics first become ill in adolescence or early adulthood may contribute to this confusion. It is possible for the patient to develop intense sexual feelings for, or delusional ideas about, the therapist. With his very poor sense of differentiation and ego boundaries, these feelings may actually represent the patient's yearning to merge with a nurturant other. The NPT needs to be alert to cues that parataxic distortions of this kind are occurring. Again, clearly stated limits are helpful. For example, the nurse might say, "It is all right for you to have personal feelings towards me, but this is a professional relationship and we need to stay very clear on that." If the patient makes more direct expressions that are seductive in nature, the nurse might say, "I think you know that this is not appropriate. I feel uncomfortable when you respond to me in a sexual way." Kahn (1984) pointed out that such overt sexual expressions also reflect the patient's resistance to emotional closeness; and she suggested interpreting these by saying, "You express these feelings in a way that's got to make me angry—I think you're trying to push me away too . . ." (p. 23).

In developing a relationship with a chronic schizophrenic patient, it is important to carefully assess the patient's capabilities, keeping in mind that most of these patients have severe limitations in socialization skills and capacity for relationships. Putting expectations too high will only add to their anxiety and frustrate the NPT. Rowan (1980) stated that for the therapist, long-term patient care requires a philosophy of realism, although sensitized by a bit of idealism. The nurse cannot work effectively with such patients without accepting the reality of the patient's situation and prevalent psychopathology. To work with these patients, the NPT needs to realize that the quality of life of one person may differ from that of another and that emotional support is a valid service for someone who is socially impaired.

## FAMILY ISSUES TO BE CONSIDERED IN TREATING SCHIZOPHRENIC OR OTHER CHRONIC PATIENTS

Traditionally, in the field of psychiatry, family dynamics are often interpreted as contributing to (or even causing) psychiatric illness. Mothers especially continue to be implicated in the genesis of psychoses such as schizophrenia. Families themselves expect to be held responsible for their relative's illness and experience tremendous amounts of guilt and insecurity. These attitudes and assumptions can lead to an almost adversarial relationship between health care professionals and families (Appleton, 1974).

Following a literature review of family responses to a member's mental illness, Kreisman & Joy (1974) concluded that this burden has been poorly assessed and that mental health professionals are not meeting family needs. Whereas past studies of families and mental illness focused on the family's role in the origin or outcome of the disorder (see Howells & Guirguis, 1984, for a summary of such studies), more recent work examines the family as a reactor to the mentally ill member. Such research questions the effects of the mentally ill member on the family and the family's ability to cope with the problems incurred by the ill member.

Hatfield (1978) felt that health care professionals demonstrate a lack of insight to the burdens the family encounters in daily living experiences with a chronically schizophrenic member. Her study revealed that such families live under considerable stress, having to deal, on a day-to-day basis, with the patient's anger, often unjustified suspicions, episodes of auditory hallucinations, nonsensical talk, and inappropriate moods. Many families complained about the intrusiveness of the patient, which often took the form of carelessness around the house, argumentativeness, physical threats, and attacks. Irregular sleeping patterns and disturbances at meal time increased family chaos.

In other families, the patient's lack of motivation, poor self-care, and lack of goals were extremely frustrating. The lives of siblings and the parents' marriage were often adversely affected. In some families the burden of care for this patient fell on one individual. Overall, Hatfield concluded that a picture of family life with a schizophrenic is marked by enduring stress.

The NPT has the unique opportunity to develop a practice that is sensitive to the difficulties families face when a mentally ill member lives in the home. Instead of approaching the family with the thought that they are the genesis of the mental illness, the NPT might approach them from a psycho-educational model (Anderson, Hogarty, and Reiss, 1980).

The psycho-educational perspective differs from traditional family therapy. In traditional family therapy, the family is viewed as an interactive system and is encouraged to deal with family interaction patterns, unresolved problems, conflicts, developmental tasks, and differentiation. Inherent in this process is the underlying assumption that the entire family system is "ill." Taking a different stance, the psycho-educational approach is designed to (1) educate the family about the patient's illness; (2) support and advise the family about the patient's progress and adaptation to the home environment; and (3) deintensify the family environment in which the patient and family live. The underlying assumption is that having a chronically mentally ill patient in the home is stressful, and both education and support are needed to help the patient and family cope. Each of these aspects of the psycho-educational approach is now discussed.

## Educating the Family

Since inpatient care facilities and community health care centers vary greatly in how they involve and teach families, the NPT needs to assess the family's level of knowledge about schizophrenia in general and the patient in particular. What have they been told about the patient's diagnosis? What is their understanding about what is wrong with the ill member? What expectations do they have now that the ill member is living at home? Anderson, Hogarty, and Reiss (1980) found that provision of information regarding theories of pathogenesis, course, outcome, symptomology, and effective management of illness decreased family guilt, anger, and other negative emotional responses. Knowledge decreases the likelihood of negative or stereotyped views of the patient, such as viewing him as "incurably ill" or "lazy." Information also helps to increase the family's understanding and tolerance of the patient's limitations and to improve their ability to set limits appropriately. There is less need to react by over-protecting or becoming judgmental toward the patient.

The NPT might develop or acquire structured materials and make these available to families. For example, a handout on medication management would be very useful. One excellent resource for educating families is Torrey's (1983) family manual in which he describes the nature of the disease, including patients' perspectives of their illness. Also included is information on diagnosis, treatment, problems of daily living, and names of family support groups available in various states.

## Supporting and Advising the Family about the Patient's Adaptation

The NPT might take the approach that while there is not firm evidence that families cause schizophrenia, families do influence how patients progress in recovery and adapt to the home situation. Just as with someone having a physical disability, the nurse counsels the family that it is important not to center the entire family lifestyle around the patient. Parents are encouraged to spend time together away from the patient to nurture their marriage and to attend to the needs of siblings.

Based on educational information given to them, families are helped to understand that it is probably necessary to decrease the patient's sensory stimulation. When first discharged from the hospital, many patients need more sleep and do not tolerate activities and the complexities of family living very well. A more isolated lifestyle may actually be better for the patient. What looks like reduced motivation may actually be a protective maneuver to avoid stimuli that the patient cannot process and respond to.

In order to reduce discouragement when progress is slow, the NPT can help the family see small gains over time and develop an accepting attitude toward the patient's limitations. She can also help the family grieve the loss they may feel as they develop a realistic view of the patient's limitations.

## Deintensifying the Family Environment

Because mental illness carries with it a stigma, families often retreat from their normal social networks when a member becomes ill. As this social withdrawal occurs, the environment within the family may become more intense. Furthermore, family research suggests that some families of schizophrenics exhibit distorted communication patterns and excessive involvement or enmeshment (Howells & Guirguis, 1984). In order to deintensify the family environment, Anderson, Hogarty, and Reiss (1980) suggest treatment sessions in which all family members are encouraged to respect interpersonal boundaries in concrete ways such as allowing family members to do things separately, speak for themselves, and recognize each person's limitations and vulnerabilities.

Attention should be given to extending the family support system and commuity network. The NPT can examine whether the extended family has been involved and how they might provide support; whether self-help groups for the family exist in the community; and whether each person in the family has a friend outside of the family system. The family should be encouraged to develop appropriate distance from the schizophrenic patient. Within the family environment, hostile, critical, and emotionally overinvolved attitudes have been shown to be related to relapses (Lukoff, Snyder, Ventura, & Nuechterlein, 1984). Problematic behavior of both family and patient needs to be openly discussed. Family members should be taught how members can tell when the patient experiences overstimulation or agitation; a plan for handling such an occurrence should be agreed upon by everyone, including the patient.

Typically, the family may be in conflict, wanting to protect the patient while simultaneously wishing to be free of him. Torrey (1983) believed that most schizophrenics eventually do better living away from home, just as normal grown children do. This is a decision that should be made carefully, and the NPT should help the family locate resources such as halfway houses and sheltered workshops. The decision for the patient to emancipate from the family should not be made until the patient has been stabilized medically for some time.

Thus, the NPT can take a very active role with the family of the chronically ill person. By operating from a psycho-educational, rather than a pathological family model, the nurse can provide support and education to help both the patient and family deal with the problems incurred by a major psychiatric illness.

## DEVELOPING A PRACTICE FOR THE CHRONICALLY ILL

While relatively rare at this point, developing a private practice for the chronically ill (whether mentally or physically ill), holds great potential for nurses. One way such a role could be developed is through contractual relationships between the nurse and community health systems. The nurse might function as a psychiatric liaison consultant for such agencies as nursing homes, hospices, home health care services, and mental health care agencies. Within this role the NPT might carry cases requiring skilled psychiatric intervention and also serve as a consultant to staff.

The nurse might also develop collaborative relationships with a private psychiatrist and/or psychologist. Through such relationships, referrals can be shared back and forth, as, for example, when a patient needs medication adjustment and supportive monitoring. In fact, good back-up and linkage systems with supportive professionals and agencies are most important. It is unrealistic to think that private practice with the chronically ill can be developed in isolation.

An NPT with research interests in this area might write a grant to study how nursing therapy for families with a chronically mentally ill member affects rehospitalization rates. Certainly, it could be demonstrated that nursing care for these patients is more cost effective than the present and more haphazard system in which many patients and their families are left unsupported in the community.

In conclusion, the NPT who enters this domain of practice needs to be a skilled, creative, and flexible practitioner. Treatment with these patients is often less traditional than the typical one-hour session. The NPT must be willing to modify the structure and process of her treatment sessions to the special needs of these patients and families. She should be willing to make home visits, develop educational materials for families, and learn about community resources. Furthermore, the NPT needs to believe that providing supportive care is a legitimate contribution to the quality of life for chronically ill individuals and families, and experience personal satisfaction in providing such service.

# REFERENCES

Anderson, C., Hogarty, G., & Reiss, D. (1980). Family treatment of adult schizophrenic patients: A psycho-educational approach. *Schizophrenic Bulletin*, 6(3), 490–505.

Appleton, W. (1974). Mistreatment of patients' families by psychiatrists. *American Journal of Psychiatry*, 131, 655–657.

Bassuk, E., & Gerson, S. (1978). Deinstitutionalization and mental health services. *Scientific American*, February, 238, 46–53.

Chapman, J. (1966). The early symptoms of schizophrenia. *American Journal of Psychiatry*, 112, 225–251.

Hardin, S., & Durham, J. (1985). First rate. *Journal of Psychosocial Nursing and Mental Health Services*, 23, 9–15.

Hatfield, A. (1978, September). Psychological costs of schizophrenia to family. *Social Work*, 356–359.

Howells, J., & Guirguis, W. (1984). *The family and schizophrenia*. New York: International Universities Press.

Kahn, M. (1984). Psychotherapy with chronic schizophrenics. *Journal of Psychosocial Nursing*, 22, 20–25.

Kane, C. (1984). The outpatient comes home: The family's response to deinstitutionalization. *Journal of Psychosocial Nursing*, 22(11), 19–25.

Kreismain, D., & Joy, V. (1974). Family response to the mental illness of a relative: A review of literature. *Schizophrenic Bulletin*, 10, 34–57.

Loomis, M. (1985). Levels of contracting. *Journal of Psychosocial Nursing*, 23(3), 9–14.

Lukoff, D., Synder, K., Ventura, J., & Nuechterlein, K. (1984). Life events, familial stress, and coping in the developmental course of schizophrenia. *Schizophrenia Bulletin*, 10(2), 258–292.

Rowan, F. (1980). *The chronically distressed client: A model for intervention in the community*. St. Louis: Mosby.

Schmolling, P. (1983). A systems model of schizophrenic dysfunction. *Behavioral Science*, 28, 253–265.

Sullivan, H. S. (1953). *Interpersonal theory of psychiatry*. New York: W. W. Norton.

Torrey, E. (1983). *Surviving schizophrenia: A family manual*. New York: Harper & Row.

# Chapter 20
# The Child As Patient

*Joyce Torpey*

The rapid decline in the American birth rate which occurred between 1960 and 1976 has been reversed; according to the National Center for Health Statistics (1982), there were 69 births per 1000 women between the ages of 15 and 44 in 1980. There are more children and young adults in the United States today than at any other time in history. More than half of the United States population is now under 25 years of age. Though the exact number of emotionally disturbed children is unknown, it is estimated that 10% of this age group requires mental health services—approximately ten million children and youths (Allen, 1978). These statistics suggest that the number of children requiring treatment from NPTs will grow over the next decade.

## GUIDING FRAMEWORK IN TREATING CHILDREN

Unless a nurse psychotherapist (NPT) wishes to severely restrict her practice, an eclectic approach is indicated in assessing and developing treatment approaches to children. No one model of psychotherapy fits all conditions of children; thus, a reasonable variety of psychotherapy techniques is an asset. Individual, group, and marital therapy; parent education; and drug therapy are approaches that may be necessary in treating children. Regardless of the NPT's particular treatment approach, a developmental frame of reference is useful. At the core of psychological development is the process of establishing a sense of self, i.e., of separating and individuating (Mahler, Pine, & Bergman, 1975). Thus, the primary objective of treatment is to promote growth, understanding of one's self and others, and the development of a separate and individuated person.

## Separation and Individuation

Problems with individuation are frequently the basis of children's and adolescents' difficulties that bring them into treatment. Moreover, children's and parents' fears and conflicts over independence and individuation often provoke behaviors that inadvertently foster dependence. (For example, children who do poorly in school are usually more fearful of growing up than of failing, as is commonly thought.) Unfortunately, since children who are brought for therapy frequently are failing, parents and teachers typically rally around to help, but in doing so may actually foster dependency and inhibit the child's growing up.

The aggressive child or adolescent is also one who is often having difficulty separating and individuating. Aggression, when controlled and in the service of ambition, can promote separation and maturation. Through the use of aggression, the child can demonstrate strength to reach out into the world and to exert his character. Children who are termed "aggressive children" and are brought into treatment, however, are typically using aggression as a defense to the exclusion of other defenses. Such aggression is perceived as obnoxious by others and interpreted as a demand that they become involved with the child. It is engaging and, as such, promotes dependency.

Parents of children with problems in individuation frequently have difficulty letting go of their child. Their conversations with their children are typically characterized by persistent questioning of the child who responds with vague, petulant answers, which in turn prompts further questioning by the parents. This cyclic pattern, if not interrupted by the NPT, fosters further dependence by the child, further invasive questioning by parents, and feelings of anger in all.

## Other Developmental Issues

In achieving individuation, the child proceeds through sequential steps of growth and development. Each phase has its conflicts, strengths, and weaknesses. In addition, the normal course of childhood produces many stresses: the losing of a tooth, the birth of a sibling, the favorite teacher announcing her pregnancy, or the death of a pet. The child's response to ordinary, yet stressful, childhood events is affected by and reflects his progress in separation/individuation (Mahler, Pine, & Bergman, 1975); cognitive development (Piaget & Inhelder, 1969); and development of psychic structures (Freud, 1966). These models of conceptualizing the child's development are useful in understanding the child's adaptation to life stresses and avenues for giving guidance, support, and education to both the child and parents. The family context of an event, including the history of other important family events, religious views, economic factors, and cultural values also influence the child's responses and adaptation to stressful and developmental events.

Caution must be taken not to view the response of children to normal developmental events or stresses as necessarily pathological. A case example may help to illustrate when a normal developmental event becomes not only a traumatic but also a pathological experience.

> John was an 8-year-old who was brought into treatment by his parents. He was often beat up at school, believed no one liked him (including his teachers), had aggressive tendencies, and was quite immature in peer relations. His parents described their relationship with their son as becoming increasingly critical and frustrating.
>
> Five weeks into treatment John's gerbil died. Although the death of a pet is a common experience for many children, for John its impact was severe and its potential for being incorporated into his pathological perception and adaptation great. His initial response was one of withdrawal. Shortly thereafter, the symptoms that prompted his treatment grew severe. John seemed frightened; he believed he was to blame for the death of his gerbil and even "deserved it."

John's loss was a normal developmental stress. His reaction and lack of healthy adaptation, however, was significant in relation to existing pathological conflicts. The intensity, as well as the length of his reactions, indicated to the therapist that this experience could and should be used in the therapeutic hour to promote growth through a reworking of the conflicts in the here and now.

This episode offered the NPT an opportunity to work with John on his distorted beliefs about himself and his world that caused him so much pain and conflict. His parents were guided in ways to provide support, understanding, and love; his thoughts and feelings on loss were explored with particular attention to his role in such events. The NPT reinforced that he was not always in control of, responsible for, or deserving of bad or sad things that happened in life. The therapist reinforced that sometimes very bad things happened to very good people.

## Ego Support

In addition to a developmental perspective, the NPT who works with children also actualizes an ego-supportive model. To have the undivided, individual attention of an understanding and accepting adult for 45 minutes every week promotes stability for the child-patient. Holding to an established pattern also promotes better ego functioning by encouraging the child to channel emotion and by providing an acceptable forum to discharge anxiety.

> Brian was a 7-year-old boy whose parents sought treatment for him because he "was having difficulty in school." Although his grades were adequate and not of concern, he was aggressive with other children. Ironically, it appeared that he caused trouble in order to make friends, or at least some contact, with others. Other children tended to pick on him and he was often the victim of group ridicule. Brian complained no one liked him.
>
> Since the family had recently moved from a distant state, Brian had attended two schools in the past year. Both his parents worked and he was tended to after school by a teenage babysitter; he had had three sitters in the past year. Brian also had a 2 year-old sister who was cared for by an older woman in the woman's home.

For Brian the overall framework for therapy was ego-supportive. The stressful events of the previous two years—starting school, the birth of a sibling, a major family relocation—promoted feelings of abrupt separation, a lack of control, and anxiety. With the help of a nurturant, consistent therapist, who listened and attended to Brian's needs, his feelings of anxiety lessened throughout the course of treatment. Prior to each therapy session Brian made a ritual of filtering water through the coffee maker to make both a pot of hot water and a pot of coffee. This act promoted a sense of control and mastery of his environment. It also provided him an opportunity for adult support and assistance when necessary. His ritual culminated in child and therapist sipping a hot liquid, which was a nurturing, shared experience, and one that promoted verbal communication. The NPT encouraged Brian to express his feelings and concerns. Those feelings were accepted, talked about, played about, and at times channeled to promote self-awareness, limit the destructive effects of his actions on interpersonal relationships, and diminish anxiety. His sense of control, as well as positive feelings about himself, grew over the course of treatment.

## Structure and Limit-Setting

Setting limits and establishing structure within the therapeutic relationship is another major aspect of the overall framework in treating children. Guidance that is firm, but not rigid, promotes reality-testing, decreases anxiety, and enhances the development of the therapeutic relationship. Although some flexibility in scheduling treatment sessions may occasionally be necessary, the time, location, and characteristics of therapy should remain as consistent as possible. Moreover, certain rules about appropriate behavior should be explicitly stated. The NPT does not allow harm to self, the child, or furnishings since such permissiveness fosters anxiety. If sessions are consistently nonproductive, there may be too many limits on the child's activity; if sessions tend to be scattered, there may be insufficient limit-setting.

## OTHER ISSUES OF CONCERN WHEN WORKING WITH CHILDREN

A developmental perspective that recognizes individuation, ego-support, and structure as primary therapeutic concerns will provide the NPT with an overall framework to direct therapy with children. Other important therapeutic issues are confidentiality, resistance, lying, silence, and self-disclosure.

### Confidentiality

Confidentiality is as important in working with children as with adults. The importance of this issue parallels the child's age; with adolescents it is an area of special concern. Although parents are privy to assessments and recommendations intrinsic to their involvement in the treatment program, all parties should be aware that there will be no reports of any family member's verbal exchanges. If necessary, the NPT can arrange a joint session of all family members who might benefit from direct exchange of thoughts and feelings. Otherwise, the only information exchanged without regard to confidentiality is that concerning patient safety, i.e., suicidal/homicidal ideation or plans of running away. The NPT directly tells children that if an issue like this arises, the child's safety will be her major concern.

### Resistance

Rarely does a child or adolescent seek mental health services; rather, children are brought for problems displayed in every aspect of their lives—home, school, and social settings. Children, especially adolescents, don't usually believe they have a problem. The NPT can view this as a form of resistance that can be treated initially by framing the objective of treatment away from the issue of the young person as the problem. A second approach to dealing with the early resistance of young people involves a new definition of freedom. Freedom is not doing whatever one wants, but rather is the ability to recognize and use options within a given circumstance. To help the young patient understand this freedom, the NPT can explore options that exist within the treatment session. Other approaches to diluting resistance include using humor and self-disclosure. However, the NPT must be cautious that the use of humor and self-disclosure do not identify her as a young person herself. Children and adolescents are distrustful of adults who try to act younger.

Dealing with the resistance of the child is illustrated in the following example:

> Diane was a 14 year-old-girl brought into treatment by her parents for consistently poor grades in school. Her parents felt she attended school for social reasons only. They reported that Diane daydreamed frequently, moved through friendships quickly, and was a "tough-talker." Prior to beginning therapy, Diane was suspended from school for hurting a handicapped child while "horsing around" at school. Diane's future goal was to be a "mud-wrestler!"

In the early sessions of treatment, Diane was not verbally spontaneous, and spoke so softly it was difficult to hear her. She sat with her leather jacket on, arms crossed, and made little eye contact. In each session, Diane did not speak to the NPT with ease, and the NPT felt as if she were "pulling teeth."

Much of Diane's defiant behavior was based on her struggle to develop autonomy and initiate separation from her family. Diane's family was characterized by poor boundary development; it was not clear where autonomy was allowed and where it was not. Her parents frequently invaded her privacy and sabotaged her emerging autonomy by robbing her of experiences through detailed and persistent questioning. Diane also perceived therapy as another of her parents' attempts to control her. If the NPT had asked for minute details or repeatedly questioned Diane beyond what was spontaneously offered, she might have felt violated or controlled, thus increasing her anger and resistance.

Diane's passive-aggressive behavior was protective; what she did not understand was that her silence and minimal answers put others in the position of demanding more answers and, therefore, of continuing to "invade her." As with all early resistance in working with children and adolescents, the NPT did not handle this by interpretation or direct attempts to eliminate it.

## Lying

Most NPTs working with children and adolescents eventually encounter the child who lies. Early in treatment such behavior can be handled as resistance; it is neither interpreted nor directly confronted. The NPT can acknowledge to the child that although confiding in strange adults can be scary, some topics can be discussed without feeling danger. Moreover, as the child comes to know and trust the NPT, lying as a form of resistance should decrease.

Once a therapeutic relationship has been established, lying may stem from the child's sense that the NPT is asking too many questions or being too authoritarian. Lying may also be reconstitutive and indicate where problems exist. Commonly such lies serve as a defense against feelings of inadequacy and a poor self-image. Lies about how wealthy or successful parents are typify reconstitutive lying.

Vague answers or non-answers (i.e., "I don't know" or shoulder shrugs) are also maneuvers that children use to keep adults at bay. If this behavior is not a part of a larger pathological picture, such as sociopathic behavior, the therapist can examine her own invasive posture. In the therapeutic process, the young person can also be taught ways to manage interpersonal communications in which he feels invaded. The NPT can help the child develop a sense of control by reviewing options in the here and now and taking action. This frequently leads to the young person's coming to understand that he can limit questioning if he finds it invasive by offering communication in an active, rather than passive, manner.

## Silence

Silence is another issue that holds special importance in treating children and adolescents. It can be very anxiety-provoking. The young person must be given time to think and respond, but silence must be monitored closely. The art of storytelling is a tradition that may prove valuable when a child is anxiously silent. Just as myths, folklore, and history have been passed verbally through generations while captivated children sat at the feet of their forefathers and mothers, storytelling continues to humanize the therapist and to establish a shared experience between the NPT and child. A story can be developed around any issue demonstrating the affects of emotion and problem-solving techniques. For example, the NPT might begin with a generalized opening such as "Once there was a boy who. . . ."

## Self-Disclosure

Self-disclosure is an important issue when working with children. It is not uncommon for a child to ask the NPT personal questions. The context of the questioning is important in determining a therapeutic response. The child may really be seeking to develop a peer-level friendship; and though some self-disclosure is advantageous, this type of friendship is inappropriate.

Questioning by the child may also signal that the young person is resisting self-exploration. Such questioning tends to focus on the therapist, directing attention away from the self, and promoting little sharing on the child's part. There is also questioning of the therapist that signals an interest in knowing the therapist's position; this may enhance reality-testing. An approach to gaining an understanding of the reasons behind the child's questioning and selecting an appropriate response is to ask the child to share four or five thoughts prompting the question before the NPT decides if and how the question should be answered.

## THE NPT'S RELATIONSHIP WITH PARENTS OF CHILDREN IN TREATMENT

It is generally accepted that children's parents and the family environment have more impact on mental health than any other aspect of their daily lives. (See also Chapter 22.) Therefore, the parent(s) must be included in the child's treatment. A treatment contract that is usually helpful is one that establishes that the child will be seen once a week individually and the parents twice per month as a couple. If an alliance is not established with the parents, they may discontinue treatment. Parental sessions are also valuable opportunities to share nonconfidential information. With their regular involvement, their child's strengths and weaknesses, and most importantly how they may assist in the treatment, can be reviewed. If the NPT establishes a treatment plan for the home, as well as for sessions, she can make use of parent sessions for feedback and re-evaluation of the home plan. Through this process the NPT can identify and dilute parental resistance.

Typically parents will present a united front, claiming that the child who is brought for treatment is the only difficulty and frustration of their family life. Often, however, it becomes clear that the marriage is suffering. Since the status of the marriage has a major impact on the quality of parenting, NPTs must become skilled at working on marital and parental issues interchangeably. (See also Chapter 24.) It is helpful for the NPT to acknowledge the considerable pain and mourning that the loss of the "perfect" child triggers for parents, and to emphasize that as parents and the most significant adults in their child's life, they are crucial in the treatment process.

# COMMON FAMILY DYNAMICS DISTURBANCES

A child who is brought for treatment frequently reflects several problems in family dynamics. The issue of boundaries is often an important one. In the family with an identified child/patient, intergenerational boundaries and authority are not stabilized; and separation and triangulation may occur. Children may hold more powerful positions than parents. Moreover, rules are used, misused, and abused; these rules may promote punishments that foster projection of blame and denial of self-responsibility. The enforcer of a family rule becomes the "bad guy" while the value of the rule and the responsibility of the rule breaker are often forgotten.

The adolescent who breaks curfew highlights this clearly. The typical parental response is to ground the child from going out for a specific period of time. In essence, the child is pulled into the home with severe limits on his independence. The teenager may project the blame for his mistake onto a friend whose watch stopped, the parent who had a difficult day and is therefore reacting harshly, or some other person or external event. The teenager grows angry with the parent who inflicts a punishment without seeing any need to change his behavior or recognize how rule-breaking of this type actually reinforces dependence. The NPT can point out the pattern of these dynamics when they occur in working with parents to establish rational and consistent sets of rules and consequences.

# DESIGNING A PHYSICAL TREATMENT ENVIRONMENT SUITABLE FOR CHILDREN

Setting up a treatment environment that is physically suitable to children requires special consideration. (See also Chapter 8.) Combination office and play areas are most practical; some demarcation of each area is helpful, but not always possible. The entire area must be safe; valuable items that might be inadvertently damaged should be removed. Toys that promote creative play are essential. Such toys might include a doll family, puppets, hero figures, animal figures, play dough, and paper and drawing supplies. Two board games that promote creativity and verbal communication are the "Talking, Feeling, Doing Game" by Richard Gardner and "The Ungame" by The Ungame Company. The use of food in treatment is an individual consideration.

# SUGGESTED INTERVENTIONS
# SPECIFIC TO CHILDREN

There are no single interventions that are helpful in every case nor major issues that are always serviced by a particular intervention. There are, however, techniques that this nurse psychotherapist found to be useful and which are offered as suggestions to other NPTs.

After establishing the initial contract, the child's interests and method of recreation can be discussed easily without provoking anxiety. The NPT can also begin to assess age appropriate involvements, strengths, thought processes, attention span, intellectual capacity, and peer relations through these early discussions. The NPT should address the reasons for which the child came into treatment, being watchful not to push the child too much. It is important that the NPT not enter power struggles over problem identification; as mentioned previously, most young people do not feel they have a problem. Often the only problem they can initially identify is being hasseled by their parents. If this is the case, the NPT can take this opportunity to reframe the nature of therapy.

Two dangers that one must avoid in the treatment of young people are creating more resistance and skewing information by being preoccupied with determining normal and abnormal behavior. Resistance usually stems from an NPT's authoritarian attitude and persistent questioning. The NPT can create a nonjudgmental atmosphere in which she shows interest in the child as a person. The NPT should communicate that she wants to get to know the young person and that her patient's input is important. Ownership and control of the sessions should be shared by the NPT and patient.

With younger children (i.e., early school age), more direction may be necessary. Many young children do not have the capacity to engage in dialogue with adults. Play therapy will probably be the treatment of choice; a formal mental status examination provides an initial assessment.

Storytelling, drawing, and projective techniques are invaluable in assessing and treating a child's problem areas. Also, there are a number of psychotherapeutic games on the market ("Talking, Feeling, Doing Game," and "The Ungame," for example) that are quite useful in working with resistant children. NPTs working with children are encouraged to explore and try these aids. Assigning tasks to children and/or parents to accomplish between sessions is also an excellent method for identifying resistance, providing an opportunity to practice what has been gained through insight, and promoting learning and self-observation outside the treatment hour.

For the family that lacks continuity and for individuals who need help to develop ego consistency, the NPT can search for the history of events. She asks in detail about another time when a similar event happened and the time before that. It can be carried further by asking parents to include similar events from their own life and families of origin. This will be difficult at first, but eventually the parents and child will learn to pay attention and become skilled at discovering patterns themselves. This technique allows the parents and/or child to process their own behavior, thus promoting a sense of control and decreasing family and child anxiety.

## SUMMARY

No one theoretical framework would serve the 10 million young people in need of mental health care, nor would one approach adequately treat the conditions of all children found in a private practice. However, fostering a holistic view of patient care and developing an eclectic approach to the diagnosis and treatment of emotional disorders of children is the NPT's forte. By maintaining a developmental perspective, and ego-supportive and limit-setting interventions while remaining vigilant to issues especially important in treating children, NPTs can improve the mental health of children and their families.

## REFERENCES

Allen, R., & Cartier, M. (Eds.) (1978). *The mental health almanac.* New York: Garland STPM Press.

Freud, A. (1966). *The ego and the mechanisms of defense.* New York: International Universities Press.

Mahler, M., Pine, F., & Bergman, A. (1975). *The psychological birth of the human infant.* New York: Basic Books.

National Center for Health Statistics. (1982). *Health, United States, 1982.* (DHHS Publication No. PHS83-1232). Washington, DC: U.S. Government Printing Office.

Piaget, J., & Inhelder, B. (1969). *The psychology of the child.* New York: Basic Books.

# Chapter 21
# The Patient with
# a Learning Disability

*Anne J. Wells*

Although disagreement exists over the number of persons with a learning disability, the nurse psychotherapist (NPT) is likely to treat a child (or adult) affected by such a deficit at some point in her practice. Figures concerning the incidence of these problems range from 1% to 40% of all children in the United States; a conservative estimate is that about 10% of all boys and girls under 18 have some form of learning disability (Silver, 1979). Boys are more likely than girls to have learning disabilities, with the reported ratio of boys to girls ranging from 4:1 to 9:1 (Silver, 1979). It is important to recognize and help learning-disabled children and their families not only because the children are at risk for problems as children, but also because they frequently experience problems later in life, including poor self-esteem, underachievement, faulty social adjustment or failure, delinquency, or psychopathology (Cantwell, 1980; Sechzer, 1977; Silver, 1979).

Mental health professionals now recognize that a number of children (as well as adolescents and adults) have difficulty learning and behaving in socially acceptable ways (Horowitz, 1981; Shelly & Riester, 1972; Wood, Reimherr, Wender, & Johnson, 1976). Often learning difficulties cluster with other symptoms and these have been labeled in various ways, such as minimal brain dysfunction syndrome (Cantwell, 1980; Sechzer, 1977; Silver, 1979) and specific learning disabilities (Brutten, Richardson, & Mangel, 1973; Lerner, 1976).

Not all symptoms occur in every child, and authors have focused upon specific learning disabilities, hyperactivity, and attention deficits. For example, Silver (1979) discussing minimal brain dysfunction syndrome, listed the primary findings as one or more areas of specific learning disability, the secondary finding as hyperactivity, and/or distractability, with short attention span (approximately 40% of cases), and the tertiary finding as emotional problems.

Sechzer (1977) listed eight common symptoms of children with minimal brain dysfunction: hyperactivity, incoordination, impulsivity, decreased attention span, impaired learning and memory, anhedonia (diminished intensity of pain and pleasure and decreased responsiveness to positive and negative reinforcement), increased attention and concentration in response to amphetamine or amphetamine-like drugs, and an increased incidence of electroencephalographic abnormalities.

Cantwell (1980) described three primary symptoms of attention deficit disorder with hyperactivity: attentional difficulties, excessive motor activity, and impulsivity. He also noted, however, that there may be such associated symptoms as specific developmental disorders, negativism, lability of moods, low frustration tolerance, low self-esteem, lack of response to discipline, and antisocial behavior.

Recently researchers have suggested that children with specific learning disabilities without hyperactivity have a different disorder than children with attention deficits, hyperactivity, and learning disabilities (Acherman, 1981; Delamater, Lahey, & Drake, 1981; Lahey, Stemtniak, Robinson, & Tyroler, 1978; Whalen, 1983). The *Diagnostic and Statistical Manual III* (1980) classified learning disabilities as either (a) attention deficit disorder (with or without hyperactivity) or (b) specific learning disabilities (e.g., developmental reading disorder, developmental arithmetic disorder, developmental language disorder, and developmental articulation disorder). This chapter discusses the treatment of children and families affected by specific learning disabilities.

## THE CHILD WITH SPECIFIC LEARNING DISABILITIES

Children with specific learning disabilities have problems that often confuse and mystify parents and teachers. Even recognizing the possibility of a learning disability can sometimes be difficult, since these children usually have average vision, hearing, and intelligence. However, they often perform poorly in school, seeming not to learn as other children their age. When parents bring these children to the NPT, their complaint most often is one of confusion and frustration; the child "seems bright enough but just is not doing well at school (or at home)." Further questioning often reveals that these children's performance fluctuates greatly. They may do some tasks well but be terrible at others (e.g., when under time pressure). They may not seem to understand instructions, get them confused, or not remember them at all. Some of these children may be clumsy, have difficulty writing, copying, playing physical games, or doing other tasks that require physical coordination. Some may be always on the move and distractible. Still others may be withdrawn and shy. Some seem socially inept, often speaking or behaving inappropriately with other children and adults.

Descriptions elicited from parents, teachers, or even the children themselves may reveal three patterns of school behavior. In the first two, the child is disruptive in school, taking the forms of clowning and teasing or not following rules. In the third pattern, the child is described as being lazy or unmotivated to work. What parents, teachers, and even the children themselves often do not recognize is that thinking of the child as bad or lazy may result from seeing the child do well some of the time but not at other times. However, these children may have difficulty controlling their behavior because of specific learning disabilities.

Information processing and learning are complicated processes in which a number of problems can arise. In brief, information is first gathered from the sensory apparatus, organized, and interpreted; often this includes integrating information from several sensory sources. Information is then stored in either short or long-term memory where it can be acted upon either immediately or later. Problems can occur at any point in this process, making learning or acting upon information very difficult. Learning disability therapists divide learning disabilities into receptive problems (difficulty acquiring information) and expressive problems (difficulty in appropriately expressing information that has already been learned). Some of these will be discussed to provide a general understanding of the problems these children face when trying to learn and to interact with others.

## Perception

One category of learning disabilities involves problems in perceiving stimuli correctly. Children can have either auditory or visual perceptual problems, or both (Brutten, Richardson, & Mangel, 1973). Children with auditory perceptual learning disabilities may have difficulty processing, recognizing, or integrating auditory information. They may be either unable to distinguish certain sounds or may consistently confuse certain sounds. For example, a child may be unable to distinguish between "cow," "how," or "now." If the child incorrectly hears or confuses words, he may make mistakes that baffle him and his teacher since neither understands the source of the difficulty. Children with auditory perceptual disabilities may also have difficulty distinguishing figure from ground. Such children may be unable to focus upon important auditory information and find themselves easily distracted by "irrelevant noise." Such children may have difficulty listening to a teacher reading a set of instructions because they are distracted by other sounds.

Children with auditory perceptual difficulties may require more time than other people to process auditory information, placing them at a distinct disadvantage. If a child cannot process information at the speed of ordinary conversation, or at the speed his teacher reads instructions, he does not comprehend what he is hearing. He may still be processing the first sentence while the speaker has gone on to the second or third sentence. The child must either miss part of what has been said or hope the speaker will repeat the message.

Children with visual perceptual learning disabilities may actually see things wrong. Information may be processed in such a way that the child receives incorrect spatial positioning of figures, words, letters, or numbers. The percepts may be seen backwards, upside down, sideways, or confused in some other manner. For example, children may see, and subsequently reproduce, letters backwards (e.g., "d" for "b") or whole words backwards (e.g., "nar" for "ran"). They face several problems. First they must learn when they make "mistakes," after which they must try to compensate for these mistakes. Sometimes they do not learn what is happening, only that they "missed the math problem again." If a child reads "$1 + 2 = 3$" as "$3 + 2 = 1$," he may only learn that his answer is incorrect. If, however, he learns what he is doing wrong, he may have a chance to compensate for "errors."

These children may not finish tasks as quickly as other children. For example, the child following several steps to figure out whether a letter is a "d" or a "b," or if the word is "nar" or "ran," will need extra time. He may appear to be "slow" to teachers or parents who do not recognize the extra work required to accomplish tasks other children do with ease.

Children with visual perceptual disabilities can also have figure-ground problems. They may have difficulty focusing upon the relevant aspects of the visual field and not being distracted by irrelevant details. This child may find it difficult or impossible to focus upon a list of the math homework long enough to copy it from the board.

Visual spatial problems may also affect some children's ability to organize themselves in space. These children may be described as being clumsy and having such problems as knocking over their milk or "running into things." They may also have difficulty playing physical games that require running, dodging, or hand-eye coordination. Some children with visual spatial problems may also have difficulty with directions or with positions (e.g., knowing their left from their right). For some, visual perceptual skills may be so problematic that they may feel disoriented, off balance, or lost when dealing with large spaces.

## Integration and Interpretation

A second category of learning disabilities involves integration and interpretation of information from different senses (Brutten, Richardson, & Mangel, 1973). For example, when learning to read and write a child connects the sound for "dog" with the visual image and then moves his fingers to reproduce the visual image. Some children may have difficulty connecting these various pieces of information. Moreover, perceptual problems in one mode may make integration of information from different sources more difficult. For example, if a child sees the word "ran" as "nar," the sounds for "ran" might confuse him. Such confusion makes learning more difficult because the information from eyes and ears does not fit together.

A second aspect of integration and interpretation involves integrating information within a sentence, several sentences, several paragraphs, or over larger units such as chapters. Sequencing within a percept, sentence, or series of sentences may pose a problem. For example, some children may confuse the sequence of letters or numbers within a single percept (e.g., "gdo" for "dog" or "476" for "764"); this can also happen with words in a sentence, within sentences in a paragraph, or in other series of information. Children who confuse the order of words in a sentence may be confused about the meaning of the sentence. Others may have difficulty following a series of instructions (e.g., following the steps to solve their math problems, to do their homework, or to do their household chores). Some children may also have difficulty following the action in a story and understanding what events preceded or followed each other. For example, when questioned about why a boy in a story left home, a child may be unable to answer because he is unsure whether the boy left home before or after his dog was missing.

Another aspect of integration and interpretation is the ability to abstract. The learning-disabled child might experience problems in learning that "red," "blue," and "pink" are colors and thus be unable to use the concept "color" appropriately in thinking, playing, and discussions. Some children have difficulty understanding the connections between various pieces of information. For example, a child may understand what the fireman, policeman, and teacher did in a story but be unable to conclude that the thing they had in common was that they were "helpful." Such children seem to have all the right information but are unable to piece parts together correctly.

## Memory

A third category of learning disability involves memory (Brutten, Richardson, & Mangel, 1973). Children having difficulty with short-term auditory memory have difficulty in remembering what they hear. They may not be able to remember homework assignments that the teacher reads to the class unless the instructions are also written on the board or on an assignment sheet. They may also be unable to remember instructions parents give them about chores unless they have a list they can reread.

Children with short-term memory deficits often have difficulty with a series of instructions. Although they may initially seem to comprehend, they may forget how to complete tasks involving several steps (e.g., math problems, test-taking, storywriting). Also, although some children seem to remember and understand a set of facts initially, they are later unable to remember what they learned. These children go over things again and again before they can retain a set of facts or a series of instructions. Some interference in the transfer of information from short to long-term memory seems to occur.

## Acting on Information

A fourth category of learning disabilities involves expressive problems, the inability to express knowledge that has already been learned (Brutten, Richardson, & Mangel, 1973). Expressive problems can be either verbal or written. For example, some children have difficulty getting their fingers to make the shapes needed to write in a readable way. Given enough time they struggle until their writing is acceptable. But with a time limit they are faced with either turning in sloppy work or only part of the assignment. Other children have difficulty expressing their ideas verbally. Again, without time pressure many are able to organize their thoughts and words in order to express what they know. But under the pressure of a parent or teacher waiting for an answer, they may be unable to organize their thoughts quickly enough to answer. Teachers and parents often do not understand that these children fail only when asked direct questions or when not allowed time to organize what they want to say.

In summary, children with learning disabilities have specific problems with processing, retaining, and acting upon information. Sometimes they learn to compensate for these problems, but this almost always involves adding several checking steps or using additional information that other children do not need. For example, one child learned to look at an alphabet list on the top of the blackboard in order to check and correctly write "p" and "q" and "b" and "d." The additional steps worked until she entered a classroom with no alphabet list on the blackboard. Another child with auditory memory and sequencing problems could only do his homework when his teacher gave him a written assignment. If the teacher merely told the child the assignment, he was unable to remember or complete his work. He also repeatedly got into trouble at home because he "forgot" to do his chores. However, when his parents learned about his problems and provided him with a written list of chores, he was able to do them without difficulty.

Children with learning disabilities struggle with additional burdens that are often difficult for parents, teachers, and the children themselves to understand. These children often become frustrated with their fluctuating ability. At times, in order to deal with their frustration and anger at self, as well as to cover their real deficits, they misbehave. They may become "the bad kid," the "clown," or give up, failing to accomplish tasks given to them. Such behavior may distract others and themselves from the fact that they cannot complete some tasks. Often parents, teachers, or other children view them as "bad," "a cut up," "lazy," or "irresponsible" (or some combination of these) as a means of explaining their inconsistent performance. However, their inconsistent performance is not due to malevolent intent or lack of motivation, but to specific deficits in information processing ability. These children are not "dumb" or "retarded" but have specific problems that make learning or acting upon that learning difficult or impossible.

## TASKS OF THE NURSE PSYCHOTHERAPIST

The NPT's first task is to be alert to the possibility of specific learning disabilities as a problem. If this is suspected, she should help the family obtain learning disability testing from a qualified learning disability diagnostician. The NPT's second task is to work with the learning disability therapist, the child's teachers, and the family to develop ways to help the child and his family deal with the specific learning disabilities found. The NPT's third task is to help the child and the family deal with problems and issues that have arisen as a result of the learning disabilities. The NPT may carry out these tasks simultaneously.

## The First Task

When the NPT is asked to treat a family with a child having problems in school (or even an adult who reports having had difficulty in school), she should be alert to the possibility that learning disabilities may either be causing or contributing to the child's problems. Often parents seek treatment because their child is acting out in school or lacks motivation. Parents may say, "I know he is not dumb; he just acts up" or "He just won't work." Parents and teachers may assume that this is an emotional or family problem because the child does well some of the time. However, this poor performance may be related to a specific learning disability that may also be accompanied by emotional and family problems associated with the learning disabilities. Before the NPT assumes that the difficulty stems from an emotional or family problem, she should carefully evaluate the information the family is sharing. If the NPT has a reason to believe that learning disabilities may be involved, she should discuss this with the parents, refer them for appropriate diagnostic testing, support them while they obtain it, and help them to understand and deal with the results. Since learning disabilities are often not considered by parents and teachers, it is important that NPTs consider this possibility before beginning treatment for emotional and/or family problems.

Only after children's specific processing problems have been identified can the NPT help them to find other ways to learn and to deal with their difficulties. The child with learning disabilities can be given appropriate learning disability therapy and/or placed in special learning situations in school that take into account his specific problems, thus helping him to develop alternative strategies for dealing with them. The NPT can then help the family and child deal with the emotional and family problems related to the learning disability as the learning disability therapist and school personnel help the child learn in a more effective way.

In order to obtain learning disability testing, the NPT may need to help the family and child work through their fears about, and resistance to, testing. This can involve working to educate the family about learning disabilities; providing them with information about where to obtain testing; or helping the family change family patterns to allow the child to obtain the testing. Some families may only need to be educated about learning disabilities. Others need to work through fears and misconceptions before they seek appropriate care. Still others must change family patterns before they can allow the child to be tested.

Often families and children may not understand just what a learning disability is and may confuse it with being "retarded" or "dumb." They usually need specific information that stresses that only specific functions of the brain may be affected, resulting in specific learning problems for the child. Closely associated with the fear that the child is retarded are fears that the child will be stigmatized if diagnosed as having a learning disbility or placed in a special classroom. The NPT may have to help the family face this possibility and weigh it against the hope that accurate diagnosis and treatment will allow the child to get the specific help he needs. At times a family may need to be confronted with the fact that if their child does not receive the help he needs (both in terms of dealing with problems in learning and emotional problems that may have resulted), not only will the child's ability to learn and function continue to be a problem, but he may also face much more serious difficulties as he grows older and continues to fail.

The NPT may also need to be aware of and help the family change various roles the child may have taken on in the family. The child with learning disabilities may have become the "problem child," the "one who needs help," the "dependent one," the "lazy one," the "bad one," or the "family scapegoat." If the child's role helps the family deal with problems such as marital conflict or fears of intimacy between the parents, there may be considerable resistance to testing or treatment that could lead to a change in the child and subsequently in the family structure. For example, if a child's inability to learn facilitates an enmeshed relationship in which one parent is overinvolved with the child and underinvolved with the spouse, suggestions for testing, therapy, and subsequent change may be met with considerable resistance. Thus, not only does the NPT need to be sensitive to the child's role in the family, but also to family issues that support the status quo.

## The Second Task

After the child's learning disability has been tested and diagnosed, the NPT needs to work with the learning disability therapist, the child's parents, and sometimes the child's teachers on a plan to help the child and family deal with the learning disability. Because the nurse has traditionally been able to act as a coordinator of health care, the NPT can work with parents and professionals in a variety of ways. These range from being the coordinator of care to being the professional who facilitates the family's dealings with other professionals and systems. The NPT can share knowledge of where to obtain testing and help the family deal with the other agencies and procedures involved. This can be done either by providing encouragement to the family or by becoming directly involved with the agencies. After the child's evaluation has been completed, the NPT can continue to work with the family and the other professionals to develop a specific plan of care.

The nurse needs to learn the exact nature of the child's specific deficits and how these affect the child's performance both at home and at school. By finding out what is wrong the nurse can help the family focus on the effects of the problem and possible solutions. For example, if a child has visual perceptual and sequencing problems but deals with auditory information well, the family might read important information (e.g., homework assignments or instructions) to the child and check written work for possible sequencing errors. Or if a child has auditory memory deficits but can deal with visual information well, the family and teachers might write down important instructions (e.g., assignments, chores, and grocery lists). They can also repeat verbal information until the child acquires it in a manner that does not imply the child is not paying attention or is dumb. For the child with verbal expressive problems parents and teachers can provide time for the child to organize answers to their questions. After asking questions, parents and teachers might be encouraged to make such comments as, "when you have thought about it, let me know what you've decided."

Several benefits accrue by helping the family to work out alternative ways of dealing with problems involving the child's specific deficits. First, this assistance clearly tells the family that there are specific problems, rather than general retardation. Second, the message is given that everyone can help the child and family cope with the problem. Finally, working out a plan to deal with the child's specific deficits provides both information about and considerable opportunity to work on problems arising from the learning disability.

## The Third Task

Several problems may arise as the result of learning disabilities, both within the child and within the family. One of the first issues which usually needs addressing is the child's and the family's fears that the child is "dumb." Everyone needs to be told directly (usually several times) that having a learning disability is not synonymous with being retarded. Sometimes focusing attention on things the child does well brings a more balanced view of the child's capacity. The technique of helping both the child and family acknowledge strengths can also facilitate work on other areas (e.g., increasing self-esteem or changing self-view and family roles).

Another possible problem is parents' guilt that they "didn't know" or "didn't get the right help soon enough." Both parents and siblings may also have guilt about how they have treated the child in the past. Parents may feel guilty about having a "damaged" child; both parents and siblings may feel guilty about their roles (either real or imagined) in the child's becoming "damaged." Such guilt may affect parents or siblings who worry that their anger or jealousy of the child may have damaged him in some way.

Parents' initial guilt that they didn't know what was wrong, or how to fix it, can be discussed and the parents helped to understand that they were not equipped to understand what was happening. Parents can be complimented on getting the testing and the help they need now, as well as be encouraged to continue the work that has been started. Initial guilt can be used to help focus upon what can be done for the child. Other feelings of guilt need to be expressed and worked through. Since the causes of learning disabilities may range from genetic factors to prenatal, perinatal or birth traumas, and early illnesses (Sechzer, 1977; Silver, 1979), each member of the family may need to realistically evaluate the basis for such guilt.

The NPT should understand that sometimes parents may need to mourn the loss of their "nondisabled child." They may need to spend a period of time grieving for what they feel might have been. This is similar to the sadness and grief that parents experience when they learn about a child's chronic illness or physical handicap. During this period, parents may look ahead and think about the child's leaving home, perhaps going to college, finding work, and establishing a family of his own. They may envision these developmental tasks as either difficult or unattainable for the learning disabled child. The nurse needs to listen carefully to discern what the parents (or the child) are actually experiencing and help them deal with the loss that is being experienced.

The NPT should help the family and child deal with changes in the child's self-view, problems of low self-esteem, and changes in the way the family views the child. In addition to family therapy, the child may need individual therapy in order to change his view of himself and increase his self-esteem. The nurse can focus specifically upon what happened to the child as a result of the learning disability; how people reacted to him; how he explained these reactions and his problems to himself; and what he thought and felt about himself. As both the child and the nurse gain understanding of the child's self-view, she can correct his misunderstandings about himself. If the child is working concurrently in an educational program designed to help him learn or is in learning disability therapy, the nurse can help him focus upon his gains and encourage him to try new ways of doing things. The nurse can remind him that new ways take time to learn, and she can support him as he works to overcome his difficulties.

Closely linked to working through self-view changes is the task of resolving specific problems that arose as the child and the family tried to deal with the learning disability (e.g., depression, school phobias, or acting out in school). Although these may have resulted from the child's attempt to deal with an overwhelming situation, the nurse will need to help the child, teachers, and the family explore feelings and thoughts, as well as change behaviors and reactions that may have become habitual. The nurse will need to seek change as she helps the child and family understand that this behavior resulted from an attempt to deal with what might have been an impossible situation. However, sometimes before change is possible, children may need to deal with their feelings and reactions to learning about their disability. For example, children who are depressed in response to their failure and the reactions of others to that failure may also need an opportunity to express their frustration and anger at both self and significant others who did not "understand and make it better." For other children, especially those who have used anger to deal with their problems, initial explanations and understanding of what was happening may be followed by a period of sadness and depression. The child may need help in facing his disappointment in himself and in others who did not understand and help him sooner.

Equally important is working with the family to develop new ways of relating to and viewing the child. Often family patterns and roles need to be altered. Some families may be eager to change their view of the child from "he's dumb" to "he's got a problem, but we can work it out." In such cases, the nurse may need only to focus upon the family's old patterns of dealing with the child and his problem, actively engaging the family in new problem-solving approaches. However, some families may not be able to accomplish this task readily. They may resist changing family patterns and roles in a way that helps the child to grow, learn, and deal with the disability. If this is the case, the family may need to work on family issues before they can handle change in the learning disabled child.

A child's learning disability may have shaped a family's way of dealing with family problems. For example, the learning disabled child may have become the "bad" or "dumb" child. This role may hide or distract from a parent's inability to provide adequate emotional support, care, and involvement. The child's need for parental support may help a parent deal with separation anxiety or the fear of being left alone. Or a parent's overinvolvement with the child may help the parents deal with marital conflict or fears of too much marital intimacy. In such cases, it may be necessary to help the family resolve these problems before the learning disabled child can leave his assigned role and grow. At this point, the

NPT may have to focus upon family problems in order to facilitate changes for the child.

NPTs who remain alert to the possibility of learning disabilities in children or adults assist persons and families to obtain appropriate testing. They support those struggling with the learning and emotional problems that such disabilities present, thus doing much to improve the mental health and quality of life for those so afflicted.

# REFERENCES

Acherman, P. T., Oglesvy, P. M., & Dykman, R. A. (1981). A contrast of hyperactive, learning disabled, and hyperactive/learning disabled boys. *Journal of Clinical Child Psychology, 10,* 168–172.

American Psychological Association. (1980). *Diagnostic and statistical manual* (3rd ed.). Washington, DC: American Psychological Association.

Brutten, M., Richardson, S., & Mangel, C. (1973). *Something's wrong with my child.* New York: Harcourt-Brace-Jovanovich.

Cantwell, D. (1980). The treatment of minimal brain dysfunction. In G. Sholivar with R. Benson & B. Blinder (Eds.), *Treatment of emotional disorders in children and adolescents* (pp. 457–482). New York: Spectrum.

Delamater, A. M., Lahey, B. B., & Drake, L. (1981). Toward an empirical subclassification of learning disabilities: A psychophysiological comparison of hyperactive and nonhyperactive subgroups, *9,* 65–77.

Horowitz, H. (1981). Psychiatric casualties of minimal brain dysfunction in adolescents. In S. Feinstein, J. Looney, A. Schwartzberg, & A. Sorosky (Eds.), *Adolescent psychiatry: Vol. IX* (pp. 275–294). Chicago: University of Chicago Press.

Lahey, B. B., Stemtniak, M., Robinson, E. J., & Tyroler, M. J. (1978). Hyperactivity and learning disabilities as independent dimensions of child behavior problems. *Journal of Abnormal Psychology, 87,* 333–340.

Lerner, J. (1976). *Children with learning disabilities,* (2nd ed.). Boston: Houghton Mifflin.

Sechzer, J. (1977). The neonatal split-brain kitten: A laboratory analogue of minimal brain dysfunction. In J. Maser & M. Seligman (Eds.), *Psychopathology: Experimental models* (pp. 308–333). San Francisco: Freeman.

Shelly, E., & Riester, A. (1972). Syndrome of minimal brain damage in young adults. *Diseases of the Nervous System, 33,* 335–338.

Silver, L. (1979). The minimal brain dysfunction syndrome. In J. Noshpitz & S. Harrison (Eds.), *Basic handbook of child psychiatry: Vol. II* (pp. 416–439). New York: Basic Books.

Whalen, C. D. (1983). Hyperactivity, learning problems, and the attention deficit disorders. In T. H. Ollendick and M. Herson (Eds.), *Handbook of Child Psychopathology.* New York: Plenum Press.

Wood, D., Reimherr, F., Wender, P., & Johnson, G. (1976). Diagnosis and treatment of minimal brain dysfunction in adults. *Archives of General Psychiatry, 33,* 1453–1460.

# Chapter 22
# The Patient Needing Improved Parenting Skills

## Kathryn R. Puskar

Patients requesting help with parenting skills pose a special challenge to the nurse psychotherapist (NPT). They may express concerns about a toddler's defiant behavior or about an adolescent's blatant rebellion. They may say, for example, "I need to know how to deal with my three year old;" or complain "I am at my wits end with my teenager!" Parents may also request help because of their own anxiety or depression in dealing with a child or because of a sense of helplessness in guiding a child through a crisis.

In this chapter, parenting is first defined as a process and a structure. Second, several common parenting problems encountered by the NPT are explored. Finally, because adolescence is such a bewildering time for parents and children alike, the chapter examines specific interventions for the NPT who counsels the parent of an adolescent.

## DEFINITION OF PARENTING

Parenting is a process involving transactions between parent and child throughout life. It requires continuous adaptation to changes within the self as a parent, parallel to and in transaction with, changes in a child. Certain developmental milestones highlight problems in the transactional processes of parenting. For example, the mother of an infant faces the challenge of a new role or the mother of an adolescent markedly changes her parenting style to adapt to her ambivalent offspring. Parenting has two major dimensions: (1) the dimension of changes in the self as a parent; and (2) the dimension of changes in the child. Parent-child conflict should be expected; it is universal.

Parenting is also a structure, having various components organized into patterns. To some extent, structure establishes the relationships between components. Parenting today reflects a variety of structures: single parent families, adoptive parent families, foster parent families, and adolescent parent families, to name only a few. According to Naisbitt (1984), one direction for the next century is a move from a society of "either/or" characteristics to a society of multiple options. The structure of traditional parenting has moved to parenting structures having multiple options, giving rise to many parenting problems. Since every parent and every child is unique, the concerns of one parent may not parallel the concerns of another. Nevertheless, certain common and ubiquitous problems affect most parents, regardless of parental structures or individual characteristics.

## COMMON PARENTING PROBLEMS

In order to identify common parenting problems that an NPT encounters, the author designed a study that included a review of selected literature on parenting problems and a pilot survey of NPTs. The literature review uncovered two main categories of general references on parenting problems. The first category included "parent-child relations" while the second was "parent education." Within the category of "parent-child relations," 267 references in one psychiatric library in Southwestern Pennsylvania were found. References in this category dealt with parenting infants, toddlers, adolescents and even considered parenting the aged. References also discussed parenting structures (e.g., parents who are divorced or gay, or parents with stepchildren or foster children). Although the NPT cannot possibly be familiar with all these references, special resources should be available for parent education and support. Kiley's (1984) *Keeping Kids Out Of Trouble* and Dreikurs and Grey's (1968) *Logical Consequences: A Handbook of Discipline* are good examples of such general references.

Under the category of "parent education," 198 references were found in the same library. This category included information on parenting problems in general and parenting problems associated with special needs of children. Books varied from what to tell one's child about birth, death, and illness, to what to tell children about sex and drugs. Various guides helped parents to deal with such problems as deafness; retardation; cerebral-palsy; stuttering; and the latch-key, gifted, autistic, or hyperactive child. Books offered guidance on how to "parent," "father," or "talk with kids." References provided instruction to parents for understanding developmental spans, for example, "Guide to the First Three Years."

The author concluded that much consumer information is available to provide parenting guidance. That so much consumer information exists suggests that parenting is one of life's critical tasks and also underscores the heavy burden parenting often becomes. Even though many resources exist for parents, the NPT will still see patients who request help with common parenting problems (e.g., exhaustion, parental disagreement, and children expressing general family anxiety), and especially if facing unique problems or the stress of developmental crises.

The selected overview of nursing literature that deals with parenting problems examined the role and function of nurses as parent counselors. Maternal-child nursing literature refers extensively to the role of the nurse in teaching, particularly prenatal classes. There is limited reference to teaching parenting skills or the role of the nurse beyond the postpartum period. Several nurses, for example, developed an assessment guide to identify women prenatally who might need extra assistance in providing parenting to promote their infants' well-being. Maternal-child nursing literature also covers the topic of parenting in relation to such special problems as adoption, fatherhood, chronic illness in children, and adolescent parenting.

The brief overview of psychiatric nursing references that address parenting problems examines the NPT's role in the area of parent counseling. Highlights of psychiatric nursing literature suggest that nursing interventions with parenting problems are addressed in various ways. Psychiatric nursing tests provide little specific information on parenting per se; others address the role of the NPT as a family therapist (Robinson, 1983).

Haber et al. (1982) and Koldjeski (1984) describe primary prevention activities of psychiatric mental health nurses geared towards parenting. Haber et al. (1982) devote a chapter to promoting mental health in families. Koldjeski (1984), in focusing on prevention, emphasizes the role that mental health professionals have in working with families, and in identifying high-risk groups. In relation to teaching parenting skills, the author states, "Parents have not been fully helped to understand relationships between the need to create family social environments that are conducive to promotion and maintenance of mental, emotional, physical, and social health and development of self-hood and self-actualization for themselves and their children" (p. 242). The mental health framework in this book emphasizes the role of psychiatric mental health nurses in providing leadership for the development of therapeutic activities designed for prevention of problems.

Burton (1983) provides an excellent resource for the NPT in her discussion of counseling strategies for helping parents. She suggests that due to the inherent stresses of parenthood, every parent is potentially abusive at times; she advises psychiatric nurses to provide parents with factual information, support, and reassurance about growth and development. Intervention strategies for nurses include assessment of parent skills and parent-child fit. She advocates teaching parenting classes at the junior high school level and conducting prenatal classes and new parent groups. Stuart and Sundeen (1983) devote a chapter to preventive mental health nursing and emphasize the role of psychiatric-mental health nurses in developing self-help groups for parents. They suggest that nurses must assess new parents' vulnerability to develop maladaptive coping responses.

To summarize, common parenting problems and teaching of parenting skills by NPTs are not extensively discussed in the nursing literature. Many references to the importance of parenting in the prevention of mental health problems in both parents and children are made. However, few specific interventions with parents who may need help are offered by nurse authors or researchers.

The second part of the study surveyed NPTs to identify parenting problems. This portion of the study explores the common problems of parenting by means of a specially designed questionnaire distributed to NPTs functioning in various outpatient mental health facilities. The NPTs were asked to identify the most common problems a therapist encounters in treating patients who need parenting skills.

The NPTs reported that parents sought counseling most often for: (1) setting limits; (2) learning how to discipline; (3) understanding realistic behavior of developmental phases; (4) learning coping resources for single and working parents (see Chapter 23); and (5) dealing with adolescents. These findings would seem to suggest that the NPT should bolster her knowledge and expertise in these five areas. For example, she might utilize her knowledge of developmental life phases to teach parents the anticipated tasks of each phase. She should be skilled in teaching parents about the purposes and techniques of limit setting. Generally, interventions by the NPT are built upon both parent and child perspectives of parenting.

# INTERVENTIONS OF
# THE NURSE PSYCHOTHERAPIST

Since parenting is a process having two perspectives, that of the parent and of the child, the interventions of the NPT who counsels the patient needing parenting skills may be classified into two broad areas. The first area considers interventions focusing on the parent perspective of the interaction and the second area deals with interventions geared to the child perspective of the interaction.

Generally, parent-perspective interventions focus upon: (1) teaching parents active listening; (2) teaching parents good observational skills; and (3) strengthening parents' skills through competence building. The following case study provides such an example.

A 27-year-old working mother of two children, ages 3 and 1, sought counseling because she was "afraid I might abuse Billy." Mrs. M. reported to the NPT that when she arrived home from work, Billy refused to be held by her. He preferred staying with the babysitter. Mrs. M. related that Billy would "yell at her" and "refused" to eat supper. Mrs. M. was encouraged to listen actively to what Billy was telling her through his behavior. Mrs. M. was asked to observe Billy's nonverbal action. Mrs. M.'s parenting skills were strengthened through education about the tasks of toddlerhood and Billy's separation anxiety related to her working out of the home. In working with Billy's mother, the NPT respected Mrs. M.'s role as a parent.

In her role as consultant, the NPT should encourage parents to avoid the pitfalls of being "too preachy," "too authoritarian," or "too permissive." NPT interventions related to the child perspective of the interaction are rooted in the nurse's knowledge of a child's growth and development. The NPT should examine the goal of the child's problematic behavior. What is the purpose of the behavior? What needs of the child are being met through the problematic behavior? Do the parents understand the purpose of the child's problematic behavior? In planning interventions, the NPT must keep both the parent and child perspectives in mind. (See also Chapter 20.)

## Interventions with the Parent of an Adolescent

The NPT who counsels the parents of an adolescent must first assess the parent's perception of the adolescent's problem since a discrepancy often exists between what the parent perceives to be a problem and what the adolescent perceives. Next, the NPT should ask the parent to explore concerns of his or her own adolescence. An offspring's adolescence may stir up the parent's own unresolved issues of adolescence.

Specific interventions of the NPT with the parent of an adolescent can be classified into parental interventions addressing the three "A's" (autonomy, ambivalence, and affect) and the three "C's" (consistency, communication, and clarity of rules/consequences) of adolescence. The NPT may ask the parent to discuss each of the three "A's" in relation to the adolescent. How does the adolescent exert autonomy? Does the parent realize that the adolescent is greatly ambivalent about becoming an adult or remaining a child? The NPT should ask parents to comment on their own observation of the adolescent's affect and nonverbal communication.

The NPT can also discuss with parents the major issues of the adolescent stages of development in order to help them understand the adolescent's behavior, typically including unpredictability, competitive struggling, and testing of limits. Adolescents, in teeter-tottering between dependence and independence, need support and external controls of their behavior as they test the limits of control systems. Adolescents also need to find firm, rational boundaries to test; thus they need to know what is expected of them and to receive honest feedback about their behavior. The adolescent who is experiencing uncertainties, conflicting emotions, ambiguity about role, and struggles with the ambivalence of independence and dependence, does not need the added burden of a family environment consisting of ambiguities, double messages, unclear rules, and uncertainties.

Another set of NPT interventions involves counseling parents regarding the three "C's" of adolescence (Puskar, 1981). The first "C," consistency, is paramount. Helping parents understand that the adolescent needs consistency because of the many issues and conflicts operating during the adolescent phase of development is a primary intervention. A fundamental adolescent attitude toward parents or authority figures was described by Stone and Church (1951):

> If the parents intervene in the child's life, they are snoopy and domineering; if they do not, they are unfeeling and neglectful. Since parents are damned if they do and damned if they do not, it appears that they cannot win. This does not mean that what they do is of no importance . . . adolescents need something to rebel against, as a way of telling themselves that they are grown-up, and parents have to provide limits as something tangible for the adolescent to fight, as well as for his own security (p. 277).

The second "C," communication, is also essential in parenting an adolescent; parents need to provide clear messages and avoid double messages. Therefore, the NPT must often help parents become aware of their own needs and feelings in their efforts to communicate clearly with the adolescent. Many times the adolescent refuses to talk, withdraws, or acts out. Parents should expect such behavior.

The third "C," clarity of rules and consequences, is important in helping the parents of an adolescent. In two-parent families, parents should be helped to concur on major rules and consequences if there is disagreement between them. The NPT can be a neutral sounding board and arbiter for parents and adolescents to reach agreement about sensible rules that protect the adolescent and the rest of the family. Often anxious parents, who are themselves conflicted, devise irrational or inconsistent rules. The adolescent needs to know exactly what the rules are and the consequences of breaking rules. Discussion of options/choices should be emphasized with involvement of the adolescent in decisions about rules/consequences. The NPT can ask parents to reflect on the following questions:

1. How consistent are you with your adolescent?
2. How you would rate and describe your communication with your adolescent; and
3. Outline consequences you have as a parent if and when the adolescent breaks rules.

In conclusion, the NPT is in a unique position to help patients improve their parenting skills. In counseling a parent of an adolescent, the NPT should: (1) discuss the common tasks of adolescence; (2) explore the "context" of the adolescent's problem; (3) sensitize the parent to the real struggle of dependence-independence that the adolescent encounters; (4) increase the parent's understanding of the adolescent's need to establish a separate identity; and (5) encourage the parent to consider the three "A's" and "C's" of adolescence. Through education of the adolescent's parents, the NPT can support them and strengthen their parenting skills. When parents become more comfortable with themselves and their adolescents, they achieve greater competency in parenting.

The NPT may be exposed to such parents' remarks as "How would you know? You are not the parent of an adolescent." Whether the NPT uses self-disclosure or not, she should empathize with the parent, acknowledging that it is difficult to be the parent of an adolescent, particularly in today's society. Adolescence is a time of accentuated change. Parents of adolescents parenting in a society with many options, have a difficult task, resulting sometimes in their need for counseling. Nurse psychotherapists can offer a holistic perspective of parents and children, sound knowledge of growth and development, and a wellness perspective to such patients.

# REFERENCES

Anthony, J., & Benedek, T. (1970). *Parenthood: Its psychology and psychopathology*. Boston: Little Brown.

Bobak, I., & Jensen, M. (1984). *Essentials of maternity nursing*. St. Louis: Mosby.

Burton, P. (1983). Parenting. In H. Wilson & C. Kneisl (Eds.), *Psychiatric nursing*, (2nd ed.). (pp. 321–341). Addison-Wesley.

Dreikurs, R., & Grey, L. (1968). *Logical consequences: A handbook of discipline*. New York: Meredith.

Erikson, E. (1959). *Identity and the life cycle*. New York: International Press.

Haber, J., Leach, A. M., Schudy, S. M., & Sideleau, B. F. (1982). *Comprehensive psychiatric nursing*. New York: McGraw-Hill.

Kiley, D. (1984). *Keeping kids out of trouble*. New York: Warner.

Koldjeski, D. (1984). *Community mental health nursing: New directions in theory and practice*. New York: Wiley.

Miller, D. (1983). *The age between adolescence and therapy*. New York: Jason Aronson.

Naisbitt, J. (1984). *Megatrends*. New York: Warner.

Puskar, K. (1981). Structure for the hospitalized adolescent. *Journal Psychiatric Nursing and Mental Health Services, 19*(7), 13–16.

Robinson, L. (1982). *Psychiatric nursing as a human experience*. Philadelphia: Saunders.

Skerrett, K., Hardin, S., & Puskar, K. (1983). Infant anxiety. *Maternal-Child Nursing Journal, 12*(1), 51–60.

Stone, J., & Church, J. (1957). *Childhood and adolescence*. New York: Random House.

Stranik, M. K., & Hogberg, B. L. (1979). Transition into parenthood. *American Journal of Nursing, 79*, 90–93.

Stuart, G., & Sundeen, S. (1983). *Principles and practice of psychiatric nursing*, St. Louis: Mosby.

# Chapter 23
# The Working Mother as Patient

*Karen Skerrett*

Census data in 1981 indicated that over half of America's mothers are employed outside the home. Even in two-parent families, 45% of the women with children under six and 54% with children under eighteen are employed (Hacker, 1983). Recent projections suggest that in the next ten years, approximately 75% of the nation's mothers will work outside the home. Clearly, parenting children—even preschoolers—is no longer a *raison d'etre* to remain at home. Who are these women who balance dual roles? What concerns and problems can the NPT help them work through? Since these mothers do not form a homogeneous group, their reasons for working, their families and social contexts, and their resources are as diverse and unique as their personal dynamics. However, several characteristics set working mothers apart from other women; thus they pose particular challenges to the nurse psychotherapist who treats them.

## THE DILEMMA OF THE WORKING MOTHER

While every mother is a working mother, the work environment that absorbs a woman's energy also shapes the nature of presenting issues and the status of her well-being. Although the full-time homemaker commonly works in several places simultaneously (for example, the community, the school, and the church), the mother employed outside the home adds these responsibilities to the demands of her job. Allowing for the impact of marital status, economic level, age, and other important variables, one distinguishing feature creates a sisterhood among employed mothers—work overload. This woman, juggling all the balls in the air at once, has been appropriately labeled "Superwoman."

The impact of the Feminist Movement, as well as other societal forces that have thrust women into more egalitarian home and work roles, have contributed to an interesting dilemma. While greater access to jobs has offered a new-found freedom, women did not anticipate that the results of this freedom could be as enslaving as their former restrictive roles. While women found themselves free to work outside the home, they were also bound by slower changing norms requiring that they still maintain a pivotal role within the home. While many highly visible and articulate spokespersons have identified the plight of employed women and urged them to stop buying the myth that they can "have it all," most working women remain conflicted. This conflict derives largely from their attempts to integrate these competing values and to establish a lifestyle that is intrapersonally congruent, rather than one which is imitative of media hype, the values of a neighbor, or the ambitions of a supervisor.

Whether the mother is of blue or white collar status and whether her income supports the family or elevates it into a higher tax bracket, virtually every employed mother's chronic complaint is that of too much to do in too little time. In this author's practice, these women present with three major mental health problems: guilt, depression, and stress.

## WORKING MOTHERS' PROBLEMS: GUILT, DEPRESSION, AND STRESS

The guilt feelings triggered by attempting simultaneously to be a competent parent and employee are commonplace. Many working mothers share this feeling, as reflected in the glib comment of one, "Guilt comes with the territory!" Despite the emergence of liberated, consciousness-raised men determined to coparent, the reality is that the woman still schedules orthodontia appointments, recalls when and what vegetables the baby last ate, and balances complicated calendar schedules of children's and parents' daily activities.

Many working women patients have identified the insidious nature of this guilt and its effects on their lives. One of the clues to this guilt is the ease with which women take on this "central switchboard" function at home. As one patient put it:

I like to think that I'm beyond feeling guilty; yet when I made myself late for work last week because I was baking a tin of brownies for my daughter's girl scout troop party, I knew that those brownies were my peace offering. I made them because I was feeling guilty about turning her down to chaperone a troop outing.

Many of these women have grown up with the model of a traditional stay-at-home mother; they apply those standards (with varying degrees of consciousness) on top of whatever maternal model they have carved out for themselves. Further, because they often hold an unrealistic picture of the mothering provided by their stay-at-home counterparts, they are sometimes convinced that their working somehow deprives their families. Rather than view their son's mismatched school outfit as a sign of his independence, the guilty mother often worries that his appearance will be judged as a sign of her neglect. The guilty mother may automatically blame herself and her unavailability for everything from her son's low grades to her daughter's not being asked to the freshman mixer. When unrealistic self-expectations are applied to work performance as well, the resultant guilt can be incapacitating. One patient, a self-confessed workaholic, described herself as constantly walking a tightrope:

Everything I do results from my attempts to minimize the guilt I'll feel in one place or the other. I have to give myself a peptalk and countless reassurances if I turn down my boss's offer of a new accounting project in favor of coming home an hour earlier every night; or I put myself through unbelievable mental gymnastics to resist a family outing in favor of a weekend business trip.

Given what they are trying to accomplish, it is not surprising to find that working mothers experience frequent bouts of depression. Very often, this depression is felt to "come out of nowhere," and to "hit with a strong force." Many are hard pressed to connect the appearance of these depressed feelings with their current life circumstances. What they do say with great consistency is that they feel depressed because they are "not doing a good enough job" in managing their lives. They characteristically blame themselves, but rarely their mates, children, or coworkers—even when this is appropriate.

Working mothers most often experience depression as either listlessness and sadness or as a more agitated out-of-control state. Many fluctuate between both poles. Depressive symptoms are often equally present among women who hold jobs through conscious choice and those who must work for economic reasons while wanting to remain at home.

The final problem that characterizes working mothers is stress. Every working woman treated in this author's practice has experienced overwhelming stress after her usual methods for dealing with it have failed. Many of these women identify that they are stressed, but few recognize specific symptoms or signs of the stress. They are thus unable to identify the limitations this stress has placed on their daily functioning. Working mothers commonly overlook recurring headaches or generalized body aches and pains as signs of stress. One patient, for example, admitted she could not remember the last day she was "headache free." When asked about such problems as insomnia, heart palpitations, angry or tearful outbursts, and forgetfulness, almost every patient recalls some or all of these symptoms regularly.

Eating disorders are also a common problem among working mothers. Many patients, not necessarily symptomatic at the time they seek help, have a history of anorexia or bulimia. If they have not been treated for these conditions previously, food continues to be a highly charged issue. Several mothers keep a tenuous control on their eating disorder out of a concern to "set a good example for the children." Many working mothers have poor nutritional habits and seldom associate their tension levels with over-consumption of coffee, minimal breakfasts, and sugar-laden lunches.

For many women, entering the work world has meant slipping into patterns of alcohol consumption similar to those of their male coworkers; thus it is essential to question carefully the drug habits of working-mother patients. One woman confessed to feeling frightened when she realized she was pushing to keep up with male colleagues' liquor intake during business luncheons, just as she was used to competing with them in other areas. Several of this author's patients have identified the availability of drugs, particularly cocaine, as a reality they never had to confront when they were home full-time with children.

Feeling out of control, expressed by virtually all of the working mothers in this NPT's practice, is often denied until some shocking event disrupts their tenuous equilibrium. For some women this event is the serious illness of a child, being passed over for work promotion, blacking out after an evening of social drinking, or being physically abused or abusive. As one patient said:

> I knew I was anxious all the time but I just kept thinking, "I'm gonna get it all together tomorrow or next week." Don and I were fighting a lot more, but I knew I'd really lost it the night he pushed me up against a door and I started throwing things at him.

It is no coincidence that what frequently brings these women to therapy is their feeling of utter exasperation, of feeling totally out of control. While one cannot generalize about complex processes, several dynamics tend to characterize working mothers who are used to feeling in control and in charge of themselves. They are goal-directed self-starters, often motivated to the point of feeling driven. Their high expectations, not only of themselves but of others, often leave them disillusioned because they and others cannot possibly measure up to their standards. They want to do a good (often perfect) job of everything: working, mothering, partnering. They find compromise in any area difficult.

Many working-mother patients are only or oldest daughters. Frequently, they have had close relationships with their fathers and are aware that they identify with and admire their fathers as role models. Some sustained an early loss in their immediate family, resulting in their assuming a position of responsibility for siblings or household chores on a regular basis. All of these women did what was necessary with characteristic competence; through therapy, however, they come to realize the costs of this earlier time. Even in the absence of early loss, they have typically been the children of parents with high expectations. These parents often placed inordinate or age-inappropriate responsibilities upon their daughters; or, because of their own emotional limitations, they required their children to nurture them. The individual profiles of patients in this author's practice support research findings on family backgrounds of achieving women, particularly the family dynamics detailed by Miller (1981).

## TREATMENT ISSUES OF WORKING MOTHERS

How can working mothers best be helped when they present for treatment? What, if any, are the salient features of their therapy? Regardless of the theoretical orientation of the NPT, treatment often focuses upon the dynamics of repressed/suppressed dependency needs. Working mothers need to learn how to accept help, to become more interdependent, and to determine when to rely upon others and when to rely upon themselves. The key problem working mothers are struggling with is self-acknowledgment of aspects of their own dependency, which is often complicated by cultural and self-imposed expectations for "superwoman" performance. The NPT can help the patient to define the struggle as one in which she can become self-possessed, as opposed to other-possessed. Woodman's (1982) *Addiction to Perfection* applies a Jungian perspective to the treatment of eating disorders, but her discussion of the perfection-istic complex can also serve as a stimulating metaphor with which to analyze the problem of working mothers.

## CASE STUDIES OF WORKING MOTHERS

Two cases, one of a working mother seen in individual therapy and one seen in conjoint and family sessions, illustrate the central issues of guilt, depression, and stress discussed above.

Kathy M., was a slim, attractive single mother in her mid-thirties. Highly articulate, she had been working as a trouble shooter/consultant for a Fortune 500 company. She sought therapy for periodic depression and a sense that her 'life was getting out of control.'

The youngest daughter of a highly successful real estate attorney, she was the 'token boy' among three female siblings. From an early age, Kathy was her father's recreational companion and business confidante. She knew from school years on that she was being groomed to take his place in the law firm. While disappointed when she chose a business career over law, he nonetheless remained her ardent advocate and mentor throughout her early career. When she was in her mid-twenties, her father suffered a series of serious financial setbacks, was hospitalized for several manic-depressive episodes, and finally committed suicide when Kathy was 32. At that time, she resumed her earlier role of family caretaker and rallied to her mother's side, hampering her own ability to deal with her private grief and loss.

Kathy had been married once to a 'workaholic who couldn't deal with his feelings.' The marriage lasted six years and produced one daughter. At the time she entered therapy, Kathy had just relocated to Chicago to be closer to her mother and to end an affair with a married man. She asked for help to maintain that separation, to deal with her daughter, and, more importantly, to cope more effectively with her mother's escalating demands.

By her own description, Kathy could barely be said to have a life of her own. She was constantly rebounding between high pressure at work and at home. She was forever juggling expectations from clients, from her daughter, or from her mother. Even though Kathy could negotiate problems between powerful corporate executives, she remained helpless to deny others' demands on her in her personal life, despite their increasing costs to her self-esteem and sense of well-being.

Highly verbal, she participated in sessions as if on a job interview. Always cordial, poised, and well-prepared with an agenda, she opened every session with a question about the NPT's welfare. She had a difficult time identifying and expressing feelings; the most painful material was responded to with a few tears that she quickly tissued away.

Her denial of any feelings of helplessness or being overwhelmed and her limited ability to appear even slightly incompetent hindered a therapeutic alliance. No matter how desperate she professed to feel or how unable she was to deny her mother's demands, scheduling time for her therapy never became a priority. She frequently cancelled sessions to attend business meetings; and when the NPT refused to juggle her appointments to accommodate her out-of-town trips, she gave up her sessions with little complaint. The more expressive, affective sessions in which she moved into threatening material were usually followed by her cancellation or a perfunctory session in which she interviewed the NPT about highly intellectual, abstract questions.

Kathy was seen for ten sessions. During that time she made some gains in her ability to detach from her mother and to deal more assertively with her demands. She had some success in interrupting her impulsive response patterns and in assessing her own feelings before responding. Kathy said she felt support for her ability to deal with her daughter and gained alternative ways to manage her periodic depression. She stopped treatment ostensibly because she felt "mostly better" and because of scheduling conflicts. However, her stopping treatment could be viewed as a function of negative transference and the threat that delving into her feelings posed to her self-esteem. For Kathy, feeling came at the expense of doing.

This case illustrates the importance of the NPT as role model. One of the critical elements the nurse therapist brings to the treatment of such patients is the ability to operate competently without compromising herself in the process. A vital part of Kathy's ability to take possession of herself and to act on her own behalf was the NPT's adherence to a clear and definite structure (such as time, place, and fee) for the therapy. Through the NPT's unwillingness to compromise essential requirements of a therapeutically-structured climate, she demonstrated to Kathy in a concrete way how she might resolve the issues explored in the sessions' content, such as taking responsibility for her own feelings and setting limits on her mother's demands.

An important point for the NPT to take into account in her function as role model relates to her attitudes about working mothers. Frequently the therapist herself is a working mother and may identify with much of what her patient expresses. The NPT may be struggling with issues similar to those of her patients or may not have examined her feelings toward women managing multiple roles. It is crucial, therefore, that the NPT recognize the influence of counter-transference; ongoing clinical supervision is very helpful in this regard. (See also Chapter 9.)

The working mother's characteristic difficulty in setting aside time for herself manifests itself not only in problems establishing a therapeutic structure, but also in the identified patient who presents for therapy. This is often a child who comes to the NPT's attention either through direct referral by a parent or school official. Despite guilt feelings and difficulty admitting that her child is having problems, the working mother is often unable to acknowledge that she needs help and to set aside time to get it. She is usually more accustomed to taking care of someone else in her family. (See also Chapter 11.) Whenever possible, the NPT should include the family of a working mother in treatment because the problems of working mothers are so embedded in relationships with significant others (Gilligan, 1982). Moreover, research has clearly identified that dense family role responsibilities are associated with increased mental distress symptoms and that women with children have more mental illness than childless women or women who feel supported in their multiple roles (Woods & Woods, 1981).

For purposes of analysis, the dual career families this NPT has treated could be classified as being of two broad types: (1) those in which one parent assumes most of the responsibility for the quality of family life and for their children's welfare; and (2) those in which neither parent takes adequate responsibility. These types reflect the boundary problems of working mothers and are characteristic of many of these family systems.

In families in which one parent assumes major responsibility for parenting, the working mother typically is "over-responsible." This marriage is usually dysfunctional to some degree, with the father being physically or emotionally unavailable. Frequently the husband is devoted to his job. While his wife may be equally ambitious, she makes accommodations in an effort to compensate for his absence. Although inwardly resentful and angry, these mothers often do not enter therapy until one of the children acts out or the working mother becomes symptomatic.

In the second type of family, both mother and father could be described as absentee parents. They are either preoccupied with the stress of their jobs or are so personally limited that they do not have the intrapsychic resources to respond adequately to the needs of a child. The H.'s serve as an illustration of this type of family.

> The H. family was a young, upwardly mobile couple who had been married eleven years and had two preschoolers. Both very ambitious, Mr. H. was the vice president of a large urban hospital and Mrs. H. worked as an advertising executive. They came for therapy because of problems with their three-year-old daughter. They described Lisa as a challenge since infancy—very aggressive and highly verbal. They had recently begun to wonder if she were 'hyperactive.' Lisa's preschool teacher described her problems of getting along with the other children and her alternating anger and withdrawal. Lisa was difficult to discipline. The parents said Lisa had suffered from sleep disturbances since she was one-year-old; it commonly took them over two hours to put her to bed. They also expressed concern that they would have similar problems with their one and one-half-year-old daughter, Maura.

Both parents held highly ambivalent feelings toward each child; they talked continually about wanting what was best for their daughters but in reality spent very little time with either of them. When they began therapy, the daughters were in child-care from 7:30 A.M. to 7:00 P.M. and with a baby-sitter three to five nights per week while the parents attended professional or community meetings. When with the girls, the parents were usually so exhausted and burdened with guilt that they were unable to set limits or consistently discipline. A vicious cycle was thus established in which the children became more demanding and the parents more overwhelmed and unable to set limits.

Treatment first centered upon providing the parents with an outlet for their feelings of frustration. Mrs. H. particularly benefitted from being able to talk about her guilt over Lisa being 'unplanned' and about what she called 'my many nonmaternal feelings.' She was very critical of her high ambitions and felt 'terrible' when she preferred to be at work than with her children. She presumed no other mother had these feelings; her sense of increasing isolation kept her from seeking out and using the support of other working mothers.

Since Mr. and Mrs. H. were both aware that they had, to some extent, neglected their children, and that this behavior corresponded to their feelings of helplessness, they responded favorably to reordering their schedules. They each limited the number of evenings they were away from the children and built into their daily routines a small amount of family time that was mutually satisfying.

The NPT and the H.'s spent many sessions working on specific behavioral problems with Lisa. The H.'s began to feel that they had some options for responding to her other than withdrawal or force. Once they began to have positive experiences with each child, the guilt lessened and they found it easier to set necessary limits. Mrs. H. benefitted from suggestions on how to play with her children; not only did Lisa blossom in response to this new dimension of her mother, but Mrs. H. reported feeling better about herself once she stopped taking herself so seriously.

Mrs. H. had a tendency, just as at work, to want to be 'in charge' to the extent that she would sabotage her husband's attempts to take over, even if she were exhausted or unavailable. Mr. H. learned to be more assertive with his wife and their parental alliance eventually strengthened.

The NPT worked with the H. family for thirteen months, seeing them one time per week. While they were initially frightened about possibly discovering they were "bad" parents, their anxiety mobilized them into an early therapeutic alliance. They benefitted from a chance to vent their long-standing frustrations and to get the NPT's reactions to their concerns. The marriage was basically sound, although lacking intimacy. It soon became clear that neither partner could maintain a deeper involvement and that their busy professional and community lives were designed, in part, to maintain distance. For this reason, and also because they expressed little interest in altering their relationship, the NPT maintained a consistent problem-solving approach centered around the unique qualities of each child and the dynamics of the sibship.

At a six month post-termination call, Mrs. H. reported that they were maintaining the majority of family changes and that most importantly, Lisa's behavior alerted the family if they started to back-slide to old patterns and needed to take steps to readjust.

# CONCLUSION

The complex pressures affecting working mothers pose a challenge to the mother to cope adaptively and to the NPT to provide adequate assistance. The NPT whose practice revolves around the restoration of human wholeness is in an excellent position to offer an alternative model for the woman distressed by overwhelming and competing demands.

The three major problems experienced by working mothers in this author's practice were guilt, depression, and stress. The majority of these mothers had many unmet dependency needs and "overmothered" partly in an effort to avoid the expression of those needs. It is crucial for the NPT in working with these individuals and families to be aware of her own conflictual feelings and the ways in which they can be managed in dealing with transference and counter-transference dimensions of the treatment.

# REFERENCES

Bermosk, L., & Porter, S. (1979). *Women's health and human wholeness.* New York: Appleton-Century-Crofts.

Collier, P. (1982). Health behaviors of women. *Nursing Clinics of North America, 3*(3), 121–126.

Dery, G. (1982). An approach to the health assessment of women. *Nursing Clinics of North America, 3*(3), 127–135.

Foley, K., Hardin, S., & Skerrett, K. (1981). The dual career nurse: Working and mothering. *Point of View, 18*(1), 17–19.

Gilligan, C. (1982). *In a different voice.* Cambridge: Harvard Press.

Greenspan, M. (1983). *New approaches to women and therapy.* New York: McGraw-Hill.

Hacker, A. (1983). *Statistical portrait of the American people.* New York: Viking Press.

Jacobson, S. (1982). Psychosocial stresses of working women. *Nursing Clinics of North America, 3*(3), 137–143.

McBride, A. (1976). *A married feminist.* New York: Harper & Row.

Miller, A. (1981). *Drama of the gifted child.* New York: Basic Books.

Parker, J., & Drew, K. (1982). Women, work and health. *Occupational Health Nursing, 7*(2), 27–28.

Piotrkowsksi, C., Stark, E., & Burbank, M. (1983, November). Young women at work: Implications for individual and family functioning. *Occupational Health Nursing, 31*(11), 24–29.

*Statistical Abstracts of the U.S.* (1979). Washington: U.S. Dept. of Commerce, Bureau of Census.

Woodman, M. (1982). *Addiction to perfection.* Toronto: Inner City Books.

Woods, N. (1982). Women's health. *Nursing Clinics of North America, 3*(3), 113–119.

Woods, N., & Woods, J. (1981). Women and the workplace. *Health care of women: A nursing perspective.* St. Louis: Mosby.
Wysocki, L., & Ossler, C. (1983). Women, work and health: Issues of importance to occupational health nurses. *Occupational Health Nursing, 3*(11), 18-23.

# Chapter 24
# The Patient Experiencing Marital Conflict

*Ruth K. Weinstein*

Traditionally nurses have had opportunities to interact with individuals and families across the life cycle in a variety of settings and circumstances. Because of this exposure, nurse psychotherapists (NPTs) are uniquely qualified to work with families experiencing disruptions in functioning. Couples experiencing the crisis of marital conflict comprise a large component of nurse psychotherapists' practice. Therefore, nurses must develop a framework for working with couples experiencing marital conflict.

This chapter describes family systems theory and its application to nursing psychotherapy. In addition, assessing the level of marital conflict, setting realistic goals for therapy, and developing therapeutic strategies for intervention are explored. This is followed by a brief discussion of marital separation and divorce mediation. Throughout the chapter clinical examples are provided to illustrate cogent points.

## FRAMEWORK FOR PRACTICE

Bowen's family systems theory is derived from general systems theory and can form a useful framework for NPT practice. Bowen (1971) conceptualized a family as a system in which relationships exist between family members. He maintained that a reaction in one family member is followed by predictable reactions in the others, in a chain reaction pattern.

Within this system, repetitive relationship patterns occur (Weinstein, 1981).

The family is viewed in the context of three generations, not just in the present. A family history, or a genogram, is obtained to help the couple gain insight into its behavioral patterns and reactiveness over time. The couple is assisted to view themselves in three interlocking dimensions: (1) as a member of an extended family system; (2) as a part of a marital dyad; and (3) as an individual searching to define him/her self.

A crucial concept in Bowen's theory is the concept of triangles (three person system) as the smallest stable relationship system in a family. In periods of calm, the dyad is the twosome with the third party, or "thing," in a distant position. However, when tension increases in the dyad, one or both members "triangle in" a third party, leading to a decrease in the couple's anxiety without dealing directly with the problem. By diffusing the anxiety into one or more triangles, the conflictual situation is superficially stabilized and meaningful change is avoided. Triangles serve the purpose of externalizing the conflict and diverting it from its original source within the marital dyad.

The concept of triangling is particularly relevant to understanding marital conflict and the emotional processes that are present in the couple system. Guerin and Fay (1984) believed that understanding the existing triangles in marital conflict is essential to being able to define the dysfunctional process in the marital relationship.

Triangles may be extrafamilial (extramarital affairs, social network triangles) or intrafamilial (in-laws, children, stepfamilies, parents) (Guerin & Fay, 1984). As the therapist becomes aware of the underlying structure and function of the existing triangles, she can map out intervention strategies to alter the dysfunctional pattern. Throughout the therapy, the therapist assesses both the level of anxiety and its influence on the couple's relationship.

A second concept from Bowen's systems theory, differentiation of self, is crucial to understanding the individual and his/her functioning in the intense, emotional system of marriage. According to Miller and Winstead-Fry (1982), "Differentiation of self classifies all people on a continuum according to the degree of differentiation between their emotional and intellectual system" (p. 24). People functioning at a higher level of differentiation are able to make decisions based on intellect and judgment rather than on pure emotions, even in highly anxious situations. People functioning at low levels of differentiation live in a feeling-dominated, relationship-oriented world; they use most of their emotional energy seeking love, approval, and togetherness. Their relationships tend to be characterized by fusion rather than intimacy (Weinstein, 1981). People tend to marry people at the same level of differentiation, though one may appear more functional than the other. An example might be the highly successful businessman whose wife is agoraphobic. Her world becomes more narrow and restrictive as his becomes more expansive.

Though it may seem a paradox, the greater the individual's sense of self, the greater the level of intimacy without fusion she/he can obtain in an emotional relationship such as marriage. The higher the level of differentiation, the greater the amount of "solid self." The solid self is a reflection of one's beliefs, values, opinions, and life principles derived and refined over time. It is the foundation for one's ability to take an "I" position and make responsible decisions and choices. The "pseudo self" is that portion of the self that is responsive to emotional pressures in the relationship and will change as the situation changes. The pseudo self is not responsive to cognitive evaluation (Miller & Winstead-Fry, 1982).

There are other important concepts in Bowen's systems theory—multigenerational transmission process, family emotional system, sibling position, and cutoffs. However, these concepts will not be discussed here. The reader is encouraged to search out this information to have a more meaningful understanding of Bowen's family systems theory.

This author believes that family systems theory is directly applicable to nursing practice. Many years ago, Peplau spoke to the importance of nurses working with families and assisting family members to differentiate themselves from each other and from the nurse (Calhoun, 1982). Today, early in the nurse's education and clinical experience, she is encouraged to view the patient both as an individual and in the context of his/her family. The individual is conceptualized as a subsystem of the family. In striving to maximize the patient's potential, the nurse assesses, counsels, and teaches the individual and significant others in his/her life. Nurses interact with families from birth to senescence, focusing on strengths and potential. Knowledge of the wellness-illness continuum, anatomy and physiology, pharmacology, growth and development, and the behavioral sciences combine to give nurses a holistic view of persons.

Marram van Servellen (1984) stated that "the nurse is a change agent affecting the structure, process and communications of individuals through strategies of support and change interventions" (p. 97). She pointed out that nurses are in two simultaneous dimensions: providing support for patients, but also striving for change. Her description of support included the concepts of caring, concern, empathy, warmth, involvement, understanding, reassurance, and constructive criticism.

Change, however, is facilitated through planned interventions that challenge dysfunctional homeostatic mechanisms, myths, and rigidity in interactional processes. Change involves restructuring.

Master's degree programs in psychiatric-mental health nursing provide students with the theoretical and clinical expertise required for working with families. (See Chapter 4.) Certification as Clinical Specialists in Psychiatric-Mental Health Nursing and ongoing supervision support the nurse's accountability to consumers. Through education, clinical experience, and supervision, the nurse continues to refine the therapeutic use of self.

## SETTING REALISTIC GOALS FOR THERAPY

Framo (1982) correctly noted that most couples who become involved in marital therapy do so in hopes of changing their mates, not themselves. They are often convinced that their mates have some serious personality or emotional problem and are incapable of loving. The NPT must help the couple move from this rigid view of therapy and establish realistic goals. Short-term goals may focus on current situational stresses while long-term goals aim to restructure the marital system.

It must be noted that short-term goals are often easier to achieve than long-term goals, because of the universal phenomenon of resistance to change that has been defined as "all those behaviors in the therapeutic system which interact to prevent the therapeutic system from achieving the family's goals for therapy" (Anderson & Stuart, 1983, p. 24). Frequently, couples enter therapy to make the present situation more tolerable rather than to make major structural changes in the family system.

Anderson and Stuart (1983) urged the therapist to push for specific goals: "What do you each want in the relationship?" "What are you willing to settle for?" "What are you willing to change?" The therapist attempts to make the couple's covert goals overt by saying what they haven't said or by using appropriate metaphors to illustrate the ongoing process. Haley's (1976) approach is to avoid abstractions by focusing on specific behaviors in order to develop a directive for change. He stated that specific goals must be formulated.

Framo (1982) believed that couples must come to terms with their irrational expectations of marriage and of their spouses. These expectations are a synthesis of sociocultural and multigenerational influences. When a person marries, he/she marries both an individual and a family. Furthermore, one marries illusions and dreams of what one thinks the other is. It has been postulated "that mate selections are made with profound accuracy and, collusively, in two-way fashion. The partners carry psychic functions for each other, and they make unconscious deals" (Framo, 1982, p. 124). Marital therapy goals suggested by Framo include partners becoming:

1. more personally differentiated;
2. more understanding of each other;
3. aware and accepting of differentness;
4. aware that realistic needs can be met;
5. able to communicate clearly and openly;
6. more likeable and more enjoyable; and
7. able to deal directly with issues.

Therapists are urged to help the couple broaden their perspective without minimizing the presenting problem (Anderson & Stuart, 1983; Haley, 1976). This can be done by respecting the uniqueness of the problem being presented, but then normalizing it in the context of family life cycle events. Therapists can also clarify issues rather than focusing only on power struggles.

The therapist assists the couple in looking at the roles they assume in the relationship. When these roles are examined, particularly in the context of their stereotypical, rigid expectations, the couple has options for modifying or abandoning these roles. In this same manner, the couple can identify and alter patterns of behavior and reactivity learned in their families of origin and perpetuated in the current relationship. Perhaps one of the most important functions of the NPT is assisting the couple to see that they have options for change. It is the challenge of therapy to enlist the couple's adaptive ability.

## ASSESSING THE LEVEL OF CONFLICT

Guerin (1982) offered a four-stage paradigm for assessing the level of marital conflict. Stage I includes those couples with a minimal degree of marital conflict. These are couples whose marriages are basically sound, their problems are relatively superficial, and each spouse appears committed to the marriage. Although anxiety levels are elevated, anxiety remains within manageable limits, reactivity levels are relatively low, criticism is low, and credibility is high. Each spouse is able to focus on his/her own issues with limited projection onto the other. Couples in this group are usually in the early stages of marriage, experiencing some difficulty negotiating a transitional period.

Stage II is made up of couples who show active relationship conflict and are experiencing moderate levels of anxiety. They have difficulty focusing on themselves and have moderate levels of projection. Communication remains relatively open and the couple shows little difficulty in doing things together. Criticism levels are higher but credibility remains high as well. Frequently, this level of conflict exists in couples dealing with a number of transition periods and clusters of stress.

Couples in Stage III are dealing with high levels of cluster stress and are experiencing severe marital conflict. Neither spouse is able to maintain a self-focus; instead there are high levels of mutual blaming and intense projection. The couples have great difficulty working together, are very critical of each other, and have little trust in each other. There is a pervasive sense of resentment and bitterness. The spouses are filled with anger, hurt, and disappointment. Neither wants to adapt to the other to avoid a struggle, which leads, in turn, to attack-counterattack behavior. Open hostility is frequently accompanied by pointed sarcasm.

In Stage IV, one or both of the spouses have already obtained a lawyer. Dissolution of the marriage appears inevitable. Sometimes the spouse who has already decided to terminate the marriage gets involved in therapy so that his/her spouse can "be left" with the therapist when the marriage actually ends.

"Fogarty's Litany" (Guerin, 1982) is a concept developed to describe the progression of responses experienced by each spouse to his/her unmet expectations. Guerin (1982) hypothesized that unmet expectations are initially experienced as disappointment but progress hierarchically to hurt, anger, resentment, and bitterness. After a prolonged period of bitterness, one or both spouses decide it is too painful to remain vulnerable to the other. Alienation sets in as hope for the future of the relationship is abandoned.

Framo (1982) also developed a classification of marital problems that is similar to Guerin's but includes more subgroups. For instance, Framo discussed couples who seek counseling because the "zing" has gone out of their relationship. These couples state that they love each other but find their relationship too predictable, that sex is routine, and there is no excitement. Framo described these as "best friends" or brother-sister marriages. Another category included couples in which one spouse is symptomatic (e.g., depressive or alcoholic). Other couples present as veterans of many years of marital and individual therapy. He called these "mental health" partners. These marriages are characterized by one or both spouses trying to be the other's therapist. Framo also had a category of long-term, chronically unhappy marriages. The relationship issues are calcified and couples feel they cannot live alone or together.

# THERAPEUTIC STRATEGIES FOR INTERVENTION

Guerin (1982) suggested a framework for intervening that coincides with his stages of marital conflict. For couples in Stage I, Guerin suggested that interventions be educational in approach as illustrated in the following example:

Sandy and Paul were a young couple who had been married for 3 years before the birth of their first child. Both spouses were in their late twenties and were eager to begin their family. Sandy was a lawyer and Paul was a computer programmer. In the first six months after the baby was born, Sandy and Paul became very disenchanted with their marriage and their ability to parent. They became involved in therapy because they were fearful that irreparable damage was occurring in their relationship. A thorough assessment of this family indicated that most of their difficulty was centered on negotiating the changes from a two-party to a three-party system. Although they had talked about the child-care/household changes that were expected, they had not anticipated the changes occurring within themselves and throughout the larger family system.

Therapy focused on discussions of transitions, realistic expectations, and role changes. Suggestions were made for reading material on life cycle changes and the young family.

Stage II couples are experiencing a cluster of stresses, for example, couples with adolescent children who are in several transition periods at the same time. They are usually in a mid-life transition, have parents at retirement age, and have adolescents seeking increased autonomy. If financial or occupational stress or illness is added, the level of anxiety increases exponentially. Unresolved issues in the areas of finances, sex, and extended family become increasingly stressful.

During therapy, Stage II couples show a tendency to project relationship problems onto each other. However, with the assistance of the therapist, they are able to develop a self-focus. The therapist can accomplish this by asking each spouse to focus on what she/he wants in the relationship. This can be accomplished as a homework assignment. The therapist then follows this up by asking each spouse, "What are you willing to do or change in yourself to accomplish this goal?"

Couples in this stage respond to the structure provided by the therapist. Marital conflict, emotional distancing and pursuit, and the interplay of individual and relationship issues can be dealt with in a fairly direct manner. Tasks can be assigned to assist each spouse to examine his/her own responses to the other's behavior and to see how one's own behavior reflects efforts to reduce personal and relationship anxiety.

Stage II couples are usually capable to responding to tasks that challenge the rigidity of the interactional system that they have created.

Andrea and Jim were a middle-aged couple with four children. Two of their children had graduated from college, one was in college, and one was graduating from high school. Andrea was very angry at Jim's over-involvement in his work as a business executive. She complained that Jim was distant and emotionally unavailable to her. She described herself as a backstage director, responsible for all the unglamorous but vital operations in the family. Jim complained that Andrea did not respect the efforts he made to maintain their financial equilibrium. He liked the fact that she arranged their social life and took care of all minor details.

In the above example, an NPT could give Jim the task of making all of the arrangements for their social activities that weekend, while Andrea would be instructed not to offer any suggestions or criticisms of Jim's plans. The couple would then be encouraged to discuss the ease or difficulty they experienced in completing these tasks. What were their reactions to their mate's behavior? How did they like the change? These tasks contribute to the couple's ability to develop flexibility in their relationship. Most importantly, therapeutic interventions with Stage II couples are aimed at increasing self-awareness and individuation.

Stage III couples are experiencing a severe level of marital conflict. It has been this author's experience that most couples seeking marital therapy fall into this category. Their relationship is characterized by open hostility, severe criticism, and little ability to maintain a self-focus. The therapist has great difficulty in helping these spouses look at their own roles in the dysfunctional process. Couples attempt to "triangle in" the therapist and utilize the sessions to hurl blame and accusations at each other. Direct confrontations on the marital conflict may be ineffectual or may intensify anxiety.

To decrease the intense reactivity, the NPT may focus on each individual's relationship with his/her family of origin. This intervention serves several purposes. First, it opens up new relationship options so that not all of the emotional intensity is in the marital relationship. In addition, each individual learns about patterns of emotional reactivity that exist in his/her family of origin. This may be very enlightening as it may reveal the origin of some of the emotional triggers currently attributed to the spouse and the marital relationship.

Framo (1981) believed that "the relationship problems that adults have with their spouses and children are reconstructions and elaborations of earlier conflict paradigms from the family of origin." (p. 346) This concept can be illustrated in the following example.

Dean initiated therapy for himself and his wife Lois after she informed him that she was very unhappy in the marriage and thought she might want a separation. They had tried getting involved in "Marriage Encounter" but this was geared to marriage enrichment and was not meant to substitute for professional intervention. Lois blamed Dean for the difficulties in the marriage; she felt he was distant and lacked understanding of her concerns. Dean felt Lois focused on her own needs and had withdrawn from him and their two children. He felt she was too engrossed in her career.

The couple made little progress in conjoint sessions. The suggestion was made to put the marital problems on the shelf for awhile and for each spouse to work on his/her family of origin. Lois was encouraged to work on the relationship with her mother; she had been the middle child of a seven-child family and had never felt close to her mother. A similar suggestion was made to Dean. These interventions proved to be very effective. Lois was able to see her involvement in repeating her mother's pattern of withdrawal when stress became too high. After reconnecting with her mother, she felt less isolated and more willing to work on the marital relationship.

While spouses are focusing on issues in their families of origin, the NPT instructs them to avoid deep "heart to heart" discussions with each other. Rather, they are encouraged to talk about topics of general interest and to get involved in activities that are fun and nonstressful. As each spouse is more able to maintain a self-focus, they can be viewed as Stage II couples, ready to look at their own reactivity in the marital relationship.

Stage IV couples enter therapy with the covert or overt purpose of terminating the marriage; one or both spouses have already engaged an attorney. When children are present in the family, this can be a crucial focus for the therapy. Families do not end when there is a divorce, but they must restructure (see Chapter 25.) Though the role of spouse may be abdicated, the role of parent must not. Therefore, the focus of therapy is to facilitate the couple's disengagement from the marriage and to decrease the trauma for the children and their grandparents. Losses permeate this stage, even when there is a potential future relationship waiting in the wings. Anger and ambivalence fluctuate during this stage. Reducing reactivity and bitterness helps to begin the emotional divorce and lessens the probability of future conflict in the areas of visitation, finances, and custody.

A new movement, divorce mediation, may offer an alternative to the traditional adversary system of divorce. When each spouse engages an attorney, a natural enemy is created in the form of the other spouse. Lawyers sometimes add to the "out to get him/her" mentality of perpetrator/victim. This focus eradicates the need for each person to "own" responsibility for his/her part of the breakup.

Divorce mediation is part of the family mediation movement. Specially trained mediators assist the couple to arbitrate their differences and negotiate a settlement. Each spouse is assisted to negotiate from a position of equal power. All financial and legal facts are shared openly. The mediator is knowledgeable in the areas of tax and family law, accounting, and state divorce laws.

This process allows each spouse to retain his/her dignity and not feel like a loser. Upon completion of the negotiated settlement, each spouse may present the agreement to an attorney as a legal safeguard. Some states (for example, California) are insisting that all couples attempt divorce mediation before coming to divorce court.

## MARITAL SEPARATION

There are a number of indicators during the course of marital therapy that could lead the NPT to suggest a trial separation. This intervention can be particularly useful when the couple expresses their hopelessness and continually threatens separation. A trial period of separation may also be indicated for couples who seem unable to reduce the frequency of their escalating conflicts. A third indicator may be the absence of emotional involvement in the marriage. It has been suggested that trial separations may be effective for each of the individuals "to gain more insight into his or her individual potential while at the same time experiencing clearly what the other person meant to him/her." (Lange & Van der Hart, 1983, p. 212)

Separation can provide an opportunity for the spouses to obtain a measure of objectivity about themselves and their marriage. Relationships have implicit and explicit contracts. The contracts are made up of a set of rules that are based on expectations and reflect motivations. Couples embroiled in conflict are unaware of the rules and how the rules operate. The separation gives each individual the opportunity to focus on him/herself and review the inter-relationships in the marriage. According to Okun and Rappaport (1980):

> The marital relationship proceeds from an intensive, romantic infatuation that is based on the needs and expectation of each partner. . . . Each partner brings to the marriage a self-concept, a concept of the spouse, a concept of the spouse's concepts, and a concept of marriage. (p. 163)

These concepts are based on perceptions, feelings, needs, and expectations, all of which need to be sorted out. Separation can provide for this reflection and sorting out.

The length of a trial separation varies, with three months being a comfortable average. There must be an explicit agreement that no final decisions will be made during the trial separation. Individual therapy or conjoint sessions should be held on a regular basis during this time.

The therapist must help the couple to negotiate specific arrangements for the separation. For instance, who is going to move out and where will she/he live? Whenever possible, these accommodations should be similar to the ones at home to eliminate this as a variable in a decision to divorce. Each spouse must be responsible for him/herself. Too much contact should be avoided except where it is essential for the continuity of care for the children. The children must be informed of the separation by both parents, and reassured that the separation is not their fault (Lange & Van der Hart, 1983). Spouses are also asked not to date anyone else during this time.

It has been this author's experience that couples given permission to separate are often more energized to work on their relationship. Being apart gives each spouse a sense of what a single life would be like. With reduction of the intense feelings that brought the couple to therapy, spouses may be able to decide if they want to end or work on their marriage.

## SUMMARY

This chapter focused on the role of the nurse psychotherapist in working with patients experiencing marital conflict. Family systems theory was offered as a framework for the NPT's practice. Assessment and intervention strategies were based on Guerin's paradigm for stages of marital conflict. Divorce mediation and the use of structured trial separation were discussed briefly. The nurse psychotherapist, because of her wholistic view of individuals and families, is uniquely qualified to provide therapy for couples experiencing marital stress.

## REFERENCES

Anderson, C., & Stewart, S. (1983). *Mastering resistance*. New York: Guilford Press.

Bowen, M. (1971). Family and family group psychotherapy. In H. Kaplan and B. Sadock (Eds.), *Comprehensive group psychotherapy*, (p. 12-40). New York: William and Wilkins.

Calhoun, G. (1982). The nurse as therapist. In I. Clements & D. Buchanan (Eds.), *Family therapy: A nursing perspective* (p. 13-21). New York: Wiley.

Framo, J. (1981). Family of origin as a therapeutic resource for adults in marital and family therapy: You can and should go home again. In R. Green and

J. Framo (Eds.), *Family therapy* (p. 341–374). New York: International Universities Press.

Framo, J. (1982). *Explorations in marital and familiy therapy.* New York: Springer.

Guerin, P. (1982). The stages of marital conflict. *The Family, 10*(1), 15–26.

Guerin, P., & Fay, L. (1984). The envelope of marital conflict: Social context and family factors. *The Family, 10*(1), 3–14.

Haley, J. (1976). *Problem solving therapy.* San Francisco: Jossey-Bass.

Lange, A., & Van der Hart, O. (1983). *Directive family therapy.* New York: Brunner/Mazel.

Marram van Servellen, G. (1984). *Group and family therapy a model for psychotherapeutic nursing practice.* St. Louis: Mosby.

Miller, S., & Winstead-Fry, P. (1982). *Family systems theory in nursing practice.* Reston, VA: Reston.

Okun, B., & Rappaport, L. (1980). *Working with families: An introduction to family therapy.* MA: Duxbury Press.

Weinstein, R. (1981, September-December). Bowen's family systems theory as exemplified in Bergman's "Scenes From a Marriage." *Perspectives in Psychiatric Care, 19*, 156–163.

# Chapter 25
# The Remarried Family as Patient

*Joan M. King*

American couples increasingly have sought divorce as an alternative to problematic marriages; however, they appear committed to marriage. During the next few decades, a predicted 40% of U.S. children will experience marital disruption from separation, divorce, and death (Bane, 1976); and a projected 11% of all children under 18 will live with a stepparent (Glick, 1980).

Families of remarriage involving children from a prior union encounter specific stresses related to establishing a new system with altered roles, relationships, and interaction patterns. Families also experience stress from competing loyalties, divergent goals, vague role definitions and/or conflict with ex-spouses and families of origin.

Many remarried families achieve a functional and rewarding family life experience, but others do not. Increasing numbers of these troubled families are seeking professional assistance. Effective family therapy requires understanding the contextual issues influencing the remarried experience. With remarriage, family boundaries, roles, and relationships must be redefined and renegotiated since roles in these families tend to be ambiguous, complex and often contradictory. Myths relating to divorce and remarriage abound; family members and therapists will be misguided if they accept these myths as truths.

# THE REMARRIAGE DEVELOPMENTAL PROCESS

Remarriage has been seen as a family developmental process involving patterned sequences that occur with regularity (Messinger and Walker, 1981; Whiteside, 1982). Each stage in this process presents a series of tasks to be accomplished. The extent of task achievement and the nature of the solutions influence resolution of the issues and tasks of later stages. Successful solutions to the tasks of one stage are problematic if automatically applied to subsequent phases. Although many of these tasks focus on adults as the family governing system, children's family life experiences are shaped by their parents' resolutions. Conversely, children influence family solutions. The remarried family developmental process occurs concommitantly with the individual developmental sequence of each member; both processes interact to shape family and individual life experience. The stages of the remarriage developmental sequence are as follows: (a) first marriage; (b) separation; (c) establishment of separate households; (d) preparation for remarriage; and (e) remarriage itself.

## First Marriage

Both functional and dysfunctional patterns of a first marriage tend to recur as marital partners separate and move through subsequent stages of remarriage. Thus, it is important to understand how spouses dealt with decision-making, conflict, and intimacy. Spouses who have been able to set aside personal differences to cooperate on family issues during the first marriage are more likely to achieve satisfactory arrangements during divorce. They are less likely to use children to play out disputes after separation.

Unrecognized, unresolved conflicts may create a second difficult marital relationship, but the tendency to replay problematic patterns is not inevitable. Individuals often mature and develop skills that improve their relationships with second partners. The new partner also shapes and influences these relationships.

## Separation

Divorce does not end the family; it alters the nature of family relationships. The tasks of separation focus on these changing relationships through restructuring family roles, relationships, and boundaries; and through grieving the loss of intimate relationships.

Family identity is based upon repeated patterns of interaction, activities, rituals, and shared memories that convey a sense of continuity over time. The family's interaction patterns and established modes of dealing with daily life occurrences are altered when one parent moves out. Subsequently, all members are involved in multiple disrupting role negotiations and in redefining family boundaries. If the family boundary is defined to include only persons living in a single household, the nonresident parent is excluded.

Extending family boundaries to include two households permits continuity of those roles that do not terminate when the marriage ends. Inherent in this process is a separation of spousal and parental roles. Ex-spouses must maintain some level of communication to meet both the adults' and children's needs for a parental relationship. However, the nature of this communication as well as the patterning of the relationship between children and nonresident parent must be negotiated. At issue is the extent and nature of the nonresident parent's involvement with children. Parents must negotiate the frequency and type of contact as well as involvement in decision-making and child rearing. These changing relationships often create stress and pain for family members, even when mutually agreeable arrangements are achieved. When children become involved in parental discord, family disruption is likely to continue over an extensive period and the child's relationship with both parents is affected adversely.

Cooperation and sharing between parents help children cope with the stress of divorce by maintaining greater consistency in parent-child relationships, by providing adult support, and by preventing loyalty conflicts. Parents' discussion of the divorce with children is an important aspect of support. Providing clear information without affixing blame or demeaning either spouse helps alleviate children's feelings of responsibility, helplessness, and confusion, while emphasizing the continuity of parental love. Providing an opportunity for children to express their feelings of loss, anger, and apprehension about the future facilitates coping.

Ahrens (1981) found great variation in relationships between divorced spouses. Relationships ranged from those characterized as "bitter enemy" to "best friend" with most being described as neutral. The discovery that many divorced spouses continue to meet their adult relationship and attachment needs through communication with one another is antithetic to the commonly held conception of this relationship as distant or hostile. Post-divorce ex-spousal bonding should not be considered automatically as an unhealthy attachment; it can be adaptive for both adults and children. A supportive, cooperative parental relationship fosters better psychological adjustment in children of divorced families (Wallerstein &

Kelly, 1980). This resolution permits both parents' inclusion in their children's lives and can be accomplished in a variety of custodial arrangements.

Divorce involves grief for all family members. Children experience a loss of intimacy when the nonresident parent is unavailable on a daily basis in the household. Adults experience the loss of marital success and an intimate relationship, even when desiring divorce. Grieving enables family members to master this loss and to enter new intimate relationships.

## Separate Households

The establishment of two residences reinforces the physical and emotional separation of spouses initiated during the separation stage. Family roles and responsibilities are renegotiated as the custodial parent adapts to being the only parent within the household. The separation of parents also elicits a need to develop or reestablish meaningful adult relationships. The tasks of this stage can be summarized: (a) reorganizing to accomplish necessary functions of daily living; and (b) establishing satisfying adult relationships.

Maintaining separate households can strain the family's financial resources and create additional stress as members' lifestyles are affected. Unemployed adults may return to the workforce to provide needed income. Families who previously had a dual income will not be burdened by this additional role, but may now have fewer options for sharing childcare and household tasks. Financial support and subsequent changes in family aspirations are frequent sources of conflict.

The custodial parent faced with multiple tasks and responsibilities of daily living once shared by two adults may reassign tasks. Children in these families often assume a larger portion of the work of family life as well as a greater degree of responsibility for themselves and other members.

The need for support and adult gratification from friends and extended family relationships continues. However, these relationships can be altered by alignments with one of the ex-spouses and the changing needs of the divorced adult. During a period when the support and pleasure of adult relationships can facilitate coping, single parents may find some previous relationships too distant or too intrusive. Mature, satisfying relationships must be maintained and new ones established. As grieving is resolved, the need for an intimate adult relationship reemerges.

Solutions to tasks of this phase have serious implications if generational boundaries are transgressed. Needs for emotional support and assistance with tasks of daily life can result in over-attachment of parent and child in a shared authority structure. Children who experience intense attachment with one parent do not readily relinquish this relationship; children may inappropriately control their parent's life through interference with adult friendships and romantic attachments. Overinvestment is less likely to occur if the child maintains a relationship with both parents and these adults are able to support one another. Parental satisfaction obtained from adult relationships also acts as a barrier to this overinvolvement. Similarly, children who assume extensive responsibility in the household may oppose their parent's romantic involvement because of the threat to their position of authority in the family.

## Preparation for Remarriage

In anticipation of marriage, the couple is faced with the task of preparing themselves, their children, and ex-spouses for the ensuing role and boundary changes. The ambiguity and complexity of these roles and relationships often create competition and conflict. Preparation can reduce conflict.

The approaching marriage may be anticipated with both pleasure and apprehension. Adults can be ambivalent about sufficiently relinquishing their independence to achieve the interdependence required for a successful marriage. They can have doubts about assuming a parental role with children who are not their own or hesitant about sharing their own parental role with the new spouse. Adults may be apprehensive about their partner's relationship with his/her ex-spouse. Ongoing ex-spouse contact may be perceived as threatening to the new marriage or stepparent role.

If both adults have children from former marriages, positive relationships need to be fostered among all children and adults in anticipation of marriage. Encouraging the development of supportive alliances can require considerable time. These relationships develop at their own pace and cannot be rushed by adult needs or time frames.

## Remarriage

Satisfying, secure, remarriage relationships emerge from a blending process. Blending is a result of new mates establishing a firm coalition and children accepting the stepparent and new family without experiencing loyalty conflicts. The interrelated tasks of remarriage are to redefine the family unit and its boundaries and to negotiate new roles and relationships.

Marriage disrupts fantasies of the divorced couple(s) reuniting. Children, ex-spouses, and extended family members are confronted with a new reality that frequently results in comfortable relationships becoming strained or conflicted.

The remarried pair must begin to develop a new family identity, one that recognizes the differences between past and present families, while providing continuity with prior family life experience. All members do not share a common identity, history, or patterns of interaction and expectations. As new patterns of daily life are established, multiple opportunities for misunderstanding and conflict are presented. Family members are unsure of their place in this new unit since they lack the familiarity of common experience to guide interactions and to interpret expectations. Sensitivity and open communication will alleviate some of the intensity of this disruption. However, only time can establish the familiarity and history required for a new family identity.

Spouses who discount prior family experience and relationships will encounter competition and conflict among members. Establishing permeable family boundaries maintains relationships with nonresident children and parents and recognizes the importances of these ties. In terms of ex-spouses, boundaries that are too permeable can impede development of a new family identity and blending. New spouses must develop a firm spousal and parental alliance that also recognizes the parental role of the ex-spouse(s).

If both parents have children from a prior union, boundaries between these two units must be relaxed to effect blending. Children are often protective of their original family roles and identity while highly sensitive to their place in the new family. The developmental age of children and prior family experience partially shape their individual responses to new family life. Particular issues may differ, but concerns about displacement and rivalry for affection are common. Sensitivity to children's concerns as well as differences in family history, expectations, and child rearing patterns facilitates relaxation of boundaries between the two units that comprise the new family.

The roles of adults and children must be redefined. Establishing a firm, supportive new spousal coalition facilitates negotiations. Two aspects of role change have particular importance for the family—inclusion of the stepparent in the authority structure and redefinition of generational boundaries.

Biological parents who are unwilling to share their authority create barriers that make it difficult for the new spouse to enter the family. Similarly, new spouses who are unwilling to assume authority tend to remain appendages to the family system. Role redefinitions are unlikely to occur or to be accepted by children unless spouses concur and support one another in this process. Children who share authority with their biological parent also challenge inclusion of the new spouse in the family. To achieve a functional spousal relationship, both parents must support the child while redefining authority as an adult prerogative.

Over-attachment of parent and child also functions as a barrier to inclusion of a new spouse. The generational boundary must be redefined to permit a spousal coalition while maintaining a more appropriate parent-child relationship. This redefinition requires the efforts of both spouses.

Child-rearing decisions, guidance, and affective bonds are important aspects of the parental role. A stepparent cannot replace a parent but must negotiate a role for him/herself that respects the rights of biological parent and child. This negotiation is a complex process influenced by family history and involves the child, step, and biological parents. Negotiations are influenced adversely by accepting as fact the myths of instant love between stepparent and child or the "ugly stepparent" image. Just as the stepparent supports the child's relationship with the nonresident parent, both biological parents must support the step relationship. Assuming a parental role as daily issues emerge does not conflict with the rights of the nonresident parent and is an essential aspect of child rearing.

Stepparents who have little experience in a parental role may encounter difficulty in assuming these functions. This lack of experience is complicated by having limited time to work out parental issues and to develop compatible spouse/parent roles before encountering situations requiring discipline. Further, child and stepparent may not share a positive bond that would ease the child's resistance to discipline. These problems are compounded by discrepancies in role definitions. The stepparent may be designated by the child as "my parent's spouse," a role that denies parental functions. Stepparents and children can encounter problems at any age, but difficulties are most volatile with adolescents.

No single pattern of blending exists for remarried families. The issues and solutions emerge from multiple factors: family composition, members' characteristics and developmental stages, and the resolution of the various tasks inherent in the remarriage process itself. The initial three to four years of remarriage is a period of adjustment (Visher & Visher, 1978).

## THERAPEUTIC ISSUES FOR THE REMARRIED FAMILY

The focus of this section is therapeutic strategies for the NPT to consider when working with the remarried family. Treatment is directed toward assessing and facilitating blending. Several issues that effect blending have been discussed earlier. These issues emerge from family efforts to cope with changes in boundaries, roles, and relationships. Assessing the remarried family involves ordering data from history, current relationships and interactions to determine: (1) the extent to which blending has occurred; (2) at what levels; and (3) from whose perspective. Effective blending occurs between spouses, between children of different unions, and between parents and children. Areas of particular concern during assessment are intimacy, authority, alliances, and exclusions. Family interactions that illustrate fixed alliances or exclusions impede blending.

## Inadequate Blending

The following family demonstrates an ineffective relationship pattern first described by Goldner (1982). The pattern involves each parent remaining closer to his/her own children than to each other. Thus the family is composed of two separate units, the spousal alliance is weak and an effective mechanism for resolving conflict is lacking.

> Mr. and Mrs. A knew each other two years before their marriage. She divorced because of physical abuse and had successfully undertaken a career in addition to caring for her two children, Ingrid, currently age 9, and 10-year-old Tom. Mr. A. divorced his first wife following desertion. Mr. A. and 4-year-old Susan lived with his parents until remarriage. Susan's grandparents assumed parental functions. During the A's courtship, he was depressed about his first marriage and found it easy to communicate with Mrs. A., who was supportive. As their relationship deepened, the couple included the children in activities that were enjoyed by all.
>
> Fidelity and nonviolence were the A's expectations for their marriage. They described their two-year marriage as happy until the past three months when the daughters began fighting. Shortly before this, all children had transferred to a school that offered special education classes for Susan.
>
> During the initial session, Ingrid and Mrs. A were involved in mutual, intense escalating accusations. Susan, who appeared depressed, sat between both parents, cried frequently, and was comforted by Mrs. A. Both Tom and Mr. A. were withdrawn. Mr. and Mrs. A. agreed that Ingrid was the problem.
>
> The parents' view of the family was inconsistent with observed interaction patterns. The A's maintained they were close and experienced no disagreement between themselves. However, Mrs. A. spoke for Mr. A. who rarely participated in family discussions. The A.'s spent little time together as a couple, stating their work and family commitments prevented this. His contributions to the family were financial support and preparing dinner while Mrs. A. worked. Decisions he made in her absence were frequently reversed when she returned and the children complained to her. Only later was Mr. A. able to express his anger that Mrs. A. did not discuss these situations with him before overriding his position. At that time, Mrs. A. expressed her concern about his limited parenting skills.

Mr. and Mrs. A. initially stated the children were treated alike. However, Mrs. A was solicitous of shy, depressed Susan; both parents were angry with Ingrid, who confronted their denial, and both ignored inarticulate, sulking Tom. The initial sessions were characterized by feelings of loss and lack of belonging. Ingrid felt isolated from the A's. She wanted to live with her father who wanted her, but not her brother. Susan's visits to her mother were anticipated with pleasure, but resulted in sadness when she observed the love her mother gave a new infant.

The major block to blending in this family occurred at the parental level. Fears of intimacy and inability to share power prevented the parents from forming a functional spousal coalition. Parental functions were maintained by Mrs. A. who undercut Mr. A's efforts in this realm. Mr. A's collusion in this process emerged from ambivalence and lack of experience in parenting. Spousal conflicts were masked by Ingrid's angry outbursts, which deflected attention from the marital relationship.

The initial overt alliances in this family were between Ingrid and Tom and between Mrs. A. and Susan. Efforts to develop a warmer relationship between Ingrid and Mrs. A. were effective, while similar efforts between Mr. A. and Tom were not. This failed effort resulted in uncovering covert alliances; both parents felt closer to their own offspring. The family was split along prior family lines. Mrs. A's guilt about preferences for her own children blocked her expressions of caring for them and resulted in an overt alliance with Susan. Susan's depression facilitated Mrs. A's caring behavior. Mr. A's abdication of parental functions inhibited demonstration of his love for Susan.

Increasing the alliance between spouses was basic to facilitating the blending process at all levels. Other important interventions were to relax the boundaries between families, increase the inclusion of Tom, and treat Susan's depression.

## Imposed Blending

A second pattern used by remarried spouses is to push too rapidly for blending (Goldner, 1982). This strategy involves parents urging their children to participate in creating an inauthentic togetherness. As parents encourage greater involvement in the new family, children resist because this participation conflicts with loyalties to the nonresident parent(s). Parental pressure escalates as children's resistance increases and initiates a spiraling repetitive process. Blending cannot occur under these circumstances and children may be extruded or withdraw from the family.

Parents may use various techniques to impose blending. For example, the child may be urged to call the stepparent "mother" or "father." Inherent in this appellation are a host of positive feelings and long-term memories. The term connotes a relationship that does not exist and loyality conflicts often ensue. The conflict can be defused if new spouses understand the child's position and cease using these terms. Children may be consulted about what they wish to call the stepparent, or parents may make the decision. In either event, it is essential to support the importance of the stepparent's position in the family.

Stepparents sometimes attempt to facilitate blending by forcing children to share cherished activities that the child considers the providence of the biological parent (Isaacs, 1982). The pleasure and meaning of these rituals cannot be transferred arbitrarily; the child may view the stepparent as an interloper in the relationship with the biological parent. Conflict can be defused if parents realize the meaning these activities hold for the child and cease their involvement. Alternative activities not previously shared with parents can become the basis for new rituals between stepparent and child. Meaningful rituals provide a pleasureable patterning of step relationships and encourage a sense of belonging and continuity that facilitates blending.

Families that attempt to impose blending frequently need help to accept that the level of integration expected of initial unions usually cannot be achieved in remarriage. Family members have differing commitments to the family as a unit and to its various members. These differences affect the integration level.

## Conflict as a Barrier to Blending

The blending process in the remarried family can be impeded by chronic conflict between the new spouse and ex-mate. These conflicts often emerge from unresolved grief. If children become involved in these disputes, their needs are negatively affected.

Ideally, the goal of therapy for families experiencing this conflict is to establish a collaborative parenting team involving both step and biological parents. If this goal is not feasible, therapy is directed toward defocusing conflict from the child. Treatment involves all parents and is not limited to the remarried family. When conflict and emotions are not too intense, joint treatment is preferable, but this requirement may be resisted. Clarifying the effect of conflict on the child and limiting treatment to parenting issues may facilitate agreement. In these volatile situations, the therapist must feel comfortable in setting firm limits and controlling conflict.

# THE REMARRIED FAMILY AND THE NURSE PSYCHOTHERAPIST

Professional nursing education and practice emphasize a broad approach to family health, one that includes physiological, psychological, and social parameters. The diversity of this generic role conception, coupled with advanced preparation in family psychotherapy, provides a distinct advantage to families experiencing blending difficulties. Family stress may affect the health and development of members, or be expressed in the arenas of work, school, and social relationships. Ineffective functioning in any area further increases family stress.

Attending to the broad range of family and individual member's behavior through direct intervention, teaching, or referral is an important aspect of service provided by the NPT. Nurses' experience in coordinating a variety of health care and social services is a further advantage. Coordination facilitates consistency and collaboration when differing professions simultaneously provide highly specialized services to the family.

The here and now therapeutic approach common among NPTs may be of primary importance to dysfunctional remarried families. The stress and pain that compels the family to seek help is highly compatible with this approach.

## SUMMARY

In summary, the family may move through the various stages of remarriage with minimal difficulty or it may encounter significant problems. Understanding the complexity of remarried family experience provides family members and NPTs guidelines to achieve blending.

## REFERENCES

Ahrons, R. (1981). The continuing co-parental relationship between divorced spouses. *American Journal of Orthopsychiatry, 51*, 414–428.

Bane, M. (1976). Marital disruption and the lives of children. *Journal of Social Issues, 32*, 103–117.

Glick, P. (1980). Remarriage: Some recent changes and variations. *Journal of Family Issues, 1*, 455–478.

Goldner, V. (1982). Therapy with remarriage families: XII. Remarriage family: structure, system, future. *Family Therapy Collections, 2*, 187–206.

Issacs, M. (1982). Therapy with remarriage families: IX. Facilitating family restructuring and relinkage. *Family Therapy Collections, 2,* 121–143.
Messinger, L., & Walker, K. (1981). From marriage breakdown to remarriage:
Parental tasks and therapeutic guidelines. *American Journal of Orthopsy-
chiatry, 51,* 429–438.
Visher, E. B., & Visher, J. S. (1978). Common problems of stepparents and their
spouses. *American Journal of Orthopsychiatry, 48,* 252–262.
Wallerstein, J. S., & Kelly, J. B. (1980). *Surviving the breakup: How children and
parents cope with divorce.* New York: Basic Books.
Whiteside, M. F. (1982). Remarriage: A family developmental process. *Journal of
Marital and Family Therapy, 8,* 59–68.

# Chapter 26
# The Abusive Family as Patient

## *Rose Odum*

Popular media, official and legal reports, clinical data, and population surveys during the past decade have made it abundantly clear in both professional and public sectors that Americans have serious problems with violence (Finkelhor, Gelles, Hotaling, & Straus, 1983; Gelles, 1979; *Time*, 1983; Warner & Braen, 1982). Because of the sensitive and often closeted nature of domestic or intrafamilial violence and abuse, its prevalence is unclear; however, the data base that does exist is impressive. Estimates of child abuse/neglect range from three to four million cases each year (Carson & Finkelhor, 1982). Wife abuse and spousal violence (including domestic rape) may occur in 30–50% of all couples (Straus, Gelles, & Steinmetz, 1980). Abuse to the elderly is less commonly reported, but studies suggest that it is becoming a serious social and health problem (Champlin, 1982; Hickey & Douglas, 1981). Increasingly, adult women in therapy for various reasons (e.g., depression, alcoholism, and sexual problems) disclose episodes of childhood incest, usually involving fathers or stepfathers (Herman, 1981).

While wives do abuse their husbands, this is more often done in self-defense and may reflect a "trapped" position of physical and economic dependency. Such violence usually occurs in women who have been abused over periods of months or years (Dobash & Dobash, 1979).

The purpose of this chapter is to outline therapeutic approaches for victims or perpetrators of abuse within a familial context. Figure 26.1 represents a model of domestic violence/abuse that includes intra- and extrafamilial factors. Abuse is defined as those behaviors that are in-

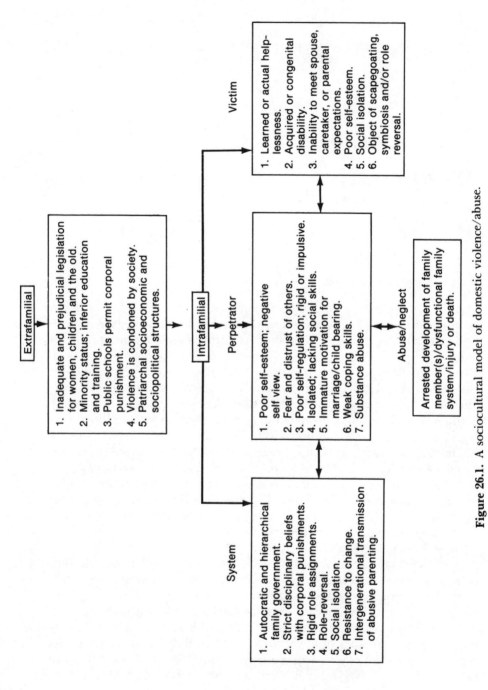

**Figure 26.1.** A sociocultural model of domestic violence/abuse.

Extrafamilial

1. Inadequate and prejudicial legislation for women, children and the old.
2. Minority status; inferior education and training.
3. Public schools permit corporal punishment.
4. Violence is condoned by society.
5. Patriarchal socioeconomic and sociopolitical structures.

Intrafamilial

Victim

1. Learned or actual help-lessness.
2. Acquired or congenital disability.
3. Inability to meet spouse, caretaker, or parental expectations.
4. Poor self-esteem.
5. Social isolation.
6. Object of scapegoating, symbiosis and/or role reversal.

Perpetrator

1. Poor self-esteem; negative self view.
2. Fear and distrust of others.
3. Poor self-regulation; rigid or impulsive.
4. Isolated; lacking social skills.
5. Immature motivation for marriage/child bearing.
6. Weak coping skills.
7. Substance abuse.

System

1. Autocratic and hierarchical family government.
2. Strict disciplinary beliefs with corporal punishments.
3. Rigid role assignments.
4. Role-reversal.
5. Social isolation.
6. Resistance to change.
7. Intergenerational transmission of abusive parenting.

Abuse/neglect

Arrested development of family member(s)/dysfunctional family system/injury or death.

tended to result in the physical or psychological trauma, pain, or arrested development of another member. Violence is a deliberate, aggressive act or pattern of acts; abuse may be exploitive or passive, as in the sexual seduction of a child or in failure to provide necessary goods and services to dependent elderly persons. This chapter does not concern institutional abuse, which may occur in day-care centers and nursing homes, or violence associated with crime.

## MYTHOLOGY OF THE "ALL-AMERICAN" TRADITIONAL FAMILY

It is highly doubtful that the functional model of family put forth by Talcott Parsons in the 1950's is adequate to examine the therapeutic needs of contemporary families (Levant, 1980). Scanzoni (1983) suggested that the traditional use of the term "family" (i.e., as the typical nuclear family with rigid, fixed roles of man-provider and woman-housewife) may no longer be the dominant sociological or clinical representation of Americans' primary social group. As the number of unmarried, single-parent, blended, or "living-together" elderly persons increases, new ideas of family dynamics and therapeutic goals emerge. Moreover, traditional families frequently become dysfunctional in a highly competitive economy requiring that many families have multiple sources of income, and in a rapidly paced technology that has brought a record number of women into such formerly male roles as lawyer, physician, legislator, and graduate student (Naisbitt, 1982). NPTs who work with violent/abusive patients must consider their own working concepts of "family."

While political conservativism exerts a powerful presence, the effects of technology, the Women's Movement, and the essential demands of a "world economy" increasingly affect intrafamilial roles and relationships (Hare-Mustin, 1978; Scanzoni, 1983). Often the family's failure or inability to adapt to forces of socioeconomic change contributes to abuse. Examples include wives who need or wish to work or pursue careers, and the increasing number of elderly parents who move in with adult children. In both cases economic need calls for flexibility and willingness to share domestic and extrafamilial responsibilities. When these adaptations are not made, frustrations may lead to spousal conflict and/or abuse to children or to elderly dependent parents. Some families fail to incorporate their concepts of traditional role models with progressive lifestyles required for survival, if not for happiness, in today's society.

Accommodation to change is much more difficult for those families whose liaisons with other social institutions, such as the church or school, reinforce sameness and rigid, fixed familial and social roles. NPTs need to help families realize that change involves adjustments in extrafamilial as well as intrafamilial relations.

## SOURCE OF REFERRAL AND CASE FINDING

Many NPTs do not advertise their services beyond the yellow pages or professional literature. Certainly few put themselves forth as experts in domestic abuse. How then do families with battered wives, abused children or elderly, or incestuous relationships come to seek therapy? Unfortunately, the answer is that such families and NPTs may not meet. Just as physicians and nurses often fail to diagnose domestic violence in the emergency room, so do family therapists and practitioners of individual psychotherapy frequently overlook abuse problems (Stank, Filcroft, & Frazier, 1979). Abuse is not generally included in the assessment process and patients may or may not disclose it. In the case of incest, adult victims may have repressed or suppressed its memory and resist associations with the thought of incestuous experiences. Furthermore, the great majority of practitioners have not been formally trained in assessing or treating incest, abuse, or violence. *DSM III* (1980) nomenclature does not even provide for this diagnostic classification, a critical problem for NPTs who apply for third-party payment.

Families will be more likely to identify themselves and seek treatment from therapists who make themselves visible in the community through presentations to organizations or writing in local publications, and who, in general, make therapy for problems of abuse public and matter-of-fact. Therapists who refuse to get involved legally (e.g., filing a child abuse report or working with a battering husband within the context of restraining orders or court-ordered therapy) will not be able to assist victims and their families. NPTs should also support community groups and activities that offer services for abuse victims or perpetrators, such as battered women's shelters, rape crisis centers, child abuse programs, offenders therapy groups, and offices of public defenders and legal assistance. The NPT should try to model a nonsexist and nonpatriarchal approach to family therapy as she becomes known in the various community agencies.

Attorneys, case workers, and affiliated counselors may also make referrals to NPTs who are known to have experience, training, and skill with abusive families (Berghorn & Siracusa, 1982; Munro, 1984). On occasion, judges will order a course of therapy as a legal recourse for spouses who have violent conflict or who abuse children. Abused children who come to the court's attention for delinquent, truant, or runaway activity may be referred with their parents for therapy. In the initial stages of therapy, such court orders can facilitate motivation for families who typically are resistant and distrustful of outsiders. Finally, referrals may come from medical clinics, family practice physicians, community nurse practitioners, ministers, and the police who encounter trauma victims of family abuse.

Often the "closeted" problem of abuse is revealed in the course of therapy initiated for some other presenting problem, such as alcoholism, depression, threat of divorce, eating disorders, or delinquency. The patient's disclosure of the abuse will be encouraged by the earned rapport and trust of the NPT after weeks or months of focusing on other clinical problems. When such disclosure occurs, the NPT should receive the information in a matter-of-fact manner, praise the patient for having the courage and trust to share the problem, and reassure the victim that she/ he is not to be blamed or shamed by the incident(s). Soon thereafter a careful history of the abusive behaviors should be taken and an assessment of the level of current danger for further abuse to occur made. Individual sessions with victims are needed to gain this detail. Some therapists have used videotapes to capture carefully the often poignant accounts of abusive activities. Concise and complete record-keeping of this material is important since legal involvement may become an issue. In many cases, well-kept records are all that will be required by the courts. For children, history-taking can include mutual storytelling, coloring books with characters representative of real life, and anatomically correct dolls or puppets (see Chapter 20 for treatment with children).

Referrals for therapy for domestic violence/abuse differ from other referrals in a number of ways. More frequently these cases will have complicated legal or medical histories. The referred patients may be resistant to disclose the current problems they face and poorly motivated to enter active therapy. They often are distrustful of the NPT's intentions and abilities to help. Individuals with histories of family violence or abuse also often live with continual separation anxiety, rejection, and an abiding fear of a real "family fracture." On the whole, these patients are difficult to engage in the traditional processes of psychotherapy or family therapy.

Each referral must also be carefully examined for the family's potential to benefit from family therapy and for their readiness to begin. For some, family therapy is not the ideal treatment; individual or group therapy may be more appropriate. Giaretto (1976) was among the first to include family therapy in the treatment of incest and this was as only one part of a multifaceted treatment program beginning with individual, group, and couple therapies. Indeed, in some instances the goal of family therapy is to help the family work through the realization that their system cannot be repaired and that separation and grief work are indicated.

## THE INITIAL PHASE OF THERAPY

The establishment of trust is the first issue in most forms of therapy and with most patients, but it is crucial in working with abusive families. Because abusive patterns so often reflect an intergenerational transmission of learned behaviors (Boszormenyi-Nagy & Spark, 1973; Spinetta & Rigler, 1972), it is unusual for the parent-child relationships to have provided the kind of security and tenderness that fosters the development of basic trust (Steele, 1980). When lack of trust is shared as a family dynamic, therapists are faced first with how to allow for prolonged periods of resistance and second with growing dependency. In a sense, these couples/families are much like infants who need to learn for the first time that a parent figure actually does have positive regard for them and that considerable giving in the form of advice, active listening, and acceptance is available. The ability of the NPT to merely give—to provide a psychologically safe place to be, without preformed expectations or recriminations—is essential during these early hours. It is the social learning-teaching of trust that must first be accomplished. As simple and straightforward as this may seem (and to some traditional therapists it may sound blasphemous), the task of getting abused and abusing patients to anticipate positive regard, consistency, and energy from the NPT is very challenging. The ability of these individuals to trust is fragile, if it exists at all.

The rationale for the NPT's "giving" demeanor is twofold. First, no psychotherapy can proceed well without at least a beginning trust in the therapist. Second, patients will not be able to extend to children or partners the capacity for trust if they themselves have not acquired this ability. Early in life, fulfillment of essential dependency needs is the condition that nurtures the capacity to trust. In abusive families this dependency is not only thwarted, but it is inverted, i.e., children are often expected to care for and to gratify the parents; and often parental expectations for the child are far beyond the child's developmental level, a phenomenon called "role-reversal." These are not the circumstances in which empathy and tenderness—characteristics of effective parenting—thrive (Helfer, Schnieder, & Hoffmeister, 1978). From this crucible of emotional deprivation emerges the future parent who is likely to abuse his/her child, the spouse who is prone to batter a partner, and the adult child who may systematically abuse an elderly parent who has reversed roles from caretaker to demanding child.

In adult abuse of the elderly, the adult-child caretaker is usually a middle-aged woman who still has children in school, cares for a husband, works outside the home, and faces numerous mid-life crises. Lifelong and unresolved conflict between the abused elderly parent and adult child is frequently reported (Rathbone-McCuan, 1980). When the siblings or spouse do not share the responsibility of providing physical and emotional care to an aging parent, the weight of the burden can cause the caretaker to lose impulse control; injuries may occur in angry shaking, jerking, and pushing, or in excessive force in lifting or turning the aged individual who may be bedridden. This middle-aged caretaker is said to reflect the emerging "sandwiched" generation, with dependents on both sides.

The primary issue of the working phase of therapy is to help individuals engaged in rigid role performances or fixed functions find ways to relax barriers to new roles. Husbands can do housework without losing their masculinity and wives can attend to career development without abandoning the family. (See also Chapter 23.) It is impressive when one sees a 6-foot-tall Vietnam veteran doing laundry, rocking an infant son to sleep, or patiently feeding an infirm parent, especially when this same man was earlier seen as rough and abusive to the entire family. The courage to try out these expanded roles derives from the trust and respect the family develops for the NPT. The nurse therapist who can evidence flexibility, avoid authoritarian and hierarchical approaches to therapy, and show genuine caring will be more able to engender role changes in otherwise isolated, rigid families.

Another approach is for the NPT to role-model flexibility while conducting some therapy sessions in the family home. "Joining," in the sense used by Minuchin (1978), is facilitated when the therapist actually sits at the dinner table or in the livingroom where the family normally interacts.

> Interventions in a family cannot be made from "outside." The therapist has to join the field of stabilized family interactions in order to observe them. He must gain experiential knowledge of the controlling power that the system exerts. Only then can he challenge the family interactions with any knowledge of the range of thresholds that the system can tolerate. (p. 94)

In these early sessions, the family is helped to feel safe in exposing its established patterns of communication and activities of daily living, even though some of these patterns will later become the focus for change.

Beginning with the family *where it is* will reduce resistance and create a feeling of acceptance. During initial therapy, the nature of change will be first order, structural, and directed to goals clear to all. Ideally the family will imprint with the NPT, meaning that members will feel rapport and begin to follow the therapist's lead as her concepts and techniques for behavioral change are introduced in the working phase. Second order change and strategic therapy techniques, such as paradox and redefinition, are usually not appropriate or successful with abusive families until and unless a firm therapeutic alliance and reliable family boundaries have been established. Logically this is more characteristic of the working phase of therapy, which is discussed in the next section of this chapter. (Most experienced NPTs realize that there is overlap between the initiating and working phases of therapy and some family members will move along more readily than others.) Table 26.1 represents a basic scheme of approaches to family therapy during various phases of progression. It should be emphasized, however, that each family is unique and, accordingly, must be assessed in each phase of therapy for readiness to respond to any approach or technique.

As the initial phase of therapy becomes the working phase, the idea of contracting is useful to further reduce resistance. The family contributes to the structure of the therapy and therein experiences some control. Contracting also provides an extension into future that enables a family to have a modified "delusion of fusion" with the therapist (Polansky, 1971).

This can mediate the separation anxiety families will develop after they have come to value the therapist. It is helpful for the NPT to keep in mind how unique the feeling of trust is for the family, and how very fearful they are of losing this positive alliance. The initial contract of the opening phase of therapy may include the number of sessions to be taken for getting acquainted, doing assessment, identifying problems, and clarifying goals and constraints. During this period, it is important too that the perpetrator of any actual abuse has been identified and confronted and his or her commitment to the therapy clarified to both family and therapist. Often this has already occurred prior to the initiation of therapy as a part of legal or medical interventions; nevertheless, it should be stated in the beginning negotiations for family therapy.

If this initial period closes with both therapist and family wanting to continue, then a second block of time for "X" number of sessions can be established. Unlike other forms of individual and family therapy, termination is not discussed until the family has had ample opportunity to have positive experiences in therapy. It is important to remember the

**Table 26.1 Structural and Strategic Methods in Therapy Concerning Domestic Violence and Abuse**

| Therapeutic process | Strategies | Techniques |
|---|---|---|
| Beginning Phase (resistance to therapist). | Assess<br>Plan<br>Contract (time, place, members) | Joining<br>Genogram<br>Mapping |
| Working Phase I (resistance to change). | Continue contract.<br>Clarify goals, expectations, limits. | More joining/establishing trust; sculpting, information giving; role-playing; modeling; assigning homework, journals, and physical exercise. |
| Working Phase II (focus on system *vs.* individuals). | Identify and redefine subsystem power issues.[a] Examine family-community boundary and context-system interface. | Role-playing; choreographing; reframing, paradox, restraining, boundary-making.[b, c] |
| Terminating Phase (resistance to/fear of autonomy). Separation from therapist. | Complete contract. Reinforce subsystem changes. Rehearse behavioral role flexibility. Refer for support services/ followup. | Role-playing; mapping projected future. Operational mourning. |

[a]For a fuller discussion of subsystem concepts, *see* Minuchin (1976).

[b]These and other techniques are discussed by Stanton (1983).

[c]*See* Taggart (1985) for a discussion of contextually defined power and domestic violence.

typical history of these individuals around parenting issues; they have greater than ordinary fears of rejection and abandonment. This has been their real experience, not their neurotic fantasy or false interpretation of a significant other's intentions. Premature discussion of termination will preclude a successful working phase of therapy. The form of the contact with the individual family should be flexible and open to negotiation throughout therapy, while retaining the structure, consistency, and predictability that is so much needed.

# THE WORKING PHASE OF THERAPY

The relative health or functional status of the family unit is directly related to the system's ability to adapt to continuously changing and shifting needs and roles of members within the group. The boundaries of the subsystems and of the family with the surrounding community must be flexible to allow for growth, expansion, change, and adaptation. The intrafamilial system factors listed in Figure 26.1 show clearly how family therapy must focus for improved function. These factors reviewed are: (1) autocratic and hierarchical family government; (2) strict disciplinary beliefs with corporal punishment; (3) rigid role assignments; (4) role-reversal; (5) social isolation; (6) resistance to change; and (7) intergenerational transmission of abusive parenting.

The subsystems most crucial in matters of family abuse are the parent-child subsystem and the spousal subsystem. In both systems there exists a maldistribution of power, responsibility, and authority. Power and authority may be differentiated on the basis of how they are assigned to members. Power can be arbitrarily assigned on the basis of gender, age, or physical and economic advantage, as in the rigid and traditional patriarchal structure. Here, father or older brother are automatically dominant, regardless of their intelligence, skill, or preparedness to perform a role's inherent tasks. Conversely, authority is awarded to the individual who evidences readiness, need, and ability to contribute in some specific way to the family good. Ideally, the individual held responsible for a given task has full authority to define how the task will be carried out, its desired outcomes, and the delegation of responsibility to family members or auxiliary services. However, in abusive families, authority is sometimes ascribed inappropriately, as in the cases of role-reversal between parent and child, or in a spouse being asked to function more like a parent than a spouse. Role reversal between an aging, dependent parent and adult child-caretaker poses particularly complex shifts in authority, responsibility, and resources.

Generally speaking, the meaning of work and of power relations and conflict resolution in families have not been adequately studied. Consequently, it is difficult to know what common practices exist and, indeed, what practices may have optimal developmental value for children and functional value for families. White and Brinkerhoff (1981), although suggesting that more research is needed, noted that the division of labor between children and adults is as conflictual as is division of labor between spouses.

In the later stages of the initial period and in the beginning working phase, the NPT can assess subsystem boundaries and power issues and use first order change techniques to facilitate greater flexibility and growth. This work is contingent upon the assumption that the family/ therapist therapeutic alliance or basic trust has developed. That alliance is, in a sense, a subsystem of its own and will help to provide a dynamic equilibrium as other subsystem dyads and triads are modified. The therapist actually applies herself as a boundary-maker during the efforts to help families restructure system properties (see Table 26.1).

In general, the processes of family therapy for situations of domestic violence/abuse can proceed in fairly standard fashion if three basic conditions are met: (1) the perpetrator has been identified and properly confronted in earlier family sessions. (Included here is assurance that any legal, civil, or criminal penalties have been met.) Family therapy is not a substitute for imposed penalties. In some cases therapy proceeds without the perpetrator during the latter's incarceration or restraining orders. The perpetrator may join the family therapy after the penalties are met if this is a goal of the entire family; (2) the therapist/family alliance, through joining, has developed; and (3) the NPT has thoroughly explored her own values about power relations based on gender and age positions in the family group. Therapists who passively or actively support rigid adherence to traditional patriarchal distribution of power will not work effectively for therapeutic change with these families, nor be able to practice primary prevention with those who have the potential to abuse (Finkelhor, 1983; Taggart, 1985). Beyond these conditions, the same judgments about such familial characteristics as verbal abilities, intelligence, insight potential, impulse control, substance abuse, obsessiveness and social support will dictate use of specific techniques or approaches.*
There is great variability among abusive families on all these characteristics and so each family must be evaluated for the methods of therapy to be employed, and indeed, whether family therapy is to be used at all.

From the activities of joining, mapping, and genograming in the initial phase of therapy, the NPT can begin to comment on the rigid and

---

*The issue of how substance abuse, especially alcohol, is related to domestic violence is complex; a thorough discussion of this and other theories of violence goes beyond the scope of this chapter. However, a simple cause and effect relationship has not been consistently documented. While some persons who drink do become abusive, others do not. The author accepts a social learning theory of violence, which holds that whether or not violence aggression is triggered in a given event will depend upon how the event is interpreted by the aggressor, the value or meaning it has in his or her perception and past experience, and how the aggression is related to his or her self-esteem and social position. For a fuller review of theories of violence the reader is referred to Chapter 2 of Campbell & Humphreys (1983).

problematic nature of the hierarchy of family government. Being a part of the system the NPT can openly observe how constricting the arrangement is for all concerned, including the enormous energy costs and alienation posed for the power holder. Role-played situations between perpetrator and victim or victim-directed sculpting can help members locate the dysfunction. Similarly, the Bowen technique of structuring and interview, so that one spouse talks while the other is prohibited, and then reversing their positions, can facilitate comparing perceptions of power differentials and the reciprocity of warmth, or lack of it, in the relationship. This has been a powerful tool in the author's practice for raising the perpetrator's consciousness regarding the self-defeating effect of abused power in a marital relationship.

Body sculpture, or one of its variations, can be effective in creating self-awareness and understanding of how all family members perceive the perpetrator and the victim. The therapeutic goals of developing insight, raising consciousness, clarifying misconceptions, and altering dysfunctional power hierarchies are enhanced by physical and graphic techniques developed in the past two decades of evolving family theory and practice. An excellent reference for becoming familiar with such techniques is *The Book of Family Therapy* (1972) by Ferber, Mendelsohn, and Napier.

Tracing the intergenerational transmission of abusive parenting or spousal roles is one concrete use for the genogram, especially when the NPT points out how this system is different from nonabusive groups. It is not unusual for families to be relatively ignorant of the fact that other families have different, nonabusive systems of family government. Abusive parents report that their fear is to "spare the rod and spoil the child"; they frequently experience a sense of righteousness during excessive corporal punishment of children that can lead to injury. Wife-batterers often have grown up in families and among friends in which the father modeled violence with his wife. The social learning of familial abusive patterns can and must be unlearned in family therapy, as well as in other social institutions of interaction.

Whether using verbal or experiential techniques, the NPT's ability to model the simultaneous skills of leadership and tenderness, firmness and empathy, reasonable anger and humor, will be more effective than the patriarchal prototype or the feminine myth as ideal roles. As a "member" of the family system, the NPT is in a position to offer advice, provide information, and enable learning about such matters as child development and parenting skills. However, since low self-esteem is characteristic of both perpetrators and victims of abuse, the NPT should not offer too much information too soon. Families can be made to feel that the therapist is condescending or critical if a teacher-posture is assumed prematurely.

When children are asked and/or coerced to act as parents, role-reversal has occurred. Some therapists (Justice & Justice, 1976) have referred to this parent-child subsystem as a symbiosis in which the parent's need for the child is excessive and the child's dependency on the parental need is great. Role-playing this reversal with both parent and child together, encouraging each to act out more age-appropriate interactions, can help to alleviate this reversal. The parents will be more likely to relinquish expectations of the child as a source of gratification if they are instructed to seek out "adult" gratifications—recreation, career interests, or hobbies. Essentially the parents are asked to develop a capacity for pleasure in appropriate adult activities that has previously been minimized. As parents find alternate appropriate sources for having emotional needs met, their expectations of the child are reduced, as is the potential for abuse to the child who fails to gratify the parent.

## THE THERAPIST'S OWN FEELINGS

After some 13 years of working with families who are abusive to members, the author has yet to find a truly effective way of dealing with rage, depression, and, sometimes, hopelessness as feelings that are stimulated within her during and between sessions. Therapists must realize that the villain is much more than one disgruntled spouse or parent; the real villain is the sociocultural matrix that allows such indiscriminate victimization, mostly of women, children and the elderly. The patriarchal society that maintains that it is men's rightful place to dominate and control others is the real source of frustration to the NPT who must contend with family violence/abuse.

However, it is helpful to note that although there were no child abuse reporting laws or protective legislation in 1972, such legislation now exists in all 50 of the United States and in many developed countries. Women and the elderly are working toward similar protections. Probably the most significant support for the NPT during the working phase of therapy is access to a group of feminist-oriented peers and/or experienced clinicians who appreciate both the scope of the problem and the energy it takes to keep one's own anger operational, i.e., anger that serves to repulse violence, but can be expressed in nonviolent ways. Some therapists find expression in political activity that advocates for women and children's rights. Others known to the author have become somewhat chronically depressed. It would be misleading to suggest that occupational hazards around the emotional well-being of the NPT are not at issue. Each NPT will definitely need to seek out a peer counselor, supervisor, or other supporter in order to work through and to maintain her own emotional reactions. (See also Chapter 9.)

In summary, the working phase is concerned with joining the family, identifying and modifying power relations in subsystems, rehearsing new patterns of communication about rules and decision-making, and finding appropriate sources for meeting emotional needs. Identifying faulty parenting, spousal-role behaviors, or intergenerational role reciprocities are also aspects of this phase of therapy with abusive families. If the NPT has been successful in joining the family, she will further be able to model leadership from a nonsexist, egalitarian position that emphasizes the individual worth and identity of every member of the group. Once consciousness of oppressive behaviors and their consequences has been raised, reinforcement for alternative behaviors becomes almost matter-of-course in the familial interactions. Families begin to feel better and, with that, resistance to change, characteristic of the working phase, begins to fade. The length of the working phase depends on many factors related to the individual strengths, resources, and needs of each family. However, because of the many unmet developmental emotional needs presented by these patients, the NPT should plan for a longer course of therapy than other patient populations may require.

## THE TERMINATION PHASE OF THERAPY

The absence of abusive behaviors in family interactions is the most crucial factor indicating readiness for entering the termination phase of therapy. If, for instance, the NPT has asked one or several members to keep daily diaries of family life experience, these can be reviewed or summarized by the member for evidence of abuse. By this time in the therapy process, the NPT will have developed a sensitivity to the potential for violence or abusive transactions. Also, it must be remembered that most American families have "heated arguments" and strong frustrations; intense and strong feelings between family members occur quite naturally. This is no less true for families who have experienced problems with abuse. Indeed, the extreme absence of feeling, characteristic of severe neglect, can be even more life-threatening, especially in children with failure-to-thrive from lack of stimulation, food, and love. The therapist must come to know the family well enough to be sensitive to the subtle differences between naturally-occurring conflict and the potential for actual violence that occurs in systems with dysfunctional power distributions. When the NPT senses danger, she should voice this and support the family's expression of their feelings, fears, and conflict. If the expression is not forthcoming, the NPT may want to hold individual sessions with members to locate the obstacle to discussion about the potential for abuse.

Criteria for assessment of readiness for termination include:

- absence of abusive behaviors
- adherence to initial contract to work in therapy
- age-appropriate emotional and physical development of children
- evidence of improved self-esteem among all members
- observed capabilities for group negotiation around decision-making
- indications of efforts to develop extrafamilial social relationships and support services
- family ability to identify resources to call upon in times of high stress (e.g., parental-stress hotlines to call)

The termination phase of therapy further addresses the boundary of family/community and the establishment of "lifelines" in social supports.

Very little research correlating treatment for domestic violence/abuse and outcomes has been done. The criteria offered above are those developed by the author over a period of years of conducting family therapy and consulting with other clinicians. These are certainly not exhaustive of all the kinds of evidence of improvement therapists might look for in a given family or community. It should be mentioned that some families never seem to respond and eventually require more stringent forms of intervention. Active evaluative research that is both prospective and longitudinal is needed to make generalizations about treatment approaches in general and family therapy in particular.

The process of introducing termination to a family who has radically changed the nature and function of basic subsystems and power hierarchy is complex. The new, more mature and autonomous behaviors may yet feel a little strange and frightening to members. Like the toddler just learning to walk, each new step is uncertain; like the adolescent leaving home, the hidden impulse to return to the secure position of childhood is strong. Old dependency needs conflict with the recently acquired sense of mastery. Like the parents of departing adolescents, NPTs may conjure up all sorts of anxieties and fears of relapse, mixed with conflicting hopes for family success. All of this operates in the shadow of old threats of loss of impulse control, socialized patriarchy, and society's tacit acceptance of use of violence and domination to resolve conflict (Campbell, 1983; Gelles, 1979).

The grief work that the loss of the NPT generates for these families cannot be treated lightly. Because the therapy has represented most members' first successful dependent-trust experience, its ending is both sad and frightening. In the author's experience this loss is expressed in much the same way as other developmental losses, such as in the loss of the dependent position in an infant's weaning process, the loss of security of a 6-year-old on the first day of school, the loss of youthful appearance for the middle-aged person. While these changes are seen as normal and necessary to development, the losses that accompany them are grieved. These expressions can include sadness and crying, irritability, and anxiety. This NPT has not, however, experienced an acting out of new violence or abuse as a reaction to carefully terminated therapy. Families who leave therapy prematurely, who never really engaged with the therapist in the first place, have been known to continue abusive patterns. Again, evaluative research is needed to assess both the outcomes and processes of family therapy with this special population.

The NPT can assess whether the identified goals of the original contract have been achieved, modified, or relinquished. Those changed behaviors that represent growth and maturity can be identified and praised. Remaining problematic behaviors can be pointed out with recommendations for continuing work. Parents should be encouraged to continue finding gratifying experiences away from their children; spouses should be reminded that they are equal partners in marriage and parenting. The termination process should evolve slowly, in a planned fashion, and with adequate opportunity for expression of feelings of loss, anger, anxiety, and affection. Some therapists may wish to send greeting cards to continue to validate the therapeutic relationship. One NPT known to the author continues to receive a Mother's Day card from a prior patient each year. While this is the only contact that remains, it seems poignant as an expression of how deeply effective the therapy had been. Referrals can be explored for temporary or intermittent services in the future, such as day care facilities, home health aides, or parental stress support groups and crisis intervention lines. The NPT may want to be sure the family still has her business card in case of future new stresses that may require supportive therapy for adaptation. The family can understand that any person in a crisis situation can become prone to violent or abusive expression; having succesful therapy does not guarantee an immunity to the effects of illness, poverty, or other crisis event.

The fears associated with separation and an autonomous future can be role-played, mapped, or just talked about. It is not unusual for members to cry, to shout, and to ask to be held during the early part of this phase. These behaviors should be allowed; it is not a time for intellectualized feelings, denial, or cold analysis. The expression of feelings is an important experience that should be valued and approved. For the family, learning to deal with the loss of a therapist who has been "parentified" earlier in the therapy can actually serve as rehearsal for the certain losses in their own family months or years later as fate or developmental crises occur in real life.

## SUMMARY

Therapy for problems of violence and abuse in families is a relatively new and challenging conceptual, theoretical, and practice issue for nurse psychotherapists and others. Violence and the will to dominate are learned at a young age in American society (Breines & Gordon, 1983; Gelles, 1979). Competition is the basis of American culture and its economic structure; how unfeeling one must be to succeed is often denied or ignored. Is it any wonder that families, crucibles for the most intense of human feeling, can become violent in a society born in violence and characterized by a sociocultural milieu that frequently condones it? NPTs who aspire to conduct therapy for domestic violence and abuse will have to think about and work through their own philosophies and values concerning aggression, dominance, and family life. Then, only with the utmost commitment and perseverence, can they thoughtfully and slowly bring about positive change with individuals for whom violence/abuse is a major problem in living with others.

## REFERENCES

American Psychiatric Association. (1980). *Diagnostic and statistic manual of mental disorders* (3rd ed.). Washington, DC: American Psychiatric Association.

Berghorn, G., & Siracusa, A. (1982). Beyond isolated treatment: A case for community involvement in family violence interventions. In J. Hansen & L. Barnhill (Eds.), *Clinical approaches to family violence* (pp. 139–155). Rockville, MD: Aspen.

Boszormenyi-Nagy, I., & Spark, G. (1973). *Invisible loyalties: Reciprocity in intergenerational therapy.* New York: Harper & Row.

Breines, W., & Gordon, L. (1983). The new scholarship on family violence. *Signs,* *8*(3), 490–531.

Campbell, J., & Humphreys, J. (1983). *Nursing care of victims of family violence.* Reston, VA: Reston.

Carson, B., & Finkelhor, D. (1982). The scope of contemporary social and domestic violence. In G. Braen & C. Warner (Eds.), *Management of the physically and emotionally abused* (pp. 3-13). Norwalk, CT: Appleton-Century-Crofts.

Champlin, L. (1982). The battered elderly. *Geriatrics, 37*(7), 115-117.

Dobash, R. E., & Dobash, R. (1979). *Violence against wives.* New York: Free Press.

Ferber, A., Mendelsohn, M., & Napier, A. (1972). *The book of family therapy.* Boston: Houghton Mifflin.

Finkelhor, D., Gelles, R., Hotaling, G., & Straus, M. (Eds.). (1983). *The dark side of families: Current family violence research.* Beverly Hills: Sage.

Fisher, L., Anderson, A., & Jones, J. (1981). Types of paradoxical intervention and indications/contraindications for use in clinical practice. *Family Process, 20,* 25-35.

Gelles, R. (1979). *Family violence.* Beverly Hills: Sage.

Giaretto, H. (1976). The treatment of father-daughter incest: A psycho-social approach. *Children Today, 5,* 2-5, 34-35.

Hare-Mustin, R. (1978). A feminist approach to family therapy. *Family Process, 17,* 181-193.

Helfer, R., Schnieder, C., & Hoffmeister, H. (1977). *Report on the research using the Michigan screening profile of parenting.* East Lansing: Michigan State University.

Herman, J. (1981). *Father-daughter incest.* London: Harvard University Press.

Hickey, T., & Douglas, R. (1981). Mistreatment of the elderly in the domestic setting: An exploratory study. *American Journal of Public Health, 71*(5), 500-506.

Justice, B., & Justice, R. (1976). *The abusing family.* New York: Human Sciences Press.

Levant, R. (1980). Sociological and clinical models of the family: An attempt to identify paradigms. *American Journal of Family Therapy, 8*(4), 5-20.

Minuchin, S., Rosman, B., & Baker, L. (1978). *Psychosomatic families.* London: Harvard University Press.

Minuchin, S., & Minuchin, S. (1976). The child in context: System's approach to growth and treatment. In N. Talbot (Ed.), *Raising children in modern America* (pp. 119-134). Boston: Little, Brown.

Munro, J. (1984). The nurse and the legal system. In J. Campbell & J. Humphreys (Eds.), *Nursing care of victims of family violence* (pp. 384-389). Reston, VA: Reston.

Naisbett, J. (1982). *Megatrends.* New York: Warner.

Polansky, N. (1971). *Ego psychology and communication.* New York: Atherton Press.

Private violence. (1983, September 5). *Time Magazine,* pp. 18-29.

Rathbone-McCuan, E. (1980). Elderly victims of family violence and neglect. *Social Casework, 61,* 296-304.

Scanzoni, J. (1983). *Shaping tomorrow's family: Theory and policy for the 21st century.* Beverly Hills: Sage.

Spinetta, J., & Rigler, D. (1972). The child-abusing parent: A psychological review. *Psychological Bulletin, 77*(40), 296-304.

Stank, E., Filcroft, A., & Frazier, W. (1979). Medicine and patriarchal violence: The social construction of a "private event." *International Journal of Health Sciences, 9,* 119-126.

Stanton, M. D. (1983). An integrated structural/strategic approach to family therapy. In D. Olson & B. Miller (Eds.), *Family studies review yearbook* (pp. 684–696). Beverly Hills: Sage.

Steele, B. (1980). Psychodynamic factors in child abuse. In C. H. Kempe & R. Helfer (Eds.), *The battered child*. Chicago: University of Chicago.

Straus, M., Gelles, R., & Steinmetz, S. (1980). *Behind closed doors: Violence in the American family*. New York: Doubleday.

Taggart, M. (1985). The feminist critique in epistemological perspective: Questions of context in family therapy. *Journal Marital and Family Therapy*, *11*(2), 113–125.

Warner, C., & Braen, R. (Eds.). (1982). *Management of the physically and emotionally abused*. Norwalk, CT: Appleton-Century-Crofts.

White, L., & Brinkerhoff, D. (1981). Children's work in the family: Its significance and meaning. *Journal of Marriage and the Family, 43*, 789–798.

# Appendix
# Guidelines for Private
# Practice of Psychiatric
# and Mental Health Nursing

The following working draft of guidelines for private practice in psychiatric-mental health nursing was developed by the former Council of Specialists in Psychiatric and Mental Health Nursing Council of the American Nurses' Association (ANA). The guidelines were approved in 1985 by the new Council on Psychiatric and Mental Health Nursing; however, they must be approved by the appropriate policy governing bodies of the Association prior to their implementation. The Council notes that the use of these guidelines must be congruent with the state nurse practice act and the statutory definition of nursing in a particular state. The actions of the nurses should not conflict with either statutory language or the rules and regulations of the state in which the nurse resides and practices professional nursing. Likewise, other legal standards for such business practices as billing should also be met.

Clinical nurse specialists in psychiatric and mental health nursing:

1. Identify themselves as members of the nursing profession and display or have credentials (R.N. licensure, diploma, certification certificate) to show if requested.
2. Are certified or in the process of becoming certified by the ANA as specialists in psychiatric and mental health nursing.
3. When advertising, use factual information regarding their qualifications and competence.

---

Readers should note that the above "Guidelines" represent a working draft. The language of the final approved "Guidelines" may vary somewhat from this draft—Editors.

4. Carry malpractice and premises liability insurance.
5. Manage financial arrangements as follows:

   a. Request a fee which is clear and understandable to the client.
   b. Complete insurance forms to facilitate reimbursement to the client or provider.
   c. Should the client be unable to pay a requested fee, negotiate a lower fee or refer to an appropriate source.
   d. Should, during the course of treatment, the client's financial circumstances worsen, making payment of the agreed-upon fee impossible, continue treatment until referral to another setting can be accomplished.
   e. Before instituting efforts to collect the unpaid fee, the therapist will either seek the client's permission to this limitation on confidentiality in advance or notify the client that the absence of payment or response by a designated date will be interpreted as permission to make a break in the confidential relationship by revealing to a collection agency, small claims court, or attorney that the client has been in therapy.

6. Outline clearly with clients the conditions of service such as frequency and duration of appointments, fee for missed or cancelled sessions, and confidentiality.
7. Conform to the ANA *Standards of Psychiatric and Mental Health Nursing Practice.*
8. Respect clients' right to confidentiality. Maintain and safeguard appropriate records. When such data are to be shared (with other professionals on referral, with courts or lawyers in case of lawsuits), inform the client in advance. When such data are used for professional publications, reframe data to prevent recognition of the client.
9. Do not engage in social, sexual, or business contacts with the client, or those close to the client. May engage in professional contacts with the client or those close to the client.
10. Are available to the client outside regular business hours in emergencies. When unavailable owing to illness, vacations, and so forth, provide a qualified substitute who will respond to emergency calls.
11. Recognize limits of statutory accountability in relation to client needs and use referrals to other professionals for necessary services such as medications or hospitalization. Collaborate with these professionals when appropriate and authorized by the client.

12. Report unethical behavior by another nurse to the appropriate body within the professional organization.
13. Respect institutional policies when granted staff privileges to continue professional services to hospitalized clients.
14. May elect to sell their practice to a professionally qualified successor.

# Index